MAO'S CHINA

BY YGAEL GLUCKSTEIN

Stalin's Satellites in Europe

MAO'S CHINA

ECONOMIC AND POLITICAL
SURVEY

BY

YGAEL GLUCKSTEIN

THE BEACON PRESS

BOSTON

FIRST PUBLISHED IN 1957

Copyright 1957 by Ygael Gluckstein

PRINTED IN GREAT BRITAIN
in 11 pt. Baskerville type
BY PURNELL AND SONS LTD
PAULTON (SOMERSET) AND LONDON

PREFACE

Scarcely any event in the past generation is of greater universal import than the rise to power of Mao Tse-tung. The need for comprehensive and accurate information about Mao's regime is obvious. This volume is an attempt to meet part of that need. However, the subject is complex and hidden behind a dearth of information which naturally adds to the difficulties of sound analysis. The hindrances to a description and analysis of what happens behind the bamboo curtain are even greater than the considerable obstacles facing the student of Soviet affairs.

Much of the evidence about Russia comes from two very different sources: tourists' descriptions and the stories of persons who had lived for long periods in Russia and then left. These two sources can be a valuable supplement to official Soviet publications. For better or worse similar sources practically do not exist for China. Students of Chinese affairs must rely almost entirely on official documents. These—the basis of this book—consist of official statements, laws and decrees; speeches of the leaders; reports and resolutions of conferences; and articles in the Chinese Communist press.

Chinese Communist literature is singularly deficient in systematic presentation of data, especially economic data. In the absence of such comprehensive statistics, I have often had to use scattered samples, to generalise from individual cases, and to make do with very rough estimates. At the same time, I have had to illustrate every point in the analysis and argument with many examples.

A plethora of fragmentary data published in the Chinese press combined with this dearth of comprehensive statements makes it extremely difficult to indicate the trend of development. There is thus a danger of obscuring the general features of the regime under an arbitrary collection of heterogeneous elements. I hope I have succeeded in avoiding such meaningless eclecticism.

The main sources for translations of official documents—laws, decrees, speeches, reports and the like—are the official daily news bulletins of the *New China News Agency* and the publications of the American Consulate General, Hong Kong: *Survey of the*

7

China Mainland Press (mimeographed, translated selections from Chinese mainland newspapers, issued almost daily), *Current Background* (mimeographed, issued occasionally), *Extracts from China Mainland Magazines* (mimeographed, issued occasionally). I have used them liberally.

I am greatly obliged to the Librarians of the British Museum, Chatham House, the School of Oriental and African Studies and the London School of Economics and Political Science, who have been unfailingly helpful.

Among those who have read all or part of the work and have made valuable suggestions are Professor T. H. E. Chen, Mrs. J. Davis, Mr. J. Menken, Mr. A. S. Newens, Dr. S. Papert and Professor K. A. Wittfogel. I wish to make it clear that while they assisted me greatly with their advice and criticism, they are in no way responsible for any error of judgment or fact that may be found in the book.

I am indebted to my teachers of Chinese at the London School of Oriental and African Studies. Were it not for the scant acquaintance with the Chinese language they imparted to me, the deficiencies of the present book would have been greater.

I also wish to thank Mr. M. Kidron for thoroughly revising the style of the book, and my wife for preparing the manuscript for print and arranging the Index.

YGAEL GLUCKSTEIN

London, February 1, 1957

ABBREVIATIONS OF
MAIN JOURNALS QUOTED

CB   *Current Background*—Translations of official documents of Communist China, issued by the American Consulate General, Hong Kong, mimeographed.

CCCP   *Ching Chi Chou Pao* (Economic Weekly)—Shanghai.

CCJP   *Ch'ang Chiang Jih Pao* (Yangtze Daily)—Hankow.

CCPR   *Communist China Propaganda Review*—issued by the American Consulate General, Hong Kong, mimeographed.

CCTP   *Ching Chi Tao Pao* (Economic Bulletin)—weekly, Peking.

CEJ   *Chinese Economic Journal*—issued monthly before World War II, Shanghai.

CFJP   *Chieh Fang Jih Pao* (Liberation Daily)—Shanghai.

CKCN   *Chung Kuo Ch'ing Nien* (China Youth)—twice monthly, Peking.

CKCNP   *Chung Kuo Ch'ing Nien Pao* (China Youth Journal)—issued for a time three times a week, then twice, now daily, Peking.

CKKJ   *Chung Kuo Kung Jen* (Workers of China)—monthly, Peking.

CKKY   *Chung Kuo Kung Yeh* (Chinese Industry)—monthly, Shanghai.

CKNP   *Chung Kuo Nung Pao* (Chinese Agricultural Journal)—twice monthly, Peking.

CMR   *China Monthly Review*—Shanghai.

CNS   *China News Service*—daily news bulletin, mainly directed to overseas Chinese.

CR   *China Reconstructs*—bi-monthly, Peking.

EBAFE   *Economic Bulletin of Asia and the Far East*—Bangkok, monthly.

ECMM   *Extracts from China Mainland Magazines*—issued by the American Consulate General, Hong Kong, mimeographed.

FEER   *Far Eastern Economic Review*—weekly, Hong Kong.

FES   *Far Eastern Survey*—formerly twice monthly, now monthly, Honolulu.

HCH   *Hsin Chung Hua* (New China)—twice monthly, Shanghai.

HCKFN   *Hsin Chung Kuo Fu Nu* (Women of New China)—monthly, Peking.

HCS   *Hsin Chien She* (New Construction)—monthly, Peking.

HH   *Hsueh Hsi* (Study)—monthly, Peking.

HHJP   *Hsin Hua Jih Pao* (New China Daily)—Chungking.

HHYP   *Hsin Hua Yueh Pao* (New China Monthly)—Peking.

HKC   *Hsin Kuan Ch'a* (New Observer)—twice monthly, Peking.

HWJP   *Hsin Wem Jih Pao* (Daily News)—Shanghai

JMCY   *Jen Min Chiao Yu* (People's Education)—monthly, Peking.

JMJP   *Jen Min Jih Pao* (People's Daily)—Peking.

KJJP   *Kung Jen Jih Pao* (Daily Worker)—Peking.

KJP   *Kwangsi Jih Pao* (Kwangsi Daily)—Nanning.

KMJP   *Kuang Ming Jih Pao* (Enlightenment Daily)—Peking.

NCNA   *New China News Agency*—daily bulletin.

NFJP   *Nan Fang Jih Pao* (Southern Daily)—Canton.

NYHT   *New York Herald Tribune.*

NYT   *New York Times.*

ABBREVIATIONS

PC	*People's China*—twice monthly, Peking.
SCCS	*Shih Chieh Chih Shih* (World Culture)—semi-monthly, Peking.
SCMP	*Survey of China Mainland Press*—Translations of official documents of Communist China, issued by the American Consulate General, Hong Kong, mimeographed, daily.
SKS	*Shanghai Kung Shang* (Shanghai Industry and Commerce)—twice monthly, Shanghai.
SSST	*Shih Shih Shou Ts'e* (Current Affairs Handbook)—twice monthly, Peking.
TCKTTH	*T'ung Chi Kung Tso T'ung Hsun* (Statistical Work Bulletin)—monthly, Peking.
TKP	*Ta Kung Pao*—daily, Tientsin.
TPJP	*Tung Pei Jih Pao* (Northeast Daily)—Mukden (Shenyang).

ABBREVIATIONS OF TITLES OF
GOVERNMENT ORGANS AND ORGANISATIONS

ACDWF	All-China Democratic Women's Federation.
ACDYF	All-China Democratic Youth Federation.
ACFL	All-China Federation of Labour (since May 1953, ACFTU).
ACFTU	All-China Federation of Trade Unions.
ACSF	All-China Students' Federation.
CC	Central Committee.
CCP	Chinese Communist Party.
CPG	Central People's Government.
CPPCC	Chinese People's Political Consultative Conference.
FEC	Financial and Economic Committee.
GAC	Government Administrative Council (since September 1954 State Council).
KMT	Kuomintang.
MAC	Military and Administrative Committee.
NCNA	New China News Agency.
NDYL	New Democratic Youth League.
PB	Political Bureau.
PLA	People's Liberation Army.
NPC	National People's Congress.

WESTERN EQUIVALENTS OF CHINESE WEIGHTS
AND MEASURES USED

Area: 1 *mow*, or *shih mow* = 0·067 hectares = 0·165 acres.

Weight: 1 *catty*, or *shih chin* = 500 grams = 1·102 lbs.

1 *picul*, or *shih tan* = 100 *catty* = 50 kgs. = 110·23 lbs.

Capacity: 1 *tou* = 10 litres = 8·8 qts. (English) or 10·6 qts. (U.S. liquid) or 9·1 qts. (U.S. dry).

Currency: 1 Jen Min Piao (JMP) or People's Bank Yuan or Chinese dollar. On March 1, 1955, there was a conversion of old to new JMP's, one new JMP being equal to 10,000 old. The official rate is £1 = JMP 6·893; 1 U.S. $ = JMP 2·4

CONTENTS

CONTENTS

14

CONTENTS

CONTENTS

PART ONE

BASIC ASPECTS
OF
CHINA'S ECONOMIC
DEVELOPMENT

CHAPTER I

THE HERITAGE: CHINA'S ECONOMIC BACKWARDNESS

Whatever path of development Mao and the Communist Party choose for China will be determined substantially by the material heritage of the former régime. This is the means they have at hand; the ends they achieve will be decisively affected by them. A study of the economy of Mao's China should therefore begin with a flashback into the past.

The overriding feature of China's economy is its abysmal backwardness and poverty. As four-fifths of the Chinese people are peasants, it might be well to begin with a short description of Chinese farming.

BACKWARDNESS OF AGRICULTURE

The density of population, measured by the number of people per unit of cultivated land, is exceedingly high. An estimate puts the number of acres of cultivated land per head of population in China at 0·45 as against 8·04 in the United States, 2·01 in Russia, 1·11 in Germany, 1·29 in France. Even Britain (0·67 acres), which is largely dependent on imports for food and agricultural raw materials, is better off than China.[1] As the proportion of population engaged in agriculture in China is much larger than in the advanced countries of the West, a comparison of the densities of the agricultural population is even more unfavourable to China than is indicated by these figures. The Chinese farm is thus truly lilliputian:

Average Size of Farm in Seven Countries (acres)	
United States (1930)	156·85
England and Wales (1924)	61·38
Denmark (1919)	39·74
Germany (1933)	21·59
Netherlands (1930)	14·28
China (1929–33)	3·76
Japan (1927)	2·67

Source: J. L. Buck, *Land Utilisation in China*, Shanghai, 1937, p. 268.

[1] A. K. Chiu, 'Agriculture', in H. F. MacNair, editor, *China*, Berkely and Los Angeles, 1946, p. 468.

While the Chinese peasant possesses little land, he has even less of the other means of production. Agricultural machinery barely merits mention. Although inhabited by more than a quarter of the world's farming population, China had in 1951 less than 2,000 tractors as against a world total of 6,130,000,[2] that is, a bare 0·03 per cent. In China there were some 120,000 acres of arable land per tractor, as against 57 in the United Kingdom, 119 in the United States, 385 in France, 469 in Czechoslovakia, 988 in U.S.S.R., 1,888 in Poland and 20,398 in India.[3] Even in India there were relatively six times more tractors than in China.

The scarcity of livestock is even more striking. A study undertaken by J. L. Buck shows this clearly. He states that only 34 per cent of all farms had oxen, 18 per cent had donkeys, 18 per cent had buffaloes, 6 per cent mules and 5 per cent horses; 69 per cent had chickens, 44 per cent hogs, 7 per cent sheep, 2 per cent goats, 1 per cent cattle, 8 per cent ducks, and 1 per cent geese.[4] The average number of draft animal units per man-equivalent in Chinese agriculture in the 'twenties was 0·48, as against 3·82 in the United States.[5]

The Chinese peasants' poverty in land is closely connected with his poverty in animals. Land cannot be spared to raise beasts. Buck shows that an acre devoted to crops for direct human consumption gives 6–7 times more food energy than when it is used for milk production, and about 19 times more than in egg production.[6] 'It usually takes about two hectares of land to raise sufficient feed for a milk cow or beef animal for a year. The food crop from the same amount of land is generally sufficient for the annual consumption of a five-member family.'[7] The raising of draft animals can no more easily be afforded. The net result is that

[2] W. S. Woytinsky and E. S. Woytinsky, *World Population and Production*, New York, 1953, p. 515.

[3] *Ibid.*, pp. 516–7.

[4] Buck, *Land Utilisation in China, op. cit.*, p. 246. Buck's works are used extensively in the present work. They are statistical studies whose limitations are explicit and obvious; dealing as they do with an illiterate peasantry, they cannot but be approximations, which serve adequately to indicate orders of magnitude rather than precise quantities. Subsequent citations from Buck's studies should be read with this consideration in mind.

[5] J. L. Buck, *Chinese Farm Economy*, Chicago, 1930, p. 231.

[6] Buck, *Land Utilisation in China, op. cit.*, p. 12.

[7] T. H. Shen, *Agricultural Resources of China*, Ithaca, N.Y., 1951, p. 143.

whereas 47 per cent of the farm area in the United States is made up of pasture, and in European countries 15–50 per cent, only 1·1 per cent of the farm area in China is pasture.[8]

The scarcity of draft animals compared with human beings makes animal labour much dearer than human labour. Thus in 1939 an agricultural worker averaged 0·58 Chinese dollars per labour day (without board), while double this amount—1·16 Chinese dollars—was paid for a draft animal.[9] When board for the worker and feed for the animal are included wages were 0·34 and 0·78 respectively (the value of board for one day's labour of a man being 0·24 dollars, while feed for the animal was valued at 0·38 dollars).[10]

The cheapness of human labour compared with that of draft animals encourages the displacement of animal by man-power wherever possible, and thus tends to make draft animals even scarcer.

China compares even more unfavourably with Western countries in the quality of its livestock than in its quantity. To give one example only, it has been calculated that a native Chinese yellow cow gives an average of 262·8 pounds of milk per year as against 9,196·8 pounds given by an average Holstein cow.[11]

In the use of fertilisers too, Chinese farms show up very badly. This is particularly noticeable in a comparison with neighbouring Japan. Japan undertakes intensive agriculture very similar to that of China, and even though its land is poorer and the average farm considerably smaller, yields are very much higher than in China. The main reason is the much larger quantity of fertilisers applied. In 1936 Japan used 3·4 million tons of chemical fertilisers[12] as against a mere 200,000 tons in China, which has a crop area about 16 times bigger than that of Japan.[13] If fertilisers were applied in China as widely as in Japan, some 50 million tons would be required, or more than double world production of chemical

[8] Buck, *Land Utilisation in China, op. cit.*, pp. 5–6.
[9] Shen, *op. cit.*, p. 373.
[10] *Ibid.*
[11] R. W. Phillips, R. G. Johnson and R. T. Moyer, *The Livestock of China*, Washington, 1945, p. 60.
[12] E. B. Schumpeter, editor, *The Industrialisation of Japan and Manchukuo*, 1930–40, New York, 1940, p. 251.
[13] Shen, *op. cit.*, pp. 36–8.

fertilisers in 1946–7 (23,939,000 tons).[14] With animals so scarce, animal manure cannot compensate for the lack of chemical fertilisers, and human excrement, or 'night soil' must be used instead. Although extensively used as a fertiliser, 'night soil' can, however, supply not more than a fifth of China's optimum needs.[15]

Pesticides to combat crop insects, pests and plant diseases are no less scarce. According to the National Agricultural Research Bureau, losses caused by insect pests and plant diseases to five winter crops in 1935–6, in terms of percentage reduction of normal yield, were as follows: wheat, 27 per cent; barley, 27 per cent; field peas, 30 per cent; broad beans, 28 per cent; oats, 29 per cent.[16] It is estimated that the rice borer alone causes an annual loss of 10 per cent of the rice crop.[17]

The Chinese peasant is well known for his intelligence and diligence. He makes the best possible use of the scarce means of production at his disposal. The limited area of the farm is exploited to the full by planting rice in seed beds and then transferring the seedlings to the field. This extends the period in which the fields are in use. By sowing one crop between rows of another already standing, one being harvested while the other is still growing, the same area is made to yield more. Double cropping is common in North China, and three or even four crops in succession are raised on the same plot in the south. Whatever animal, vegetable and human refuse is available is conscientiously put to use as manure. Systematic irrigation, mainly by hand or foot pumps, is carried out. Mud is dredged from river beds to fertilise the fields; soil transferred from one part to another; terracing is practised widely; and every scrap of land utilised.

These methods of increasing the yield involve of course great exertion, and indeed the amount of labour the Chinese peasant invests in each unit of land is many times what the farmer in Europe or the United States puts in. Buck says:

[14] U.S. Department of Agriculture, quoted in G. F. Winfield, *China: The Land and the People*, New York, 1948, p. 287.
[15] *Ibid.*, pp. 264–5.
[16] National Agricultural Research Bureau, Nanking, *Crop Reports*, August 1936, p. 232.
[17] J. L. Buck, *Some Basic Agricultural Problems of China*, New York, 1947, p. 8.

The man-equivalent required to grow one acre of wheat is 26 days compared with 1·2 days in the United States: one acre of cotton in China 53 days compared with 14 days in the United States: one acre of corn 23 days compared with 2·5 days in the United States.[18]

Despite the great investment of labour, the yield, even per unit of land, let alone per unit of labour, is on the whole not at all high, as can be seen from the following table:

A Comparison of Yields of Crops in China with Yields in Other Countries (in quintals per hectare)

Wheat		Rice		Corn		Cotton	
Denmark	33·1	Japan	30·7	U.S.A.	16·3	Egypt	4·5
Belgium	25·3	China	25·6	Italy	15·8	Mexico	4·4
Britain	21·2	U.S.A.	16·8	Argentine	13·8	Brazil	3·0
Japan	13·5	Argentine	16·8	Rumania	13·1	U.S.A.	2·0
France	13·1	India	16·5	China	7·5	China	1·8
U.S.A.	9·9					India	0·9
China	9·7						
India	8·1						
Argentine	6·2						
Russia (European)	5·9						

Source: Buck, *Chinese Farm Economy, op. cit.*, p. 208.

Compared with the extensive agriculture of the U.S.A. or Russia, the yield per acre in China is not low, but compared with the more intensive agriculture of Europe it is very low indeed.

Even more significant is the low yield per unit of labour in China. Buck states that 'production per unit of labour in the United States is apparently at least twenty-five fold greater than in China.'[19]

The extreme poverty and primitivity of Chinese agriculture and the very low output per hour of work are accompanied by mass underemployment in the countryside. Except for short busy seasons, many of the Chinese peasants, especially in the north, often find themselves without any work to do. It has been estimated that 168 million people were underemployed in 1925.[20]

A low level of productivity gives the peasant a very low standard of living. Peasant homes are mud and bamboo huts without

[18] Buck, *Land Utilisation in China, op. cit.*, p. 14.
[19] Buck, *Chinese Farm Economy, op. cit.*, p. 423.
[20] 'Unemployed in China', CEJ, December 1931.

ceilings below the raftered roofs; the earth serves as their floor and greased paper replaces glass in the windows; kerosene lamps are a semi-luxury, homes usually not being lit; and the same roof shelters man and beast. Food consists almost entirely of grain and vegetables, hardly any meat being eaten. Clothing consists of cotton cloth and straw sandals. Disease is rife, illiteracy almost universal.

These bare facts show plainly that redistributing the national income and wealth cannot by itself improve the conditions of the people in any great measure. As long as the overwhelming majority are engaged in agriculture and the productivity of labour in agriculture is as low as it is today, no real improvement in their conditions is possible.

INDUSTRIAL BACKWARDNESS

China is very backward industrially not only in comparison with Europe and North America, but also when compared with some of her neighbours, such as Japan, or even India.

One measure of the level of industrial development is the amount of mechanical energy consumed. In 1937 the energy consumed *per capita* (coal-equivalent, in metric pounds) was 170 in China as against 190 in India; 600 in Egypt; 760 in Yugoslavia; 860 in Rumania; 2,000 in Poland; 2,340 in Japan; and 13,310 in the United States.[21] The consumption of steel shows a similar picture. Steel consumption per head in 1950 was (in metric pounds): China, 2; India 11; Japan 111; U.S.S.R., 278; United Kingdom, 556; United States, 1,130.[22] The output of cement in China in 1952 was 2·9 million tons[23] against 2·7 million in India (in 1950).[24] The output of electricity in 1950 in China was 2,250 million kwh. against 5,063 million in India and Pakistan, and 38,840 million in Japan.[25] The number of spindles in China at the beginning of 1951 was 4 million against 10·8 million in India (or 3 times more *per capita* in India than China).[26] The number of

[21] Woytinsky, *op. cit.*, pp. 299, 942.
[22] *Ibid.*, p. 1124.
[23] Li Fu-chun, *Report on the First Five Year Plan for Development of the National Economy of the People's Republic of China in 1953–57*, delivered on July 5 and 6, 1955, at the Second Session of the First National People's Congress, Peking, 1955, p. 32.
[24] Woytinsky, *op. cit.*, p. 825.
[25] *Ibid.*, p. 967.
[26] *Ibid.*, p. 1067.

looms in December 1936 was 56·2 thousand in China against 201·5 thousand in India and Ceylon.[27]

It has been calculated that gross manufacturing output in 1936 was 19·9 times greater in Germany than in China, 19·0 times in the United Kingdom and 61·6 times in the U.S.A.[28] The value of the net output per factory worker in the U.S.A. (1935) was 19·3 times greater than in China (1936), 9·5 times greater in Germany (1936), and 8·5 times greater in the United Kingdom (1935).[29] Comparison of a handicraft worker's output in China with that of a factory worker's in the West shows the difference to be even greater, as the output per handicraft worker in China was 2·6 times smaller than the output per Chinese factory worker. And so, 'one day's work of an American worker will be equivalent to fifty days' work of a Chinese handicraft worker'.[30]

A Chinese economist has estimated that in 1933 there was in the United States an average of about 600 times more industrial capital *per capita* than in China, or more than 900 times more of manufacturing capital alone were considered.[31]

To gauge the industrial level of China, especially in relation to Mao's plans, the most cogent comparison is between the level reached by China on the eve of Mao's coming to power and that reached by Russia on the eve of the Bolshevik revolution. A Chinese Communist economist who made such a comparison gave the following results:

Comparison of Industrial Production in China in 1943 and in Russia in 1913

	Unit	China	Russia	Ratio between
		(1)	(2)	(1) and (2)
Steel	1,000 tons	1,200	4,200	1 : 3·5
Iron	1,000 ,,	1,915	4,200	1 : 2·2
Coal	1,000 ,,	52,647	29,050	1 : 0·6
Electricity	1,000 kw.	2,500	1,100	1 : 0·44
Acid	1,000 tons	300	338	1 : 1·1
Spindles	1,000 spindles	5,000	7,668	1 : 1·5
Railways	1,000 kms.	30	73	1 : 2·4
Petroleum	1,000 barrels	330	9,000	1 : 27·2

Source: Wang Hai-chi, *Economy of New Democracy* (Chinese), Shanghai, 1950, p. 6.

[27] Woytinsky, *op. cit.*, p. 1068.
[28] Pao-san Ou and Foh-shen Wang, 'Industrial Production and Employment in Pre-War China,' *The Economic Journal*, September 1946.
[29] *Ibid.*
[30] *Ibid.*
[31] Tso-fan Koh, *Capital Stock in China*, New York, 1942, p. 19.

Thus even in absolute terms, China's industrial output on the whole lagged well behind that of Russia in 1913. Per head of population China was much worse off, her population being four times as big as Russia's at that time.

TRANSPORT

Transport is an essential requisite for industrial development, and China's lack of facilities in this sphere is one of the worst bottlenecks holding up her advance. Her transport lags far behind that of the West or even India. Prior to the Second World War, railway density in a few countries was as follows:

	Length of Railroads (kms.)	Area per km. of Railroad (sq. kms.)	No. of people per km. of Railroad
China	22,940	540·8	25,300
India	66,185	61·9	5,878
United Kingdom	32,309	6·9	1,483
United States	381,079	20.6	345

Source: U.N., *Economic Survey of Asia and the Far East, 1947*, Shanghai, 1948, p. 113.

China was much poorer even than India in rolling stock, having (in 1948) 2,477 locomotives and 35,000 wagons as against India's 8,488 locomotives and 285,300 wagons (in 1938).[32]

China's position as regards other means of transport is no better. Thus in 1946 China had about 34,000 trucks,[33] as against more than double—87,810—in India (in 1950).[34] Again, in 1947, there were in China 16·2 thousand passenger motor vehicles as against 90·1 thousand in India.[35]

NATIONAL INCOME

The backwardness of China's agriculture, industry and transport compound to make an extremely low national income. It has been estimated by Ta-chung Liu that for the years 1931–6 consumption *per capita* in China was only 36·6 U.S. dollars (current prices) as against 404·8 in the United States, i.e., Chinese consumption was 11·1 times smaller.[36] The difference between

[32] U.N., *Economic Survey of Asia and the Far East, 1949*, New York, 1950, pp. 60, 62.
[33] *Report of the United Kingdom Trade Mission to China, October to December, 1946*, London, 1948, p. 204.
[34] U.N., *Economic Survey of Asia and the Far East, 1950*, New York, 1951, p. 263.
[35] *Ibid.*
[36] Ta-chung Liu, *China's National Income, 1931–36*, Washington, 1946, p. 16.

26

China and the U.S.A. is seen to be even greater when other items of the national income, e.g. investment, are included. Gross national product *per capita* in 1931–6 was 26·3 times greater in the U.S.A. than in China. Since then the national income in the U.S.A. has doubled while in China it has hardly risen at all.

Most specialists on the economy of China tend to think that Ta-chung Liu greatly overestimated the national income of China. Colin Clark estimates that the net income produced per head of working population in China (1933–5) was 138 International Units;[37] in India (1944–5), 246; in U.S.S.R. (1937), 379; in Hungary (1938–9), 408; in Poland (1938), 508; in Japan (1940), 600; in Great Britain (1947), 1,383; in United States (1947), 2,566.[38] A United Nations estimate also puts China's national income much below that even of India, being 27 U.S. dollars in China (in 1949) as against 57 in India (1948–9) and 100 in Japan (1949).[39]

The obverse of the same coin is the small amount of capital. This is both cause and result of the low national income. Colin Clark calculates that during the period 1935–8 real capital per head of the working population was 180 I.U.'s in China as against 580 in India, 1,350 in Japan, 2,740 in France, 4,360 in the United States, and 5,000 in the United Kingdom.[40]

Low national income per head means a low level of consumption. The following table serves as a rough guide to general nutritional standards:

Annual Per Capita Consumption of Some Foodstuffs in 1934–8 (metric pounds)

	Meat, Milk. and Eggs	Fish	Sugar	Fats and Oils
United States	483·8	10·2	98·8	44·2
United Kingdom	395·0	24·2	98·2	39·6
Poland	387·8	4·0	17·0	14·8
India	137·8	3·2	29·8	6·6
China	28·8	5·6	2·4	12·6

Source: Woytinsky, *op. cit.*, pp. 290–1.

[37] Clark defines the 'International Unit' as 'the amount of goods and services which 1 dollar would purchase in U.S.A. over the average of the period 1925–34'.

[38] C. Clark, *The Conditions of Economic Progress*, Second Edition, London, 1951, pp. 47, 63, 115, 116, 124, 126, 137; the figure for U.S.S.R. is from the first edition (London, 1940), p. 86.

[39] U.N., *Economic Survey of Asia and the Far East, 1950, op. cit.*, p. 112.

[40] C. Clark, quoted in I.L.O., *The Economic Background of Social Policy, including Problems of Industrialisation*, New Delhi, 1947, p. 74.

On the whole the nutritional level of China is not only very low compared with the advanced countries but even lags behind India.

As regards clothing the consumption level in China is much the same as in India, but much lower than in Japan or Western countries.

Annual Per Capita Consumption of Cotton in 1934–8
(metric pounds)

United States	20·0
United Kingdom	25·6
U.S.S.R.	8·2
Japan	21·0
India	2·6
China	3·0

Source: Woytinsky, *op. cit.*, p. 294.

The consumption of services is also extremely low in China. Thus, for instance, medical services compare very unfavourably with other countries. The number of doctors per 10,000 people (around 1940) was, in the United States, 12·9; United Kingdom, 10·6; Japan, 9·0; Czechoslovakia, 7·7; U.S.S.R., 7·6; Poland, 3·9; India, 0·8; China (excluding Manchuria), 0·3.[41] Practically the whole of the rural population of China as well as more than half the urban population are tended only by the traditional 'medicine men'.[42]

[41] Woytinsky, *op. cit.*, p. 229.
[42] Li P'ei-san, 'Adopt the Correct Attitude Toward the Medical Legacy of the Fatherland', HH, October 2, 1955; ECMM, 15.

CHAPTER II

GENERAL PROBLEMS OF THE ECONOMIC DEVELOPMENT OF CHINA AND THEIR SOLUTIONS

CAPITAL REQUIREMENTS

For China to pull herself out of her all-pervading poverty, large amounts of capital are needed. It is possible to give some idea of the magnitude of the sums required.

A group of United Nations experts dealing with the economic development of backward countries in general, estimated the amount of capital that would be required for a very modest increase in national income ($1\frac{1}{2}$ per cent per annum per head of population). They assume that populations would grow by 1 per cent per annum, a rate actually below that of Chinese population growth.[1] Secondly, 1 per cent of the total working population would transfer into non-agricultural employment each year. In a sense, such a rate of transfer is rather high, since it would increase industrial output by more than 10 per cent per annum. On the other hand, it would still not be high enough to reduce the absolute number of persons engaged in agriculture. Neither is a 10 per cent annual increase in industrial output unusual for countries which are just beginning their industrial development.

To achieve these targets, the underdeveloped countries, with 1,527 million people, would need an annual investment of some 19 thousand million U.S. dollars, 'which is about 20 per cent of the national income of these countries in 1949'.[2] This 19 thousand million U.S. dollars covers only the direct needs of industry and agriculture. 'The total capital requirements, including the capital required for social overheads, greatly exceeds $19 billion.'

[1] Chinese Ministry of the Interior investigations conducted in certain typical areas comprising an aggregate of some 30,180,000 people, showed a birth rate of 3.7 per cent, and a death rate of 1.7 per cent, making the natural rate of increase 2 per cent (Pai Chien-hua, '600,000,000 People—A Gigantic Force in Our Nation's Socialist Construction Work', JMJP, November 1, 1954); ECMM, 9.

[2] U.N., *Measures for Economic Development of Underdeveloped Countries*, New York, 1951.

In applying the results of this report to China some reservations must be made. The bias in the Report is on investment in light industry, where the amount invested is much smaller per employed person than in heavy industry, while in China the emphasis is on heavy industry.[3] Secondly, the Report did not take into account unproductive investments, such as those in the armament industry and defence. Thirdly, national income *per capita* in the underdeveloped countries covered by the Report was some 60 U.S. dollars, while in China it was (in 1949) only 27 U.S. dollars, and in 1956 probably some 40 U.S. dollars. If, to achieve the modest targets envisaged in the Report, some 20 per cent of national income would have to be saved annually, then to achieve comparable targets for China, some 30 per cent of the national income would have to be saved, or about 8 milliard U.S. dollars. Such a rate of accumulation is unprecedented.[4]

China has had, to date, only an infinitesimal rate of accumulation. Although estimates of her capital stock and its accumulation are even less reliable than other Chinese statistics, we might perhaps gain some idea of their magnitude from an estimate advanced by Ou Pao-san. He estimated capital investment for the years 1931–6 as follows: 1931, 698 million yuan; 1932, 808 million; 1933, a net disinvestment of 24 million; 1934, disinvestment of 617 million; 1935, disinvestment of 573 million; and 1936, an investment of 1,472 million.[5] The highest figure— for 1936—is equivalent to some 400 million U.S. dollars at 1936 prices, or about 800 million at 1952 prices (of this sum more than half was investment by foreign capital). National investment, domestic and foreign, as a percentage of total national income was, in 1931, 2·8; 1932, 3·3; 1933, –0·1; 1934, –3·1; 1935, –2·7; 1936, 5·5. India, with a higher income level than China showed, in 1949–50, an estimated rate of investment of 8 per cent.[6]

[3] See pp. 52–5.
[4] The rate of accumulation in other countries in the past was as follows: Britain: 1860–9, 16·6 per cent; 1900–10, 12·2 per cent; 1919–24, 8·1 per cent; 1925–30, 7·6 per cent; 1934–7, 7·0 per cent. United States: 1900–10, 14·3 per cent; 1919–24, 12·2 per cent; 1925–30, 10·9 per cent; 1934–7, 5·0 per cent. France: 1870–9, 6·0 per cent; 1900–10, 9·0 per cent; 1913, 12·5 per cent; 1925–30, 11·2 per cent. Germany: 1900–10, 19·1 per cent; 1925–30, 7·7 per cent; 1934–7, 11·8 per cent. Japan: 1919–24, 21·9 per cent; 1925–30, 19·8 per cent; 1934–7, 21·9 per cent (Clark *op. cit.*, First Edition, p. 406). Even Stalinist Russia, with its forced savings, was far from reaching the rate of 40 per cent. Thus the First Five Year Plan envisaged an investment in

In order to syphon off as much of the rural population as would decrease the absolute number of agriculturists and thus decrease the pressure of population on limited agricultural resources, a much larger amount of capital would be needed, and a rate of saving considerably higher even than 30 per cent.

China is in the clutches of a vicious circle. Her national income is too low to provide for significant capital accumulation. But without such accumulation her national income cannot grow rapidly. The possibility of breaching this circle, and the way of doing so are crucial for Mao Tse-tung's plans for the economic development of China.

POSSIBILITIES OF SAVINGS IN AGRICULTURE

With four-fifths of the population engaged in agriculture, one naturally looks in this direction for the saving of a considerable portion of the capital needed for the country's industrial advance.

The first point of enquiry is to assess the possibility of enlarging agricultural output as a source of capital accumulation.

The growth of agricultural output would seem to depend, first of all, on an extension of the cultivated area. However, the outlook is a very limited one, and progress in this direction is dependent on initial large investments of capital. There are hardly any large plains in China like those of the American Middle West. The greater part of the country is broken up by rugged mountains and bare hills. The only considerable tracts of good agricultural land are the fertile plains of the lower Yangtze River, the great delta of the Yellow River and Central Manchuria.

1928–9 of 22·6 per cent of the national income, and in the last year of the Plan (1932–3) a maximum of 33·6 per cent. (*Five Year Plan of National Economic Construction of U.S.S.R.* (Russian), Moscow, 1930, Volume II, Part 2, p. 38). Actually, according to official statistics, in 1929, 22·6 per cent of the national income went to investment, in 1932, 24·2 per cent (A. K. Suchkov, *Revenues of the State Budget of U.S.S.R.* (Russian), Moscow, 1945, p. 9), while the Plan for 1942 aimed at 28·3 per cent (*Problemy Ekonomiki*, October, 1940, p. 67).

[5] Ou Pao-san and Associates, *China's National Income in 1933*, (Chinese), Shanghai, 1947, Vol. I, pp. 173–4.

[6] This relates to the share of gross investment in gross national product. (Derived from Mukharjee and Ghosh, 'The Pattern of Income and Expenditure in the Indian Union. A Tentative Study', *Bulletin of the International Statistical Institute*, 1951. Quoted in W. W. Rostow, *The Prospects for Communist China*, New York, 1954, p. 279.)

The loess lands of the northwest could be very fertile if there were more adequate rainfall. In North China as a whole, good crops can be expected only once in three or four years when rain comes at the right time and in the right quantities. In other years the peasants suffer either from too little rain and hence drought and even famine, or from torrential rains and floods. Manchuria offers almost the only possibility for large-scale agricultural colonisation. Southern Manchuria is, indeed, already over-crowded, but not the north and west. Here, however, settlers will suffer from scanty rainfall and extremely cold winters. As has been remarked: 'The cream of Manchuria is already occupied.'[7]

With few exceptions the Chinese peasant has not left any spot of arable land, however marginal, uncultivated. Land that in Europe or North America would be considered uneconomic is planted with crops in China where labour is plentiful and cheap and the need to eke out an existence compelling. It is true that some of the marginal lands from which even a Chinese peasant cannot raise a living could be cultivated with the help of machinery, or be turned into grassland, but this demands initial investments in transport facilities needed to carry the products to the market. It would demand also considerable investment in machinery, housing, power, etc.

The cost of reclaiming waste land is very high, and at the moment practically prohibitive. Thus the present Minister of Agriculture, Liao Lu-yen, said in a report on March 3, 1955:

'. . . State investments in agriculture do not run to a large amount in the First Five Year Plan. Without large investments and quantities of machines, it is impossible to reclaim waste land on a large scale. According to the standard of state mechanised farms, JMP 40–50 investments at least are required for reclaiming one *mow* of waste land, which means JMP 4,000,000,000–5,000,000,000 investments for reclaiming 100,000,000 *mow* of waste land, a sum that is beyond our financial means at the moment.'[8]

It is thus clear that the reclamation of waste land for extending the cultivated area cannot serve as an *initial* step towards the solution

[7] G. B. Cressey, *China's Geographic Foundations*, New York, 1934, p. 231.
[8] NCNA, Peking, March 9, 1955.

of the basic difficulty facing economic development—the scarcity of capital. Undoubtedly such an extension would be possible and necessary in the long run, but it is dependent on prior development and cannot be the starting point for it. [9]

It would hardly be an exaggeration to say that no country in the world is in such dire need of afforestation simply in order to maintain its agriculture, not to speak of extending it, as China. Growing population pressure and the need for fuel and building materials has led, through the years, to steady encroachment of the forest area by the peasants. Deforestation is a main cause of the silting up of the rivers and hence of floods. By upsetting the hydrological balance, deforestation also leads to disastrous droughts. Furthermore, by removing protective vegetation it allows soil erosion to take place, thus rendering large areas unfit for cultivation. Climatologists are of the opinion that the desert area of North-Central Asia is expanding outwards from the Gobi towards the coast, a process helped by deforestation. A large portion of the hills of China is eroded to rock bottom or at best will grow only scant grass or weeds. Erosion is a grave problem, especially in the Yellow River area. In the rice growing areas of South and Central China deforestation has also proceeded far, but here the innumerable terraces have checked erosion quite effectively.

Whatever the importance of afforestation for preserving agriculture and enlarging its output, it can, however, have only a very long-term effect. Within the space of a few years, or even decades, it cannot help to solve the capital scarcity. Indeed, it may even aggravate the problem by diverting some of the precious capital available.

The case of water conservancy is hardly any different.

There are other ways of increasing agricultural output—by the use of more fertilisers, more and better irrigation and drainage, better seed selection, introduction of better strains and varieties, more and better animals, the control of plant and animal diseases, pest control, etc.

[9] The Communist authorities are so conscious of the great scarcity of good land which does not need big initial capital investment for cultivation that in order to save small corners of it, they encourage cremation, (see, for instance, the article, 'Minister of Interior Expresses Views on the Question of Burial' JMJP, October 21, 1952), although in face of deep-seated beliefs no laws are laid down to enforce it.

A generous use of fertilisers can make a big difference to output, as neighbouring Japan clearly showed. There, between 1880 and 1920, the combined unit yield of six major crops rose by nearly 50 per cent.[10] A wide application of fertilisers, however, is dependent upon a number of factors that presuppose certain large investments of capital. Electricity, needed to draw nitrogen from the air, and to make superphosphates from the extensive sources of phosphates discovered in Yunnan Province, is a key to their production. Cheap transport is also vital, to carry fertilisers at economic prices into the far interior. Here again, investments in electricity for fertilisers, and in transport, beneficial as they would be to production, and hence to income and savings in the long run, have the immediate effect of aggravating the capital scarcity. Another great impediment to the use of fertilisers is their cost. In Japan fertilisers make up 22 per cent of production costs, or 27–33 per cent of the peasants' money costs.[11] A precondition for as wide a use of fertilisers as in Japan is the existence of a large urban market for the peasants' products. Without a big industrial population with a rising standard of living, the peasant cannot market his products well, and so has little cash with which to buy fertilisers. This situation is very pertinent to industrially backward China. The wide use of fertilisers presupposes industrialisation as an accomplished fact. Thus we come up against another facet of the vicious circle: the use of fertilisers can produce surpluses, aid capital accumulation and industrialisation, but the existence of a developed industry is a prerequisite for the use of fertilisers.

Other means for increasing agricultural output, such as the use of better seeds, better animals, etc., are cheaper and demand relatively little initial investment. These therefore can more easily be put into effect to increase agricultural output.

But even assuming a rise in agricultural output, this does not guarantee the creation of surpluses that can serve the needs of capital accumulation and industrialisation. First, the increase in agricultural output may be paralleled by an increase in the rural

[10] B. F. Johnson, 'Agricultural Productivity and Economic Development in Japan,' *Journal of Political Economy*, December, 1951.
[11] J. H. Boeke, *The Interests of the Voiceless Far East*, Leiden, 1948, p. 41.

population. When food is scarce and the birth rate high, as in China at present, more food may simply result in more people living on the same standard. Only when the rise in incomes is really rapid and very considerable does it check population increase. Otherwise economic advance may be rapid enough to check the death rate but not the birth rate.

China is entering the so-called 'vital revolution', or more precisely, its first half. During this stage (through which Western Europe passed during the nineteenth century) the death rate declines steeply (as a result of better sanitary conditions, health services, etc.), while the birth rate hardly falls. The natural increase of population is therefore very high. In the second half of the 'vital revolution'—the stage which Western Europe has reached—the birth rate falls quickly. When Europe entered the vital revolution (at the time of the industrial revolution) its total population was relatively small (187 million in 1800),[12] and the density of population was very low, so that the increasing numbers did not bear too heavily on agricultural output. In addition, a considerable portion of Europe's population migrated,[13] mainly to North America, and produced enough food in its new homes for both itself and to supply some of Europe's requirements. Thirdly, a considerable portion of Europe's food requirements during the first phase of her 'vital revolution' was supplied by the agrarian countries of Asia and Africa. Now, China has a much larger population—more than three times as large as Europe's at the time of its industrial revolution—with a much higher density, practically no openings for migration, and no sources of food imports. It is true that demographic phenomena are subject to a demonstration effect, such as the adoption of Western birth control practices,[14] so that it is fairly safe to predict that the time-lag between the two halves of the vital revolution will be much

[12] Woytinsky, *op. cit.*, p. 34.
[13] At least 65 million people left Europe between 1820 and 1930. (*Ibid.*, p. 72).
[14] In July 1954 the Ministry of Health drew up regulations concerning improvement in the problem of contraception and birth control (KMJP, December 19, 1954). These regulations, unwilling altogether to flout the Soviet ban on abortions, put such slight restrictions on this practice as to make it virtually free. The stipulations are: 'Abortion is allowed in cases where continued pregnancy is medically considered undesirable, where the spacing of childbirth is already too close and where a mother with her baby only 4 months old has become pregnant again and experiences difficulty of breast-feeding. The operation may be done upon the joint application of the

shorter in China than it was in the West.[15] Nevertheless, unless there is a *quick* and marked rise in living standards, population increase will not be checked, but on the contrary will parallel the increase in food output and China will have to cope with the full explosive potentialities of the 'vital revolution's' first phase, at least in the short run.

Even if the rise in agricultural output were not paralleled by an increase in the number of mouths to be fed in the countryside, there is nevertheless another threat to the agricultural surpluses which may prevent them reaching the towns to feed new industrial workers, to supply raw material to industry, or to be exported in exchange for imported machinery. The first reaction of a peasant to a rise in output where food is scarce is to fill his stomach. Only after satisfying his hunger does he show any interest in increasing the sale of his goods, and then in the first instance only in order to buy industrial consumer goods. Having satisfied his appetite for these, he will take an interest in buying producer goods—chemical fertilisers, improved ploughs, etc. Indeed, it is only when increased output is likely to benefit the peasant in one of these two ways that he shows real zeal in production. But if the increased agricultural output per head goes to fill the rural belly, there will be no agricultural surpluses for industrialisation. And if the surpluses that do collect are available only in exchange for industrial consumer goods, industry will

---

couple, the certification of a doctor and the approval of the responsible organisation to which they belong. If the reason is special work or too heavy work (or study), any request for operation must first be certified and endorsed by the key personnel of the responsible organisation and also approved by a medical organisation.' (*Ibid.*) Instructions on the use of contraceptives appear in the official press. See, for instance, the article, 'How to Treat the Question of Contraception', by Cho O-fen, CKCN, February 16, 1955 (SCMP, 1017); On March 7, 1957, the Minister of Health, Li Teh-chuan, announced the legalisation of abortion and sterilisation. (NCNA, Peking, March 7, 1957).

[15] Thus, while it took France over 70 years to experience a drop in her birth rate from 30 to 20 per thousand, Sweden and Switzerland 40 years, and England and Denmark about 30 years, it took twelve years (from 1924 to 1936) for the Bulgarian birth rate to fall from about 40 to 26 and for the Czechoslovakian rate to fall from 35 to 26. While the birthrate in Central and Southern Europe in 1922–3 was as high as that of Western and Northern Europe in 1881–5, 13 years later, it had reached the 1911 level of those same countries. (R. R. Kuczynski, 'The International Decline of Fertility', in L. Hogben, editor, *Political Arithmetic, A Symposium of Population Studies*, London, 1938, p. 53.)

have to concentrate upon the supply of those goods, that is, the emphasis in industrial development must be on developing light industries. But where the emphasis is put on the development of consumer goods, the process of economic growth is slow.

The vicious circle preventing the use of agricultural surpluses for capital accumulation can be broken by organising the peasants in large collective farms under centralised State control, and thus enabling the State to take away a large portion of the agricultural output. When the State granaries are filled, the surplus agricultural population can be put to capital construction, which is one of the few activities where labour serves as a satisfactory substitute for capital. For instance, the TVA scheme in the United States was built with an army of bulldozers, tractors, mechanical shovels, concrete mixers and the like, while a similar complex on the Huai River in China is being built by millions of peasants who use practically no machinery at all. However unproductive such labour may be, it is very economical where human labour is abundant and cheap and capital equipment scarce and dear. However built, these public construction works are a valuable contribution to the capital fund of the country.

State-imposed collectivisation of agriculture, though it can successfully break the vicious circle of poverty—insignificant capital accumulation—continued poverty, is also, at least partially, weakened by the deleterious effect of population growth which adds to the poverty of the country and places impediments in the path of its economic advance.

HEAVY VS. LIGHT INDUSTRY

A number of factors makes it advantageous for China to put the emphasis on light industry in the course of its industrialisation. It seems logical that projects which yield immediate increases in productivity, or at least in which the time lag between investment and the rise of productivity is shortest, should be preferred. It also seems logical to stress investments with a low capital intensity, i.e., those which demand relatively less capital investment per worker employed. Both of these requirements are satisfied by light industry. Only at a much later stage of development, when income levels should have risen considerably as a consequence of higher productivity, should developing backward countries like China turn to projects which demand larger investments and longer periods of gestation. In other words, these countries should concentrate on light industry from which, after a time, will come the resources—as well as the demand—for heavy industry. This was the line of industrial development in the Western capitalist countries. Thus, in Great Britain, the mother of modern industrial capitalism, for instance, the ratio of capital invested in the consumption goods industries to that invested in the capital goods industries between 1851 and 1924 change as follows:

Year	Ratio
1851	4·7: 1
1871	3·9: 1
1901	1·7: 1
1924	1·5: 1

Source: Woytinsky, *op. cit.*, pp. 415–16.

This development, with light industry as the pioneer of heavy industry, is the most rational and least burdensome to the peoples of the economically backward countries, and is the basis for the sequence of stages recommended by the Industrial Development Working Party of United Nations Economic Commission for Asia and the Far East:

(1) Extractive and light industries, notably light engineering industries, to supply needed consumer goods and to serve as a training ground for engineers so essential for the installation, maintenance and servicing of machinery and power-driven equipment;

(2) Transport, communications and a suitable network of electric power supplies, to open up new areas and to speed the process of industrialisation;

(3) Subject to conditions being favourable, the development of medium and heavy metallurgical processes, and of chemical industries (fertilisers);

(4) Manufacture of simple power tools and machinery, electrical goods and equipment; assembly of road vehicles and transport equipment generally, etc.;

(5) Heavy industries, such as shipbuilding, manufacture of locomotives, rolling stock, road vehicles, etc.;

(6) Manufacture of heavy and precision engineering equipment, including electrical equipment.[16]

The advantages of concentrating initially on the development of light industry become particularly clear when it is borne in mind how big the role of artisan output is in satisfying the Chinese peasants' needs. A *People's Daily* editorial states that handicraft products constitute '60–80 per cent of the total industrial goods bought by the peasants . . .'[17] The number of people engaged in handicrafts at the beginning of 1954 was estimated to be 25·4 million, or with their dependants, 100 million.[18] The capital invested in small workshops is extremely small. Thus it was found that the capital invested per worker in the workshops of the county town in one *hsien* in Hopei Province before the war averaged 95 Chinese dollars.[19] The capital turnover was very rapid; the value of goods produced in a year was 9·5 times bigger than the capital investment. Annual profit was 2·8 times the total capital.[20] It has been estimated that the value of the annual output in the Shensi handicraft co-operatives in 1939 was 25·2 times larger than the capital invested.[21]

However, it became clear even before Mao's rise, that handicrafts and peasants' domestic industries would lose in competition with modern machine industry unless they themselves were modernised, used better equipment, and above all, had cheap electricity, technical advice, and better financial and marketing facilities. All these are beyond the power of the village to give. State help is therefore a question of life and death for the handicraft industries.[22]

[16] U.N. ECAFE, *Interim Report and Recommendations on Industrial Development by the Working Party*, New York, 1948, p. 11, mimeographed.

[17] NCNA, Peking, September 20, 1953.

[18] Lo Yuan-chen, *Economic Transformation in the People's Republic of China* (Russian), Leningrad, 1955, p. 160.

[19] S. D. Gamble, *Ting Hsien, A North China Rural Community*, New York, 1954, p. 323.

[20] *Ibid.*, p. 294.

[21] E. Snow, *Scorched Earth*, London, 1941, Volume II, p. 315.

[22] An example of successful small-scale industry is that of Japan. Home industry using electric power and modern equipment forms the core of Japan's many light industries. It has been estimated that 65 per cent of the total value produced and 57 per cent of the total value of merchandise exported by Japan in 1933 were accounted for by products of medium and small industries ('Handicrafts and Small-scale Industries in Asian Countries', *International Labour Review*, Geneva, July–December, 1950). In 1930, 53 per cent of all the people employed in industry in Japan were in factories

Whether Mao's government put the emphasis on developing small mechanised home industries or on developing large manufacturing industries producing consumer goods, the amount of capital needed for industrialisation in either case would be considerably smaller, and employment opportunities considerably larger, than if the emphasis were put on heavy industry. But these factors—capital costs and employment opportunities—are not the sole, nor indeed the major elements involved. Mao's decision as to the desirability of concentrating on light or heavy industry is largely influenced by other considerations derived in the main from the international situation, and from the role Mao's China hopes to play in it. The following quotation deals with this aspect of the problem of the sequence of stages in industrial development in backward countries:

> Whether or not the Asian countries are able to adopt the most advantageous sequence of stages in economic development will . . . depend, first, upon the prospect of world peace and, secondly, upon the possibility of obtaining capital equipment from the advanced industrial countries. Under threat of war the policy adopted in regard to capital formation is bound to be dominated by considerations of national defence and military preparedness. . . . The difficulty of obtaining capital equipment from abroad may also force these countries to adopt a different sequence of economic development: in the early stages, instead of concentrating their capital resources on the development of essential consumers' goods industries, including agriculture, they may have to divert a large portion of their limited resources to the expansion of their own capital goods industries whose production costs are, furthermore, likely to be appreciably higher than those of similar industries in the advanced countries. [23]

with fewer than 5 workers, 59 per cent in factories with fewer than 10 workers, and 70 per cent in factories with fewer than 50 workers (Chen Han-seng, *Gung Ho!*, New York, 1947, pp. 60–2). Some of the economic-technical disadvantages of small-scale production were partially offset by the fact that many of the small producers were, in fact, part of large financial and administrative organisations. The work of small-scale industries is thus integrated with that of large factories. Big companies supply the small producers with equipment, raw materials, working capital, specifications, technical advice, etc., and they collect, assemble and market the finished product (*ibid.*). Again, in many branches of industry, electric power reduced the size of plant, and machines suitable for small-scale production were specially invented.

[23] International Labour Organisation, Asian Regional Conference, *Report of the Director-General*, Geneva, 1949, pp. 45–6.

With Mao's bureaucracy in control of the commanding heights of the economy—industry, transport, banking—with great political power in hand and a compelling urge to make the country an independent economic-military power, the advantages of industrial development with a bias towards light industry are disregarded. Mao cannot but attempt to vie with the advanced countries and build, on the weak foundations of the backward economy inherited from the past, a new, gigantic, advanced, heavy industrial structure.

The collectivisation of agriculture is an important factor in this set-up. Unwilling or unable to build light industries as a foundation for heavy industry, industry becomes all the more dependent on resources created by agriculture. At the same time, as industry is incapable of providing the goods for which the peasant is willing to exchange his produce, agricultural surpluses have to be extracted by other means, above all via the collective farm. Thus the twin brother of a bias towards heavy industry is the forced collectivisation of agriculture.

Certain features of labour policy derive directly from this. A substantial rise in the industrial workers' living standards becomes impossible. Yet it is imperative for the success of the drive towards industrialisation to raise the productive efficiency and enthusiasm of the workers, and this means raising their living standards. This dilemma is a basic feature of Peking's labour policy, leading to the use of a dual technique of persuasion (highly disproportionate material and moral prizes for successful workers, in other words, Stakhanovism) and pressure (extremely harsh punishments for the violation of labour discipline).[24] Again, an emphasis on heavy industry makes for a widespread use of forced labour,[25] for it is bound up with great constructional activity where unskilled manual labour serves admirably. With food and industrial consumer goods so scarce, the attraction of labourers becomes more difficult than their conscription, the push replaces the pull.

An emphasis on heavy industry also gives the rulers—the Party and State bureaucracy—a specific role to play. The process of capital accumulation, the subordination of consumption to it, must appear to the majority of people as alien to their interests and yet

[24] See pp. 213-18.　　　　[25] See pp. 287-92.

41

inescapable. The 'Guardians' must therefore take to themselves exclusive power to chart the necessary path of economic advance, and to judge where the people's real interests lie. A socio-political dictatorship is born.

The greater the pressure of industrial advance and the greater the emphasis on heavy industry, the stronger becomes the resistance of the people—especially the peasantry—to the regime. Also the greater the international economic, political and military tensions, the more insistent is the need for heavy industry, the more totalitarian becomes the regime, and the more extreme the means it uses to control the populace.

The thread running through the entire economic and political development of Mao's China is the effort of an élite to goad the people into building a magnificent economic-military machine on a backward, narrow agricultural foundation, to jump from medieval times to the supersonic age.

CHAPTER III

ECONOMIC ACHIEVEMENTS AND AIMS[1]

THE REHABILITATION OF THE ECONOMY

The Communist regime was successful in rapidly restoring the economy of the country. In 1949, after more than a decade of war and civil war, industrial production reached its lowest ebb. According to a Communist source, industrial production in 1949 was only some 56 per cent of its pre-1949 peak.[2] Food production was about 25 per cent below the pre-1949 peak.[3]

The Communist press claims that by 1952 China's output had already greatly surpassed previous production peaks.

Industrial and Agricultural Production, 1949–52
(*Pre-*1949 *peak* = 100)

	1950	1951	1952
Electricity	78	117	143
Coal	59	77	95
Petroleum, crude	51	82	119
Pig iron	49	80	102
Steel ingots and castings	69	—	} 148
Structural steel	67	—	
Cement	66	115	133
Cotton yarn	100	108	141
Cotton cloth	109	115	167
Paper	115	150	223
Sugar	48	90	119
Food crops	91·8	100·5	109·9
Raw cotton	83	131	156

Source: 'Economic Development in Mainland China, 1949–53', EBAFE, November, 1953.

This table exaggerates the achievements of the Chinese economy in the period between Mao's rise to power and the end of 1952 by falsifying pre-1949 peak levels. Thus, for instance, the pre-war

[1] Changes in the organisation of the economy—State ownership of industries, collectivisation of agriculture, etc.—are dealt with on pp. 148–73, 187–208.

[2] This figure is based on the index compiled by the Financial and Economic Committee, GAC, 'Economic Development in Mainland China, 1949–53'; EBAFE, November, 1953.

[3] Li Shu-cheng, 'New China's Achievements in Agricultural Production During the Past Three Years', *New China's Economic Achievements, 1949–52*, Peking, 1952, p. 188.

peak figure used for cotton output was 860,000 metric tons. The 1952 output of 1,304,000 was therefore some 56 per cent higher. In fact the 1936 output of cotton in China proper (i.e., excluding Manchuria) was substantially higher, being estimated at 1,031,950 metric tons.[4] To this must be added the output of Manchuria. Cotton output in 1952 was thus only some 15 per cent higher than the pre-war peak.

If the necessary correction in the basic pre-1949 data were to be made, it is very probable that the output of pig iron, electric power, sugar, soya beans and wheat actually did not reach past peak levels. It is also doubtful whether the pre-1949 peak was reached by steel and crude oil production. Differing estimates of output by various authorities make it practically impossible to reach any sound conclusions in this respect. For instance, the *Great Soviet Encyclopaedia* gives the figure for steel output in the peak year as 1 million tons.[5] Another authority put the 1944 figure at 1,200,000 tons.[6] Yet another gives the pre-1949 peak output of crude steel in the whole of China as 923,000 tons.[7]

Another consideration should be taken into account in evaluating the achievements of Mao's regime in reaching—or nearly reaching—pre-1949 peaks of production by 1952. The actual out-

---

[4] Shen, *op. cit.*, p. 308.
[5] *China* (Russian), from *Great Soviet Encyclopedia*, Second Edition, Moscow, 1954, p. 65.
[6] *Report of the United Kingdom Trade Mission to China, etc.*, *op. cit.*, p. 59.
[7] NCNA, Peking, September 21, 1955. The unreliability of Communist statistics in a comparison of production levels under Mao with pre-1949 peak levels is clearly shown by a juxtaposition of figures given in two articles in *People's Daily*, comparing 1951 output with the presumed pre-1949 peak. The first article is by Sung Shao-wen, 'The Achievements in the Chinese People's Construction in the Past Two Years' (JMJP, October 6, 1951). The second is by Li Fu-chun, 'Reconstruction and Development of the Industry of our Country in the Past Three Years' (JMJP, October 2, 1952).

1951 Production as Percentage of Peak pre-1949 Level

	Sung Shao-wen's Article	Li Fu-chun's Article
Pig iron	64·0	104
Steel ingots	97·0	155
Coal	69·2	90
Electric power	94·5	115
Cement	107·0	148
Cotton yarn	105·9	144
Cotton cloth	113·5	161
Paper	155·0	234

put of industry, especially heavy industry, at the pre-1949 peak level, was considerably below the existing plant capacity. This point is of some importance.

A very large amount of capital was invested in Manchuria—as much as 11,000 million yen—during the Japanese occupation.[8] Of course this was not immediately followed by a rise in industrial production. Investments in new mines and steel mills, in power stations, etc., do not yield large returns until a few years after they are made. Owing to a lack of equipment and skilled labour during the war, output continued to lag far behind investments. Thus, while Japanese-occupied Manchuria had a pig iron capacity of 2·5 million tons,[9] actual peak output was only 1·7 million tons. Crude steel production capacity during the war was more than 1·5 million tons,[10] while actual production was probably less than 1 million tons.

Had the plants built by the Japanese in Manchuria been completed according to plan, the output capacities of heavy industry would most probably have been about double the actual output in pre-1949 peak years. This is of special importance, as the overwhelming portion of China's heavy industry, and more than half of all China's modern industry was, and still is, situated in Manchuria.[11] The fact that industrial capacity under the Japanese was far above actual output, made it possible for China by 1952 to reach, or almost reach, the pre-1949 peak output without great capital investments. Nevertheless, the restoration of industrial production was no mean feat, especially when it is recalled that a large part of the equipment of Manchurian industry was dismantled by the Soviet army of occupation.[12]

Agriculture was also restored. Its output did not drop as badly as that of industry during the war and the subsequent civil war. In addition, Nature proved beneficent. Whereas the countryside

[8] U.S. State Department, *United States Relations with China*, Washington, D.C., 1949, p. 600.

[9] J. B. Cohen, *Japan's Economy in War and Reconstruction*, Minneapolis, p. 127.

[10] *China, op. cit.*, p. 65.

[11] 'According to approximately accurate figures, North-east China in 1943 produced 49 per cent of the entire country's coal output, about 87 per cent of pig iron, 93 per cent of steel products and 78 per cent of electric power. Manchuria had 42 per cent of the total railway tracks of the country' (presumably including Taiwan, otherwise 48 per cent) (NCNA, July 4, 1950).

[12] See pp. 391–3.

in 1949 suffered from grave natural calamities, 1950, 1951 and 1952 enjoyed very favourable weather and, consequently, good harvests.

At the end of 1952, China's economy—industry as well as agriculture—was practically rehabilitated. It was then that Peking decided to launch its First Five Year Plan.

THE FIRST FIVE YEAR PLAN (1953–7): INDUSTRIAL OUTPUT TARGETS

China is extremely secretive about detailed economic information. Virtually all the statistical information given is unrelated and usually presented in the form of percentage figures. No reliable bases for systematic statistical computation are offered and it is thus quite impossible to determine with any degree of accuracy how these percentages should be translated into absolute figures. Some light was let into this statistical obscurity by the publication of the first systematic annual report by the State Statistical Bureau in September 1955.[13] Further illumination followed with the first report on the Five Year Plan delivered by Li Fu-chun, Vice-Premier and Chairman of the State Planning Commission, on July 6, 1955. Although this report was made some two and a half years after the launching of the Plan, it is a useful aid to the student of China's economy. But even here the veil of secrecy is barely lifted. Peking, in her First FiveYear Plan, is clearly following the example of the mature Russia, rather than the Russia of 25 years ago.[14] However, information on some key points of the Plan is given. The table on the opposite page gives information about the industrial output targets of the Five Year Plan and actual output in 1952 and 1955:

From Chou En-lai's report to the Eighth Congress of the Chinese Communist Party,[14a] it seems that on the whole the Five Year Plan's targets of industrial output will not only be reached but even considerably surpassed.

[13] NCNA, Peking, September 28, 1953.
[14] In Russia, as time goes by, information about the Plans becomes less and less. The First Five Year Plan was published in four volumes (and an Appendix) totalling 1,947 pages; the second in two volumes totalling 1,315 pages; the third in one volume of 232 pages; and the fourth is a pamphlet of 95 pages; the fifth is a long article, and so is the sixth.
[14a] NCNA, Peking, September 16, 1956.

		1952	1955 (actual)	1957 (goal)
Steel	000 tons	1,350	2,853	4,120
Coal	000 ,,	63,530	93,064	113,000
Electricity	000,000 kwh.	7,260	12,278	15,900
Crude petroleum	000 tons	436	966	2,012
Cement	000 ,,	2,860	4,503	6,000
Machine-made paper	000 ,,	370	589	650
Cotton piece goods	000 bolts	111,630	103,000	163,720
Machine-processed sugar	000 tons	249	410	686
Generators	000 kw.	30	108	227
Electric motors	000 ,,	640		1,050
Lorries	Number	—		4,000

Sources: Li Fu-chun, *op. cit.*, p. 32; and 'Communique on the Fulfilment of the National Economic Plan for 1955', by State Statistical Bureau, NCNA, Peking, June 14, 1956.

The rate of industrial growth aimed at is somewhat less than that achieved by Russia in her First Five Year Plan.[15] Indeed, so meagre are China's initial resources that even after her First Five Year Plan she will still be far behind Russia's level of production not only after its First Five Year Plan, but even before it was started. This can be seen clearly from the following table:

Per Capita Output of Different Goods in China and Russia

		China 1952	China 1957 (target)	Russia 1928	Russia 1932
Power supply	kwh.	12·71	25·20	32·50	81·70
Steel	kg.	2·36	6·53	27·60	35·80
Cotton mill spindles	spindles per 100 persons	0·99	1·15	4·90	4·80
Cotton cloth	meters	6·70	8·85	18·00	16·30
Grain	kg.	286·95	305·74	475·20	421·50

Source: Yang Chien-pai, 'A Comparative Analysis of China's First Five Year Plan and the Soviet Union's First Five Year Plan', TCKTTH, August, 1955; ECMM, 10.

China will need a number of Five Year Plans in order to reach the Russian level of even the pre-Plan era. Though the rate of

[15]

	China Index for 1957 (1952: 100)	China Yearly Rate of Increase	Russia Index for 1932 (1928: 100)	Russia Yearly Rate of Increase
Value of gross industrial output	198·3	14·7	202·0	19·3
Output of large-scale industry	207·0	15·7	230·0	23·2

Source: Yang Chien-pai, 'A Comparative Analysis of China's First Five Year Plan and the Soviet Union's First Five Year Plan', TCKTTH, August, 1955; ECMM, 10.

growth may be swift, it may yet mean very little in absolute quantities.[16]

To see the industrial production targets of the First Five Year Plan in proper perspective, one cannot do better than compare them with those of the projected Second Indian Five Year Plan (1956/7–1960/1).[17]

		China		Per Cent.	India		Per Cent.
		1952	1957	Increase	1955–6	1960–1	Increase
Steel	000,000 tons	1·3	4·1	205	1·3	4·68	231
Coal	000,000 ,,	63·5	113·0	78	38·0	60·0	58
Electricity	000,000 kwh.	7,260	15,900	118	11,000	22,000	100
Cement	000,000 tons	2·9	6·0	110	4·28	13·0	202

Sources: For China: Li Fu-chun, *op. cit.*, p. 32. For India: Government of India *Second Five Year Plan*, 1956, pp. 59, 336.

The table shows quite clearly that the Chinese Five Year Plan is hardly, if at all, more ambitious than the Plan of non-Communist India.

It is most probable that the industrial production targets of the Chinese Five Year Plan will be fulfilled, even overfulfilled. But even then it will be only a short step on the very long road of industrialisation. It has taken Russia some five Five Year Plans to catch up on the 50 years' development lag separating her from the advanced industrial centres of the West (and she has not yet reached the latter in output per head of population); it will probably take twice the time for China to build a comparable industrial civilisation.

---

[16] This was shown clearly in the growth of output of basic materials between 1933 and 1943:

		1933*	1943†	1943 as per-centage of 1933
Crude steel	000 tons	25	923	3,692
Pig iron	000 ,,	606	1,801	297
Coal	000 ,,	28,378	61,875	217
Petroleum	000 ,,	91	320	352

* JMJP, September 24, 1949. Lo Yuan-chen, *op. cit.*, p. 41.
† NCNA, Peking, September 21, 1955.

[17] The First Indian Five Year Plan, 1950/1–1955/6, was mainly a plan of reha-bilitation, as at its beginning the country was still dislocated by war and partition. It is, therefore, much more suitable to use the Second Indian Five Year Plan to compare with the First Chinese Five Year Plan, both being the first Five Year Plans for *development*.

LARGE CAPITAL INVESTMENTS

Even prior to the inauguration of the Five Year Plan, quite considerable capital investments took place. The State budget was the main source of the capital funds. It devoted the following sums to national economic construction:

	In milliard JMP (old currency)[18]	In millions of U.S. dollars at official rate of exchange
1950	17·3	660
1951	35·1	1,534
1952	73·1	3,194

Source: Wang Tzu-ying, 'Our Public Finance', TKP, January 29, 1955.

Of the above-mentioned sums, a certain, quite large, portion was devoted to capital construction. Thus, in 1952, as much as JMP 37·1 milliard (old currency),[19] or, expressed at the official rate of exchange, some U.S. $1,635 milliard, represented the state's gross capital investment.

The First Five Year Plan trained its sights even higher. The state is to contribute JMP 76,640 million (new currency) toward 'economic construction and cultural and educational development' during 1953–7, of which JMP 42,740 million will be allocated to capital investment.

This sum represents an average annual investment rate of JMP 8,548 million, or, at the official rate of exchange, some U.S. $3,650 million. As a matter of fact capital investment was: 1952, JMP 3,711 million; 1953, 6,505 million; 1954, 7,498 million; 1955, 8,212 million.[20]

When using these figures the following considerations should be borne in mind. First, Chinese investment figures include reinvestment of depreciation allowances (these probably account for more than 10 per cent of gross investment).[21] Secondly, the official

[18] On March 1, 1955, there was a conversion of old to new JMP's, one new JMP being equal to 10,000 old.
[19] NCNA, Peking, September 21, 1955.
[20] NCNA, Peking, June 14, 1956.
[21] Thus, in U.S.S.R. which, like China, had a quick capital accumulation, the rate of net investment in non-war years was calculated to be 75–88 per cent of the rate

49

rate of exchange of the JMP is no indication of its real purchasing power, as can be seen by its low black market valuation—60·8 per cent of its official dollar value in 1954.[22] However, to counterbalance these factors, the figure covers *State* investments only, and thus excludes whatever limited private investment is undertaken in agriculture.

Whatever the reservations, an annual capital investment of some 3 milliard U.S. dollars is no mean achievement for China, especially when the sum is compared with the paltry investments of the 1930's.[23]

It has been stated by Minister Po I-po that gross capital investment in 1952 made up 15·7 per cent of the national income; in 1953, 18·3 per cent; in 1954, 21·6 per cent; in 1955, 20·5 per cent; in 1956, 22·8 per cent.[24] Compared with other countries, and especially under-developed countries, this rate is very high. It considerably exceeds the net investment targets envisaged in the Second Indian Five Year Plan, which are set to rise from 7 per cent of the national income in the first year of the Plan to 10 per cent at its close.[25] (The rate of gross investment should thus be some 9–10 per cent in the first year and 12–13 per cent in the last.)

The rate of capital investment in China is, however, below that visualised—and realised—in Russia's First Five Year Plan. There an investment of 22·6 per cent of the national income was planned for the first year of the Plan, and 33·6 per cent for the last year.[26] According to Soviet authorities, 22·6 per cent of the national income did actually go to investment in 1929, and 24·2 per cent in 1932.[27]

---

of gross investment (N.M. Kaplan, 'Capital Formation and Allocation', in A. Bergson, editor, *Soviet Economic Growth*, Evanston and White Plains, 1953, p. 45).

[22] Calculated from F. Pick, *Black Market Yearbook, 1955*, New York, 1955, p. 95.

[23] See p. 30.

[24] Po I-po's speech to the Eighth National Congress of the Chinese Communist Party, NCNA, Peking, September 18, 1956. However, from figures on the previous page, it is clear that Po I-po's figures are probably exaggerated.

[25] Government of India, *Second Five Year Plan, op. cit.*, p. 92.

[26] *Five Year Plan of National Economic Construction of U.S.S.R.*, (Russian), Moscow, 1930, Third Edition, Volume II, Part 2, p. 38.

[27] *The Second Five Year Plan for the Development of the National Economy of the U.S.S.R. (1933–7)* (Russian), Moscow, 1934, Volume I, p. 427.

In absolute terms the level of capital investment in China is modest. Gross investment comes to some 6 U.S. dollars per head of population annually. As against this, the Plans of the East European satellites, projected gross annual investments *per capita* at 45 U.S. dollars (at 1948 prices).[28] China's achievement looks even smaller in comparison with the countries of Western Europe. Thus, for instance, in 1948, net investment *at 1938 prices* (which are about half of 1948 prices) in Western Europe was: Norway, 55 dollars; Sweden, 42; U.K., 36; Denmark, 32; Netherlands, 27; France, 16; Belgium (1947), 16; Italy, 10.[29]

In face of China's extreme backwardness, Mao finds it difficult during the first Five Year Plan to allocate as great a percentage of the national income to investment as did Stalin in his time. However, he goes even further than Stalin in allocating the major portion of capital investment to industry. 58·2 per cent of all capital invested during the first Five Year Plan will be allocated to industry,[30] as against a corresponding figure of 41 per cent for U.S.S.R. during its first Plan.[31]

Of course the greater the share of industry in total capital investment, the greater is the rate of industrial growth. One of the 'secrets' of the Soviets' astonishing tempo of industrial growth is to be found in the bias of Soviet investments towards industry. The 41 per cent ratio for the Soviet First Five Year Plan compares with a 19·1 per cent ratio in the U.S.A. for the years 1880–1912.[32] Of course this means the neglect of housing and other nonproductive capital investments.[33] By accentuating, even more than did Stalin, the bias towards capital investment in industry as a share of all capital invested, Mao hopes to achieve quick industrial growth—quick in terms of China's present backwardness—no matter what the price to the people.

[28] U.N., *Economic Survey of Europe in 1948*, Geneva, 1949, p. 203.
[29] *Ibid.*, p. 48.
[30] Li Fu-chun, *op. cit.*, p. 23.
[31] N. M. Kaplan, 'Capital Formation and Allocation', in Bergson, *op. cit.*, p. 52.
[32] *Ibid.*, p. 54.
[33] The share of housing in the total capital invested in U.S.S.R. was particularly small, being 9·2 per cent during the First Five Year Plan, 9·1 per cent during the Second, and 8·2 per cent (goal) during the Third, as against 26·0 per cent in U.S.A. for the years 1880–1912, 24·6 per cent for 1920–9, and 13·5 per cent even during 1930–40, which were largely years of depression (*ibid.*, p. 61).

THE BIAS TOWARDS HEAVY INDUSTRY

The quicker the rate of industrial growth des ired and the more limited the investment, the more will investment be concentrated on heavy industry. Mao's China shows this bias in an extreme form. Investment in consumption goods industries as a percentage of total industrial investment during the Five Year Plan period is planned to be 11·2, even lower than in Russia during her First Five Year Plan (14·1).[34] As these figures refer to *gross* investment, that is, without taking into account depreciation of existing capital, it is doubtful if the Plan envisages *any* net investment at all in light industry. Even the meagre investment planned is liable to be preyed upon and diverted to other uses. Chia To-fu, Minister of Light Industry, in a speech to the National People's Congress on July 23, 1955, said:

> ... in the spring of this year, in accordance with the directive of the CCP Central Committee and the State Council, we re-calculated the needs of society, possible supply of raw materials and the production capacity of existing light industry of all types, cut and deferred some capital construction projects that could be cut and deferred and that were included by the textile industry and light industry in the Draft Plan. The funds thus saved, if invested in heavy industry, will be enough to build a tractor plant capable of producing 15,000 tractors per annum and two oil refineries capable of producing 1,000,000 tons of oil each per annum. This measure is entirely necessary and correct.

And:

> Recently, the Ministry of Light Industry, the Ministry of Textile Industry and local industrial departments, in accordance with the economy directive of the CCP Central Committee and the State Council, for the second time slashed capital construction plans and investments for the last three years of the Five Year Plan after studying and examining each item. The total amount of investments slashed on these two occasions amounted to 30 per cent of the original capital construction appropriations.[35]

[34] Li Fu-chun, *op. cit.*, p. 47.
[35] JMJP, July 26, 1955. Actually the small capital investment in light industry is not the only bottleneck in its development. The other bottleneck, and for a time

However, things went too far, and in 1956 it was decided that the rate of capital investment in light industry should rise, lest workers' enthusiasm for production wane, with grave effects on general economic growth. The Government decided that "the ratio of heavy-industry investment to light industry should be changed from 8:1, as originally fixed in the Five Year Plan to 7:1,"[35a] that is, the share of light industries in all capital investment in industry should be raised from 11·2 per cent to 12·5 per cent. In justification for this change, the *People's Daily* suddenly blurted out the truth:

> In proportion to population, the output of our light industry is still lagging behind many countries. Take the textile industry, for example. Our cotton mills output has to be increased fourfold before we catch up with the Soviet Union of today, and has to be more than doubled before we catch up with India of today. Our wool, jute and silk mills output has to be increased by nearly forty times before we catch up with the Soviet Union of today, and has to be increased nearly threefold before we catch up with India of nearly four years ago.[35b]

However, even with this new shift, it is very doubtful if the total new capital invested in light industry exceeds the

---

the more pressing one, is the shortage of raw materials, which caused a very low utilisation rate of existing equipment in light industries. Reporting on local State industry a *People's Daily* editorial wrote:

'. . . the equipment utilisation rate is only 60 per cent in the case of the sugar-refining industry . . . in the Central-South region; the equipment utilisation rates of certain key industries in Honan are as follows: textile, 82·2 per cent; oil and fat, 63; flour, 58·9. . . . Equipment utilisation is only 54·42 per cent in the case of the textile industry and 21·16 in the case of the match industry in Anhwei Province. The position is more or less the same in other districts' (JMJP, November 11, 1954; SCMP, 737).

Similarly Chia To-fu reported:

'As to the State-operated textile industry, while utilisation of equipment once reached 96 per cent, it dropped to 76 per cent in 1955 on account of the poor cotton harvest.' 'Utilisation of equipment during 1954 was less than one third in the case of tobacco and matches, only about 50 per cent in the case of oil and fat and wheat flour, and about 60 per cent in the case of leather' (JMJP, July 26, 1955; ECMM, 13).

The shortage of raw materials was starkly revealed after the 1954 floods which 'caused a decline of production in 1955 from the 1954 level as follows: over 600,000 pieces of yarn, 18,000,000 pieces of gunny bags, 180,000 cases of cigarettes. Oil production will also be 180,000 tons less than the Plan' (*ibid.*).

[35a] JMJP editorial, July 9, 1956.
[35b] *Ibid.*

depreciation of existing capital, that is, if any *net* investment takes place at all.

With hardly any capital invested in light industry, its share in the total industrial output is bound to go down. In 1933, capital goods made up 17 per cent of all the country's industrial output.[36] Then came the tremendous Japanese investments in industry—mainly heavy industry—in Manchuria and North China, which raised the percentage considerably. But with the Soviet looting of Manchuria at the end of the war and the general effects of the civil war later, heavy industry suffered badly compared with light industry. So that the output of the capital goods industries in 1949 was 30 per cent of the pre-1949 peak, while that of the consumer goods industries was 70 per cent.[37] Since the establishment of Mao's regime with its restoration of industry and its emphasis on heavy industry, the share of producer goods in the total industrial output has grown. From 28·8 per cent in 1949[38] it rose to 46 per cent in 1955.[39] As practically all industrial investment during the present Five Year Plan is in heavy industry, the share of capital goods in the aggregate output of the modern industrial sector will leap forward and certainly be bigger than the share of light industry as soon as the investments mature. The output of capital goods will then form a higher percentage of total output than is the case in most other countries, including the very advanced ones.

Ratio of Capital Goods Industries to Consumer Goods Industries in Net Output

China	1957 (plan)	1 : 1·2
Britain	1924	1 : 1·5
France	1921	1 : 1·5
Germany	1925	1 : 1·1
Japan	1925	1 : 2·4
U.S.A.	1920	1 : 0·8

Sources: For China: Calculated from Li Fu-chun, *op. cit.*, pp. 34–5. For other countries: Woytinsky, *op. cit.*, pp. 415–16.

The only countries with a higher percentage of industrial output made up of capital goods will be Russia and her European

[36] B. G. Boldyrev, *The Finances of the People's Republic of China* (Russian), Moscow, 1953, p. 8.

[37] 'Economic Development in Mainland China, 1949–53', EBAFE, November 1953.

[38] NCNA, Peking, September 21, 1955.

[39] Li Hsien-nien, *Report on the 1956 State Budget*, NCNA, Peking, June 15, 1956.

satellites.[40] There can be no doubt that one of the main factors in the very high rate of industrial growth in the U.S.S.R. was the fact that a very large portion of the capital invested in industry went into capital goods industries and not into consumer goods industries. A machine to produce machines is of greater weight in capital-formation than a machine producing, say, shoes for the people to wear. The bias towards large investments in producer goods industries at the expense of the consumer goods industries is derived from the combined circumstances of an urge for quick industrial advance grafted upon a backward economy. The tendency is to be seen in India, too, a non-Communist country.[41] In China, under a totalitarian bureaucracy, this tendency is revealed in its starkest form.

THE BURDEN OF THE MILITARY BUDGET

A very important factor in Chinese industrial growth, affecting it adversely, is the unproductive expenditure on armaments, which consumes a substantial portion of the national income. Even if one does not include any of the investments in heavy industry, directed, at least in part, to enhancing the military might of the country, and limits oneself to what is included under the

[40] In Russia, the following was the division of the gross output of industry into capital goods and consumption goods (in percentages):

	1913	1928	1932	1937	1940	1942 (goal)
Capital goods	33·3	32·8	53·3	57·8	61·0	62·2
Consumption goods	66·7	67·2	46·7	42·2	39·0	37·8

(Y. Gluckstein, *Stalin's Satellites in Europe*, London, 1952, p. 76).

As regards the countries of Eastern Europe the following was the share of capital goods in the output of industry (in percentages):

	1938	1952
Bulgaria	23·0*	43·9
Czechoslovakia	40·0†	62·0
Poland	47·0†	55·8
Rumania	36·8	57·4
Hungary	34·9	63·0‡

* 1939; † 1937; ‡ 1953.

(G. Kohlmey, *Der Demokratische Weltmarkt*, Berlin, 1955, p. 178).

[41] The Second Five Year Plan of India visualises that 83·7 per cent of all the net capital invested in large and small industry will be devoted to capital goods industries (Government of India, *Second Five Year Plan, op. cit.*, p. 416).

item 'national defence' in the budget, the military burden appears quite considerable.

National Defence Expenditure
(in milliard JMP, old currency)

1950	28,273
1951	50,605
1952	42,777
1953	56,790
1954	52,635
1955	64,999

Source: Wang Tzu-ying, 'Our Public Finance', TKP, January 29, 1955; SCMP, 1113; and NCNA, Peking, June 15, 1956.

At the official rate of exchange this was, in 1950, 1,346 million U.S. dollars; in 1951, 2,211; 1952, 1,868; 1953, 2,424; 1954, 2,246; 1955, 2,746.

Defence expenditure eats up a sizeable portion of the national income:[42] in 1952, 18·1 per cent; in 1953, 15·9 per cent; in 1954, 15·2 per cent; in 1955, 16·2 per cent. This is a very high percentage indeed. By comparison, defence outlay in Ceylon (1951–2) was about 0·95 per cent of the national income; in the Philippines (1950–1), 1·6 per cent; in India (1950–1) about 2 per cent.[43] Even Western countries in the midst of the 'cold war' spend a smaller percentage of their national income on the military budget than does China. Thus in 1955 the United States spent 9·8 per cent of the gross national product; United Kingdom 8·2; France 7·5.[44]

The heavy burden borne by China in her military budget stands in clear relief when compared with the expense on the same count in the Western countries during their industrialisation. It is much greater than it was in Russia too at the beginning of her industrialisation. In 1928 the military budget made up some 2 per cent

[42] Figures for defence expenditure are given in the table above. The national income is calculated from the figures of gross capital investment and its proportion of the national income, given by Minister Po I-po (see p. 50). From what is said in note 24 it is clear that these figures are somewhat exaggerated.

[43] I.L.O. Asian Regional Conference, *Report of the Director-General*, Geneva, 1953, p. 15.

[44] U.N., *Economic Survey of Europe Since the War*, Geneva, 1953, p. 60. Of course, as the net national income is a relatively much smaller proportion of the gross national product in advanced industrial countries than in backward ones, it is clear that the share of defence expenditure in the net national income of China is not much bigger, or perhaps not at all bigger, than the respective figures for the Western countries.

of the gross national product of the U.S.S.R.[45] At that time the number of soldiers in Russia was 562,000.[46] As against this, in Mao's army there were 4·9 million men in 1949, and even after the modernisation and streamlining of the forces, the number was as high as 2·2 million in 1956.[47]

TRANSPORT

The cardinal importance of the transport system for industrial development is quite obvious. At the same time transport can be a serious drain on capital resources needed for development. Conscious of this fact the Soviet Government for a long time did not do much more than maintain and replace the railway system it had inherited.[48] Even then, transport and communication took a considerable part of total investments: during the first Five Year Plan (1928–32), 18·7 per cent; during the second (1933–7), 19·0 per cent; and during the third (planned, 1938–42), 20 per cent.[49] The Peking government intends to follow in Moscow's footsteps by spending as little as possible on transport. But even then Peking will have to devote a considerable portion of her capital resources to this end—in fact a proportion comparable to that devoted by Soviet planners to the same service. Transport, posts and telecommunications will take a projected 19·2 per cent of all capital investments during the first Five Year Plan.[50] The Plan aims at the construction of 4,084 kms of new railway lines. The number of locomotives will increase by 550, the number of goods wagons by 33,720, and the number of passenger wagons by 1,437.[51] These are relatively modest targets. If this were to remain China's rate of railway construction it would take many Five Year Plans to reach even the level of India.

Peking can hardly afford to follow Moscow in limiting herself to maintaining existing railways. The length of railways inherited by Stalin was, in absolute terms, some 3½ times more than that

[45] Rostow, *op. cit.*, p. 322.
[46] *Great Soviet Encyclopaedia* (Russian), Volume 47, Moscow, 1940, p. 787.
[47] NCNA, Peking, September 19, 1956.
[48] In 1928 the length of railroads in U.S.S.R. was 76·5 thousand kms. and in 1937, 86·4 thousand kms., an increase of less than a thousand kms. a year.
[49] A. Baykov, *The Development of the Soviet Economic System*, Cambridge, 1946, p. 421.
[50] Li Fu-chun, *op. cit.*, p. 23.   [51] NCNA, Peking, August 22, 1955.

inherited by Mao, and per 1,000 population, 13 times more. The Chinese quandary is aggravated by the fact that Peking has embarked on an extensive rather than an intensive type of railway development. The main lines under construction are the Lanchow–Alma–Ata line connecting China to Russia via Sinkiang; the Chining–Ulan Bator line, connecting China, the Mongolian People's Republic and Russia; the Paoki Chengtu line connecting the North West with the South West; the Paotow–Lanchow line connecting the Inner Mongolian Autonomous Region and North West China; the Yintang–Amoy line connecting Kiangsi and Fukien provinces in the South. Most of the new lines will run through very sparsely populated territories, a large part of them desert. This construction is largely motivated by military considerations. Its economic significance will grow, but the new lines will become a paying proposition only after a very long period.

AGRICULTURAL OUTPUT—TARGETS AND ACHIEVEMENTS

Li Fu-chun gave information about the agricultural output targets of the Five Year Plan from which the following table is derived:

		1952 I	1957 II	Percentage Increase 1952–7 III
Grain [52]	000,000 *catties*	328,000	385,600	17·6
Cotton	000,000 *piculs*	26·1	32·7	25·4
Jute and ambary hemp	000,000 ,,	6·1	7·3	19·7
Cured tobacco	000,000 ,,	4·5	7·8	76·6
Sugar cane	000,000 *catties*	14,200	26,300	85·1
Sugar beet	000,000 ,,	960	4,270	346·4
Oil-bearing crops	000,000 *mow* sown area	85	118	37·8

Source: Figures in Columns II and III from Li Fu-chun, *op. cit.*, p. 36. Column I calculated from this data.

Communist authorities claim that the output of grain in 1952 was 9 per cent higher than in 1936.[53] This is a remarkable achievement. But the increase in grain output was outstripped by the increase in population. If we assume, conservatively, that China's population has grown by 1 per cent annually, then in

[52] Under the heading of 'grain' are included not only grain proper but also peanuts, peas, beans and potatoes. [53] Li Fu-chun, *op. cit.*, p. 36.

1952 it was some 17 per cent bigger than in 1936, or proportionately greater by 8 per cent than the increase in food crops. Again it should be remembered that China was an importer of grain in 1936—obtaining about 1 per cent of her needs from abroad—while in 1952 she was a net exporter. Under Mao's regime, the death rate is reported to have declined so much that the rate of population increase is some 2 per cent per annum.[54] Thus even if grain consumption per head is kept down to the 1952 level it would require an aggregate output some 10·4 per cent higher by 1957—the last year of the first Five Year Plan—merely in order to keep abreast of the additional 12 million mouths a year. As the urban population, whose grain consumption is higher than that of the rural population, is scheduled to rise considerably, grain output should expand even more than this figure. Besides, grain exports are needed to pay for imports that are vital for industrialisation.

According to Teng Tzu-hui, Vice-Chairman of the State Planning Commission and Director of the Rural Work Department of the CC, CCP, the Five Year Plan aimed at an increase of 30 per cent in grain output in order to fill the backlog of the past 15 years and to cope with future needs.[55] Two years later, in 1955, sights were lowered considerably, however: Li Fu-chun declared that by the end of the Five Year Plan a 17·6 per cent increase in annual grain output over 1952 was projected.[56] It is not yet safe to predict that even this revised target will actually be reached. Much is dependent on the weather. Actual output of leading agricultural crops was as follows:

		1952	1953	1954	1955	1957
			Actual	Output		Target
Grain	000,000 catties	327,830	333,660	339,030	367,986	385,600
Cotton	000,000 piculs	26·1	23·5	21·3	30·4	32·7
Jute and ambary hemp	000,000 ,,	6·1	2·8	2·7	5·1	7·3
Cured tobacco	000,000 ,,	4·5	4·3	4·6	6·0	7·8
Sugar cane	000,000 catties	14,200	14,420	17,180	16,220	26,300
Sugar beet	000,000 ,,	960	1,010	1,980	3,192	4,270

Source: For 1952–5: NCNA, Peking, June 14, 1956; 1957 target from Li Fu-chun, op. cit., p. 36.

[54] Pai Chien-hua, '600 Million People—A Gigantic Force in our Nation's Socialist Construction Work', JMJP, November 1, 1954; ECMM, 9.
[55] Teng Tzu-hui, 'Basic Tasks and Policies', in Mutual Aid and Co-operation in China's Agricultural Production, Peking, 1953, p. 27.
[56] Li Fu-chun, op. cit., p. 36.

On the whole the Chinese Five Year Plan proposes to devote a much smaller share of State capital resources to agriculture than the First Soviet Five Year Plan. Agriculture, forestry and water conservancy will take up some 7·6 per cent of all the state capital investment in China,[57] while in Russia their share was 19·4 per cent.[58] While Soviet agriculture was to a considerable extent mechanised by the end of the first Five Year Plan, having at the time 210,900 tractors,[59] China expects her first tractor to come off the production line in 1959 (in July 1955 there were only 2,758 tractors in the country).[60] Even the Indian Second Five Year Plan, while not aiming at the mechanisation of agriculture, projects the allocation of a much greater share to agriculture and irrigation than does China's Plan—19·7 per cent of the total net capital investment[61] as opposed to China's 7·6.

A comparison of China's agricultural targets with India's achievements under the First Five Year Plan and her targets for the second is interesting.

Percentage of Increase in Output

	China's F.Y.P. (target)	India First F.Y.P. (actual)*	India Second F.Y.P. (target)
Grain	17·6	28·0	15
Cotton	25·4	35·5	31

* Provisional estimates.

Sources: For China: Li Fu-chun, *op. cit.*, p. 36. For India: Government of India, *Second Five Year Plan, op. cit.*, pp. 58, 256.

The great increase in agricultural output in India during its first Five Year Plan was due, in the main, to the good luck of two contiguous favourable monsoons. As both China and India are quite helpless in face of the caprices of Nature, it is very probable

[57] Li Fu-chun, *op. cit.*, p. 23.
[58] Baykov, *op. cit.*, p. 421.
[59] *Ibid.*, p. 202.
[60] Calculated on the basis of 15 h.p. per tractor (Lai Jo-yu, 'Strengthen Leadership over Peasants, Boycott Bourgeois Influence on Peasantry', KJJP, November 22, 1955). As a matter of fact this calculation 'on the basis of 15 h.p. per tractor' is a statistical abstraction. The actual number of tractors must be considerably smaller. Thus, in U.S.S.R. the number of tractors in 1955 'on the basis of 15 h.p. per tractor' was 1,439,000, while the actual number of tractors was only 844,000, or 41·3 per cent lower (*The National Economy of U.S.S.R. Statistical Collection* (Russian), Moscow, 1956, p. 144). I have been unable to find figures for the actual number of tractors in China.
[61] Government of India, *Second Five Year Plan, op. cit.*, pp. 51–2.

that the differences shown in the table between the Plan of the one and the achievement and plan of the other are merely accidental. One conclusion, however, certainly can be reached: China's targets for agricultural production as outlined in her Five Year Plan are not very revolutionary, when compared with her neighbour India.[62]

However, the level of agricultural output, important as it is in determining the pace of industrial growth, is far from being decisive. A much more weighty factor is the size of the surplus that can be syphoned off from agriculture and turned into new capital. The size of these surpluses can vary greatly without any variation in aggregate agricultural output. Different institutional organisations of farming can produce different amounts of agricultural surpluses

[62] The references to the Second Indian Five Year Plan showing quite a close similarity between its production and investment targets and those of China's First Five Year Plan may quite easily lead to some wrong conclusions. The first is that there are no great differences between the Chinese and Indian Plans; secondly, that an economic plan embodying the same basic elements and with the same emphasis as that of Peking can be realised in the framework of a political democracy. The two conclusions are connected. As a matter of fact there are actually big differences in the economic and social circumstances in which the Plans are to be realised in the two countries as well as in the design of the Plans: (1) The capital and national income of India are somewhat higher than those of China. (2) India gets much more foreign aid at present and expects to get more in the future than China. Between March 1951 and January 1956—roughly the period of her First Five Year Plan— India received 306·7 crores of rupees, approximately 650 million U.S. dollars, not including the American wheat loan of 190 million U.S. dollars obtained in 1951-2 (*The Times*, London, January 26, 1956); the draft of the Second Five Year Plan includes expected foreign aid of 1,100 crores of rupees, approximately 2,310 million U.S. dollars (Government of India, *Second Five Year Plan, op. cit.*, p. 92). (3) Unlike China, India intends to preserve a mixed economy; no private capitalist is to be expropriated. During the Second Five Year Plan 61 per cent of net capital investment will be in the State sector and 39 per cent in the private (*ibid.*, p. 57). (4) No forced mass collectivisation is projected for India, although voluntary organisation of agricultural producer co-operatives is encouraged. (5) No forced labour camps are provided for in India (although the proposed organisation of a National Labour Force may create, even if on a smaller scale, something similar to the mass of peasants compulsorily mobilised by Peking to do its construction works). (6) In India, unlike China, emphasis is put on handicrafts to extend employment to the fullest, for which purpose excises are levied on machine products and on handicraft products subsidised (in the case of cloth), and special fields reserved by law for handicrafts.
Despite the material advantages which India possesses compared with China, the present writer doubts very much whether the Plan will not strain the resources of the country too far, lead to bitter conflicts between the different elements in the mixed economy, rising inflation and social tensions which may undermine the political democracy as well as block the path of progress of the Plan itself. It appears that in an underdeveloped country the success of a Plan similar in targets of output and investment to that of China or India—with insufficient foreign aid—must depend on the institution of an all-embracing totalitarian control of economy and society.

from the same productive resources. Thus, for instance, a given agricultural technique with a given level of productivity will produce greater surpluses if organised in large latifundia rather than in small farms, or if organised in State-controlled collective farms rather than in individual peasant holdings. For Peking's ambitious economic plan, therefore, it is much less important to know how much the peasants produce than to know what share of the peasants' product will come under State control. Peking's efforts at increasing agricultural surpluses and its control over them—from the State monopoly over trade in grain and cotton to the organisation of collective farming—will be dealt with elsewhere.

WATER CONSERVANCY WORKS

The future development of agriculture will be greatly affected by the tremendous water conservancy works now under construction by masses of conscripted peasants. There are numerous reports of the size of the labour armies mobilised. Fu Tso-yi, Minister of Water Conservancy, stated on October 28, 1951:

> During the two years (October 1949–October 1951) a total labour force of 10,370,000 workers was mobilised for various conservancy projects, assisted by 320,000 troops from the People's Liberation Army.[63]

Another report stated that on the Shu Wi River projects alone, 1 million peasants worked for $3\frac{1}{2}$ years.[64] Again, on the Huai River project, nearly 3 million peasants were working in 1951.[65] Some time later Fu Tso-yi stated that 'about 20 million people took part in water conservancy work in the past three years'.[66] In 1951–2, a total of 4,600,000 peasants worked on the Huai River project.[67] In the months April–June, 1954, 4,100,000 peasants

[63] JMJP, October 30, 1951; CB, 147.
[64] *Shanghai News*, June 14, 1952.
[65] CMR, October 1952.
[66] Fu Tso-yi, 'Great Achievements in China's Water Conservancy Work During the Past Three Years', *New China's Economic Achievements, etc., op. cit.*, p. 196.
[67] *Young Builders of China*, Peking, 1953, p. 68.

were conscripted in Manchuria for dyke repairing.[68] In February–March 1955, 4,400,000 peasants worked on the dykes of the lower reaches of the Yellow River.[69]

With these labour armies, spectacular results are achieved. Thus in the first three years after the establishment of the People's Republic of China (1949–52), '1,700 million cubic metres of earthwork, equal to the digging of ten Panama Canals, or 23 Suez Canals', were moved.[70]

The greatest project, now well under way, is the harnessing of the Huai River. Its aim is to rid the Huai Valley, an area of some 220,000 sq. kms., with a population of approximately 60 million, of floods. This complex project will, in addition, increase the irrigated area, produce hydro-electric power, and improve navigation on the waterways. It was to have been completed in 1955,[71] but the fact that the 1954 flood caused as much damage in the Huai Valley as ever before showed that Peking's time-table was not as scheduled. It seems certain that the harnessing of the Huai River will remain a problem for many years.

Other conservancy works carried out on a large scale are on the Ching-chiang (the section of the Yangtze between Chih-chiang in Hupeh and Ch'eng-ling-chi in Hunan), the Kuan-t'ing reservoir on the Yungting River (near Peking and Tientsin), on the Yu and Shu Rivers in East China, and the Jao-yang and Hun Rivers in Manchuria.

A project which promises to dwarf all others is the harnessing of the Yellow River, for which plans are afoot. The same session of the National People's Congress which deliberated upon the First Five Year Plan also heard and discussed a *Report on the Yellow River Project*, delivered by Vice-Premier Teng Tzu-hui.[72] This magnificent multi-purpose project envisages a series of dams and reservoirs on the main river and its tributaries, large-scale soil and water conservation work, and above all afforestation in areas in the Yellow River Basin, principally Kansu, Shensi and Shansi

[68] TPJP, July 19, 1954; SCMP, 894.
[69] NCNA, Chengchow, May 10, 1955.
[70] Fu Tso-yi, *op. cit.*
[71] *Ibid.*, p. 199.
[72] NCNA, Peking, July 19, 1955.

Provinces where loss of soil and water constitutes a grave problem. It is expected that with the completion of the scheme, the irrigated area in the basin will increase from the present 1,100,000 hectares to 7,733,000 hectares or to one-fifth of the Yellow River Basin area. The scheme will provide a tremendous amount of electricity, some 110,000 million kwh a year, or ten times the country's total electricity output in 1954. It will also make a big section of the river navigable: 500-ton tug-boats will be able to sail from the estuary to Lanchow. According to Teng Tzu-hui, the whole project of water and soil conservation will take fifty years. The initial phase of preventing floods, generating power and irrigating the land, will take, according to Teng, some three Five Year Plans, i.e., up to 1967. During these three Five Year Plans, it is expected to increase the irrigated area by 2 million hectares, and the output of electricity by some 9,800 million kwh, or nearly as much again as the country's total output of electricity in 1954. Investment in the first phase will amount to some JMP 5,324 million spread over fifteen years, or about JMP 361 million a year. This is very impressive indeed.

FOREIGN ECONOMIC RELATIONS

During the late 'twenties and early 'thirties—the first stages of her industrialisation—Russia imported machinery and technicians for her newly-built factories and mines on a large scale. Their decisive importance for industrialisation was reflected in the fact that despite unfavourable conditions in the world market during the depression, Russia did not cut her imports but even expanded them considerably at the time.[73] China, with a far smaller capacity to manufacture complex capital goods, is even more dependent on their import than Russia was.

China's ability to pay for her imports depends on her ability to export. This dependence was less absolute before the war, as there were a number of invisible exports (above all, remittances from overseas Chinese). Thus before the war, the import of goods could

[73] The volume of imports in 1931 was 77·0 per cent higher than in 1928, and in 1932—the last year of the First Five Year Plan—15·3 per cent (A. Baykov, *Soviet Foreign Trade*, Princeton, 1946, Appendix, Table 1).

normally surpass by far the export of goods, as can be seen from the following table:

China's Foreign Trade (in million U.S. dollars)

	Imports	Exports	Surplus of Imports over Exports
1928	849·1	703·9	145·2
1931	487·4	309·2	178·2
1935	513·8	334·6	179·2
1939	825·8	503·8	322·0

Source: M. I. Sladkovsky, *An Outline of the Development of China's Foreign Economic Relations*, (Russian), Moscow, 1953, p. 288.

Thus in the years 1929–39, average annual imports exceeded exports by as much as 42·3 per cent.

Since Mao's rise to power some items in the balance of international payments, such as the nearly complete abrogation of remittances of foreign business profits and interest payments on foreign loans, have changed to China's advantage. But against this must be placed a decline in the capital flow from abroad. In the years 1931–6 receipts from 'foreign loans and investments and profits from abroad' and 'foreign expenditures in China' averaged 290 million Chinese dollars a year,[74] or about 80 million U.S. dollars, at current value. Even more important were the remittances from overseas Chinese. In the years 1931–6 the average annual income from this source reached 291·4 million Chinese dollars,[75] or about 105 million U.S. dollars, a sum that went very far (two-thirds of the way) towards covering the import surplus. The flow of these remittances from abroad has been reduced to a trickle,[76] and practically the only source of foreign capital remaining to Mao is Russia.

How large are the credits that Moscow grants Peking? When Mao went to Moscow in February 1950, he was given a loan of 300 million U.S. dollars spread over 5 years from January 1, 1950. This is not a large sum. In 1938–9 Chiang Kai-shek contracted a loan of 250 million U.S. dollars in Moscow.[77] As prices in 1938–9 were about half those in 1950, Chiang's loan was worth as much

[74] Ta-chung Liu, *op. cit.*, p. 69.
[75] *Ibid.*
[76] In 1954 it was estimated to be less than U.S. $700,000 a month (FEER, August 26, 1954). However, this is surely an under-estimate. The actual amount was probably four to five times bigger.
[77] Sladkovsky, *op. cit.*, pp. 214–15.

as 500 million U.S. dollars at 1950 prices. Even relatively small Poland received a loan of 450 million dollars from Moscow in 1949.

In October 1954 another long-term Soviet loan was granted to China. This time it was quoted in roubles and amounted to 520 million.[78] According to the official rate of exchange this is equal to 130 million U.S. dollars.[79] (At a realistic rate of exchange the value of the loan is, of course, considerably smaller.)

In September 1953 Russia promised to help China build 141 key industrial plants.[80] These included joint iron and steel enterprises, non-ferrous metallurgical enterprises, coal mines, petroleum processing plants, machine building factories, motor vehicle factories, a tractor building factory and power plants. They are the backbone of China's Five Year Plan. Contrary to the general impression created by Chinese propaganda literature directed toward the outside world, that part of the equipment for the 141 plants that came from Russia was neither a gift nor even a loan, but had to be paid for immediately in goods, as was made clear by the *People's Daily*:

> In the case of the 141 huge projects . . . which the Soviet Union has helped us to construct or renovate, the equipment for these factories and mines was all obtained through trade by exporting our agricultural, native, special and mineral products.[81]

(Other equipment, amounting to 30–50 per cent of the total for these 141 enterprises will be produced in China.)[82]

In October 1954 Russia promised to help China build a further 15 industrial enterprises. Possibly the 520 million roubles credit was for this purpose. Further credit may also have been given by Russia to China. But the fact that the two credit grants mentioned (those of February 1950 and October 1954) were hailed as acts of great generosity, suggests that other credit grants, if there were any, were not big.

---

[78] PC, January 16, 1955.
[79] Only one-fifth of this at the black market rate.
[80] NCNA, Peking, September 15, 1953.
[81] JMJP, February 7, 1954.
[82] JMJP, March 10, 1954.

Again, on April 7, 1956, A. I. Mikoyan, on visiting China, signed an agreement by which Russia undertook to help China build a further 55 industrial enterprises, supplying her with equipment, the services of designers, and other technical assistance, to the value of about 2,500 million roubles.[83] According to the official rate of exchange this is equal to 625 million U.S. dollars. From the official communique it appears that a part—but it is not clear what part—of this large sum was given as a loan.

Another form of Soviet economic aid to China is the construction of a number of common Soviet-Chinese enterprises. According to an agreement signed in Moscow on March 21, 1950, three mixed Sino-Soviet companies were to be established, one for the prospecting, production and refining of oil in Sinkiang, another for the mining of non-ferrous metals in Sinkiang, and lastly a civil aviation company flying the routes Peking–Chita, Peking–Irkutsk, and Peking–Alma Ata. Some time later, another mixed company was established—the Dairen Shipbuilding Company. For a number of years the companies were active, but then, on October 12, 1954, after negotiations carried on in Peking, it was agreed to dissolve them as of January 1, 1955, all their property being transferred to China. The value of the Soviet share was to be refunded to Russia in the form of goods over several years.[84]

The niggardly credits, together with the fact that Soviet exports to China, it seems, have not exceeded her imports from China,[85] suggest that the loans were mainly used for paying for Soviet arms during the Korean War, and for Soviet specialists since then. There are thousands of such specialists in China, and

[83] NCNA, Peking, April 7, 1956.

[84] NCNA, Peking, October 12, 1954.

[85] The balance of China's foreign trade with Russia and Eastern Europe is favourable. This can be inferred from the following data: Russia's share in China's foreign trade was as follows: 19·84 per cent of all China's imports as against 26·58 per cent of her exports in 1950; 44·7 per cent and 51·51 per cent respectively in 1951 (NCNA, Peking, September 29, 1951). The corresponding figures for the East European satellites were: 1·37 per cent and 3·87 per cent in 1950, and 25·3 per cent and 26·43 per cent in 1951 (ibid.). It is thus clear that in 1950 and 1951 the value of Chinese exports to Russia as well as to her East European satellites was larger than her imports from these countries. Again in 1952 we are informed that while U.S.S.R. took 54 per cent of China's exports, she delivered only 53 per cent of her imports (A. M. Smirnov and N. N. Liubimov, editors, Foreign Trade of U.S.S.R. (Russian), Moscow, 1954, p. 238). If China's foreign trade was favourable, as the Chinese press contended, it is clear that also in 1952 as well as in 1950 and 1951, China delivered more goods (in value) to Russia and her European satellites than she received from them.

in face of China's poverty in technicians, their help in the industrialisation of the country should not be underrated.

In addition Russian universities give education to thousands of Chinese.[86]

Total Russian credit to China is therefore some 60–100 million U.S. dollars annually, a sum much lower than annual receipts from invisible exports before the war. Mao's China can therefore not pay for an import bill two-fifths bigger than the value of her exports and must balance her foreign accounts. Thus in 1950, for the first time in 73 years, exports exceeded imports by 9·34 per cent.[87] The Chinese press has since reported that the balance of foreign trade continues to be active, but has not given exact data. The Chinese leaders commend this fact, although in fact an export surplus in an economically underdeveloped country is no advantage. Russia indeed was lucky in being able to import more than she exported during her First Five Year Plan, and to run up a balance of payments deficit.[88]

The absolute size, in value, of China's foreign trade is as follows:

China's Foreign Trade (in million current U.S. dollars)

	Import	Export	Total
1928a	849·1	703·9	1,553·0
1939a	825·8	503·8	1,329·6
1950b			1,190
1951b			2,310
1952b			2,320
1953c			2,160
1954d			2,260
1955e			3,100
1956f			3,830
1957 (plan)g			3,850

a Sladkovsky, op. cit., p. 288.

b Estimate of British Council for the Promotion of International Trade, China's Foreign Trade, London, 1954, p. 11.

c Calculated from Chou En-lai, Report on Government Work, NCNA, Peking, September 24, 1954.

d 'Communique on Fulfilment of 1954 State Plan', NCNA, Peking, September 22, 1955.

e Kung Yuan, Vice-Minister of Foreign Trade, in an article in TKP (September 3, 1956), stated that the value of China's foreign trade in 1955 was 2·6 times that of 1950.

[86] NCNA, August 6, 1956.

[87] NCNA, Peking, April 12, 1951.

[88] The foreign indebtedness of Russia increased from 485 million gold roubles in 1928, to 1,400 million gold roubles in 1932 (the gold rouble was then equivalent to 0·5146 U.S. gold dollars) (Baykov, Soviet Foreign Trade, op. cit., p. 50).

f Chou En-lai, in his report to the Eighth National Congress of the Communist Party of China (NCNA, Peking, September 16, 1956), says that it is estimated that China's foreign trade in 1956 was some 65 per cent higher than in 1952. The 65 per cent is added to the estimated 1952 level.

g Yeh Chi-chuang, Minister of Foreign Trade, in a speech to the National People's Congress (NCNA, Peking, July 28, 1955), speaks of an expected rise of 66·5 per cent in China's foreign trade between 1952 and 1957. The 66·5 per cent is added to the estimated 1952 level.

As international prices in 1950–5 were more than double pre-war,[89] it seems safe to state that China's foreign trade, even in 1956, was scarcely higher than before the war. And as the pre-war foreign trade balance was markedly passive, while it has not been so since Mao's rise, China's imports even in 1956 must have been markedly lower than they were before the war. What applies to 1956 will apply to 1957 as well, whether the Plan is fulfilled or not. However, as practically no data are published, it is difficult to calculate changes in the total value of imports and exports, and the total trade turnover more exactly, and these general conclusions must suffice.[90]

[89] U.N., *Yearbook of International Trade Statistics, 1954*, New York, 1955, p. 20.

[90] The Communist leaders, for obvious reasons, try to paint a very different picture of China's foreign trade. Accordingly Nan Han-chen, President of the People's Bank of China and Chairman of the China Committee for the Promotion of International Trade, claimed that the total value of China's foreign trade in 1951 far exceeded the pre-war level (Nan Han-chen, 'China Offers Trade to All', CR, July–August, 1952).

To prove his contention he gave some specific quantitative data for selected exports in 1951. It is instructive to compare these figures with exports of the same commodities in some pre-war years (in thousand metric tons):

	1951a	Pre-war Year
Soya beans	2,480	about 3,000 (1938)b
Tea	100	41·6 (1938)c
Tung oil	100	131 (incl. perilla, etc., 1936–8 average)d
Antimony	20	17·6 (1935)b
Eggs and egg products	70	105 (1933–7 average)e
Groundnuts	250	201 (1936)b
Raw silk	10	10 (1936)f
Coal	7,430	4,862 (1936)f

a *Ibid.*

b *Report of United Kingdom Trade Mission to China*, etc. *op. cit.*, pp. 62, 79, 100.

c U.N., *Economic Survey of Asia and the Far East, 1948, op. cit.*, p. 58.

d U.N., *Economic Survey of Asia and the Far East, 1950, op. cit.*, p. 383.

e Shen, *op. cit.*, p. 346.

f U.N., *World Economic Report, 1951–2*, New York, 1953, p. 129.

A few years later, arguing that exports do not constitute too much of a burden on the people, the Minister of Foreign Trade, Yeh Chi-chuang, revealed that 'in 1954,

The composition of China's exports has changed very little since before the war. During the five-year period before 1937 nine leading agricultural exports accounted for about 85 per cent of the value of total exports of China proper. In Manchuria agricultural products made up a similar proportion of exports.[91] The composition of China's exports at present are practically the same as at that time. Thus in the years 1953–5 vegetable oils, animal produce, tea, and foodstuffs together accounted for 60 per cent of the value of China's exports.[92]

The composition of imports, however, has changed drastically. In 1935–7 foodstuffs, tobacco, etc., made up 18·1 per cent of the value of all imports; other consumer goods 24·4 per cent; together 42·5 per cent.[93] Capital goods made up 30·3 per cent of all imports, and raw materials 27·3 per cent.[94] Detailed analysis of the items included under the heading 'capital goods' shows that often many of the imports were for the needs of light industry or even for personal consumption, and only a small portion was real machinery. Thus, in 1935–7, machines and hand tools together made up only 10 per cent of all imports.[95] As against this, in 1953, 87 per cent of China's imports consisted of means of production,[96] and in 1954, 88·5 per cent.[97] Machinery, including machine tools, motors, drills, cranes, building machinery and vehicles formed more than half the total import.

The direction of China's foreign trade has changed radically since before the war. Both before 1937 and between 1945 and 1949, Russia and Eastern Europe accounted for less than 1 per cent of China's foreign trade. Since the establishment of the People's Republic of China, under the impact of the attraction to

the tea exported by China was only 65 per cent of the 1936 level, while raw silk was only 32 per cent of the 1931 level' (Yeh Chi-chuang, Speech to National People's Congress, NCNA, Peking, July 28, 1955). It is obvious that the quantitative data for selected exports given by Nan Han-chen do not support his contention that China's exports in 1951 exceeded pre-war levels.

[91] Shen, *op. cit.*, p. 338.
[92] HCS, March 3, 1956; ECMM, 36.
[93] Chih Tsang, *China's Post-war Markets*, New York, 1945, pp. 114–15.
[94] *Ibid.*
[95] *Ibid.*
[96] TKP, October 6, 1954; SCMP, 920.
[97] 'Several Questions Concerning China's Foreign Trade', CCTP, August 1955; ECMM, 4.

Moscow on the one hand and the West's embargo on the other, the share of Russia and her European satellites has increased tremendously. In 1950 it was 26 per cent; in 1951, 61 per cent; in 1952, 72 per cent; in 1953, 75 per cent; in 1954, 80·55 per cent.[98]

As trade relations with Russia and her European satellites are now decisive for China, it is worthwhile expanding somewhat on the subject. Economically, Moscow's bargaining position is much stronger than Peking's in the trade between them. Russia imports soya beans, oil seeds, tea, tin, antimony and tungsten from China, and exports to China capital goods and industrial raw materials. It is obvious that China is much more dependent on her imports from Russia than Russia is on her imports from China. This is especially so since the Western embargo has prevented China from obtaining the capital goods she needs anywhere but in Russia and her East European satellites, while Russia can get most of the goods she imports from China elsewhere, as they are not strategic materials. Besides, in the bargaining relations between a highly industrialised economy and a backward agricultural country, the former has generally an overwhelming economic superiority.[99] The fact that 80 per cent of China's trade is with Russia and her East European satellites, accentuates this dependence.

There is no doubt that China has found Russia a very hard bargainer indeed in the trade negotiations which have taken place annually between them since the establishment of the Chinese People's Republic. New agreements have been reached only after very long negotiations. Particularly lengthy and arduous were those which took place immediately before the launching of China's ambitious Five Year Plan. On August 17, 1952, Chou En-lai arrived in Moscow, heading a delegation including the Chairman, Deputy Chairman and General Secretary of the Financial and Economic Committee, GAC, the Minister and Deputy Minister of Heavy Industry, the Minister of Fuel Industries and the Deputy Minister of Communications. More than a

[98] Shih I-t'ao, 'It is Time to Call off the "Embargo"', SCCS, October 5, 1955; ECMM, 18.
[99] Rostow, op. cit., p. 254.

month later Chou returned to Peking, leaving four out of the seven members of the delegation in Moscow. These were strengthened in October by another delegation, led by Liu Shao-chi and including four highly placed economic officials, which came to Moscow ostensibly to attend the 19th Congress of the CPSU. A little later another mission, led by the Minister of Foreign Trade, Yeh Chi-chuang, arrived in Moscow and stayed there until March 1953.

That the Chinese found the negotiations hard going was clear not only from the number and importance of the people sent to Moscow and the duration of the negotiations, but also from the fact that prior to their conclusion, Peking was forced to announce (mid-January 1953), a downward revision of 30 per cent in the targets for new construction in the first year of the Five Year Plan. It was only on March 26, 1953, that Moscow appeared more 'co-operative', and it was announced that 'recently' a new agreement of economic aid to China had been signed. (This was three weeks after Stalin's death. It seems that with Stalin's departure, Mao's stature grew considerably in the Moscow-Peking axis.)

Since then the annual trade agreements between Russia and China have been signed after relatively short negotiations.

The spirit pervading the Sino-Soviet trade agreements is most clearly revealed in the relative prices charged. There is very little information about this. Officially, trade between Russia and her satellites on the one hand, and China on the other, is conducted through bilateral barter agreements valued in roubles. What relation rouble prices bear to world market prices is impossible to say, though it is claimed that they are equivalent to world market prices. There are, however, some indications that the terms of trade are not very advantageous to China. Thus, the informed Hong Kong journal, *Far Eastern Economic Review*, writes the following:

Pig bristles and tung oil, which were the major items in China's exports before the war, have been offered in Western European markets, including Rotterdam, at prices below the market prices in Shanghai and Tientsin. Since the Soviet Union is the exclusive agent for Red China's export goods, Moscow's marketing of pig bristles and tung oil at such low prices indicates that it bought the Chinese products at even lower rates. . . . On the other hand, the imports Red China is receiving from the outside world through Soviet Russia have been found to be priced two to ten times higher than those of the similar Western products available in Hongkong. Chinese Communist purchasing agents have been forced to pay more than H.K.$50,000 for a Soviet Zis 4-ton truck in Tientsin. The price for a comparable 5-ton truck of Western make is less than $15,000 in Hongkong. However, the export of Western trucks from Hongkong to Red China is prohibited. Czechoslovakian saccharine, also imported through Soviet Russia, is sold at H.K.$106·40 per pound in Tientsin. German saccharine of equal quality is obtainable at $6·60 per pound in the British colony.[100]

Again, the Yugoslav Communist paper, *Borba*, reported that U.S.S.R. was paying $70 per ton for soya beans bought in Manchuria while the world market price was $120.[101]

The fact that Russia and her satellites re-export soya beans and oil seeds to the West has probably become especially annoying to China in the last three years or so, as she has been experiencing increasing difficulties in supplying her own needs. In 1953 she stopped supplying soya beans to Japan, and had to impose a general embargo on the export of certain oil seeds. Incidentally the fact that hog bristles and tung oil have been resold by Russia and her satellites suggests that China's exports of these goods go beyond the needs of the Soviet bloc—a factor which weakens Peking's trade bargaining position *vis-à-vis* Moscow still further.

One reason for Russia and her East European satellites serving as a go-between between China and the West is that the Western Powers' trade embargo is much more rigid towards China than towards the other members of the Communist Bloc. At the same time China sells Far Eastern rubber to Russia. This explains the fact that re-exports of rubber from Britain to the U.S.S.R., which totalled about 88,000 tons in 1952, fell to 27,000 tons in 1953, and to only 4,000 tons in 1954. There were no direct exports

---

[100] FEER, November 27, 1952.
[101] *Borba*, Belgrade, February 25, 1950.

to U.S.S.R. from Malaya, Indonesia or Ceylon, either in 1953 or in 1954.[102]

There are a number of factors affecting Russia's aid to China which can be touched on only very briefly. First, the capital resources available to Russia herself are quite inadequate to satisfy an insatiable, economically backward giant set upon rapid industrialisation like China. (When it is remembered that in the trade in machinery and equipment between Russia and her satellites Russia is a *net importer*, exporting in 1953 to the value of some 200 million U.S. dollars and importing to the value of 700–750 million dollars,[103] her relative poverty in surpluses of capital resources becomes plain.) Secondly, Moscow knows well that an equal volume of investment will mature much more slowly in China than in Russia herself or in Eastern Europe. A third factor, of an economic-political nature, is Russia's desire to keep China as economically dependent upon her as possible, which makes her not over-anxious to see a big increase in Chinese industrial power.[104]

To sum up, China's foreign trade, despite its rise since the establishment of the Chinese People's Republic, is still extremely low—smaller *per capita* than in any other country.[105] This backwardness is largely the result of difficulties in extracting considerable surplus products from the population. It is partly due to the

[102] U.N., *World Economic Report, 1953–4*, New York, 1955, p. 149.
[103] U.N., *Economic Survey of Europe in 1954*, Geneva, 1955, p. 118.
[104] As economic aid produces very different results to military aid, one may well understand the niggardliness of Russia's 1950 credit compared with the considerable military aid rendered to China by Russia during the Korean War. Aid in the form of military supplies as a matter of fact increases the dependence of the receiving country on the giver.
[105] *Value of Trade Per Capita in 1951 (in current U.S. dollars).*

U.K.	368·11
France	205·17
U.S.A.	163·42
West Germany	138·20
Ceylon	93·94
Egypt	66·88
Japan	38·86
India	10·33
Ethiopia	5·56
China (1951)	4·00
China (1955)	6·00

Sources: For China: From Table given on p. 68, For other countries: U.S. Department of Commerce, *Foreign Commerce Yearbook, 1951*, Washington, 1953, p. 719.

difficulty of translating available surpluses into imports of capital goods, which, in turn, is partly a result of the virtual drought in capital inflow from abroad, partly a result of the Western trade embargo and partly the result of Russian trading practice. However, the industrialisation and general economic growth of the country depend to a large extent precisely on the development of her foreign trade.

Low productivity, the meagreness of foreign economic aid and the objective of quick industrialisation will force Peking to mulct relentlessly any source which can provide the wherewithal to pay for necessary imports. She is bound to increase pressure on the people (and above all the peasants) to create and hand over larger surpluses to the State. Thus the bottleneck in foreign trade only serves to enhance the exploitation and the totalitarianism.

PART TWO

THE COUNTRYSIDE
UNDER MAO

CHAPTER IV

AGRARIAN REFORM

LAND RELATIONS PRIOR TO THE AGRARIAN REFORM

In a report to the Central Committee of the Chinese Communist Party on December 25, 1947, Mao Tse-tung gave figures on land ownership in China. These have formed part of every statement on agrarian reform issued since. He said: 'Landlords and rich peasants . . . make up approximately only 8 per cent of the population (reckoned in families), but the land they hold generally makes up from 70 to 80 per cent of all the land.'[1] The frequency with which these figures have been repeated by the Communists has persuaded even many non-Communist observers to accept them at face value, thus helping to disseminate them even further.

Whether they are true or not is of the utmost importance, as the effect of agrarian reform is largely dependent on land tenure prior to it. In order to judge these figures, it would be well to compare them with the following: first, estimates of land tenure made by non-Communist experts; secondly, estimates of land tenure made by Communists before Mao's statement; thirdly, other relevant information published by Chinese Communist spokesmen since this statement.

The most prominent non-Communist land specialist, J. L. Buck, conducted a survey of 16,786 peasant holdings in 168 localities, in 154 *hsien*, in 22 provinces in China (1929–33). The survey showed that of the total farm area, 28·7 per cent was rented (12·7 per cent in the wheat region, 40·3 per cent in the rice region).[2] C. C. Chang, another non-Communist expert, estimates that 51·7 per cent of the agricultural land of China was worked by owners, 22·1 per cent by part owners and part tenants, and 26·2 per cent by tenants. The proportion of tenants varies greatly regionally: 40 per cent in South China, 13 per cent in North

---

[1] Mao Tse-tung, *On the Present Situation and Our Tasks*, Appendix to O. B. Van der Sprenkel and Associates, *New China: Three Views*, London, 1950, pp. 161–2.
[2] Buck, *Land Utilisation in China, op. cit.*, p. 194.

China and 30 per cent in the North East.[3] According to Franklin L. Ho, land tenure prior to Mao's land reform presented the following picture:

	South China		North China	
	Percentage of total farming population	Percentage of land owned to total land	Percentage of total farming population	Percentage of land owned to total land
Landlord	3	30	2	18
Rich peasant	7	27	6	21
Middle peasant	23	23	18	30
Poor peasant	67	20	74	31

Source: F. L. Ho, 'The Land Problem of China', *The Annals of the American Academy of Political and Social Science*, July 1951.

Other non-Communist experts arrive at similar conclusions, namely, that the landlords owned a minority of the land even if a not inconsiderable minority—or somewhat under a third.

Estimates published by Communist writers prior to Mao's statement also conflict sharply with it. According to an investigation carried out in 1926–7 by the Wuhan Government—in which the Minister of Agriculture was a Communist—the distribution of land ownership in China was as follows:

	Size of Holdings (mow)	Percentage of Population	Percentage of Cultivated Land
Poor peasants	1–10	45	7
Middle peasants	10–30	24	13
Rich peasants	30–50	16	17
Small landlords	50–100	10	20
Big landlords	over 100	5	43

Source: A. K. Chiu, 'Agriculture', in *China*, edited by MacNair, *op. cit.*, p. 473.

If people who owned 50 *mow*, or less than 10 acres, are counted as 'landlords'—which is obviously ridiculous—then landlords formed 15 per cent of the population and owned 63 per cent of the cultivated land. If the term landlord includes only those who owned more than 100 *mow*, they formed 5 per cent of the population and owned 43 per cent of the land. Bukharin gave the following table of land ownership in China at the 15th Conference of the C.P.S.U. (1925):

[3] C. C. Chang, in *The China Critic*, Shanghai, September 25, 1930.

Size of Holding	Percentage of Families	Percentage of Land
1–20 *mow*	49·5	15
20–40 *mow*	23	22
40–75 *mow*	15	25
over 75 *mow*	11	36

Source: *Fifteenth Conference of the All-Union Communist Party (B)*, Russian, Moscow-Leningrad, 1927, p. 25.

The same figures were repeated in 1940 by a Soviet economic expert on China.[4] In 1945 another Communist authority, Chen Han-seng, gave the following table of land ownership in China proper.[5]

	Percentage of Total Number of Families	Percentage of Total Acreage Owned
Landlords	3	26
Rich peasants	7	27
Middle peasants	22	25
Poor peasants	68	22

Source: Chen Han-seng, *The Chinese Peasant*, London, 1945, p. 13.

According to these Communist estimates, therefore, landlords owned 26, 36 or 43 per cent of the land. This too is a far cry from Mao's statement.

But the best proof that Mao's figures are quite groundless is provided by other relevant figures published by the Communist authorities today. Peking claims that the total amount of land distributed under land reform was 700 million *mow*.[6] In 1954 the total cultivated land in China was over 1,640 million *mow*.[7] One-ninth of this area should be added to arrive at a figure for the total agricultural area. (Farmsteads, graves, ponds, woodland, etc., took up 10·4 per cent of the land in the samples given in J. L. Buck's survey).[8] The total agricultural area of China is then some

[4] A. I. Ostrovskaya, 'The Agrarian Question in China', in V. M. Alekseev and Associates, *China*, Russian, Moscow-Leningrad, 1940.

[5] It is interesting to note that a few years later, after Mao's figures on land tenure were publicised, Chen Han-seng, now an important government official in Peking, gave a totally different estimate of land tenure prior to land reform: 'Before the land reform, the landlords, who constituted only 5 per cent of the rural population . . . owned between 50 and 60 per cent of all agricultural land in the country' (Chen Han-seng, 'Land Reform Uproots Feudalism', CR May–June, 1952).

[6] This figure is now given in all Communist sources. See, for example, *New China's Economic Achievements, op. cit.*, p. 171.

[7] NCNA, Peking, September 21, 1955.

[8] Buck, *Land Utilisation in China, op. cit.*, p. 172.

1,800 million *mow*. If we assume that all the 700 million *mow* distributed in the land reform was cultivated—a lenient assumption—land distribution affected some 43·7 per cent of the total. Included in the redistribution was land belonging to foreigners, temples, ancestral shrines, etc., which, according to J. L. Buck, formed about 7 per cent of the total;[9] also included were some plots taken from rich peasants.[10] Thus, all in all, landlords' property taken and redistributed made up from a quarter to a third of all agricultural land in China.

A similar conclusion may be arrived at by a different method of calculation. All Communist authorities agree that prior to land reform landlords used to get 25–30 million tons of grain value-equivalent in rent.[11] As China's grain output in 1936 was 150 million tons,[12] rent made up at most 16–20 per cent of the country's grain output. (If other agricultural output were added to the grain output figure, the share of rent would decline correspondingly.) Seeing that the landlord normally took at least half the tenants' yield, it is clear that landlords' land rented to peasants did not make up more than a third of all China's agricultural land.

THE MYTH OF CHINESE FEUDALISM

Having gained a rough idea of the proportion of agricultural land owned by landlords prior to land reform, let us try to find out how many landlords there were and the size of their holdings.

Estimates of the percentage of landlords in the agricultural population vary considerably. Thus, as we have seen, the Wuhan Government (1926–7) figure was 5 per cent; Bukharin gave the percentage as 11; Chen Han-seng as 3. Even the lowest estimate

---

[9] Buck, *Land Utilisation in China*, p. 192.

[10] See below p. 85.

[11] 'In the past peasants paid landlords 30 million tons of grain in rent annually' (NCNA, September 18, 1952). Chen Han-seng corroborates this: rent collected in the past by landlords was 'the value-equivalent of 30 million tons of grain' (Chen Han-seng, 'Industrialisation Begins', CR, January–February, 1953). Or, according to another Communist author, peasants paid landlords 'an estimated 25 million tons of foodstuffs' (Wu Ta-sing, 'Raising Agricultural Production', CR, May–June, 1952).

[12] Li Fu-chun, *op. cit.*, p. 36.

puts the number of landlord families prior to land reform at some 3½ million, or about 18 million people.[13]

The average holding of a landlord family and the extent to which it exceeded that of the average peasant before land reform were, according to the different Communist estimates quoted above, as follows:

	Average holding of Land-lord's Family (mow)	Average holding of Land-lord compared with that of average peasant
Wuhan Government	120	14 times as large
Bukharin	48	5 times as large
Chen Han-seng	140	12 times as large

Comparison between these figures and their equivalents for any European country at a time when feudal land tenure prevailed reveals a *fundamental difference* between land tenure in China and land tenure in feudal Europe. To cite one instance only: at the end of the nineteenth century, there were some 28,000 big land-lord families in Tsarist Russia, owning an average of 2,227 dessiatins (26,000 *mow*) of land each, or about 202 times more than the average peasant.[14] Indeed, China's landlords were not only much greater in number and smaller in stature than Euro-pean feudal lords; they were in fact not *feudal* landlords at all. It is necessary to bear this in mind in order to understand Mao's agrarian reform as well as the development of rural China there-after, particularly in view of the Communists' constant attempt to project feudalism into Chinese rural society. Actually China has not been feudal, by any definition, for more than 2,000 years. During this time, the Chinese have bought and sold land freely. As early as 350 B.C., in the State of Ts'in, a land law established private ownership of land, with freedom to buy and sell.[15] With

[13] The mass nature of landlordism may be indirectly derived from Teng Hsiao-ping, who stated that those deprived of electoral rights—almost all of them landlords, but not all the landlords—made up 1·64 per cent of the population (NCNA, Peking, June 19, 1954), or with their families, some 10 million people.

[14] V. I. Lenin, 'The Agrarian Question in Russia at the End of the Nineteenth Century', *Works*, (Russian), Fourth Edition, Volume XV, pp. 57–9.

[15] K. A. Wittfogel, *Wirtschaft und Gesellschaft Chinas;* Leipzig, 1931, pp. 384–5.

The author owes a great debt for his understanding of ancient Chinese society to the works of K. A. Wittfogel: *Wirtschaft und Gesellschaft Chinas*; *The History of Chinese Society*. Liao, Philadelphia, 1949 (in co-operation with Fêng Chia-shêng); 'The Foundations and Stages of Chinese Economic History', *Zeitschrift für Sozialforschung*, Paris, 1935; 'Die Theorie der orientalischen Gesellschaft', *Zeitschrift für Sozialfor-schung*, Paris, 1938. Professor Wittfogel informs me that through further research

the unification of the country in 216 B.C., full private ownership of land became a common institution over the whole of China. Where land is bought and sold freely, where the toilers are not tied to it, in other words where serfdom does not exist, the agrarian order, according to practically all schools of economic thought, that of Marx included, cannot be defined as feudal. The absence of feudalism in China is due to her typical form of agriculture. Highly intensive garden cultivation demands great diligence, attention to detail and intelligence, and is thus incompatible with the compulsions of slavery or serfdom. Hence, ever since Chinese agriculture has been based mainly on irrigation, i.e., since about the fourth century B.C., there has been no widespread slavery or serfdom.[16] Ancient Egypt and Babylon followed the same pattern for the same reason.[17] The slaves that did exist in China were not engaged in agricultural production, but were household slaves.[18] Real feudalism (containing elements of tribalism), with serfs tied to the land, no private property in land and the prohibition of its purchase and sale, is to be found only in some very primitive and isolated border regions where intensive agriculture and irrigation are practically unknown, such as among the Pai Yi people of Yunnan, the Kamba of Sikang,[19] or in a sector of Northern Kiangsu.[20]

One should, of course, be wary of concluding that because the Chinese landlords were usually small by European standards, and were not feudal, the relations between them and the peasants were more harmonious than in feudal Europe, and that the powder of agrarian revolution was dampened. On the contrary, as one scholar has aptly observed: 'A landowner need not possess half a million acres to be extortionate; in fact, slender means may invigorate his greed.'[21] These characteristics of China's land-

---

he has come to the conclusion that Chou China (1122–255 B.C.) was already not feudal. An elaboration of this point is to be given in a new book by Wittfogel called *Oriental Despotism*. I was not able to consult this work when preparing my book.

[16] *Ibid.*, pp. 392–410.
[17] *Ibid.*, pp. 395–9.
[18] *Ibid.*, p. 405.
[19] See Chen Han-seng, *Frontier Land Systems in Southernmost China*, New York, 1949, mimeographed.
[20] Wittfogel, *op. cit.*, pp. 392–3.
[21] E. V. G. Kiernan, *British Diplomacy in China, 1880–1885*, Cambridge, 1939, p. 236.

lordism did, however, impart some peculiar features to Mao's agrarian reform and thus are destined to affect the future of agriculture in China, and hence her whole development.

MAO'S AGRARIAN REFORM LAW

The law which shapes the course of agrarian reform in nearly the whole country is the *Agrarian Reform Law of the People's Republic of China*, promulgated by the Peking Government on June 30, 1950.[22] The salient items of this law are:

> The land, draught animals, farm implements and surplus grain of the landlords, and their surplus houses in the countryside shall be confiscated . . .
> The rural land belonging to ancestral shrines, temples, monasteries, churches, schools, organisations and other land owned by public bodies shall be requisitioned . . .
> Land and peasant dwellings in the countryside which are owned by industrialists and merchants shall be requisitioned . . .
> Land owned by rich peasants and cultivated by themselves or by hired labour, and their other properties, shall be protected from infringement.
> Small portions of land rented out by rich peasants shall remain untouched. But in certain special areas, the land rented out by rich peasants may be requisitioned in part or in whole with the approval of the people's governments at provincial or higher level.
> If the portions of land rented out by rich peasants of a semi-landlord type exceed in size the land tilled by themselves and by their hired labour the land rented out should be requisitioned . . .
> Land and other properties of middle peasants (including well-to-do middle peasants) shall be protected from infringement.[23]

As 'feudal' landlords are very numerous and the great majority of them are small owners, the dividing line between them and the other strata of the rural population is not very clear. The Chinese Communist leaders were thus compelled to define in minute detail the class status of the rural population. As landlords, rich peasants of a semi-landlord type, rich peasants, well-to-do middle

[22] *The Agrarian Reform Law of the People's Republic of China*, Peking, 1951.
[23] *Ibid.*, pp. 2–4.

peasants, poor peasants, and farm labourers have different roles to play in the agrarian reform, the definition of their class status is of fundamental importance. To assist in this task the GAC issued *Decisions Concerning the Differentiation of Class Status in the Countryside* (August 4, 1950), according to which:

1. A landlord is 'a person who owns land, but does not engage in labour or only engages in supplementary labour and depends on exploitation for his means of livelihood'. 2. A rich peasant is 'one who owns better means of production and some floating capital and takes part in labour himself, but is constantly dependent on exploitation for a part or the major part of his means of livelihood'. 3. A middle peasant is 'one who depends wholly or mainly upon his own labour for his living. If his income from exploitation does not exceed 25 per cent, he shall be considered as a middle peasant or well-to-do middle peasant'. 4. A poor peasant is 'one who, in general, has to rent land for cultivation, and is exploited by others in the form of land rent, loan interest and hired labour'. 5. A farm labourer is 'one who generally has neither land nor farm implements, and depends wholly or mainly upon the sale of his labour power for his living'.[24]

On the face of it, the criteria for determining class status might seem clear enough. But when the Government proceeds to elaborate on the definition of class status,[25] the borderline between the classes becomes extremely hazy. The *Decisions* are so complicated, and the boundaries between the classes so blurred, that in many cases it is extremely difficult to determine whether a person is a landlord or a rich peasant; still more absurd, whether he is a middle peasant or even an agricultural worker, or a landlord.

The *Decisions* states: 'A person shall be classified as a landlord who owns land, but does not engage in labour or only engages in supplementary labour, and who depends on exploitation for his means of livelihood.'[26] What kind of labour determines whether a person is a peasant or landlord? The labour which

[24] *The Agrarian Reform Law of the People's Republic of China*, Peking, 1951, pp. 19–24.
[25] *Ibid.*, pp. 25–56.
[26] *Ibid*, p. 19.

defines the class status of a peasant is, we are told, 'labour employed in the main forms of agricultural production, such as ploughing, planting, reaping and other major items of labour in production'.[27] The labour that defines the class status of a landlord is

> auxiliary labour which plays only a part of secondary importance in production, such as helping with weeding, vegetable-growing and taking care of draught animals.[28]

The difficulty of determining exactly the borderline between these two kinds of labour is apparent from the same *Decisions*:

> In the course of land distribution and investigation many mistakes have been committed in connection with the problems of labour and supplementary labour. By mistaking labour for supplementary labour, some have been wrongly classified as landlords: by mistaking supplementary labour for labour, others have been wrongly classified as rich peasants.[29]

The seriousness of such a 'mistake' is clear when it is borne in mind that landlords were to have much of their property expropriated, while rich peasants were not! But even if a family is credited with having participated in 'major agricultural labour', it is still not safe to conclude that this is not a landlord family.

> Where a landlord family has some members who are engaged in major agricultural labour all the year round, or at the same time hires labourers to cultivate part of its land, the said family shall be classified as a landlord family and not as a rich peasant family if the major part of its land is rented out and the rented-out land is three times or more the size of the land cultivated jointly by the family and by hired labourers (for instance, 150 *mow* of land rented out and less than 50 *mow* cultivated by the family and by hired labourers); or in a case where the family possesses large landholdings and the rented-out land is twice or more the size of the land

[27] *The Agrarian Reform Law of the People's Republic of China*, Peking, 1951, pp. 26–7.
[28] *Ibid.*, p. 27.
[29] *Ibid.*

cultivated jointly by the family and hired labourers (for instance, 200 *mow* rented out and less than 100 *mow* cultivated by the family or hired labourers).[30]

Let this not draw one to the erroneous conclusion that the class status of the whole family is landlord. No,

> the status of those members who take part in labour, if their position in the family is not a dominant, but a subordinate one, should be appropriately determined as labouring people in order to distinguish them in status from other family members who do not participate in labour.[31]

No clue is given, however, how to determine whether the position of a person in a family is 'dominant' or 'subordinate'. Again,

> In one family, for instance, if there is a person in the rural area who has, for three years, depended on land rent and loan interest as his major means of livelihood, then the said person is a landlord. If there is another person who has, for one year, depended on the sale of his labour power as his main means of livelihood, then the said person is a worker.[32]

Worker and landlord in one and the same family! How flimsy the border!

Or take another question. What is the class status of a landlord who marries a worker? A whole section of the *Decisions* deals with the problem, but for the purpose of demonstrating the difficulty of differentiating the classes when they are not in fact very different, the posing of the question alone suffices. Imagine discussing the class status of landlords who married into workers' families during the Great French Revolution! Where feudal landlordism really exists, the peasants do not need to be told how to recognise it!

Where the widest cleavage—between landlord and labourer—demands such careful scrutiny to be detected, how are the nar-

[30] *The Agrarian Reform Law of the People's Republic of China*, Peking, 1951, p. 22.
[31] *Ibid.*
[32] *Ibid.*, pp. 50-1.

rower borders, between 'well-to-do middle peasants' and rich peasants, between 'well-to-do middle peasants' and simple middle peasants, and so on, to be discerned at all?

INDUSTRIAL AND COMMERCIAL ENTERPRISES OWNED BY LAND-LORDS

Unlike the landlords of feudal Europe, those of China were widely engaged in trade, usury and industry; hence, one of the most important issues connected with the agrarian reform was the attitude to be adopted towards industrial and commercial enterprises owned by landlords. A few instances will clarify the issues involved. In Southern Kiangsu in 1930, 22·36 per cent of big landlords engaged in trade as their chief occupation, and 7·45 per cent in industry.[33] In Szechwan Province, a survey undertaken by J. L. Buck showed that 31 per cent of the landlords were also merchants.[34] The position in Kwangtung was described by Fang Fang, Vice-Chairman of the Provincial Government:

> In Canton, the majority of industrialists and merchants are either landlords also engaged in industry and commerce, or industrialists and merchants who are also landlords. Among the owners of oil processing mills in Canton, for instance, some 90 per cent of them are landowners. The percentage of such industrialists and merchants is even greater in the small cities right next to the rural areas.[35]

The landlords being thus two-sided, the Communist leaders had to decide whether they would destroy both sides, expropriating their land and also confiscating their industrial and commercial enterprises, or not. They decided against the double bill. The *Agrarian Reform Law* states:

> Industry and commerce shall be protected from infringement.
> Industrial and commercial enterprises operated by landlords and the land and other properties used by landlords directly for the operation of industrial and commercial enterprises shall not be confiscated.[36]

[33] Chen Han-seng, *The Present Agrarian Problem in China*, Shanghai, 1933, p. 19.
[34] J. L. Buck, *An Agricultural Survey of Szechwan Province*, Chungking, 1943, p. 13, mimeographed.
[35] NFJP, August 11, 1952; CB, 211.
[36] *Agrarian Reform Law, op. cit.*, p. 2.

The mass nature of the landlord class and the hazy boundaries separating landlords from peasants inevitably had an effect on the actual execution of land reform. These effects are:

1. Mass opposition of landlords to the reform—unheard of during the Russian revolution, the French revolution or any other anti-feudal revolution;

2. Repeated errors in the determination of class status, and the need to carry out prolonged and careful examinations and revisions of already executed land distribution;

3. Further strengthening of the role of Party and State cadres in directing the land reform.

Let us take each point in order.

MASS OPPOSITION OF LANDLORDS TO AGRARIAN REFORM

People were classified as landlords *en masse*. In the country as a whole, some 5 per cent of all the rural population was declared landlord. In some areas the percentage was much higher. In Hupeh Province, for instance, about 20 per cent of the rural population were classified as landlords and rich peasants.[37] It is not surprising then that their opposition to land reform was carried out on a mass scale. The following excerpts are culled from Chinese press reports of events which are symptomatic and which could not have happened were it not that the landlords showed a violent and continuous mass opposition to land reform.

Liu Jui-lung, Vice-Chairman of the Agrarian Reform Committee, East China MAC, reported:

> After land was distributed, the landlords dared to launch a counter-attack, tearing up notices and posters and forcibly taking back land, farm implements, draft animals, foodstuffs, and houses which had already been distributed to peasants.[38]

Again, in the Central-South region, three years after 'Liberation':

> Since the conclusion of agrarian reform, there have appeared in various areas such phenomena as law-defying landlords staging counter-attacks against the peasants, carrying out counter-settlement

[37] CCJP, February 19, 1951.   [38] HWJP, March 19, 1951; CB, 92.

moves and resisting the system of reform through labour service. In the Ta He Liu Chuang *hsiang* in Chio Shan *hsien* in Honan, for instance, in the one or two years following the conclusion of agrarian reform, of the 101 landlord households, 24 carried out counter-settlement of accounts with the peasants . . .

Such phenomena have also been widely reported from other areas.[39]

Another report from the same region states:

According to statistics given by Linhsiang *hsien* in Hunan Province, there have been over 220 cases of landlords' sabotage during the production campaign. In Yangshan *hsiang*, Liling *hsien*, Hunan, landlords regained their water mills and clothing previously distributed to peasants, and smashed peasants' furniture. In Mamiao *hsiang*, Honan Province, nine families of the landlord class counter-attacked against the peasants and got back 62 *mow* of land, three houses and portions of their livestock and farm implements.[40]

The extent of opposition to the land reforms resembles more closely the 'liquidation of kulaks' in Russia during the late 'twenties and early 'thirties than the overthrow of the landlords during the Revolution.

ERRORS IN LAND REFORM AND REPEATED RE-EXAMINATION

In 1948 Mao Tse-tung wrote:

In many places many labouring people who did not engage in feudal exploitation or only engaged in slight feudal exploitation were erroneously placed in the landlord or rich-peasant category, thus the area of attack was erroneously expanded . . .[41]

Again, in carrying out the agrarian reform in the suburban areas of Peking, the mass of the peasants proved that in fact they did not know how to distinguish between landlords, and rich or even

[39] CCJP, August 20, 1952; CB, 216.
[40] CCJP, May 31, 1952; SCMP, 369.
[41] Mao Tse-tung, 'Significance of Agrarian Reform in China', *China Digest*, June 1, 1948.

middle peasants. For instance, in three villages, among families expropriated

> only four families were landlords (one family was despotic landlord), and the rest consisted of four families of rich peasants and 18 families of middle peasants.[42]

Reporting on land reform in the Central-South Region on November 16, 1951, Tu Jen-sheng, a member of the Agrarian Reform Committee of the region stated:

> In order to find out the conditions in areas where land reform had been completed, we conducted re-examination of land reform in over 1,100 *hsiang* last summer. Only 20 per cent of the *hsiang* completed the work satisfactorily.[43]

But even among this 20 per cent, 'wrong classifications of peasants' status were widely found'.[44]

Three years after 'Liberation', T'ao Chu, Secretary of South China Sub-Bureau of the Central Committee, CCP, could state:

> During the six-month period from now to the spring sowing season next year, our major attention must still be directed to the re-examination of the work of agrarian reform where it has been completed . . .[45]

And again, two months later, Fang Fang, Vice-Chairman of Canton Provincial People's Government, stated:

> Viewed from the standpoint of the distribution of land, agrarian reform has been concluded in areas containing three-fourths of the population of the province, and the whole movement is thus drawing to its close. But viewed from the standpoint of the re-examination of reform work carried out, the task has only been concluded in areas containing one-ninth of the population of the province, and thus the whole movement may be considered to have only begun.[46]

[42] *General Report of Peking Municipal People's Government on Agrarian Reform in Peking Suburban Areas*, approved by GAC on November 21, 1950; CB, 72.
[43] CCJP, December 9, 1951; CB, 157.
[44] *Ibid.*
[45] NFJP, October 28, 1952; CB, 226.
[46] NFJP, December 25, 1952; CB, 226.

Thus despite the most meticulous definition of class status, innumerable errors in classification are still committed, and years after the reform, it is still found necessary to separate the sheep from the goats. This involves vigorous activity by the courts which deal with cases connected with the movement. According to one report, in 124 *hsien* (out of more than 2,000 *hsien* in the country) the People's Courts had to deal with 143,761 cases connected with agrarian reform in the six months between November 1950 and April 1951.[47]

ROLE OF CADRES IN LAND REFORM

Because of the tremendous number of landlords, the blurred dividing line between landlords and peasants and rich and middle peasants, and above all because of the totalitarian character of Maoism, land reform could not be allowed to develop spontaneously. It had to be planned and directed by the cadres. As was emphasised:

> In areas where the land reform is to be carried out, it is necessary that the Party cadres for land reform are, both in quantity and quality, capable of grasping local reform work without letting the masses indulge in spontaneous activities.[48]

A report on land reform work in the suburban areas of Peking repeated the injunction and mentioned an example that should be followed:

> Spontaneous struggles by peasants must be firmly prevented in agrarian reform . . . Pending the arrival of an agrarian reform work team, no official action was permitted, and only policy, publicity and preparatory work were permitted.[49]

The substitution of bureaucratically-directed activities for spontaneous plebeian revolution calls for a large number of cadres. In East China as many as 170,000 special cadres were trained to

---

[47] NCNA, Peking, November 14, 1951.
[48] HKC, December 10, 1950; CB, 63.
[49] *General Report of Peking Municipal People's Government*, etc., *op. cit.*

carry out the agrarian reform.[50] Similar armies of officials were recruited and trained in other regions of China. An Tzu-wen, Minister of Personnel, reported: 'When agrarian reform was introduced, about 300,000 agrarian reform workers were organised into work corps each year.'[51]

The main stages in the actual execution of agrarian reform are these:

First, rents and interest payments are cut. Although the property rights of the landlords are not touched for a number of seasons, the rent paid by tenants is cut by 25 per cent, with the provision that the new rent is not to be more than 37·5 per cent of the harvest. In addition interest on loans is reduced. For the period, covering many months, during which this policy is being put into practice, the landlords' influence in the village is weakened, and they are rendered more and more isolated. After this preparatory stage, agrarian reform proper can start. The wheels start turning when the land reform teams come to the village. Their first job is to install telephones to maintain constant communication with the higher administrative bodies. Next they make propaganda for land reform and select the 'positive elements' who would be the key members of future organisations in the village. Then mass 'anti-despot meetings' in which one or several landlords, carefully selected by the cadres, are harangued and denounced, are organised. At the accusation meetings the cadres play an important part in manipulating the mass hatred, a role described as follows by a professor who participated as a cadre at such a meeting:

We are instructed by our leaders to scatter among the crowd at the meeting. Our tasks are: when the peasants are at a loss as to how to argue with the landlord, we should give the peasants some ideas to speak up: when the peasants become incensed and want to resort to rough measures, we should exhort them to be calm.[52]

After the accusation meetings comes the definition of the class

[50] HWJP, March 19, 1951; CB, 92.
[51] NCNA, Peking, September 30, 1952.
[52] Feng Yu-lan, 'Lessons (Learned) in My Participation in the Land Reform', HH, April 1, 1950, quoted by Chao Kuo-chun, 'Land Reform Methods in Communist China', *Papers on China*, Harvard, Mass., Volume 5, May 1951.

status of the population. This too is done at mass meetings. Disputed status is passed on to higher authorities for decision. A preliminary list is then posted up in the village for a few days, during which time amendments can be proposed to the work team. The revised list is submitted to the *chu* or *hsiang* agrarian reform committee for approval, after which it becomes final.

Each peasant now has to state the productivity of each plot of his land, the final assessment being made by the cadres. He further reports the number of members of his family, and the amount of land and number of implements he owns.

The actual expropriation of the property of those defined as landlords, and part of the property of certain rich peasants, and its distribution among the other peasants, now take place. The property distributed—land, implements, livestock, grain, etc.—is registered, and the file submitted to the *chu* or *hsiang* government for ratification.

Some months later all the findings are once more cast into the melting pot for re-examination.[53]

Contrast this long, involved, manipulated performance with the following description of a typically spontaneous peasant revolution in a Russian village:

> One September day in the fateful year 1917 . . . a man climbed a telephone pole, and cut the minute thread of communication which joined a manor house . . . with the towns, the police-offices, and the barracks . . . the two elements—peasant and proprietorial —were left momentarily to react upon each other in isolation: and within a few hours the estate had been looted, the mansion was in flames, and somewhere within the fiery circle the master of the house lay dead.[54]

WHAT DID THE PEASANT GAIN FROM LAND REFORM?

Liao Lu-yen, Minister of Agriculture, states in an article entitled, 'The Great Victory in Land Reform during the Past Three Years':

[53] For a very good description of the actual agrarian reform in a particular village, see Hsiao Ch'ien, *How the Tillers Win Back their Land*, Peking, 1954.
[54] G. T. Robinson, *Rural Russia under the Old Régime*, London, 1932, p. 64.

About 300 million peasants, including those in the old Liberated Areas or between 60 and 70 per cent of the nation's agricultural population, have received economic benefits from the land reform. Some 700 million *mow* of land have been distributed.[55]

The figure of 700 million *mow* is repeated by all Communist spokesmen. But the figure of 300 million peasants (including their families) sharing in the land reform has to be revised in the light of the 1953 census which showed the agricultural population of China to be considerably larger than was previously thought. But even if we accept the figures quoted by Liao Lu-yen, it is clear that each person sharing in the land reform received on an average only a little more than 2 *mow*, or a third of an acre. In many areas much less than this was distributed. In Kwangsi Province, for instance, an average of 1·3 *mow* per person was distributed in the land reform carried out in the winter of 1950 and spring of 1951.[56] Likewise, according to a report presented on November 21, 1951, by Teng Tzu-hui, Vice-Chairman, Central-South MAC, in a part of the region where agrarian reform had been completed (including the whole of Honan, the major portions of Hupeh, Hunan, and Kiangsi, and portions of Kwangtung and Kwangsi) the average amount of land distributed was 1·1 *mow* per head of the agricultural population.[57] Worse still, a report from East China (November 20, 1951) stated that 'in the more densely populated areas, the share *per capita* was from 0·7 to 1 *mow*.'[58]

If, however, we pass from the statistical average to the individual peasant families, there is no doubt whatever that for millions of them, particularly those who in former times were landless tenants and hired labourers, the land reform came as a tremendous, and most welcome, revolutionary change. They became owner-peasants, even if very small ones. In addition the crushing burden of rent was reduced over the whole country by some 25–30 million tons of grain. The combined effect on millions of peasants was one of deeply felt satisfaction. However, this need not obscure the hard fact that the average peasant today does not

[55] *New China's Economic Achievements, 1949–1952, op. cit.*, p. 171.
[56] KJP, October 12, 1951; CB, 142.
[57] CCJP, December 13, 1951; CB, 142.
[58] CFJP, November 29, 1951; CB, 160.

own more than some 3½ *mow* of land, barely sufficient to eke out the most meagre existence.

Passing from the land of the peasants to other means of production, we find again universal poverty, particularly where draught animals are concerned. In this sphere the effect of the agrarian reform was infinitesimal. The report on Kwangsi Province, already cited, stated that in the areas where land reform was accomplished in winter 1950 and spring 1951, the 'magnificent' number of 87,000 draft animals was distributed among more than 2 million peasants ('thereby generally solving peasants' difficulties in production').[59] Similarly, in the suburban areas of Peking during land reform 229,892 peasants acquired 1,743 draft animals,[60] or 1 among some 130 peasants. Likewise, the report of Teng Tzu-hui cited above shows that the 60 million peasants of the Central-South region who had already shared in the benefits of agrarian reform at the time the report was delivered, received 780,000 draft animals,[61] or one per 80 peasants. In another report summing up the results of land reform in the whole country, Teng Tzu-hui wrote that between 1950 and 1953, in East, Central-South, North-West and South-West China, i.e., in an area comprising some three hundred million peasants, a total of 2,960,000 head of draft animals were confiscated and distributed among the peasants.[62]

All in all, the productive forces gained by the peasants during the agrarian reform were hopelessly inadequate. A study of five villages in north China where land reform had been carried out clearly brought home this point. In these villages 740 peasant households (61 per cent of the total) had no draft animals; 637 households (53 per cent) were lacking in important implements, and 178 households (15 per cent) owned land averaging less than one *mow* per head, 47 households owning only half a *mow*.[63]

---

[59] KJP, October 12, 1951; CB, 142.
[60] *General Report of Peking Municipal People's Government,* etc., *op. cit.*
[61] CCJP, December 13, 1951; CB, 142.
[62] Teng Tzu-hui, *The Outstanding Success of the Agrarian Reform Movement in China,* Peking, 1954, p. 15.
[63] Min Wan-lan, 'The Agricultural Production in the Old Liberated Areas', HCH, July 1, 1951.

CHAPTER V

AGRICULTURAL TAXATION

Of the many burdens borne by the Chinese peasants, one of the most onerous is the agricultural tax. It would take us too far afield to review Mao's agricultural taxation policy prior to the establishment of the People's Republic of China, or even since then. Only the prevailing system will therefore be described. This was established by the Government Administrative Council on June 16, 1952, when it promulgated the *Directive on the Collection of the 1952 Agricultural Tax.*

The *Directive* distinguished between three areas—North-East China, North China and the rest of the country. In the North-East a *pro rata* system of tax that had been in force until then, varying between 21 and 23 per cent of the harvest (except for Jehol Province, where it was 15 per cent), was to continue during 1952. In North China the rate was fixed according to the area of the holding, which makes it practically impossible to calculate exactly what percentage of the gross output is taken as tax. In the rest of China, the tax was progressive, ranging between 7 per cent for an average peasant income of 150 catties of grain per head to 26 per cent for incomes of 1,550 catties and over. [1]

The *Directive* announced that in 1953 the tax in North-East and North China would be brought into line with the system prevailing in the rest of the country. This was duly enforced. As it is quite unlikely that this change sought to lighten the burden of taxation on the peasantry in 1953—the first year of the Five Year Plan—it stands to reason that the present rate of tax must yield at least as much as the former *pro rata* system did, i.e., in the case of the North-East (except for Jehol Province) 21–23 per cent of the harvest.

A different calculation gives a similar result for the whole country. The average output of grain per head of the whole population was some 550 catties in 1952, or per head of the agricultural population alone, some 650 catties. If we exclude

[1] JMJP, June 19, 1952; SCMP, 359.

peasants who do not grow grain but industrial products, herds-men, etc., who, together with their families, number some 40–50 million people, the average output of grain *per capita* of grain-growing peasants is some 900 catties. A peasant family with this income must yield 20 per cent of the harvest in tax at current taxation rates.[2] The tax is levied on gross agricultural income; obviously the peasant's net income—after deducting the cost of seeds, fertilisers, etc.—will suffer a larger cut.

In cases of low yield caused by natural calamities—drought, flood, hail, etc.—which are not uncommon in China, the rate of tax is cut, but only slightly. According to the *Measures for Reduction in and Exemption from Agricultural Tax in Respect of Calamity-Stricken Peasants* promulgated on August 14, 1952, peasants who lose 60 per cent or more of their crop are 'to be exempt from all agricultural tax;' those that lose between 50 and 60 per cent of their crop are 'to be given a 70 per cent reduction in the agri-cultural tax;' those that lose between 40 and 50 per cent of their crop are 'to be given 50 per cent reduction in the agricultural tax;' those that lose between 30 and 40 per cent of their crop are 'to be given 35 per cent reduction in the agricultural tax;' and those that lose between 20 and 30 per cent of their crop are 'to be given 25 per cent reduction in the agricultural tax. If loss of crop is less than 20 per cent, no reduction in tax shall be given.'[3] This is an extremely heavy burden for calamity-stricken peasants. Yet the provisions of the law are frequently overlooked by the cadres who, according to the repeated testimony of the press, tend to deviate widely from it in the direction of increasing the peasants' tax burden. What decides their activities when collecting taxes is the 'assigned quota of agricultural taxes to be collected' from an area, a figure set by the higher authorities, rather than the formal tax-rate schedule. The Central Government decides the total amount of agricultural tax to be collected in a year and assigns tax quotas to each province; the provincial government allocates the 'assigned quota' among the *hsien* (counties); the

---

[2] It comes as a surprise to read what the Minister of Agriculture, Li Shu-cheng wrote in the English language *People's China*: 'The (agricultural) tax this year (1952) takes only 12 per cent of the peasants' gross income . . .' (Li Shu-cheng, 'Achieve-ments in Agriculture', PC, October 1, 1952).

[3] NCNA, Peking, August 20, 1952; SCMP, 399.

hsien government allocates its own quota among the *hsiang* (an administrative unit, containing a few villages); and finally, the cadres in each *hsiang* allocate the quota among the peasant households. If the assignments of the higher authorities are large, the official list of tax rates has to be ignored in practice.[4]

If the State's demand is not reason enough for local cadres to extort more from the peasants than provided for by law, there is another factor which encourages them—the wide margins for arbitrary decisions and collections due to the difficulty of calculating the 'gross agricultural income' of a family. Proof of this may be culled at will from the Chinese press. The *People's Daily* has the following to say:

> There was no small number of defects in the collection of the agricultural tax in 1952. For instance, the production norm remains uneven and varies from place to place, so that some peasants shouldered heavier burdens than did other peasants. This has been particularly conspicuous in border areas. In 159 pairs of *hsiang* standing opposite each other in Honan and Anhwei Provinces, with the exception of two where the norms are approximately equal, twenty-seven *hsiang* in Honan Province had their production norms fixed at a lower level than opposite *hsiang* in Anhwei Province, the difference ranging between 5–30 per cent . . .[5]

A month later the *Southern Daily* reported from another part of the country:

> According to investigations in Chungshan *hsien* and Kuikang *hsien*, the peasants said that the annual production norm had been raised every year. They said that 'the norm has been increased from 350 *catties* per *mow* to 400 *catties* and then to 500 *catties*, higher every year'. Some peasants in Chiehyang *hsien* feared that 'after increasing production, the burden of the agricultural tax will be increased'. In some villages the peasants said that 'the government appealed for greater production because it wanted to increase the agricultural levies'.[6]

[4] See, for instance, GAC (*Directive on Agricultural Taxation During 1953*, adopted on June 5, 1953 (NCNA, Peking, August 30, 1953); SCMP, 642.
[5] JMJP, January 11, 1953; SCMP, 505.
[6] NFJP, February 19, 1953; SCMP, 527.

Many known excesses are connected with the cadres' arbitrary methods of tax collection. Hsi Chung-hsun, secretary of the North-East Bureau of the Party, said in a speech on May 20, 1951, that during the collection of agricultural taxes, 'the practices of indiscriminate beating, scolding, punishment, threats, arrests, etc., are frequently employed in promoting the work of collection'.[7] Another paper reports:

> In the matter of tax collection, the demand for fulfilment of the task, inadequate check-up of work and inadequate implementation of policy have resulted in such law-breaking acts in various districts as commandism, beatings, arrests and forced suicide, etc.[8]

No wonder the peasants often 'hold that paying the grain tax is like paying rent to the Government'.[9]

It is also not to be wondered at that the work of collecting the agricultural tax does not run very smoothly. Thus Po I-po, Minister of Finance, said:

> The work of collecting public grain met with both open and secret sabotage by bandits and reactionaries organised by the Kuomintang. According to incomplete figures, more than 3,000 cadres sacrificed their lives in the course of collecting public grain.[10]

Thus far we have dealt with the agricultural tax. Actually the peasants are liable for many other taxes also. Po I-po listed some of them in a speech on the *Draft Budget for 1950*:

> A considerable portion of the taxes, such as in the case of the salt tax, customs duties, commodity tax, business turn-over tax, and the tax for slaughtering animals is borne by the consumers, most of whom are peasants.[11]

A quick glance at a few items on the list will show what a burden these taxes are for the peasant. A decision (June 1, 1950) of the GAC Financial and Economic Committee fixed the salt tax at

[7] NFJP, June 9, 1952; CB, 158.
[8] TKP, April 12, 1953; SCMP, 555.
[9] NFJP, February 19, 1953; SCMP, 527.
[10] *New China's Economic Achievements, 1949-1952, op. cit.*, p. 90.
[11] *Ibid.*, p. 43.

between JMP 30,000 per picul in the North-West and JMP 70,000 per picul in North and East China. The market price of salt in Shanghai on January 24, 1952, was JMP 111,500 per picul.[12] The salt tax is particularly burdensome, as the peasant, lacking other condiments, uses salt liberally. The commodity tax weighs heavily too, as the following list, issued by GAC on December 26, 1952, makes clear:

Tobacco leaf, cut	40 per cent
Native tobacco leaf	40 per cent
Superstitious paper	80 per cent
Fire crackers	20 per cent
Drinks	40 per cent
Sugar	30 per cent
Tea	20 per cent
Woollen yarn and thread	20 per cent
Silk	20 per cent
Native cloth	3–7 per cent
Vegetable oil	10 per cent
Matches	15 per cent
Cigarettes	90–120 per cent
Wines	20–80 per cent

Source: JMJP, December 31, 1952; SCMP, 509.

[12] C. K. Chao, compiler, *Source Materials from Communist China*, III, Cambridge, Mass., 1952, pp. 36–7, mimeographed.

CHAPTER VI

SOME OTHER FACETS OF THE PEASANT SITUATION

THE 'SCISSORS'

An important factor affecting peasants' welfare is the relation between the price of the agricultural goods the peasant sells and the industrial goods he has to buy. In present-day China the terms of this trade have changed to the detriment of the peasant. The 'scissors'—to use a term borrowed from the Soviet Union— of prices of agricultural and industrial goods has opened and is much wider today than before the war. To hide this fact the Chinese press generally refrains from comparing present-day with pre-war prices, even though it readily indulges in comparisons of present-day prices with those prevailing in the last few years of Kuomintang rule, when the 'scissors' was even wider than it is today.[1] Nevertheless from time to time items of information enter the Chinese press which show the urgency of the problem.

Thus, according to the Nankai University's Institute of Economics at Tientsin, if the period of July 1936 to June 1937 is taken as the base of 1, after the rocketing inflation of Kuomintang rule, prices in the third week of December 1949 were: food, 11,600; agricultural foodstuffs, 12,293; animal products, 10,089; other agricultural products, 5,886; while manufactured consumers' goods stood at 13,676.[2] Similar information is included in another paper:

'It can be shown that the average difference in the rates of exchange between yarn and textiles on the one hand and grain and cotton on the other in the large or medium cities of China (Shanghai, Tientsin, Hankow, Changsha, Tsinan, Changchow, Sian, Taiyuan, Shihchiachuan and Paoting) increased from 0·9 per cent to 16·7

[1] See JMJP, November 15, 1953; December 11, 1953; March 1, 1954; SCMP, 768. TKP, March 18, 1954; SCMP, 768.
[2] FEER. January 26, 1950.

per cent between the end of June and the end of August. A similar comparison between yarn and grain shows an increase of 13 to 64 per cent from August 1936 to August 1950 in the four cities Shanghai, Tientsin, Tsinan and Taiyuan, while a comparison between textiles and grain in the same cities over the same period shows an increase of 43 to 73 per cent.[3]

The Nankai Institute calculated that if the period from July 1936 to June 1937 were taken as the base of 1, the average price index for four categories of agricultural products stood at about 18,500 during the last week of January 1951, while the price of manufactured goods stood at about 35,800.[4] During 1951 the prices of industrial goods continued to rise more rapidly than those of agricultural products. The Nankai Institute calculates that the wholesale price index of cotton yarn and cotton cloth in the six large cities (Tientsin, Shanghai, Hankow, Canton, Chungking and Sian) in the first half of September 1951 was 23·2 per cent higher than at the end of 1950, while the price of grain and other foodstuffs increased during the same period by only 11·4 and 9·7 per cent respectively.[5] Two years later there was no amelioration. An article entitled 'Mass Reaction and Problems after Land Reform', written by the Investigation Section, Kwangtung Provincial Land Reform Committee, says:

> The peasants remarked that in the field of production materials, fertilisers cost an equivalent of 118 *catties* of grain per *picul* before liberation; now they cost 262 *catties* of grain. Cakes of sesame husks used to cost 118 *catties* of grain per *picul*; now they cost 150 *catties*. Bean-cakes have gone up in price, and farming tools are also much too expensive. A plough used to cost 18 *catties* of grain; now it costs 40 *catties*. In the field of daily necessities, in the past one *picul* of grain could be converted into four suits of coarse cloth; now it fetches only two suits.[6]

A month later a *People's Daily* editorial assured the peasants that the Government stood for 'the policy of the gradual reduction

[3] *Wen Hui Pao*, Shanghai, January 1, 1951.
[4] NYT, February 19, 1951.
[5] Chang Yu-chiang, 'Brilliant Achievements in the Domestic Trend of our Country in 1951', CCCP, January 24, 1952.
[6] NFJP, February 19, 1953; SCMP, 527.

of the scissor differences in prices for industrial and agricultural products'.[7] But the fact that no figures have since been published about changes in their relative prices of agricultural and industrial goods, makes it doubtful whether this statement has had any practical results.

The above refers to relative prices of industrial and agricultural goods in the free market. As practically the whole of the market-able agricultural product is compulsorily purchased by the State at very low prices,[8] the 'scissors' is in fact much wider than it seems.

THE PEASANTS LACK CREDIT

Peasant poverty in land and other means of production—live-stock, agricultural implements, fertilisers, etc.—renders their need for cheap and abundant credit very urgent. This need becomes acute during the oft-recurring calamities of crop failure, death of a draft animal, sickness, death and so on. Births and weddings, the latter especially, also call for expenses that are often beyond current incomes. Peasants need credit for maintaining production, not to speak of enlarging it.

In the past, the peasant poverty and the scarcity of capital led to his involvement in heavy debts for which exorbitant interest was demanded. A study of 16,786 peasant holdings in 168 locali-ties and 38,256 farm families in 22 provinces of China showed that during 1929–33 the average rate of interest was 2·7 per cent per month or 32 per cent per annum.[9] Indeed, 'It is not un-common to find places where farmers borrow one bushel of wheat in February and pay back two in June. It is certainly common to borrow one bushel and pay one and one half for the same length of time'.[10]

The agrarian reform hardly reduced the urgent need for credit. At the same time, however, it stopped up the traditional sources of peasant credit in that the landlord-usurer ceased to exist and the

[7] JMJP, March 26, 1953; CB, 240.
[8] See pp. 134-5, 141-3.
[9] Buck, *Land Utilisation in China, op. cit.*, p. 463.
[10] L. T. K. Wu, 'Merchant Capital and Usury Capital in Rural China', FES, March 25, 1936.

merchant-usurer became more circumspect in advancing loans. Prior to land reform these were the two main sources of peasants' credit.[11]

During the last few years, attempts have been made by State and credit co-operatives to bridge the gap. But the amounts and terms offered are far from favourable to the peasant. Dealing with the length of the loan, a GAC *Directive on Issuance of Farming Credit* of July 7, 1953, states:

> The periods of repayment of farming credits should be separately stipulated according to the different purposes for which they are intended. In some cases, the credits are to be issued in the spring and to be repaid in the autumn. In some cases the credits are to be repaid in 1, 2, 3 or even 5 years by instalments.[12]

The amount of State credit given to the needy peasants is extremely small. The GAC's *Directive* states:

> In principle, the amount should not exceed 10 per cent or 20 per cent of the total earnings in a year.[13]

In 1956 the planned state agricultural loan was as much as JMP 3 milliard (new currency).[14] This is about JMP 6 (new currency) per head of the agricultural population, or the munificent sum of 18 shillings!

In addition to State loans, peasants can obtain loans from credit co-operatives. But this is also a rather limited source. In 1955 there were more than 160,000 credit co-operatives with a membership of 76 million households. The co-operatives granted loans of over JMP 780 million during the year.[15] This amounted to an average of about JMP 10 (new currency) per household, i.e., about £1 10s., or 6 shillings per head.

The loan from the co-operatives is not wholly an addition to the

---

[11] A survey carried out in 1934 by the National Agricultural Research Bureau, Nanking, covering 2,268 rural communities in 22 provinces showed that of all the peasants' creditors, 42·6 per cent were landlords and rich peasants, and 38·1 per cent were merchants. (Wu, *ibid.*)

[12] NCNA, Peking, September 1, 1953; SCMP, 645.

[13] *Ibid.*

[14] NCNA, Peking, March 14, 1956.

[15] TKP, March 5, 1956; SCMP, 1250.

state loan, since a good portion of the former represents relending of funds made available by the state.

These figures should be compared with the results of the survey made by J. L. Buck in 1929–33. At that time the *annual* credit extended to the peasant borrower totalled 80 yuan per peasant holding, or about £4 10s. 0d. If all peasants are included—those who did not take loans too—the annual credit per holding was 31 yuan, or about £1 14s. 0d.[16] Prices at that time being about one third of those at present prevailing, the real value of £1 14s. 0d. in 1929–33 is nearer £5 today.

The small scale of State lending to peasants compels the Government to permit private loans. Furthermore, it prevents the imposition of any legal restriction on the rate of interest. The GAC's *Directive on Issuance of Farming Credit* (July 7, 1953) says:

> At the present moment when the State bank is still not in a position to fully satisfy peasants' needs for loans and when credit co-operatives have not been universally developed, free borrowing in the countryside is still what the peasants need and should be permitted to exist and develop, and mutual help and mutual relief and repayment of loans should be promoted. It is difficult to restrict the interest rates of private loans simply by laws and ordinances.[17]

And clearly, as the risk attached to loans given by private persons is greater than that attached to State or credit co-operative loans, the rate of interest will be exorbitant. When the East China Bureau of the CCP on September 18, 1949, ordered all debts to be paid unless the rate of interest was usurious (in which case only the principal need be paid) it defined the term 'usurious' as a rate higher than 15 per cent a month, or 180 per cent per annum![18] Reports such as the following are quite common:

> Last spring, peasants of five villages in Sunchiang *hsien* borrowed usurious loans amounting to JMP 110,000,000 from unscrupulous merchants: after autumn harvest, they repaid JMP 180,000,000.[19]

[16] Buck, *Land Utilisation in China, op. cit.*, p. 462.
[17] NCNA, Peking, September 1, 1953; SCMP, 645.
[18] CFJP, September 18, 1949.
[19] JMJP, December 30, 1953; SCMP, 727.

Or again,

> According to investigations of Chiangning *hsien*, Kiangsu Province,
> the rich peasants, by loaning 1 *picul* of rice (without husk) in the
> spring, get 3 *piculs* of rice (with husk) in the autumn . . . The
> interest more than doubles the capital loaned.[20]

Natural disasters, even when relatively mild, shoot up the
usurious rate of interest. The Hankow *Yangtze Daily*, describing
the effect of summer famine in Hunan Province, said:

> In the special districts of Lingling, Changsha, Hengyang, etc.,
> usury has developed in the rural districts on account of the pre-
> valence of summer famine. There, quite a great number of peasants
> have started mortgaging their land and selling their houses, draft
> animals, and farm implements. In the 6th village of the Yangliu
> *hsiang* in Chitung *hsien*, middle peasant Chen Yun-hung lent out two
> *piculs* of rice and demanded four *piculs* in return as principal and
> interest after the autumn harvest. In Shatien *hsiang* of the 5th *chu*
> in Tao *hsien*, there was a middle peasant who lent out one *picul* of
> paddy and demanded five *piculs* of new paddy crops in return after
> the autumn harvest.[21]

The benefit derived from State or co-operative loans is often
diminished by reservations attached to their use. They are frequently given for the stipulated purpose of buying a plough, or
digging a well, etc., and for this purpose only. This 'special aim
for each loan' decided by State Bank or Credit Co-operative
bureaucrats, sometimes leads to ludicrous results and personal
tragedies. Thus, in a bout of self-criticism, Hu Ching-yun, Vice-
Manager of the People's Bank of China, revealed:

> In a number of places, loans were not granted on the basis of the
> people's needs for production and living, and the targets were ful-
> filled through coercion and commandism. In some places where
> wells could not be sunk, loans were extended to compulsorily sink
> wells. In some places where no dykes could be built, loans were
> extended to build dykes. Though the people in some places could

[20] JMJP, November 23, 1954; SCMP, 959.
[21] CCJP, July 9, 1952; SCMP, 379.

not use the 7-in. ploughs, loans were granted to compulsorily purchase such ploughs. As a result, the wells sunk have become 'wells
to look at'; the dykes built have been called the 'great despot dykes'
by the people, and the ploughs have become 'hanging ploughs'.
In recovering the loans, compulsion was used, thereby bringing
about the death of several persons.[22]

A few months later, the GAC again unwittingly revealed the
bureaucratic mismanagement of loans in its *Directive on Issuance of
Farming Credit* which called for the return of

> all modern farming implements, apparatus, insecticides and water-
> wheels loaned to the peasants without their agreement, which are
> found unsuitable for use or unacceptable to the peasants and which
> are still lying idle in peasants' hands.[23]

When collecting debts, the cadres are not in the habit of
approaching the peasants with kid gloves. Excesses abound. One
report described how

> when collecting debts compulsory repayment was demanded and
> the peasants were forced to sell their cattle, farming tools and land
> holdings for repayment. . . . At Shenchow, Honan . . . 13 peasant
> households were forced to sell their cattle for repayment of debt.
> When collecting debts, the Wangmo bank branch threatened to
> detain the chiefs of teams of peasants' associations unless the debts
> owed by their groups had been repaid.[24]

Similarly,

> 57 cadres of the bank in Chiahsing in Chekiang were repeatedly
> guilty of beating up the masses and as many as 174 peasants became
> victims. When collecting debts at Kaoshan *hsiang*, Huaiyuan *hsien*,
> Anhwei, bank cadres bound and imprisoned the peasants who were
> unable to repay their debts. The bank cadres announced: 'Whoever
> wants an extension of credit, stay here one night.' Cadre Chiao
> Ho-hsien forced peasant Yuan Chien-ying to repay his cattle loan,
> and Yuan was forced to go to a hill at night and hang himself.[25]

[22] TKP, March 19, 1953.
[23] NCNA, Peking, September 1, 1953.
[24] TKP, March 24, 1953; SCMP, 571.
[25] *Ibid.*

These are probably extreme cases. But the mere possibility of their occurrence shows how the crying thirst for credit, unquenched by the meagreness of the loans, gives the cadres unwarranted power.

To make the plight of the peasants even more severe in the matter of credit, the State Bank and the Credit Co-operatives very often insist on the peasants depositing savings. Tientsin *Ta Kung Pao* states:

> Some districts, disregarding peasants' financial conditions and ability to save, blindly launched savings emulation drives . . . In Luchen of Shansi, a call for JMP 10,000 savings for each person was raised. The peasants commented: 'This looks like a poll tax!' . . . Savings were turned into 'exorbitant taxes'.
>
> A case was reported in Kunshan, Kiangsu, where peasants were bound and an aged woman forced to commit suicide when savings quotas were apportioned. At Hsuchiatun, 4th *chu*, Port Arthur and Dairen, savings quotas were apportioned according to land holdings and villager Hsu Chentien killed himself for being unable to take the quota. Bank cadres of Tachiao *chu*, Hochiang *hsien*, Szechwan, compelled the masses to buy savings bonds in such a way as to affect peasants' livelihood and force suicides. Similar cases have also been reported in Yangyuan of Chahar, Sungtao of Kweichow and Kienshui of Kiangsu.[26]

Another article said:

> In Huanyen *hsiang*, the cadres held meetings every day in the homes of those peasants who were unwilling to join the co-operatives or who subscribed less shares. Forced into a situation where there was no alternative, the peasants had to submit with a deep sigh: 'These meetings every day hinder production. Better take two shares and let the matter drop.' . . . The work team of Shulan Party Committee in Kirin deducted shares from the grain proceeds when purchase of grain was made. Those country folk who did not take shares or could not make deposits were subjected to criticism and abuse as stupid elements at mass meetings. A peasant and his family members cried the whole night for being 'called upon' to deposit

[26] TKP, March 24, 1953; SCMP, 571.

10,000 *catties* of grain. Seeing that they cried, the work team increased the quantity to 15,000 *catties* on the following day and told them cruelly: 'Since you cry, deposit more.' In the view of many peasants, demand for co-operative capital and deposits looks like collection of debts by the 'King of Hell'.[27]

In Yuhsien, Chahar, cadres

compelled peasants of 40 households to continue meetings for seven nights in succession, and the peasants were thus forced to sell out their draft animals or relief grain in order to buy savings bonds. In Kaotang, Shantung, militiamen kept sentry during mass meetings and would not let out those who did not buy savings bonds. The masses called the savings bonds 'exit passes'. Some peasants of Hopei were heard to say: 'Bring your quilts when going to a meeting: if you are not permitted to go, sleep at the place of the meeting'.[28]

This extortion of the peasants' money sometimes takes the form of 'insuring' his cattle. For instance,

In Hunan Province, the cadres demanded compulsory insurance of all draft cattle in a *hsiang* and intimidated the peasants, saying: 'If the insurance money is not paid up, the cattle will be taken away.' The people called the insurance premium 'cattle tax'.[29]

NEW CLASS DIFFERENTIATION IN THE COUNTRYSIDE

Against a background of poverty in means of production, with his meagre income eaten into by crushing taxation, by an unfavourable price-ratio of the goods he sells to the goods he buys, suffering from a lack of credit with its attendant usury, having hardly any margin of reserves, any misfortune such as drought, death of a draft animal or illness, can force the peasant to sell his property, even his land. Thus the stage is set for the pauperisation of the mass of the peasants.

This pauperisation of the many can help the few to get rich quickly. The land reform having stopped up one gap through

[27] TKP, March 24, 1953; SCMP, 571.
[28] *Ibid.*
[29] TKP, March 19, 1953; SCMP, 539.

which the resources of the peasants percolated, enables at least some of the peasants, for some time, to improve their conditions and even accumulate some wealth.

But before going into the effect of land reform on social differentiation in the village, the great differences of income between the peasants in the different regions of the country should be examined. According to the *People's Daily* the differences between average incomes of peasants in different areas are tremendous:

> According to available data, the average *per capita* agricultural incomes in the various areas in the Northeast are: Northern Manchuria, approximately 1,845 *catties* per annum (of principal local foodstuffs; the same applies hereafter); Southern Manchuria, approximately 845 *catties*; Jehol Province, approximately 504 *catties*.
> . . . In the barren and mountainous regions in Western Hupeh, Western Hunan and Northern Kwangtung, the average individual income is only 300–400 *catties* per year. But in rich regions like those surrounding Lake Tai Hu (Kiangsu), those near Lake Tung Ting (Hunan) and those in the Chengtu plains (Szechwan), the average individual agricultural income reaches 1,000 *catties* or more.[30]

Even if the 'averages' in different areas did not hide great local variations in income, the differences in income among the various regions must themselves lead to increasing social stratification. In some areas the peasants manage to save and improve their welfare and wealth, while in others they become poorer. These variations in output in different regions are not, of course, new. They were a factor in social differentiation among the peasantry before the agrarian reform as well. But then its effect was somewhat slowed down by the fact that the landlord managed to squeeze out a larger share of the produce when it was grown on better land, or in areas nearer markets or railways, and so on. Land reform removed this factor which tended to preserve the equality of poverty in the countryside.

Of much greater significance, however, is the social differentiation within the peasantry of each area, within each *hsien*, *chu* or even *hsiang*. There is a great deal of evidence to show that this process has been greatly accelerated since land reform. This is

[30] JMJP, July 7, 1952; SCMP, 385.

best seen in areas where the most radical type of agrarian reform was carried out under the pre-1949 slogan of 'equal distribution of all land'. Not only were landlords completely expropriated at that time, but rich peasants too had their surplus land, livestock and agricultural implements, houses, etc., confiscated. It is thus obvious that the rich peasants now living in these 'old liberated areas' must be mainly not heirs of the past, but a new crop altogether. How the peasantry of these areas became stratified can be seen from the following examples.

A *Report on Investigation of Conditions in Five Villages in an Old Liberated Area in Shansi Province* describes the situation five years after land reform. It says:

> Since land reform, 96 peasant families in the five villages have sold a total of 284·11 *mow* of land to pay for wedding and funeral expenses, and the like. Ninety-nine peasant families have bought land. Private ownership of land, natural calamities, and other inevitable misfortunes have caused a small portion of peasants to lose labour and land and become once again impoverished. On the other hand, another small portion of peasants has risen in status. This is the reason for emergent rural class distinctions.
>
> In Su-ko village, as 20 per cent of the total families in the village have amassed fortunes, and purchased land, the price of land is now double the price in pre-war years. When it is impossible to buy land, the peasants make money by practising usury, collecting interest in kind which sometimes reaches as high a rate as 60–180 per cent per annum. Such a practice, while not universal, is worthy of our attention.[31]

A similar picture was presented by Yen Chia Ts'un village in Shansi Province, a village awarded the title of 'Bumper-crop Model Village' by the Central Government. It was 'liberated' in 1947 and equal distribution of all land was carried out. In 1952 it showed the following picture: of 126 households in the village, '11 are newly impoverished households and poor peasants' and '10 per cent have become upper middle peasants'.[32] This situation was not peculiar to Shansi but was characteristic of the whole

[31] JMJP, November 11, 1951; CB, 143.
[32] JMJP, July 19, 1952; SCMP, 394.

of North China. Thus Liu Lan-tao, Chairman of the North China Administrative Committee, complained that 'a considerable number of peasants sold their land and became impoverished shortly after the land reform'.[33]

That the rise of rich peasants, including Party members, has gone far is clear from the fact that the North China Bureau of the CCP had to issue special provisions admonishing against 'the hiring of labour, issue of loans, engagement in commercial enterprises, and renting out of land by members of the Party':

Should any member of the Party . . . still persist in the employment of labourers and engage in exploitation, and thereby is transformed into a rich peasant or any other exploiting element, he shall be expelled from the Party.

No member of the Party may issue loans . . .

A member who derives his main income from loans, and loans at usurious interest rates, shall be expelled from the Party.

A member of the Party who derives his main income from the renting out of land and has been transformed into the status of a landlord shall be expelled from the Party. . . .

Buying land for renting out, or for cultivation with hired labour, and dealings in land with a view to profit shall be severely criticised and prohibited.[34]

Similar conditions existed in other places where 'equal distribution of all land' had been practised a few years earlier. An investigation into the economic conditions of five villages in Heilungkiang Province in the North-east carried out in December 1952 showed that of all households, new rich constituted 3·03 per cent; upper middle, 23·31; middle, 48·36; poor and hired labourers, 24·27; others 1·03. In this province exploitation is rampant.

Generally, exploitation takes the following forms, the making of loans at high interest rates, speculation in livestock and grain, hiring labourers to operate secondary productions, hiring labourers under the pretence of recruiting relations or keeping footmen, and hiring a great number of temporary labourers, (five new rich

[33] JMJP, March 14, 1953; SCMP, 535.
[34] JMJP, February 26, 1953; SCMP, 532.

peasants in Kungnung village hired 7 permanent labourers and 400 temporary labourers in 1952) . . . rich peasants' exploitation activities are prevalent and conspicuous. In Kungnung village, the amount of grain loaned by six rich peasant households constituted 48 per cent of total grain loaned in the whole village, the interest rates all being above five per cent (per month).[35]

On the other hand,

Poor peasants constitute 24·27 per cent of all households in the five villages . . . their farmlands, 14·23 per cent; their farm animals, 4·35 per cent; their big carts, 4 per cent; and their farm implements, 3·24 per cent of the total holdings.[36]

Among the direct reasons for impoverishment the following are pointed out:

(1) Poor households short of labour because of disability, injury, death and illness (constituting 15·52 per cent of poor and distressed households), (2) the newly re-settled afflicted households (constituting 29·9 per cent), (3) those overburdened with old debts and having little money of their own (constituting 8·62 per cent), (4) those in debt due to building of houses and marriage (constituting 9·22 per cent), (5) those who have no horses or whose horses have died (constituting 15·5 per cent . . .)[37]

Party members and Government officials in these five villages are not free of the taint of exploitation:

Of the 14 Party members in Yuanhai Village, only two females have not participated in exploitation. Five Party members have hired labourers and another five have made loans at high interest rates. The secretary of the Party Branch, Kuo Chung-hsiao, has hired labourers to do heavy work for three years on end. . . . Bad people have got into the Party, the Government and the Youth League, all of which are sometimes dominated by rich peasants.[38]

A similar picture of increasing peasant class differentiation in the countryside in North-east China as a whole five years after

[35] JMJP, June 8, 1953; SCMP, 602.   [37] Ibid.
[36] Ibid.   [38] Ibid.

land reform, was given by Kao Kang, at the time head of the Manchurian Administration, in a speech on January 10, 1952. He speaks about

> rapid development of the practice of usury and growing speculative activities in rural villages. According to the results of investigation made in the Heilungkiang and Sungkiang areas, 60–70 per cent of the rural families are involved in loans at usurious rates, and part of them change their own line into doing speculative business, with even some of our Party members doing this, to the detriment of rural production work.[39]

Another sentence in Kao Kang's speech hints at the extremes which had been reached:

> If Communist Party members all hire labour and give loans at usurious interest, then the party will become a rich peasant party.[40]

In the areas 'liberated' after the beginning of 1949, where land reform was not directed against the rich peasant economy, social stratification is partly a heritage of the past, and partly a new creation. There is, however, ample evidence to show that class differences increased considerably in the years after land reform. The following report comes from the South-Central regions of China:

> In areas south of the Yangtze, the season of summer famine has again arrived.
> Certain impoverished peasants whose capital reserve is scanty, have run out of food. They subsist from day to day on what little they manage to earn. In the Hsuangchiao *hsiang* of Chitung *hsien*, Hunan Province, the peasants of two food-short families have sold their rice seedlings . . . The seedlings on three-fifths of a *mow* were sold only for half a *picul* of rice. In the Chang-chia Branch of the Peasants' Association of the Szeyenchiao *hsiang* in Tao *hsien*, the impoverished peasants and farm hands, totalling 118 families, have sold 17 out of their 22 head of draft animals that were given to them during agrarian reform.
> In Chuantang *hsiang* of the 5th *chu* in Chitung *hsien*, poor peasant

[39] CB, 163, p. 59.   [40] *Ibid.*, p. 60.

Teng Hsiang-fu sold 0·4 of a *mow* of land from the total 2·9 *mow* received from the recent land reform, because he had nothing to eat. The sale brought him only 0·7 *picul* of rice. In Changchiang *hsiang* of the 8th *chu* in Tao *hsien*, poor peasant Chu Chih-chia exchanged 0·5 *mow* of his high-grade land with some one for inferior land of a similar size in order to obtain 200 *catties* of rice to maintain his living. . . . Similar incidents also prevail in other localities.[41]

Similar reports come from other parts of the same region: 'According to a survey of 16 villages in the counties of Huihsien, Tenchin, Tsiyuan, etc. (in Honan Province) conducted in June 1952, out of the 3,753 families, 185 families sold their land. . . .'[42]

At the other end of the scale, the rich peasants are seeking spheres other than agriculture in which to invest the growing sums brought in by their farms. As an example,

In one *hsien* city in Kwangsi Province, 91 shops were opened by peasants. A militia captain in Kiangsu Province drew up a 100-word personal '5 year plan' for becoming a rich peasant in three years and a landlord in five years. A '5 year plan' drawn up by another *tsun* cadre provides for hoarding grain and extending loans first, then building houses and buying land and grain and transforming himself from a poor peasant into a rich peasant.[43]

Naturally Peking will view the concentration of economic power in the hands of individual peasants unfavourably. The rich peasants—or kulaks, to use the widely known Russian term— threaten to divert surplus wealth into their own hands, to the detriment of State capital accumulation. The kulak is no less disliked for political reasons, as he is usually the leader in the village society and the organiser of local interests, independent of the Central Government.

As land reform tends to encourage the aggrandisement of the kulak, Peking follows close on its heels with measures to counteract it. The most important and radical measure is the collectivisation of agriculture.

[41] CCJP, July 9, 1952; SCMP, 379.
[42] JMJP, November 16, 1953; SCMP, 701.
[43] JMJP, March 1, 1954; SCMP, 759.

NATURAL CALAMITIES

The age-old scourge of famine, caused mainly by droughts and floods, continues to plague the Chinese peasants. A study made by the University of Nanking shows it to have been an almost annual visitor in one part of the country or other for as long as can be traced: in the 2,019 years between 108 B.C. and A.D. 1911, 1,828 years were afflicted with the scourge.[44] J. L. Buck's investigations show an average of 3·6 famines in the northern wheat region and about 2·5 in the rice region of the south within the lifetime of his informants.[45] Deaths due to famine during the past century are estimated at a hundred million people.[46]

Floods and droughts are of greatest frequency in North and East Central China, especially in the former. When, as often happens, the two strike in one season, famine ensues. The Yangtze rice-wheat area also suffers—to a lesser extent—from famines, two very severe cases having occurred within living memory, following the great flood of 1931, and the worse one of 1954. Manchuria escapes the floods, but not droughts.

The backwardness of the transport system aggravates the effect of natural calamities. When food has to be carried by porters, long hauls are impossible, as the porter would soon eat up his pack. In this regard W. H. Mallory writes:

> Relief cannot be brought . . . to a district beyond fifty to one hundred miles from the source of supply if the grain is carried. In localities where the roads are serviceable for wheelbarrows this distance can be increased two and one-half times.[47]

Another factor which aggravated local famines in the past was the tax levied on interprovincial traffic in food by local militarists. This naturally discouraged the transport of food from one region to another.

Mao's regime tends to affect the incidence and impact of natural calamities in two contradictory ways. It mitigates the

[44] W. H. Mallory, *China: Land of Famine*, New York, 1926, p. 1.
[45] Buck, *Land Utilisation in China*, *op. cit.*, p. 125.
[46] G. Cressey, *Asia's Lands and Peoples*, quoted in G. F. Winfield, *op. cit.*, p. 73.
[47] Mallory, *op. cit.*, p. 34.

impact by uniting the country administratively and developing the transport network. It thus extends the area of food distribution and almost wipes out purely local famines. This can be, and in fact has been, achieved quickly. Furthermore the long-run effects of Mao's efforts to extend irrigation and drainage will bring about such an increase in the area cultivated—and even more, in the area irrigated—and in the yield, that a more regular supply of food is bound to follow. An even more long-run improvement in the food situation will be flood control and the harnessing of rivers.

There are, however, a number of important factors on the negative side. First, in its zeal to acquire the resources needed for rapid industrialisation, Mao's regime may leave the peasants with insufficient reserves of food. The same policy is also liable to dampen the peasants' eagerness for production, and even their desire to keep reserves of food, for fear they will be snatched away by the State. These negative factors are bound to become more important as industrialisation gathers speed.

However that may be, it seems safe to predict that the day of major famines with their hundreds of thousands—sometimes millions—of dead, has gone, even though food margins are small. (India, which is also extremely poor, has not seen a major famine for a long period, the exceptional famine of 1942 being caused mainly by wartime transport difficulties). But though the famines may be alleviated, the natural calamities which cause them will continue to visit Chinese agriculture in one region or another, as it is still quite beyond the power of any regime to contain the gigantic forces of nature within the space of decades, let alone years. Communist propagandists thus expose themselves to ridicule when they claim spectacular achievements in changing the face of nature. Dealing with one of the regions most affected in the past, Vice-Premier Tung Pi-wu stated: 'The 55 million people in the Hwai River Valley have freed themselves from now on of the grave threat of floods.'[48] Fu Tso-yi, Minister of Water Conservancy, went one better, generalising about conditions in all of China: 'The danger of disastrous floods which were a scourge to the Chinese people for thousands of years has been

[48] NCNA, Peking, September 30, 1951.

basically removed. . . .'⁴⁹ N.C.N.A. repeated this grandiose asser-
tion, declaring that China 'has now, in the main, once and for all,
freed her five hundred million population from the many thousand
years' old flood menace.'⁵⁰

These statements are for foreign consumption. Reports for home
consumption, which have to be swallowed by those who have
suffered, are less extravagant. A few random quotations will
illustrate this. A conference of *hsien* magistrates of North China
(September 19–30, 1951) referred in a resolution to the following
fact:

> More than 10,000,000 persons in the North China region have
> been affected by the serious famine situation during the current year,
> especially in the provinces of Chahar and Suiyuan.⁵¹

East China was equally devastated by the 1951 floods:

> In the whole of the East China region, a total area of 22,238,707
> *mow* of land was affected by floods.
> In Shantung Province, heavy rainfall was reported continuously
> from the latter part of July 1951 to the middle part of August. The
> plains were covered with several feet of water, and the flood situa-
> tion was serious. . . . A total of 3,954,000 persons in the province
> was seriously affected by the floods, which also accounted for the
> collapse of more than 280,000 buildings.⁵²

A report from South China:

> In the first half of 1952, there were serious calamities in Kwangsi
> Province. Beginning from March, a seasonal spring famine developed.
> Of the 1,770,000 persons affected by the shortage of grain through-
> out Kwangsi Province, 600,000 needed relief before they could tide
> over the famine period.⁵³

Of South-west China in the spring of 1953, the Chungking *New
China Daily* wrote:

⁴⁹ *New China's Economic Achievements, 1949–52, op. cit.,* p. 195.
⁵⁰ NCNA, Peking, September 13, 1952.
⁵¹ JMJP, November 17, 1951; CB, 148.
⁵² CFJP, December 1, 1951; CB, 160.
⁵³ NFJP, August 6, 1952; SCMP, 394.

According to reports received from various localities, at present spring famine has affected 133 *hsien* in the South-west region. Statistics based on reports from 70 spring famine stricken *hsien* show that more than one million people are suffering from food shortage. . . . In Shihfang *hsien* in Szechwan province, some families in difficulty were found to be selling their land and unharvested crops in order to tide over the famine, and in the districts of P'engan, Shehung, Chiachiang, P'ushan and Meishan, serious cases of suicide and death resulting from hunger and cold have been discovered.[54]

In 1953 again North China suffered from drought. The *People's Daily* wrote:

It is estimated that in Hopei Province farmlands on which seeds cannot be sown on account of drought amount to over 12,000,000 *mow*. Similar conditions exist in some parts of the provinces of Shansi and Suiyuan.[55]

Other calamities followed too.

Since last winter, the principal wheat-growing provinces—Anhwei, Kiangsu, Honan, Shantung and Shansi—have been hit by cold spell, late frost, insect pests or hailstorm: wheat production dropped and certain early spring crops (broad beans, peas, etc.) suffered damage in a number of areas. In some areas in the North, spring drought is not yet over, making it still difficult to do timely sowing of autumn crops. In some areas south of the Yangtze, incessant rainfall has led to rotting of young plants.[56]

Among other things, the article proposes to the peasant 'to collect such substitutes as wild herbs to use as food during the period of shortage before autumn harvest'.[57]

Again, a *People's Daily* editorial in May of the same year speaks of 'millions of famine-stricken people' who need relief-food 'to tide over the spring famine'.[58] After the spring famine, many areas suffered a summer famine, later an autumn famine. A *People's Daily* editorial of February 10, 1954, speaks of the need to supply

[54] HHJP, March 24, 1953; SCMP, 561.
[55] JMJP, April 15, 1953; SCMP, 564.
[56] JMJP, May 17, 1953; SCMP, 577.
[57] *Ibid.*
[58] JMJP, May 29, 1953; SCMP, 587.

grain 'to famine-stricken peasants constituting about 10 per cent of the rural population'.[59]

But these catastrophes pale before the 1954 floods. In the most disastrous pre-war flood year, 1931, the inundated area was 26·3 million acres or some 158 million *mow*. In the 1948 flood under Kuomintang rule, described by Communist sources as 'the most catastrophic ever'—120 million *mow* of land were inundated.[60] As against this, the 1954 floods inundated an area of 'over 160 million *mow*'.[61] This is about 10 per cent of the cultivated area of the country. Li Fu-chun described them as such 'great floods ... in 1954 as had never been met before for a hundred years'.[62] If the density of agricultural population in the affected areas is taken as no more than the national average, some 50 million peasants must have suffered. But most probably a larger number were affected, as the population density in the inundated areas is greater than the national average. Again 1956 had even worse floods, typhoons and droughts than 1954.

These natural calamities, over which the Peking rulers have so little control, coupled with the permanent narrowness of the margin of agricultural surpluses, straitens the Communist Supreme planners' room for manœuvre considerably.

POVERTY-STRICKEN PEASANTS FLOW INTO TOWNS

Disguised unemployment, one of the worst curses in the countryside, cannot be eliminated without large-scale industrialisation extending over decades; the present regime can barely have begun to deal with the question. Add to this the many different calamities visiting the villages; the undoubted fact that the standard of living in the towns is much higher than in the country; the seemingly unlimited opportunities for employment in factories, construction works and so on in the towns; and one may well understand the powerful urge impelling the peasants to flock to the towns. The weight of evidence suggests that this influx is much beyond the requirements of industrialisation and the

[59] JMJP, February 10, 1954; SCMP, 753.
[60] Boldyrev, *op. cit.*, p. 106.
[61] NCNA, Peking, September 27, 1954.
[62] NCNA, Peking, July 5, 1955.

wishes of Peking. It plays havoc with food supply, and aggravates the financial difficulties of the State, for it is much cheaper to feed people in the country than in towns.

The *People's Daily* complained editorially: 'Rural surplus labour in a considerable number of areas has recently been found moving blindly towards the cities.' The rural cadres are blamed: 'Not only did these cadres not dissuade the peasants from blindly moving into the cities, but they adopted an irresponsible attitude of "out of sight, out of mind".' The editorial goes on to show the plight of the unfortunate immigrants into the towns: 'When they go to the cities blindly without being able to find work for the moment, they will be compelled to sell their clothes and bedding and will become displaced persons.' The obvious reply that peasants who brave hunger and cold to go to the town probably have nothing better in the village, is ingeniously evaded by the notion that the rural unemployed are really *not unemployed at all*: 'Surplus labourers in the villages are not unemployed persons; they have land and food.'[63]

The reasons put forward for this migration are interesting. *New China Daily* of Chungking explains it thus: 'The reason why the majority of peasants abandoned their spring farming is due to their loss of self-confidence and their mistaken belief that farming in no longer profitable.'[64] A GAC *Decision on the Labour Employment Problem* puts forward this reason: 'Despite the agrarian reform the insufficiency of arable land space remains basically unchanged.'[65]

The *People's Daily* editorial quoted above presses for a solution:

> The People's Governments in various places should pay close attention to this matter and take effective steps immediately to dissuade the peasants from moving blindly into the cities. Especially in winter should the peasants be prevented from blind movements so that they may be spared from unfortunate accidents resulting from hunger and cold.[66]

A *Directive on Dissuasion of Peasants from Blind Influx into Cities* issued by the GAC on April 17, 1953, advises the following measures:

[63] JMJP, November 26, 1952; SCMP, 468.
[64] HHJP, March 2, 1953.
[65] NCNA, Peking, August 13, 1952; SCMP, 388.
[66] JMJP, November 26, 1952; SCMP, 468.

All provincial and municipal people's governments should immediately notify the *hsien, chu* and *hsiang* governments as well as peasants' associations to patiently dissuade the peasants who prepare or ask to enter cities from so doing. . . .

Further:

Except those in possession of official documents issued by factories, mines and building construction companies, confirming that they are contract workers, all peasants desirous of entering cities to find employment shall not be issued certificates of introduction by the *hsien, chu* and *hsiang* governments.[67]

And what of those who have already arrived in town?

Except those needed by the work units, all peasants who have entered cities should be persuaded by the labour and civil affairs departments of the people's governments, in conjunction with trade unions and other relevant organs in the districts of their residence, to go home.[68]

Following upon this the New China News Agency announced from Chungking that 'the Government organs in Chungking are now working conscientiously to solve the problem of the blind influx of peasants into the city.'[69] A key role in 'solving the problem' was taken by the security police:

Now the Chungking Municipal Bureau of Labour has made concrete arrangements, and the public security sub-bureaus in various *chu* in Chungking will be responsible for carrying out registration work.[70]

Again and again it is reported that peasants who migrated to the towns are taken and sent back to the countryside. Thus, for instance, between April and October, 1955, 'over 558,000 persons were sent out of Shanghai to the countryside'.[71]

[67] NCNA, Peking, April 17, 1955; SCMP, 554.
[68] *Ibid.*
[69] NCNA, Chungking, May 2, 1953; SCMP, 563.
[70] *Ibid.*
[71] NCNA, Shanghai, November 16, 1955.

A couple of months later it was announced that '60,000 persons were sent out of Canton into the countryside' recently.[71a]

ARBITRARY INTERVENTION OF CADRES IN PEASANTS' FARMING

The most important and far-reaching intervention of cadres in peasant production is their pressure to build co-operatives. This will be dealt with later. In the present chapter some examples of cadres' intervention in production still based on the individual farm will be given. These are taken from press and news agency reports covering a couple of months only.

A report from Shantung Province states that

peasants had great misgivings in cultivating S cotton. In mobilising the peasants to cultivate this type of cotton during the spring of 1952, the leadership cadres of Tsangshan *hsien* . . . forced the peasants uniformly to cultivate S cotton. The upshot was that many peasants adopted a perfunctory attitude towards the matter. Some planted S cotton and local strains intermingled with each other: some planted a little S cotton at both ends of their field but continued to plant local strains in the inner part of their field. After the cotton plants had grown up, the Tsangshan *hsien* magistrate Chang Tso-chen (member of CCP Tsangshan *hsien* committee) mistakenly gave orders at 6 *chu* and *hsiang* cadres' conferences 'to uproot the local strain of cotton' and raised the slogan 'early compulsion better than late compulsion'. By the time he had ordered the 'uprooting of local strain of cotton' for the sixth time, it was already mid-June when cotton blossomed and grew young ears. . . . On numerous occasions *hsiang* and *tsun* cadres as well as peasants came to the *chu* offices with requests not to uproot the cotton, but these *chu* cadres, instead of listening to the peasants, let *hsiang* cadres with militiamen, NDYL members and primary school pupils pull up cotton plants everywhere.[72]

A few days later, An Tzu-wen, Minister of Personnel, said:

During the campaign for the drilling of wells to prevent drought in Shantung . . . some *chu* and *hsiang* cadres allotted tasks to the

[71a] NFJP, February 4, 1956.
[72] NCNA, Tsinan, January 29, 1953; SCMP, 503.

masses on the basis of households, proceeded to mark the land with circles, and forced the masses to drill wells in accordance with the circles drawn. Some even posted militia men in the villages and inhabitants were concentrated and forced to work on the drilling of wells. There were even cases when market towns were suddenly blockaded, and the people attending the markets detained and forced to work on the wells. The wells thus drilled were generally not usable. In Chucheng *hsien*, more than 20,000 wells were drilled, but less than 5,000 were usable, and less than 300 were actually used. . . .

Similar cases of forcing people to drill wells were reported from Jehol and Hopei. As a result of the use of force and command, in 1952 5,416 wells were drilled in Ningchin *hsien* in Hopei, but water was found in only about 1,000 of them. In the Tientsin administrative district, 70,000 wells were drilled, and 40,000 of them were unusable.[73]

A couple of days later a *People's Daily* editorial again referred to the question and gave the following picture of violence committed against the peasants:

Law-breaking acts such as illegal detention and tying up of peasants and even public accusations against peasants in meetings and parading of them in streets have happened not only during the process of promoting improved strains of cotton and modern farming implements last year, but also during the mobilisation of the masses to sink wells for prevention of drought and to prevent frost damage . . . In some cases, even deaths resulted from such persecution.[74]

A similar story comes from Kwangsi Province in the South:

In Junghsien our comrades personally watched the masses do sparse sowing. But the minute the cadres left, the peasants sowed more seeds on the field. The peasants complained, 'You people simply come to give us trouble and waste our time. You live on public grain and fear no starvation. Who is going to make up our losses should your method result in failure?'[75]

[73] NCNA, Peking, February 9, 1953; CB, 251.
[74] JMJP, February 11, 1953; SCMP, 512.
[75] NCNA, Nanning, April 19, 1953; SCMP, 591.

From the South-West region:

> Some *hsien* rigidly defined the number of seedlings and the space between holes—7–8 inches between holes and only 4–5 plants in each hole. . . . In Chingtsin, Hochiang and Fushun *hsien* of Szechwen, there have been instances where cadres, bringing with them rulers, went to the field and forced those peasants whose plants exceeded the limit of 7–8 inches in distance, to pull out the plants and plant the seedlings anew. They indiscriminately branded peasants as 'stupid', 'conservative' and 'backward'.[76]

Again *People's Daily* wrote:

> In the past, some localities blindly introduced modern ploughs without finding out whether such new farming implements are suitable for local peasants and without teaching them the way to use them, with the result that these modern ploughs were kept idle after they were received by the peasants. Blind promotion of close-planting method also led to the practice of 'outwardly close-planting but actually wide-planting'.[77]

It is fitting here once more to mention the GAC *Directive on Issuance of Farming Credits* of July 7, 1953, quoted above,[78] which admitted that in many cases loans given to the peasants were actually imposed on them for purposes they did not wish.

PEASANT CORVÉE

The work done by millions of conscripted peasants—above all in water conservancy—has already been referred to.[79] One aspect has not been dealt with—the payment for the work. It is very difficult to know exactly what this payment amounts to. One sympathetic British observer states: 'These peasants laboured for nothing.'[80] Another friendly observer states that the standard wage for the Huai River project 'was set at two pounds of rice for every cubic metre dug at ground level and carried seventy

[76] JMJP, May 27, 1953; SCMP, 583.
[77] JMJP, October 20, 1953; SCMP, 681.
[78] See p. 109.
[79] See pp. 62–3.
[80] B. Davidson, *Daybreak in China*, London, 1953, p. 66.

127

yards away'.[81] In all probability the peasants are paid nothing for their labour in some cases, and are given some food in others. This is certainly the case in road repairs. Thus the *Provisional Rules Governing Repairs of Highways by Civilian Labour* promulgated by GAC on May 31, 1951, states:

> in general, no ration or allowance shall be given to highway re-pairing civilian labour in principle, but in the case of districts with special conditions of civilian labour coming from remote places the Provincial People's Government may, according to local conditions, stipulate measures for granting appropriate allowance . . .[82]

(Incidentally, the same *Provisional Rules* state that it is the duty of civilian workers to bring their own ordinary tools for repairing the highways.) Even where paid, a wage of two catties of rice per cubic metre dug and carried 70 yards away, as in the Huai River project, is extremely low, even by Chinese standards. The average output per worker in conservancy works is one and one-third cubic meters of earth work per day,[83] so that an average of only two and two-thirds catties of rice will be earned in a twelve-hour workday.[84] J. L. Buck's survey of 1929–33 showed that the average daily wage of agricultural workers in China was equal to the value of 7 kilograms or 14 catties of rice.[85] Today, too, agricultural labourers receive a wage much higher than the 'wage' paid to workers on conservancy projects. Thus it was reported that the average wage of hired farm hands in eight representative *tsun* in Kwangsi Province in 1951 was equal to 1,522 catties of grain per year.[86]

It is not surprising then that human labour is preferred to machinery which cannot compare in cost. Read a description of work on the Huai River project by the friendly observer pre-viously quoted:

[81] W. G. Burchett, *China's Feet Unbound*, London, 1952, p. 157.
[82] JMJP, June 4, 1951.
[83] NCNA, Changsha, March 27, 1953.
[84] The weight of a cubic metre of earth is some 3,000–4,000 lbs. At $1\frac{1}{3}$ cubic metres per day this is 4,000–6,000 lbs., or, say, $1\frac{1}{2}$–$2\frac{1}{2}$ long tons, to be carried 70 yards. It is doubtful if the energy contained in $2\frac{2}{3}$ catties of rice is equal to the energy output required for this labour.
[85] Buck, *Land Utilisation in China, op. cit.*, pp. 305–6.
[86] CCJP, July 25, 1952. SCMP, 392.

Team members (women also) took their turns in digging and carrying. Each individual on this part of the project dug an average of four tons of earth a day, and carried it 70 yards up to the top of the dyke wall. He marched an average of eight miles a day, carrying for half the distance between 80 and 100 pounds of earth in his baskets. Engineer Chang Tsoying smiled when I expressed amazement at the vast amount of work done with wooden spades, a few picks, stone rammers, wicker baskets and bamboo poles.

'What mechanical equipment we had, we abandoned as too costly,' he said. 'We had a number of five and a half horse-power diesel operated pumps. We used them for a while, but we found that they pumped 36 cubic metres of water an hour, whereas hand-operated water-wheels pumped 30 cubic metres and we could move 14 cubic metres with bucket brigades. But for the cost of shifting one cubic metre by diesel pump we could shift 22 cubic metres with the water-wheels and 14 with buckets.'[87]

Imagine women carrying 80–100 lb. of earth for a distance of about four miles a day! Compare this with the Soviet Labour Code of 1922 which prohibited the employment of women 'in particularly heavy and unhealthy production . . .'[88] and with the order (November 14, 1923) of the Commissariat of Labour and the Supreme Economic Council which prohibited the employment of women for work consisting *entirely* of carrying or moving loads exceeding 10 lb.; the carrying of loads up to 40 lb. was allowed only if it was directly connected with the woman's normal work, and if it did not occupy more than one-third of her working day.[89] In China, however, where the evil effects of carrying heavy weights, especially for women, are concerned, the authorities turn a blind eye. If it is cheap, it is good!

Nevertheless, a job on conservancy work is not wholly unwelcome for the conscripted peasants. As it is done mainly during the slack season, the income from it, even if it amounts only to some food, is a net gain.

[87] Burchett, *op. cit.*, p. 159.
[88] Labour Code, 1922 (Russian), Moscow, 1922, Article 129, p. 18.
[89] 'Women Workers and their Protection in Russian Industry', Geneva, *International Labour Review*, October 1929.

CHAPTER VII

STATE MONOPOLY OF TRADE IN GRAIN AND OTHER AGRICULTURAL PRODUCTS

THE MARKETABLE SHARE OF THE AGRICULTURAL OUTPUT

Speedy industrialisation requires an increase in the marketed portion of agricultural output. It is this portion that supplies the needs of the urban population and provides raw materials for industry and exports. But the output of agriculture generally increases at a much lower rate than the growth of industry or the rise in the town population or the growth in export requirements, while the portion of his yield that the peasant is inclined to sell not only fails to increase, but—owing to the immediate effect of land reform—even decreases. Whereas, before land reform the landlord used to sell the major portion of the grain and other agricultural products he received as rent, after it this source of supply dries up. The Chinese Communist leaders are well aware of the effect that land reform has on the marketed food supply. As early as 1951, prior to the completion of land reform in Szechwan, the local Communist paper stated:

> After the Reduce-Rent and Refund-Deposit Campaign and the Land Reform Campaign have been carried out in rural districts, consumption of grain will increase, and the amount of commercial grain will decrease.[1]

A *People's Daily* article dealt with the experience of Russia:

> The Soviet Union during a transition period may serve as reference for us. Before the revolution the portion of food supplies marketed reached 26 per cent, that is to say, of the total volume of food produced, more than one-fourth was marketed food. But in the period from 1926 to 1927, the portion of marketed food dropped to only 13 per cent. The basic cause of this difficult situation, according to the analysis of Stalin, was the transformation in the agricultural structure of the Soviet Union, which had passed from the

[1] HHJP, November 16, 1951; CB, 146.

economy of large landlords and the economy of rich peasants which produced marketed food in large quantities, to the economy of the small peasant and the economy of the middle peasant, which produced only limited quantities of marketed food. [2]

Unwilling to draw the lesson and apply it to Chinese experience, the article concludes: 'Due to the lack of overall figures, we are as yet unable to pass judgment on the movements of marketed food in our country after Liberation.'[3] However, investigations carried out in certain villages in Hunan showed that while before 'Liberation' the peasants marketed some 30 per cent of the grain they produced, after it the proportion dropped below 20 per cent'.[4] The 'scissors' crisis—the lagging of agricultural prices behind industrial prices—further discourages the peasant from putting his product on the market. When he is not offered a cheap and plentiful supply of industrial goods in exchange for his food, he prefers to eat rather than sell.

Naturally, the quicker the pace of industrialisation, the greater the discrepancy between the supply of agricultural goods and the State's demand for them. Hence since the inauguration of the First Five Year Plan in 1953, China has suffered a practically uninterrupted food supply crisis.

PRELUDE TO THE ESTABLISHMENT OF THE STATE GRAIN TRADE MONOPOLY

In 1953 grain output was a little higher than in 1952—166 million tons as against 164 million tons. This was far below plan, the goal for 1953 being 178·5 million tons, a projected increase of 14·6 million tons.[5] State purchasing fell even further short of the target. This a *People's Daily* editorial had to admit:

Although gross grain output has not decreased, State target of grain purchase was not fulfilled according to schedule in many districts following autumn harvest of 1953 while grain sales far

[2] JMJP, November 21, 1954; SCMP, 965.
[3] *Ibid.*
[4] Pan Ching-yuan, 'Two Years of Planned Purchase and Planned Supply of Grain', HCS, September 1955; ECMM, 9.
[5] NCNA, Peking, September 25, 1952.

exceeded the plans, thus bringing about an unbalance between purchase and sales.[6]

To add to the State's difficulties, while grain purchases from the peasants fell short of the plan, grain sales exceeded it. During the autumn of 1953, a season when food supplies usually reach the market in quantity, this divergence showed itself clearly:[7]

1953	Percentage of Purchase Plans Fulfilled	Percentage of Sales Plans Fulfilled	Excess of Sales Over Purchases (percentage)
September	80·11	118·47	10·72
October	72·17	120·42	41·22

Under such conditions, market prices are naturally far in excess of official ones. In September and October 1953, 'the market grain price was 3 per cent to 30–50 per cent higher than the official level in the main grain-growing areas of Hunan, Kiangsi, Anhwei, Shantung, Hopei and Shensi'.[8] The *People's Daily* attacked merchants in Changning, Hunan, who offered peasants JMP 17,000 per *tou* of grain instead of the official price of JMP 12,000. So sternly does the State look upon such acts that it condemned three merchant speculators to death on December 3, 1953.[9] Black-market prices today are higher than ever. 'Wheat price for a time went to JMP 2,400 per catty (against official price of JMP 800) in Takiang *hsien*, Honan.'[10]

The State's reply to the food crisis was the imposition of a State grain trade monopoly.

THE STATE GRAIN TRADE MONOPOLY

On November 19, 1953, the GAC adopted an *Order for Enforcement of Planned Purchase and Planned Supply of Grain*.

Grain-producing peasants should sell their surplus grain to the State according to the types of grain, purchasing price and quotas of planned purchase fixed by the State.

[6] JMJP, March 1, 1954; SCMP, 770.
[7] TKP, March 2, 1954; SCMP, 770.
[8] NCNA, Peking, December 16, 1954; SCMP, 952.
[9] JMJP, March 7, 1954; SCMP, 774.
[10] NCNA, Peking, January 6, 1955; SCMP, 969.

All private grain merchants shall without exception not be allowed to deal privately in grain, but may be commissioned by State grain departments to sell grain on their behalf under strict State supervision and control. [11]

The State made it abundantly clear that it would not resort so much to the carrot as to the stick in order to get the amount of grain needed. It was no longer to be left to the peasants to decide how much they wished to sell to the State.

Control figures of planned purchase and planned supply should be properly determined . . .

(a) Control figures applicable to administrative regions shall be determined by the GAC Committee of Financial and Economic Affairs on the basis of the national control figures fixed by the State Planning Committee.

(b) Control figures applicable to provinces, administrative districts and *hsien* shall be determined by the governments of upper level.

(c) Control figures applicable to *chu* and *hsiang* (or *tsun*) shall be determined by *hsien* governments. Control figures applicable to *hsiang* (or *tsun*) should be publicly announced to the masses . . . [12]

The price paid was to be decided by the Central authorities.

At the same time the *Order* established a grain rationing system in the cities and a modified form of grain rationing in 'market towns, industrial crop areas, famine areas and rural villages in general'. [13] Carried out in this manner, State grain trade has little in common with the voluntary sale of grain by peasants to the State, and is very close to being an agricultural tax pure and simple. Hence 'the enormous role of political work is fully demonstrated in the actual operation of grain purchase'. [14]

A mass of cadres and activists takes part in propaganda for the State grain trade monopoly. Thus, during the grain purchase campaign of 1954,

[11] NCNA, Peking, November 19, 1953; SCMP, 701.
[12] *Ibid.*
[13] *Ibid.*
[14] JMJP, November 23, 1953; SCMP, 704.

according to incomplete figures, 8,270,000 CCP and NDYL members, basic level cadres and activists in Hopei, Shansi, Liaotung, Chekiang, Honan, Hupeh, Kiangsi and Kwangsi conducted extensive propaganda among the peasants after studying the general line.[15]

The cadres do not limit themselves to political propaganda in support of the State grain trade monopoly. While they are about it they do the actual purchasing of the grain. A *People's Daily* editorial speaks of 'the tireless efforts of millions of cadres in the collection of the grain tax and the purchase of grain'.[16] Nor is their activity confined to a few days or even weeks but lasts for months. The *People's Daily* states that 'As a matter of fact, the Party committees of various places have to devote at present from 6 to 8 months of their time every year to the work of centralised buying and selling.'[17] The work is not found to be easy. Cadres are quoted by the *People's Daily* as saying: 'Of all kinds of work, grain work is the most difficult.'[18]

Where compulsion is the rule, the courts gain prominence:

When the policy of unified purchase and sale of grain was first enforced, the people's courts throughout the country set up over 1,000 circuit courts to give legal protection to the work and to ensure the smooth progress of the measure, as well as to prevent attempts at sabotage by counter-revolutionaries, speculation of unscrupulous merchants and unlawful acts of depraved elements.[19]

The price the State pays for the grain is far below the price at which it sells. Peasants in Hupeh, for example, were paid JMP 500 per catty of wheat,[20] and in Szechwan JMP 700 per catty of rice.[21] At the same time wheat was being sold at JMP 1,200 per catty in the towns,[22] rice at JMP 1,515 per catty in Shanghai and JMP

[15] NCNA, Peking, December 16, 1954; SCMP, 952.
[16] JMJP, March 20, 1954; SCMP, 776.
[17] JMJP, May 8, 1955; SCMP, 1050.
[18] JMJP, May 10, 1955; SCMP, 1050.
[19] JMJP, May 20, 1954; SCMP, 817.
[20] JMJP, April 19, 1954; SCMP, 828.
[21] NCNA, Peking, December 14, 1954; SCMP, 952.
[22] CNS, December 24, 1954; SCMP, 958.

2,070 in Peking.[23] The peasants are thus paid only from a third
to less than half of the retail price of grain in the urban markets.
This gross exploitation is second only to the exploitation of Soviet
agriculturists conducted through obligatory deliveries.[24] The
Chinese peasant gets a much better deal; but then China is only
at the beginning of her industrialisation.

Because of the obligatory nature of the grain sale to the State
and the low prices paid, the peasant sees only a difference *in
degree* between the State agricultural tax and the State purchase of
agricultural products. The *People's Daily* accordingly pleads with
the peasants to renounce the erroneous view 'that it is not in the
interests of the peasants to sell their grain to the State'.[25]

One manner of getting round the State grain trade monopoly
is by illicit brewing. The Tientsin *Ta Kung Pao* gives some
examples of the extent of this practice:

> 60 per cent of the households in Liaolan *hsien* and 63 per cent of
> the households in Yentien *tsun*, Chiaohsien, were illicit distillers.
> Of the 15 *tsun* of Jushan *hsien*, 126 households were found distilling
> 800 *catties* of liquor without permission. In Chenning *hsien*, Kwei-
> chow, 15,000 *catties* of illicit wine liquor were discovered on two
> occasions: in Wuteh *hsiang*, Shihchien *hsien*, 1,004 moonshiners were
> found in 5 days.

> 150 households in Tienchiao *hsiang*, Shuangho *chu*, Chinchai *hsien*
> of Anhwei, collectively distilled liquor without permission. Peasants
> of Lienhsien, Kwangtung, used 300,000 *catties* of grain for wine
> making and liquor distilling during last autumn; 85 per cent of all
> households in the *hsien* were guilty. 1,332 households in the 6th *chu*,
> Lienchiang *hsien*, consumed 76,000 *catties* of grain for wine making
> and liquor distilling in a little more than 10 days. In Szechwan . . .
> it is estimated that they (the illicit peasant brewers) would consume
> 100,000,000 *catties* of grain more than local State-operated distil-
> leries each year.[26]

[23] B. Shastri, 'Impressions of Communist China', *Socialist International Information*, January 30, 1954.
[24] In Russia, in 1935, the price fixed by the Government for obligatory delivery of oats, which it was reselling at the retail price of 55–100 kopeks per kilogramme, was 4–6 kopeks per kilogramme; figures for rye were 60–100 kopeks and 4·6–6·9 kopeks respectively; for farina (of poor quality) the retail price was 60–70 times the procurement price of wheat (N. Jasny, *The Socialised Agriculture of U.S.S.R.*, Stanford, 1949, pp. 374–5).
[25] NCNA, Peking, January 7, 1954; SCMP, 726,
[26] TKP, February 20, 1954; SCMP, 760.

A necessary corollary of the State monopoly of the grain trade is consequently the State monopoly of alcohol.

Another method used by the peasants for cheating the State monopoly is debasing quality, supplying grain which has a 'high water content and many impurities'.[27]

THE 1953–4 GRAIN CRISIS IS OVERCOME

The establishment of the State grain trade monopoly in November 1953 solved the grain supply crisis for a time. The Chinese Communist press trumpeted its victory on the grain front repeatedly.

Thus in April 1954, one Communist paper wrote:

> After the enforcement of the planned purchase of food, in November 1953, the State purchased 85·52 per cent more grain compared with October, the quantity purchased being 41·2 per cent in excess of the quantity sold. In December the purchases were 72·22 per cent in excess of November, and the quantity purchased was 112·74 per cent in excess of the quantity sold. In January 1954 the purchases were 41·54 in excess of those of November 1953, and the quantity purchased was 61 per cent in excess of the quantity sold.[28]

A few months later Chang Nai-ch'i, Minister of Food, reported:

> The figures for purchases have increased. The purchases made between July 1953 and June 1954 went up 77·78 per cent, as compared with the same period of the previous year, while the grain in the State granary at the end of June this year increased by 51 per cent, compared with the same period last year.[29]

The blare of self-praise proved shortlived. A few months later the food crisis struck with even greater force than in 1953–4.

THE 1955 GRAIN CRISIS

In 1954 China suffered from unusually heavy floods and the State had to make additional purchases of grain from peasants

[27] JMJP, June 19, 1954.
[28] TKP, March 2, 1954; SCMP, 770.
[29] NCNA, Peking, September 26, 1954; SCMP, 918.

in some areas in order to supply the flood victims. Throughout the year, the supply situation remained precarious, and peasants' uncertainty about supplies turned to alarm. 'Grain sales began to rise abnormally both in urban and rural districts in September 1954,'[30] the crisis reaching its peak in March and April 1955. On April 30, 1955, NCNA stated: 'According to latest reports from various parts of the country, there is a crisis in planned marketing of grain in many areas.'[31]

On April 28, 1955, the State Council and the Central Committee, CCP, together issued a *Directive on Intensified Reorganisation of Planned Marketing of Grain*, in which they tried to explain away the grain crisis as a pretence on the part of the peasants to be short of grain in order to get more from the State:

> The main situation in rural districts where excess sales are made is that whereas peasants who are short of grain are buying grain, peasants who are not short of grain are also buying grain and that those who ought to buy less want to buy more and those who ought to buy later want to buy early and that each and all cry of 'grain shortage'. Many peasants who are not short of grain sold their surplus grain to the state at the time of State purchase but are buying back as much grain as possible after State purchase is over ... In such a situation, certain peasants, mainly poor peasants who are genuinely short of grain, fail to obtain the full guarantee of supply.[32]

Accordingly the *Directive* calls for a cut in the sale of grain to peasants:

> Experience of many districts proves that if 'additional efforts' are made to reorganise the planned marketing operations, the tense situation can be alleviated at once. Grain sales can generally be reduced by 20, 30 and even over 50 per cent and peasants who are actually short of grain can be ensured of proper supplies. It follows that if correct, firm and effective measures are taken in good time, it is entirely possible to ensure that the sales quota will not be exceeded.

[30] Chen Yun, 'On the Question of the Unified Purchase and Distribution of Grain', Speech to the National People's Congress, July 21, 1955, NCNA, Peking, July 21, 1955; CB, 339.
[31] NCNA, Peking, April 30, 1955; SCMP, 1041.
[32] NCNA, Peking, April 28, 1955; SCMP, 1041.

The *Directive* calls upon 'those buyers who bought more than was justified to return part of their purchase in order to make grain available for supply to food-short households'. To implement the *Directive* and relieve the crisis in food supply, an official of the Ministry of Food declared that 'if house to house appraisal is carried out, those households which are actually short of grain can be properly supplied with grain and quantities of grain that should not be supplied and may be reduced, can be reduced.'[33] He even adduced proof: 'In 56 *hsiang* of Soochow administrative district, Kiangsu, where additional marketing of grain was completed, the quantities of sale applied for by the peasants have generally been reduced by 30 per cent and in some cases by 70 per cent.' Further results from other areas:

> Sungtien *hsiang*, Wenhsi *hsien*, Shansi, had asked the State to supply 10,170 *catties* of grain over and above quotas: after reorganisation of planned marketing of grain, not only was demand for more supplies withdrawn but 6,200 *catties* of grain was made available as reserve. In the case of seven *hsiang* and five *tsun* in Liangshan, Yuncheng and Chuyeh *hsien* of Shantung, planned marketing of grain was reorganised, as a result of which an additional 59,000 *catties* were supplied to 243 grain-short households while 620 peasant households voluntarily cut their grain demand by 475,000 *catties*.[34]

Ten days later (on May 2), Yen Ta-kai, Deputy Governor of Hopei, quoted a number of similar cases. For instance:

> Originally, Chienku *hsiang* of Ningho *hsien* demanded 50,000–60,000 *catties* of grain: after penetrating work, only 2,050 *catties* were issued and the whole problem was settled.[35]

Kwangtung followed suit. As an official of the Food Bureau of the Province stated:

> Whereas daily sales in the province averaged 4,200,000 *catties* in excess of plans during the first half of April, the figure dropped

[33] NCNA, Peking, April 30, 1955; SCMP, 1041.
[34] JMJP, April 24, 1955; SCMP, 1043.
[35] NCNA, Paoting, May 3, 1955; SCMP, 1043.

to 2,800,000 *catties* during the period April 11–20 and to 780,000 *catties* during the period April 21–25.[36]

In Kiangsi the Secretary of the CCP Provincial Committee, Yang Shang-kui, declared:

> According to returns, average daily sales on April 11–15 dropped by 18 per cent compared with the first five days of April and those on April 21–27 dropped further by 13 per cent compared with April 11–15 or 30 per cent compared with the first five days of April.[37]

As a result of these steps the State sale of grain was cut throughout the country, and the *People's Daily* could record with satisfaction:

> During May, a month normally reporting the largest volume of consumption, the sale of food in the whole country registered a reduction of more than 1,200,000,000 *catties* compared with April.[38]

The peasants, however, were far from satisfied. Their clamour even affected some of the rural cadres, who, according to Vice-Premier Liu Wen-hui, cried: 'Alas, the peasants have no food, and the situation is very bad,' and 'state purchase is too much and state supply is too little, the peasants are short of food.'[39]

A *People's Daily* editorial advises the peasants to follow 'the "eat what is available" principle, try to minimise consumption of miscellaneous grain and rice'.[40] Communist leaders continued to argue that the peasants who clamoured about the grain crisis were exaggerating or even inventing a crisis. For instance, Ou Pai-chuan, Vice-Governor of Kweichow told the National People's Congress: 'The overwhelming majority of people who

---

[36] NCNA, Canton, May 2, 1955; SCMP, 1043.
[37] NCNA, Nanchang, May 4, 1955.
[38] JMJP, June 18, 1955; SCMP, 1078.
[39] NCNA, Peking, July 28, 1955.
[40] JMJP, July 7, 1955.

cried shortage of grain did not really lack grain.'[41] Similarly, Vice-Premier Liu Wen-hui said at the same session of the National People's Congress:

> It is clear that the 'grain shortage' was in fact not a real shortage but a false shortage, that no shortage was genuinely experienced by peasants, but that counter-revolutionaries, law-breaching landlords and rich peasants fanned up agitation for grain, and that it was not a question of crisis in supply but a question of a man-made crisis. . . . Such are the facts. But some of us, not analysing various kinds of hearsay and taking the wind as the forerunner of rains, echoed others' cry of 'grain shortage'. . . . In fact, State purchases are not too much, nor are supplies too small: only the grain is in the hands of the State, and rich peasants and unscrupulous merchants can no longer do speculative business.[42]

THE 'THREE FIXED'

Fearing that the imposition of obligatory deliveries had gone as far as to threaten to extinguish the incentives to produce completely, Peking decided on the policy of 'three fixed' (*san ting*)—fixed production, fixed purchases and fixed sale. According to the 'three fixed', the State establishes a production norm for each grain-producing household, determines the quota to be collected in taxes and purchases from each household, and fixes the quantity which each grain-deficient rural household may purchase from the State. These norms remain constant for a number of years. The 'three fixed' policy was first discussed in a *People's Daily* editorial in March 1955. After much deliberation, the State Council promulgated (August 25, 1955) *Measures for Unified Purchase and Unified Supply of Grain in Rural Districts*. The central points in the decree are:

> The quantities of grain delivery and sale fixed for each household in 1955 will remain unchanged for the next three years in normal circumstances; that is, State purchase of grain will not be increased if output has increased. The quantities of grain supply to grain-short households will be fixed once every year. (Article 4.)

[41] NCNA, July 28, 1955; CB, 356.   [42] *Ibid.*

State unified purchase of grain from surplus-grain peasant house-holds should, in general, account for 80–90 per cent of their surplus grain (Article 14).[43]

But a number of loopholes are left by the decree for the Government to change the amount of grain obtained from grain-producing peasants or sold to grain-deficient rural households. For instance,

> In case of serious calamities in one province or autonomous district of several provinces, that prevent the State grain receipt and sale plans being balanced, the State Council may designate the bumper harvest provinces and autonomous districts to increase their purchases appropriately (Article 28).

Or,

> After they have been fixed, the figures of unified purchase from and planned sale of grain to peasant households will generally not be subjected to readjustment for three years, beginning from 1955, on account of births, deaths and increase or decrease of livestock. If, however, as a result of marriage, death, going away and returning home of persons and as a result of increase or decrease of live-stock, the original amount of grain consumption shows marked deficiency or surplus, readjustments may be made in the unified purchase of the next year (Article 29).

WHAT PORTION OF THE GRAIN OUTPUT IS ACQUIRED BY THE STATE?

In trying to argue away the food crisis, Vice-Premier Chen Yun unwittingly revealed many facts concerning the share of grain produce taken by the State. He argued, first, that the State has to supply food to a tremendous number of people, 100 million in cities and industrial and mining areas, 30–40 million in industrial crop areas, 50 million food-deficient peasants, 12 million engaged in pastoral, fishing, salt and forest activities, and 40 million in calamity-stricken areas: altogether about 240 million people.[44]

[43] NCNA, July 28, 1955; CB, 356.
[44] NCNA, Peking, July 21, 1955.

The State supplied them with 40·4 million tons of grain (husked) in the year July 1954 to June 1955. Grain for export came a bad second, a total of 1,750,000 tons of grain and soya beans being exported in 1954. Altogether, in the year July 1954—June 1955 the State acquired, in the form of grain tax and compulsory purchases, a total of 52 million tons of grain (unhusked), or about 44·6 million tons of husked grain. This constitutes 30 per cent of the total grain output of the country. If we exclude the portion sold by the State to grain-deficient peasants, the State took 18 per cent of all the grain produced.

Chen Yun uses this figure to prove that the State does not take too high a portion of the grain output. But it means little or nothing, as the grain allocated to grain-deficient households is not given free, but in exchange for other agricultural products. The real level of State acquisition is therefore not 18 per cent, but 30 per cent.

The 52 million tons of unhusked grain taken (in taxes and obligatory deliveries) from the grain-producing peasants, is far more than the landlords used to take in rent (25–30 million tons).[45] Of course the peasants used to pay taxes as well, but these were much smaller than the amount of rent. Today, however, the peasant is paid for part of what he gives the state, although badly.

The figure of 30 per cent seems to compare unfavourably with the equivalent figure for the Soviet Union, which, in 1938, was 17 per cent.[46] However, if payments for services rendered to kolkhozes by the State-owned Machine Tractor Stations are included—they certainly are in part a modified form of tax—the State share of the gross grain output of the kolkhozes would be 33 per cent,[47] which compares more closely with the figure for China. This is, of course, only a very rough comparison, as it is not known what portion of what the Chinese peasant gives is actual tax, what price he gets for the obligatory deliveries and how these compare with the Russian kolkhoznik's position.

Chen Yun's figures deal with gross output. The State share obviously constitutes a much larger percentage of the net output.

[45] See p. 82.
[46] A. Arina, 'Kolkhozes in 1938', Moscow, *Sotsialisticheskoe Selskokhoziaistvo*, December, 1939.
[47] *Ibid.*

After deducting from gross output only the allocation to seed reserves and fodder, the State share is nearly half of the rest.

There is little consolation to be derived from Chen Yun's statement that for the year July 1955—June 1956 and for a further two years after it the amount of grain taken in taxes and obligatory deliveries would be fixed at a slightly lower figure—43·25 million tons of husked grain, instead of 44·6 million tons, as in 1954–5 (or some 50 million tons of unhusked grain). The deliveries are still high enough to cause great bitterness among the peasants, which the government is quick to put down to 'provocation'. As a high official of the Ministry of Food said: 'The allegation of some people to the effect that this tense (food) situation is caused by the government's taking away all the grain is obviously a malicious provocation incompatible with facts.'[48]

Finally, Chen Yun suggests the following measure to alleviate the permanent food crisis and guard against future famines:

> On the basis of normal consumption, if each one of us will economise consumption to the extent of half an ounce a day, in one month we shall save one *catty* per person. There are six hundred million people in the country, and each year we shall save between 6,000 and 7,000 million *catties* of grain. This economy measure must be steadfastly adhered to over a long period, and by a certain time, we shall have a definite amount of grain stored up capable of coping with possible emergencies. To economise half an ounce of grain a day, on the basis of normal consumption, is within our possibilities, and such economy means that the people in the whole country are storing up grain to guard against a big famine. I believe that if there is promotion and regular publicity, so that everybody recognises the significance of the storage of grain, the awakened Chinese people will be capable of achieving such an objective.

Special attention was to be paid to 'economising' the consumption of grain in the towns.[49]

---

[48] Hong Kong, Communist daily, *Wen Hui Pao*, June 17, 1955; SCMP, 1073.
[49] For measures of grain rationing in towns, see pp. 261–3.

STATE TRADE MONOPOLY OF OTHER AGRICULTURAL PRODUCTS

The first trade to follow grain in becoming a State monopoly was the trade in oil-bearing products, also in very short supply. The decree effecting this states:

> The State will continue to enforce planned purchase of oil-bearing materials and peasants must sell oil-bearing materials to the State according to the quantity and price fixed by the State. Any surplus of the oil-bearing materials (kept by the peasant for own use) which is left after fulfilment of state purchase plans, and which they want to dispose of, may be purchased by supply and marketing co-operatives or may be used by the peasants for exchange for grain on the State-controlled grain market, but private merchants are not permitted to do such business.

In addition, peasants must 'sign production plans for oil-bearing materials'.[50]

The Communist press made it clear that the shortage of edible oil is not a temporary phenomenon but is there to stay. Thus the Tientsin daily, *Ta Kung Pao*, stated that the highest output of edible oil after 'Liberation', 'reached only over 80 per cent of the peak level' before the war, and 'the unbalanced state of supply and demand of edible oil will remain in China for a comparatively long period of time....'[51]

A national conference called to deal with the problem (October 25–November 3, 1954) sought to increase the extraction rate from oil-bearing crops by improving the work of oil mills.[52] But again, as in the case of the grain crisis, the main emphasis is on frugality, on the need to avoid extravagance in consumption.

A short time later a state monopoly of trade in cotton and cotton goods was established. Nor are other agricultural goods neglected by the State and its agents, the marketing and supply co-operatives. These even control products that are not officially a State monopoly, through 'advance purchase contracts'. For in-

---

[50] NCNA, Peking, September 19, 1954; SCMP, 894.
[51] TKP, May 30, 1954; SCMP, 834.
[52] NCNA, Peking, November 3, 1954.

stance the GAC Committee for Financial and Economic Affairs issued a Directive on March 23, 1954, which instructs the All-China Federation of Co-operatives to purchase through advance purchase contracts products such as tea, ramie, jute, hemp, silk and wool. The co-operatives are instructed to advance a certain amount of money at the time of the signing of the contract to encourage the peasant to sell.[53] Poverty and the crying need for credit, especially at the time of sowing, which is when the contracts are made, forces the peasant to avail himself of the advance and thus enables the State to buy agricultural products very cheaply. Besides, the peasant has no other openings for sale.

A second important arm of the State in securing control over agricultural products is the 'link contract'. Under this contract the co-operatives undertake to supply farm implements, materials or consumer goods on condition that the peasant delivers a certain amount of agricultural goods of a certain quality and at a fixed price. Such contracts are made, in the main, between the co-operatives and members of mutual-aid teams and agricultural producer co-operatives.

DIFFICULTIES FACED BY THE STATE AGRICULTURAL TRADING MONOPOLIES

The State trading monopolies come up against numerous difficulties. First, the number of peasants is so vast and the transactions so minute that it is extremely difficult to keep track of them.

This is especially so when the peasant does his own selling at the market instead of relying on middlemen. Such cases are very numerous. For instance, in one *hsien* in Shantung,

Among the total traders of eleven markets, in one market day, 69·8 per cent of them came to sell their own service and products, both agricultural and handicraft . . .

Inquiry into thirty-seven farm families shows that thirty-three rely entirely upon the periodic markets for disposing of their agricultural products; and only four, whose farms are larger than the rest, sell about 25 per cent of their grains directly to merchants.[54]

[53] NCNA, Peking, March 27, 1954.
[54] Hsiao-tung Fei, *China's Gentry*, Chicago, 1953, p. 100.

In addition to this multitude of trading peasants are millions of pedlars who go from one tiny market or fair to another. A writer described a rural market in southernmost China (in 1940):

> Market days are distributed among several villages in the same vicinity, four or five places in turn holding the market. There is a fixed place for this market either in, or immediately on the outskirts of, the village, to which place 'pedlars' flock from as far as ten miles away. . . . A market is attended by between 30 to 1,500 people; the number of pedlars at each market runs from fifty to five hundred as a rule, each carrying with him, or her, commodities usually worth only two Chinese dollars *in toto*.[55]

In Hopei Province, at the turn of the 'thirties, there were an estimated 6,500 pedlars in one *hsien* alone.[56] If a similar number of pedlars did business in each of the other 2,000 and more *hsien*, their total number in the country would be about 14–15 million. A huge number to control!

The number of shopkeepers is also extremely large. Despite all the effort put into State and co-operative trade since the inception of the new regime, there are still—according to a recent estimate—2,410,000 private shops employing 3,500,000 people in the rural areas.[57] There are about 10,000,000 employees in private retail establishments throughout the country.[58]

In an attempt to overcome this difficulty and strengthen State control over the trade in agricultural goods, the State first of all restricted the number of markets in which grain, cotton and vegetable-oil crops could be transacted. The *People's Daily* stated the purpose of this measure: 'The number of markets should not be too many because too many markets would not be easy to control. . . .'[59] This policy was effectively carried out, with the result that the number of local grain markets is today very small. 'According to incomplete returns from 20 provinces, 12,513 primary grain markets were established by early May,' which,

[55] Chen Han-seng, *Frontier Land Systems in Southernmost China*, op. cit., pp. 55–6.
[56] Gamble, *Ting Hsien, etc.*, op. cit., p. 279.
[57] JMJP, February 4, 1955; SCMP, 999.
[58] Tseng Shan, 'Struggle for the Fulfilment of Tasks in Commerce in the First Five Year Plan', SSST, July 25, 1955.
[59] JMJP, May 18, 1954; SCMP, 822.

considering the vastness of the territory, is an insignificant number.[60] Secondly, the State seeks to integrate the activities of private merchants with those of supply and marketing co-operatives and State commercial companies. This is done through the State monopolising the wholesale trade and turning private merchants into wholesale as well as retail agents.[61] Above all, the State's efforts to consolidate control over the market in agricultural products are made through the marketing co-operatives. These are not to be confused with what is normally understood by marketing co-operatives in the West. Western co-operatives are independent bodies of self-mobilised and active farmers which, by fostering improvements in marketing methods, by taking advantage of the economies inherent in large-scale marketing, and by opening more direct connection between producers and consumers, assure their members better prices for their products than would otherwise obtain, and so help the small capitalist farmer to prosper. In contrast, the marketing co-operatives in China are not independent bodies at all, but simply State agencies for controlling the peasants. Instead of securing for their members the maximum possible price, they serve to assure the State of the cheapest possible supplies.

But even with all these measures, the State cannot hope to gain complete control over agricultural output or increase its share of this output at a rate geared to the requirements of swift industrialisation as long as there are more than 100 million individual holdings. In order to do so the State must collectivise agriculture.

[60] JMJP, May 24, 1954; SCMP, 822.
[61] See, for elaboration of this, Sun Chung-ta, 'Some Forms of State Capitalist Commerce', JMJP, May 15, 1955.

CHAPTER VIII

THE COLLECTIVISATION OF AGRICULTURE

TYPES OF MUTUAL-AID TEAMS AND AGRICULTURAL PRODUCER CO-OPERATIVES

Peking has trodden carefully in its effort to eliminate individual peasant farming and has refrained from forcing the immediate and widespread establishment of the Soviet-type collective farm (kolkhoz) or State farm (sovkhoz). For the first five years of his rule Mao did little more than encourage the formation of peasants' mutual-aid teams and, later, agricultural producer co-operatives, as halfway stations on the way to complete collectivisation.

These mutual-aid teams and agricultural producer co-operatives can, with local variations, be classified into three main types.

The first and simplest is the seasonal mutual-aid team. Consisting of three to five households or, in rare cases, seven or eight, and organised to meet seasonal or special needs, it functions only during the busy seasons and dissolves at other times. It is formed chiefly to make up for the shortage in draft animals, implements or manpower in the busy season or in times of emergency. This type of mutual aid perpetuates traditional Chinese mutual-aid practices.[1]

The second type is the year-round mutual-aid team, which is somewhat more advanced than the first. It usually consists of six or seven households but sometimes comprises as many as twenty. Some of these teams have accumulated a certain amount of common property, such as implements and cattle. This, however, is not owned equally by all members of the team. Each member subscribes a certain amount, some more some less, and

---

[1] That mutual aid in agriculture, especially in the form of common ownership of draft animals, was very common in the past is shown by many writers: among others, Wittfogel, *Wirtschaft, etc., op. cit.*, pp. 158–9; *Agrarian China*, London, 1939, pp. 72–3, 82; Hsiao-tung Fei and Chih-i Chang, *Earthbound China*, London, 1948, pp. 36, 64, 144; M. H. Fried, *Fabric of Chinese Society. A Study of the Social Life of a Chinese County Seat*, New York, 1953, pp. 117–21.

gets interest in proportion to his share. If he leaves the team, he is free to withdraw his investment. Some teams of this type combine mutual aid in agriculture with mutual aid in rural subsidiary occupations on a year-round basis, adopting simple common production plans. This type of mutual aid also accords with traditional mutual-aid practices.

Mutual-aid teams are thus extremely small organisations. At the end of 1953 there were some 47 million peasant households organised in about 10 million mutual-aid teams[2]—an average of less than five households per team.

The third type is the agricultural producer co-operative. This is much larger in scale and involves a higher degree of co-operation than is practised by the other two types. Its distinctive feature is its common pool of land, though even here each peasant continues to be the private owner of the share he contributes. In June 1956 the average number of households in agricultural producer co-operatives was about a hundred.[3] This type includes the main characteristics of the second type, such as the combination of agriculture and side occupations, a certain amount of planning in production, ownership of some property, such as farm implements and draft animals in common. These are, however, more strongly marked than in the second type. Peasants are free to join or leave a co-operative, taking with them the property they brought into the common pool.

OWNERSHIP OF PROPERTY AND DISTRIBUTION OF INCOME IN MUTUAL-AID TEAMS

The mutual-aid teams are much more akin to private peasant holdings than to the Soviet kolkhoz in their property relations. In the latter practically all the land belongs to the kolkhoz, as do the horses, and all the important implements, except for tractors, combine-harvesters and similar large machines which are the property of the State-owned Machine Tractor Stations. The individual kolkhoznik owns no draft animals, but only a tiny plot of land and some simple tools. The difference between mutual-aid teams and the kolkhoz was emphasised ceaselessly by the

[2] JMJP, January 1, 1954.   [3] NCNA, Peking, June 19, 1956.

Chinese Communist leaders until a couple of years ago.[4] For instance, Po I-po, at the time Minister of Finance, wrote in the *People's Daily*:

> . . . the present mutual-aid team is a kind of organisation of voluntary exchange at parity prices built on the foundation of private property, generally designed to protect and not to weaken or negate private property.[5]

Taking this affirmation of peasant private property as their leit-motif for some time, the Communist authorities did not attempt to alter the prevailing rate of exchange between human labour, which is plentiful and cheap, and draft-animal labour which is not. Thus a 'typical model mutual-aid team' in a village in North Anhwei is described in the following terms:

> The members of the team have devised a rational method of dividing the work and counting workdays; it is a credit system based on the principle of 'equal pay for equal work'. Credits are awarded on the basis of 10 points for a first-class labourer's work-day, with 8 points for second class, and 6 points for third. A labourer's half work-day is 5 points. The draft animals are also divided into classes, with 20, 18, and 16 points per work-day per head.[6]

A draft animal's workday is thus equal to two or more labourers' workdays. Equal pay for equal work, indeed! Again, reports on the organisation of mutual-aid teams in a village in Hunan Province state: 'Each unit of animal labour was reckoned as $4\frac{1}{2}$ units of human labour.'[7]

Thus affirmation is given to the fact that where capital is scarce but human beings plenty, labour is willy nilly subordinated to capital, private or otherwise. This lends support to the great law of social change: in the last analysis the relations between people, including the mode of distribution of the social product, are determined by the wealth, the productive forces of the society.

[4] This emphasis changed with the drive towards complete collectivisation initiated in 1955. See pp. 157-9.
[5] JMJP, June 29, 1951; CB, 161.
[6] Kiang Chen-yo, 'Mutual Aid in Agriculture', CMR, March, 1952.
[7] Hsiao Ch'ien, *op. cit.*, p. 137.

OWNERSHIP OF PROPERTY AND DISTRIBUTION OF INCOME IN AGRICULTURAL PRODUCER CO-OPERATIVES

For a number of years the Communist leaders emphasised those characteristics of agricultural producer co-operatives which might make them more acceptable to peasants attached to their private property, and stoutly denied any similarity between them and the Soviet-type collective farm. Thus, for instance, Kao Kang said in a speech to a North-east Rural Work Conference (October–November 1952): 'Unlike the Soviet collective farms, our mutual-aid and co-operative organisations are still built on the foundation of private ownership.'[8] Similarly the *Decisions on Mutual Aid and Co-operation in Agricultural Production* adopted by the Central Committee, CCP, on February 15, 1953, stated: 'Co-operation and mutual aid at present means collective labour practised on the basis of an individual economy (private ownership of property by peasants) . . .'[9] To make it absolutely clear to the individualistic peasant that there was to be no infringement of the right of private property when he pooled his land, the *Decisions* stated explicitly: 'Members withdrawing from a mutual-aid team or from a co-operative are entitled to withdraw their investments in capital and reserve funds.'[10] The Communist leaders also made it abundantly clear that a peasant, even while a member of an agricultural producer co-operative, is not bound to pool anything besides land unless he wants to, and then only for full monetary compensation. As Teng Tzu-hui, Director, Rural Work Department, CC, CCP, explained in an address before the Second National Congress of NDYL (July 2, 1953):

> The co-operatives now developed in different areas only transfer the one major production material, land, and with the voluntary assent of the peasants, from private cultivation to common utilisation by the co-operatives. Other production materials, like farm tools and draft animals, are still the private property of the peasants, and the co-operatives may only hire their use, or else purchase them at a price, but cannot use them without payment

[8] JMJP, December 23, 1952; SCMP, 482.
[9] *Mutual Aid and Co-operation in China's Agricultural Production*, op. cit., p. 3.
[10] *Ibid.*, p. 15.

of consideration or transfer them to common property without compensation.[11]

The price paid for draft animals and tools is the prevailing market price at the time of purchase.

The peasant might also be anxious lest a considerable portion of the income of the agricultural producer co-operative go not to increase his own property, but the commonly held property. The Communist authorities again did their best to allay his anxiety. Thus, the above-mentioned *Decisions* stated:

> . . . the amount of reserve funds and public welfare funds should never be too large a percentage of the annual income of the mutual-aid teams or agricultural producers' co-operatives. Generally speaking, 1–5 per cent would be a comparatively reasonable amount; in time of a poor harvest, however, the accumulation of reserve funds may be discontinued.[12]

However, since the turn in Peking's policy at the end of 1955 towards the quick and complete organisation of the peasantry in agricultural producer co-operatives,[13] the emphasis in the definition of their role has shifted from their private property element to their *collectivist* element. This was made quite clear in the *Draft Model Regulations for Agricultural Producer Co-operatives*, adopted by the Standing Committee of the National People's Congress on March 17, 1956.[14] The essence of the agricultural producer co-operative was defined thus:

> An agricultural producer co-operative is a collective economic organisation of labouring peasants and is organised by the peasants under the leadership and with the help of the Communist Party and the People's Government, based on the principle of voluntariness and mutual benefit. It makes unified use of members' land, draft animals and farm tools and step by step turns these means of production into communal property. It organises its members to perform common labour and divides the gains of members' common labour in a unified manner (Article 1).

[11] JMJP, July 23, 1955; CB, 255.
[12] *Mutual Aid, etc., op. cit.*
[13] See pp. 157–9.
[14] NCNA, Peking, March 17, 1956.

The *Regulations* leave no doubt that the agricultural producer co-operatives are meant to be a halfway house to the collective farm (Article 3). The aim is clearly to make all land the property of the common farm and gradually to cancel payment for past land ownership:

> Land belonging to members must be placed at the unified disposal of the agricultural producer co-operative . . .
>
> In consideration of members' needs to grow vegetables and other garden crops, members may have small plots of land for their own use. The size of land kept by each member household should be determined by the number of persons in each household and the amount of land in local areas, but the maximum amount of land kept by each person may not exceed 5 per cent of the average amount of land owned by each person of the village (Article 17).

As regards the rent paid to a peasant for his land:

> At the preliminary state of the co-operative, the agricultural producer co-operative shall pay proper dividends, out of its annual income, to members according to the amount and quality of their land turned over to the co-operative.
>
> The income of an agricultural producer co-operative is derived from the labour, not from the land ownership, of its members. The dividend for land, therefore, must be lower than the payment for agricultural labour so that all members of the co-operative can be encouraged to take an active part in the labour of the co-operative. But at the preliminary stage of an agricultural producer co-operative, dividend for land should not be fixed too low because it is desirable to absorb peasants with more and better land into the co-operative and to enable members who own land but lack manpower to earn appropriate incomes (Article 18).

To discourage peasants from asking for rent for the land they contributed to the agricultural producer co-operative, the following article is included:

> If members acquire dividend for their land, they should pay the agricultural tax. If agricultural tax is paid by the co operative, then

dividend for members' land should be correspondingly reduced (Article 19).

In dealing with other means of production, the *Regulations* seems wary of antagonising the individualistic peasant too much and therefore allows for an equitable price to be paid by the co-operative, but the aim of complete collectivisation is not hidden.

> Principal means of production required by the agricultural producer co-operative, other than those belonging to a member, should be placed under the unified disposal or unified management of the co-operative with proper payment made to the owner, and, with agreement of the owner, should be gradually turned into communal property by the co-operative . . . (Article 25).

We have seen that the *Decisions* of February 15, 1953, prescribed that the reserve fund should in general be in the range of 1–5 per cent of the income of the co-operative. The new *Regulations* increase this share considerably:

> The amount of reserve funds should in general not exceed 5 per cent of the actual income of a co-operative . . . at the initial stage of a co-operative, and may gradually be raised to 10 per cent along with the development of production. In the case of co-operatives producing industrial crops, however, reserve funds may be slightly increased (Article 64).

Contrary to the *Decisions* of February 15, 1953, which allowed 'complete freedom for members to withdraw both their invested capital and their contributions to the common fund', the new *Regulations* states:

> Reserve funds, welfare funds and other communal property accumulated by the co-operative may not be dispersed. A retiring member can only, according to Article 15 of these Regulations, take with him his private means of production and withdraw his shares' funds and investments and may not distribute and take away any communal property accumulated by the co-operative (Article 68)[15].

[15] NCNA, Peking, March 17, 1956.

Nevertheless, it must be emphasised that the agricultural producer co-operative is still not a kolkhoz, the element of private property being much stronger. At the present stage the co-operative owns only a small portion of the means of production, and the individual peasant is free to withdraw from it taking with him the property he brought with him.

Indeed, even if all the land, livestock and other means of production were owned collectively, the resulting institution would still be very different from the Soviet kolkhoz, the basic difference between the two being in the technique of production: the kolkhoz is dependent on State-supplied tractors and combine-harvesters, the Chinese agricultural producer co-operative is not. At the end of her First Five Year Plan, Russia had 210,900 tractors;[16] in China at the end of 1955 there were less than 2,000[17] and she is not expected to produce any before 1959. By then the organisation of agriculture in collective farms will have been virtually completed. In the same way as a factory cannot be broken up and divided amongst its workers, so also a mechanised kolkhoz cannot be broken up into peasant holdings (as the Nazis learned to their chagrin, for when they toyed with the idea of breaking up the kolkhozes in their zone of occupation they found that there were not enough horses for individual farming to replace the tractors). The Chinese non-mechanised agricultural producer co-operative, even the Chinese collective farm, is a much more frail organism. It can readily dissolve into its constituents.

Again, the Chinese agricultural producer co-operatives are too small and their number much too big—compared with the Russian kolkhozes—to serve as tools for efficient centralised State control over farming. The size of the average farm in pre-war China was 3·76 acres.[18] As the average number of households in the agricultural producer co-operatives is about a hundred,[19] the size of the average co-operative is some 350–400 acres. Such a unit is not large when

---

[16] Baykov, *The Development of the Soviet Economic System, op. cit.*, p. 202.
[17] See p. 60.
[18] Buck, *Land Utilisation in China, op. cit.*, p. 268.
[19] Vice-Premier Teng Tzu-hui's report to the National People's Congress, NCNA, Peking, June 19, 1956.

compared with privately owned farms in a number of Western countries.[20]

Compared with the Soviet kolkhoz with its 9,000 or more acres, the Chinese co-operative is quite small.

Comparison of the number of co-operative farms controlled by Peking and Moscow is equally instructive. There are 1,080,000 agricultural producer co-operatives in China.[21] As against this, there were 254,000 kolkhozes in Russia at the beginning of 1950,[22] when even this number, proving too large for efficient centralised control, was pruned to 87,500 by amalgamating the small kolkhozes.[23] (The Khrushchev plan for *agro-gorods*, which was not fully realised, aimed at amalgamating the kolkhozes even further.) It is out of the question for Chinese agriculture—technically backward and intensive as it is—to be reorganised in large units comparable to those in Russia. This factor alone would seriously undermine efficient control over the countryside by Peking.

Peking, however, has no alternative policy for agriculture. For Mao the agricultural producer co-operative is the chrysalis from which a new butterfly—the kolkhoz—will emerge. That many a chrysalis dies without turning into a butterfly is beside the point.

PEKING DETERMINED TO ORGANISE AGRICULTURE IN
PRODUCER CO-OPERATIVES

Between 1949 and 1953 Peking concentrated its propaganda on organising peasant households in mutual-aid teams. It was only after the 1954–5 grain crisis that real efforts were made to pass from the elementary form of mutual-aid team to that of the agricultural producer co-operatives. The development is shown clearly in the table on the opposite page.

As late as autumn 1954 agricultural producer co-operatives comprised only 1·9 per cent of all peasant households. Even more insignificant was the number of collective farms. At the time there were only 17 such farms with a couple of thousand members.[24]

---

[20] Thus the average farm in England and Wales (1924) was 63·18 acres, and in the U.S.A. (1930), 156·85 acres. (Buck, *Land Utilisation in China, op. cit.*, p. 268.)
[21] NCNA, Peking, May 7, 1956.
[22] *Pravda*, March 11, 1950.
[23] *The National Economy of U.S.S.R. Statistical Abstract* (Russian), Moscow, 1956, p. 100.
[24] HH, March 2, 1954; SCMP, 807.

	Percentage of Peasant Households in Mutual-aid Teams		Percentage of Peasant Households in Agricultural Producer Co-operatives
	Teams of all types	Year-round teams	
1950*	10	—	—
1951*	over 20	2	—
Middle 1952†	34	7	—
Nov. 1953‡	43	10·3	0·57
Autumn 1954§	58·4		1·9

* Cheng Lin-chuang, 'The Development of Agricultural Producer Co-operatives and Mutual-Aid Movement in China', HCS, April 3, 1955.
† NCNA, Peking, August 29, 1952.
‡ NCNA, Peking, January 14, 1954.
§ NCNA, Peking, September 21, 1955.

As the grain crisis of 1954–5 became acute, Peking began a serious drive to organise the mass of the peasants in agricultural producer co-operatives and even went so far as to establish numerous collective farms. By July 1955, 14 per cent of all peasant households were already organised in agricultural producer co-operatives.[25] On July 6, Li Fu-chun set the Five Year Plan target as the organisation of about a third of all peasants in agricultural producer co-operatives.[26] Some three weeks later, however, on the 31st of the same month, Mao Tse-tung, in a report delivered to a meeting of Secretaries of Provincial, Municipal and Area Committees of the CCP set the target higher: by 1957 more than half the peasants were to be members of agricultural producer co-operatives and by 1960 all of them were to be.[27] Mao lashed out at cadres and Party members who showed milk-and-water enthusiasm for collectivisation: '. . . some of our comrades are tottering along like a woman with bound feet, always complaining that others are going too fast'. They are 'picking on trifles, grumbling unnecessarily, worrying continuously . . .' They 'think that several hundred thousand small semi-socialist agricultural producers' co-operatives that have sprung into being have "gone beyond practical possibilities" . . .' 'They think that the present situation of the co-operative movement is critical.'[28] A couple of

[25] Speech by Liao Lu-yen, Minister of Agriculture, to National People's Congress, JMJP, July 26, 1955.
[26] Li Fu-chun, op. cit., p. 66.
[27] Mao Tse-tung, 'The Question of Agricultural Co-operation', PC, November 1, 1955.
[28] Ibid.

months later Chen Po-ta, one of the chief Party theoreticians, reproved 'some comrades', saying, 'their interest in the preservation of the economy of the small peasant is greater than their interest in leading the Socialist transformation of agriculture'.[29] Vice-Premier Chen Yi used even harsher words against Rightist elements who argued 'on the question of the co-operativisation of agriculture within the Party during the past three years': 'They did not proceed to develop agricultural co-operatives, but rather extensively undertook the reduction and dissolution of co-operatives. They did not lead the masses to take the road of Socialism, but rather dragged the masses away from the road of Socialism. They did not lead the peasants to rid themselves of the influences of capitalism, but rather encouraged the peasants to take the road of capitalism.'[30]

Following the new directive, the cadres set about organising agricultural producer co-operatives with the utmost possible speed. And so, from encompassing 16·9 million families, or about 14 per cent of all peasant households in July 1955, the agricultural producer co-operatives came in June 1956 to embrace over 108 million peasant households, making up 90·4 per cent of all peasant households in China; of these 73 million, or 61·1 per cent of all peasant households, were in higher-stage co-operatives, and 35 million, or 29·3 per cent, in elementary co-operatives.[31]

Collective farms are also being organised on a significant scale. Thus in the last months of 1955 350 agricultural producer co-operatives in Peking suburban areas have been changed into 220 collective farms.[32] In Liaoning Province, North-east China, there were already by the end of 1955 about 4,000 collective farms; 2,000 collective farms in Heilungkiang Province in the North-east, 10,000–15,000 in Hopei (North China) and 3,400 in Anhwei Province were expected to be forthcoming by the spring of 1956. There were already by the end of 1955 more than 2,000

[29] Chen Po-ta, 'Explanations on the Draft Resolution on the Question of Agricultural Co-operation', Report submitted to the 6th Plenary Session of the CC, CCP, on October 14, 1955, NCNA, Peking, October 18, 1955.
[30] JMJP, November 13, 1955; SCMP, 1177.
[31] Vice-Premier Teng Tzu-hui's Report to the National People's Congress, NCNA, Peking, June 19, 1956.
[32] NCNA, Peking, January 12, 1956.

collective farms in Shansi (North China).[33] Altogether there were more than 29,000 collective farms in the whole country by the end of 1955.[34] On the basis of these achievements, Mao Tse-tung showed a not unjustified optimism when he stated that by 1959 or 1960 the whole of China's agriculture would be organised in collective farms.[35]

It seems, however, that the peasants' 'voluntarily' joining agricultural producer co-operatives show less enthusiasm for the co-operativisation of agriculture than Peking and its agents. Their attitude is clearly indicated by the large-scale slaughter of livestock, in which they follow in the footsteps of their Russian counterparts. The Russian peasants who 'voluntarily' joined kolkhozes when they were introduced on a mass scale at the turn of the 'twenties showed their opposition by slaughtering their livestock *en masse*. Thus between 1928 and 1933 the number of horses in the kolkhozes and individual farms declined from 33·4 million to 14·9 million; the number of cattle from 70·4 to 33·7 million; hogs from 25·9 to 8·9 million; sheep and goats from 145·9 to 41·8 million.[36] Slaughtering in China is carried out on nothing like the vast scale it was in Russia, chiefly because the Chinese agricultural producer co-operatives—unlike the Soviet kolkhoz—leave the overwhelming majority of livestock in the possession of the peasants as their private property. However, notwithstanding Peking's assurances that the peasant's livestock would not be taken away from him, but at worst would be bought at some future date for an 'equitable price', he still shows a very definite inclination to sell for slaughter or himself slaughter and eat his livestock before joining the co-operative. Thus a *People's Daily* editorial entitled 'Stop the Falling Prices for Draft Animals' said:

. . . since the beginning of winter, in many areas where peasants have been selling draft animals in large numbers, the prices for such draft animals have dropped, the price declines being particularly marked for mother animals and infant animals. In the Kiaochow administrative district in Shantung, prices for animals dropped an average of 30 to 40 per cent compared with the same period last year, while young animals were worth still less, a calf that sold for

[33] NCNA, Peking, January 12, 1956. [35] NCNA, Peking, January 2, 1956.
[34] NCNA, Peking, January 13, 1956. [36] Jasny, *op. cit.*, p. 324.

between JMP 30 and 40 last year being sold now for only from JMP 5 to 10. In Shansi, prices of small animals in some areas dropped by two-thirds compared with the normal figures for the year. In some areas in Hopei and Honan, similar conditions were also reported. Some peasants and speculative merchants saw that prices for draft animals were excessively low, and resorted to indiscriminately slaughtering such draft animals.[37]

Three days later another paper described the serious situation in an editorial entitled 'Take Action Immediately to Protect Draft Animals':

> At the moment, a new situation has emerged in the livestock market in the rural areas. In many areas the peasants are selling their draft animals, especially small animals, in large numbers. Due to the fact that there are many sellers and few buyers, the prices for small animals have dropped drastically, and butchers, in order to profiteer, are taking the opportunity to slaughter small draft animals in large numbers. From the situation reflected in the purchase of oxhides by the State, cattle slaughtered during this year has shown an increase of more than 70 per cent compared with the same period last year, and calves have constituted a very large portion of the animals slaughtered.[38]

The slaughter of animals led the State Council to issue an urgent *Directive on Protection of Young Animals*, which points out that 'if all-out efforts are not exerted now for the protection and heeding of young animals, then in a short while the existing old draft animals will have served their usefulness, and there will not be sufficient strong animals to take their place.' It went on to decree a number of measures to stop the slaughter of animals.[39]

But it seems that all the exhortations did not put an end to the evil. And about six months later we find a *People's Daily* editorial complaining bitterly:

> It has been a widespread phenomenon in the agricultural producer co-operatives in the different places during the period of last

---

[37] JMJP, December 18, 1955; SCMP, 1200.
[38] TKP, December 21, 1955; SCMP, 1200.
[39] NCNA, Peking, December 26, 1955; SCMP, 1202.

winter and the spring of this year that the draft animals have become thin and weakened or have died.[40]

Again, Chen Yun stated that the number of pigs in the country declined from 100 million in June 1954 to 80 million in June 1956.[40a]

Another deleterious effect of forced collectivisation in China may be the decline of sideline production in the rural areas, such as handicrafts, fishing, etc. This could be of great importance, as the income of the Chinese 'peasants from sideline production generally makes up about one-third of their total income.'[41] It was noted that from the winter of 1955 to the spring of 1956 'in many areas sideline production registered a great decline. In some areas income from sideline production dropped by between one-third and half of original figures.'[42]

If Peking were to decide to effect complete, fully-fledged collectivisation on the Soviet model, the peasants' reaction would most likely be even more serious than it is at present.

THE EXPERIENCE OF STATE FARMS

The experience of running State farms during the last few years must have been a cautionary sign for Peking when she decided on collectivisation.

On April 1, 1955, there were 101 mechanised State farms in China, with a planted acreage of 2·8 million *mow*,[43] or an average of 27,000 *mow* (about 4,500 acres) per farm. Their equipment, mainly inherited from the former Japanese farms of the Northeast, is quite impressive. According to data compiled during the first half of 1953, 59 mechanised State farms with a cultivated area of more than 2 million *mow* were equipped with 1,763 tractors and 348 combine-harvesters.[44] They employed a total of 56,000 workers and employees, including technicians, drivers, administrative and political personnel.[45] Extensive (in Chinese

[40] JMJP, May 17, 1956; SCMP, 1302.
[40a] NCNA, Peking, March 10, 1957.
[41] JMJP, editorial, May 24, 1956; SCMP, 1302.
[42] *Ibid.*

[43] JMJP, April 1, 1955. Non-mechanised State farms, whose number exceeds 2,000, are not dealt with, as they are small, primitive organisations, and do not serve as the vanguards and pathfinders that the Chinese Communists seek.

[44] Hua Shu, 'The Socialist State-owned Agricultural Economy of China', HH, March 2, 1954; SCMP, 807. [45] *Ibid.*

terms) farming is the rule, as the cultivated area per worker averages some 40 *mow*. In a number of the more mechanised farms the average is even bigger. Thus, 'In the 8 mechanised farms directly controlled by the North-east State Farms Control Bureau, the workers directly engaged in production averaged, in 1952, the cultivation of 225 *mow*, and this was increased to 300 *mow* in 1953'.[46] Similar information is given regarding a State farm in Heilungkiang Province: 'With the equipment of 98 tractors, and 100 combine-harvesters which it possesses, this farm requires only 604 people to work an area the size of the normal cultivated area of a *hsien* with 100,000 inhabitants.'[47]

Reports from these farms paint an unremitting picture of inefficiency, waste and loss. The North-east Bureau, CC, CCP, in a *Decision on Strengthening the Work of State Farms*, issued in September 1952, described the financial failures of the State farms in the region under its jurisdiction as follows:

> . . . the absolute majority of the State farms today are not properly managed . . . On the one hand, the production per unit of cultivation is small, and on the other there has been too much loss and waste. Added to these facts have been the excessive numbers of non-productive personnel, and the huge costs of transportation, all contributing to high production costs, and providing the principal cause for incomes not balancing expenses.

Again, the *Decisions* grumbled that 'attention was not paid to land in accordance with the needs of mechanised operations'. It complained about the 'lack of enforcement of the fallow and of rotation crops systems, the impurity of seeds, inadequacy of disinfection processes, failure to proceed with cultivation in good time leading to growth of weeds'.

> . . . there were also such conditions as the unbalanced assignment of machinery equipment with an overabundance of power machines and a lack of working machines, improper care of machinery equipment and lack of regular inspections and repairs and failure to

[46] Hua Shu, 'The Socialist State-owned Agricultural Economy of China', HH, March 2, 1954; SCMP, 807.
[47] Shang Tang, 'Heilungkiang, The Northernmost Province', Hong Kong, Communist daily, *Wen Hui Pao*, June 7, 1955; SCMP, 1069.

operate such equipment according to technical instructions. Accidents became numerous, creating serious damage and waste, and lowering the efficiency of the equipment. In some farms, the tractors were employed only to the extent of from 20 to 25 per cent of their capacity. . . .

. . . losses from waste reach alarming figures—losses through damage to machinery, death of horses, waste of fuel, desolation of arable land, and alarming losses in the processes of harvesting and husking.[48]

Lin Feng, First Deputy Secretary of the North-east Bureau of the CC, CCP, emphasised:

The chief defects in the State mechanised farms may be seen in the comparatively low productivity and enormous waste, which have combined to make costs excessive and turn the farms into losing propositions.[49]

This reproof brought about no improvement. Half a year later Lin Feng cited some examples to show that the management of the State farms were still blundering happily along:

The leading comrades in some farms still harbour an attitude of bureaucratism. They neither thoroughly examine nor understand conditions . . . For example, last year a certain farm lost money, but by February of this year the leaders of that farm still did not know how much had been lost. At first, they said that it was JMP 800,000,000, then JMP 3,200,000,000, when actually it was JMP 3,700,000,000. Again, in March another farm announced that it had lost over JMP 400,000,000, but now it reports that the loss is over JMP 1,600,000,000. . . .

. . . in 1952 capital was invested in the Wulitien farm on the basis of estimated average output of 550 *catties* of cotton per *mow* (and 1,000 *catties* per *mow* for abundant production areas). But the result was that the output was 60 per cent less than the original estimate, while the cost was 40 per cent more than the amount planned. In the Lut'ai farm, fertiliser was applied to rice crops on the basis of estimated output of 1,000 *catties* per *mow*. . . . Only

[48] JMJP, December 10, 1952; SCMP, 485.
[49] JMJP, December 11, 1952; SCMP, 490.

75 per cent of the estimated output was fulfilled, but the cost exceeded the estimate by 23 per cent . . .[50]

The issue of the paper in which Lin Feng's article was published complained of excessively large investment of capital per unit of land in State farms:

> In the past three years, the investment in capital construction in three subsidiary farms has constituted approximately 80 per cent of the total investment. If this is divided according to acreage, an average of JMP 1,210,000 has been invested in one *mow*. With regard to housing and irrigation only, JMP 3,160,000 has been invested in one *mow* in the Wulitien farm, JMP 2,150,000 in the Hsuangch'iao farm, and JMP 510,000 in the Lut'ai farm (the average for this farm has been low because of its large area). The investment in capital construction has been so large that no matter how large the output per unit acreage, it will still be difficult to get rid of the burden of the large amount of annual depreciation.[51]

If a similar investment per *mow* to that of Wulitien farm were made over the whole country, housing and irrigation alone would, in three years, reach JMP 5,000,000,000,000,000 (old currency) or £75 milliard, or £25 milliard per annum—a sum about six times the total national State budget.

The position had hardly changed 15 months later. Li Shucheng, Deputy to the National People's Congress, summed up the working of the State farms thus:

> Lack of experience and 'expansion' mentality in running State agricultural enterprises have led to high production costs, low output and huge waste, thereby weakening the demonstrative role that is supposed to be played by State agricultural enterprises.[52]

A year later the *People's Daily* had to admit that 'of the 101 State-owned mechanised farms throughout the country' only 'nearly 50 farms reported working profits . . . the situation of waste remains very serious in the State-owned mechanised farms'. The

[50] CKNP, June 25, 1953; SCMP, 634.
[51] *Ibid.*
[52] NCNA, Peking, September 26, 1954; SCMP, 918.

same complaints recur: 'The State-owned Lut'ai Farm . . . reported waste amounting to JMP 120,000 last year . . .' (i.e., some £17,000).

The State-owned 'May 4 Farm' blindly carried out capital construction, wasted large amounts of capital funds, delayed the task of cultivation, violated natural conditions so that the harvest for the major portion of the crops was bad, large numbers of livestock perished, and large quantities of machinery and equipment piled up and was damaged. In 1954, the said farm reported a total loss of JMP 620,000 from . . . wasteful spending,

(i.e., nearly £100,000).

In the farms in the Yellow River flood area, although repeated reorganisations had been carried out, the non-production personnel still constituted more than 34 per cent of all personnel, or more than half the personnel directly employed in production.

In some farms the utilisation rate of the land is not high, with larger areas ploughed but smaller areas sown, and resowing is not carried out where such is possible, and the custody of the harvested grain not properly attended to. The State-owned Tung Pei Farm, for instance, reaped an average harvest of 550 kilograms of soya beans per hectare last year, and sustained an average loss of between 70 and 80 kilograms per hectare.

No wonder that 'peasants in the vicinity of such farms said, "The farms are very fine indeed, but we cannot copy their examples". This shows that such farms produce very little influence as models for the peasants around them'.[53]

KHRUSHCHEV'S WARNING

While China's experience of mechanised extensive farming over the past few years should serve as a warning to Mao to beware of large-scale collectivisation, the fate of Soviet agriculture over nearly a generation should serve as an even greater warning.

The output of grain in Russia in 1938 was 16 per cent higher

[53] 'Eliminate Waste in State-owned Mechanised Farms', JMJP, August 14, 1955; SCMP, 1119.

than at the beginning of collectivisation in 1928. But this advance was not due—except to a very small degree—to an increased yield per acre, but rather a result of an increase—of 11 per cent—in the sown area.[54] More significant from the standpoint of Chinese intensive agriculture, is the impact of collectivisation on a branch of Russian agriculture which is in the main intensive—livestock breeding. Nothing could better highlight the crisis in this branch of Soviet economy than Khrushchev's report to the Plenary meeting of the Central Committee of the Communist Party of the Soviet Union, delivered on September 3, 1953. He painted the situation in sombre colours, giving some alarming figures on the development of livestock:[55]

Livestock Population of the U.S.S.R.
(millions of head on January 1, in comparable territory)

	Total	Cows	Pigs	Sheep and Goats	Horses
1916	58·4	28·8	23·0	96·3	38·2
1928	66·8	33·2	27·7	114·6	36·1
1941	54·5	27·8	27·5	91·6	21·0
1953	56·6	24·3	28·5	109·9	15·3

Khrushchev went on to say that 'districts which had long been famous as butter suppliers are now producing less butter than before. Siberia, for instance, produced 75,000 tons of butter in 1913, and only 65,000 tons in 1952.'[56]

Vegetable farming, another intensive branch of agriculture, shows the same trend (although here, unfortunately, Khrushchev confined himself to a pre- and post-war comparison only, and omitted mention of the pre-collectivisation output). 'The vegetable crop area today is 250,000 hectares less than in 1940.'[57]

When Khrushchev gave this report the population of Russia was bigger by some 50 million than it was in 1916, while the livestock population was smaller!

Khrushchev's Report was not published in the Chinese press and probably remained unknown even to many high Chinese bureaucrats. Instead Mao instructed his cadres to study Chapters

[54] Gluckstein, *op. cit.*, pp. 111–12.
[55] N. S. Khrushchev, *Measures for the Further Development of Agriculture in the U.S.S.R.*, Moscow, 1954, p. 21.
[56] *Ibid.*, p. 26.
[57] *Ibid.*, p. 37.

9–12 of Stalin's *History of the CPSU (Bolsheviks), Short Course*. These chapters describe the forced collectivisation and industrialisation in Russia as one great success story.

WARNING FROM EASTERN EUROPE

Recent experience in Russian-dominated Eastern Europe serves to underline the warning with regard to collectivisation even where extensive, not intensive, farming (grain production) is concerned.

Agriculture in Eastern Europe has reached quite a high level of mechanisation. The 1953 position as regards tractors, for instance, is quite impressive:

	Number of tractors (thousands, in 15 h.p. units)	Hectares of Arable Land per 15 h.p. unit
Bulgaria	13·5	308
Czechoslovakia	30·7	159
East Germany*	55·9	105 on farms served by MTS and 21 on State farms
Hungary	14·0	379
Poland	45·3	325
Rumania	23·3	386
China	2·8	60,000

* Machine Tractor Stations and State Farms only.
Sources: For Eastern Europe: U.N., *Economic Survey of Europe in 1954*, Geneva, 1955, p. 273. For China: KJJP, November 22, 1955.

Eastern Europe uses also a considerable amount of fertilisers, as can be seen from the following table:

Fertiliser Supplies per Hectare of Area (kg. of pure content)				
Czechoslovakia	1948–9	31·1	1952–3	51·0
East Germany	1948	62·0	1954	123·0
Hungary	1949	4·0	1953	6·6
Poland	1948–9	17·7	1953–4	30·8

Source: U.N., *Economic Survey of Europe in 1954*, Geneva, 1955, p. 274.

In China the application of fertilisers (*not* pure content) is some 2 kg. per hectare. (Of course, China uses night-soil on a large scale, while European countries do not.)

Notwithstanding the better supply of machines and fertilisers, grain output in *every one* of the Eastern European countries mentioned in the first table has not risen, but has declined since collectivisation. In the 1934–8 period they produced 42·8 million tons of grain annually; in 1951–3 they produced only 37·5 million tons,[58] a decline of 12·4 per cent. Eastern Europe, which was a big exporter of grain, has become a net importer.

Chinese agriculture cannot hope to obtain a comparable amount of machinery, fertilisers and the like in the foreseeable future, which should make its rulers very apprehensive of the effects of collectivisation. This warning gains weight from the fact that even with their fine achievements in agricultural mechanisation—the backbone of large farming—the Eastern European governments still tread very carefully along the path of collectivisation. Up to the present the agriculture of Eastern Europe is still based in the main on the small individual peasant farm.[59]

To note the warnings from Russia and Eastern Europe is one thing; to act upon them is another. Is the scope for manœuvre in China big enough to allow large-scale and rapid industrialisation without the collectivisation of agriculture?

COLLECTIVISATION AND MECHANISATION OF AGRICULTURE

The technical backbone of collectivisation in Russia and Eastern Europe is the tractor, and one of the main differences between collectivisation there and its prospects in China lies in the suitability of machines to their very different type of agriculture.

First, the ratio of labour to land in China is very different from that in Russia and Eastern Europe. With labour so plentiful it would pay to use machinery instead of people in very few operations. Even if machines were cheaper, it is doubtful whether their

---

[58] U.N., *Economic Survey of Europe in 1954*, Geneva, 1955, p. 120.
[59] *Area of Co-operative and State Farms in Eastern European Countries as Percentage of Total Area.*

East Germany	December 1954	18 per cent*
Poland	December 1953	20 per cent*
Rumania	June 1954	20 per cent†
Hungary	April 1954	31 per cent†
Czechoslovakia	December 1953	44 per cent†

* Percentage of agricultural area.
† Percentage of arable area. (*Ibid.*, p. 61).

use would be justified from a socio-economic standpoint unless the labour saved found other productive employment. Regarding the first factor, J. L. Buck found that it cost 10·43 Chinese dollars to plough one hectare with a tractor in 1925, as against approximately 4·00 Chinese dollars when a water buffalo was used.[60] The problem of productive employment for the labour power released by machines is, and promises to remain, a long term impediment to the economic use of agricultural machinery, except in cases where machinery relieves the seasonal labour bottlenecks of harvesting and planting. Another obstacle to the use of tractors is the extent of irrigation, which covers nearly half the cultivated land. However, in opening up new lands in areas of extensive agriculture, especially Manchuria, this factor would not exist.[61]

Besides these general difficulties, the topography of China does not lend itself easily to the use of machines. China is a very mountainous country with relatively small flat areas and a rough terrain unsuited to extensive mechanised cultivation. North China, particularly Manchuria, is an exception. Indeed, conditions in Manchuria favour mechanisation. A short growing season demands very intensive work at the time of ploughing and again during the harvest. Manchuria could be transformed into an agricultural area similar to that of the Middle West in the United States and South Canada.

While not underestimating the difficulties of mechanising agriculture in China, one should also not underestimate the possible long-term results of such mechanisation, especially when it affects the operations that have to be done during the busiest seasons. As it is, with present production techniques and the seasonal labour bottlenecks which they entail, it is very nearly impossible to enlarge the cultivated area per family, and, as only

---

[60] Buck, *Chinese Farm Economy, op. cit.*, p. 315.

[61] The threshing machine promises better results than the tractor. Cost data on small threshing machines calculated at the University of Nanking show that they can thresh as cheaply as the flail. Furthermore, they come into use precisely when a shortage of labour is most keenly felt, during the harvest season. (*Ibid.*, pp. 315–16.)

Another machine that could be successfully used in irrigation or drainage is the internal combustion engine. Rice requires a great quantity of water, so that it is economical to use water pumps when fields are either elevated or far from the source of water. (*Ibid.*, p. 316.)

the more fertile soil can—without a change in technique—support a family, much of the land that could otherwise be cultivated remains uncultivated. The results are increasing density of the agricultural population, labour power wastage, low productivity and other evils. The mechanisation of certain operations which take place in the busiest season could break this vicious circle.

As far as China as a whole is concerned, it is only *after* the ratio of labour to land is radically changed that the general mechanisation of agriculture can become a paying proposition. As there are no immediate prospects of decreasing the agricultural population in absolute terms, and as the agricultural area cannot be increased significantly, at least for the coming generation or two, the general mechanisation of Chinese agriculture—of main operations and in all regions—seems not to be economically feasible. A move in the direction of rapid collectivisation would, in view of these problems, produce a tangled and complex situation.

In Russia, the First Five Year Plan saw the large-scale mechanisation of agriculture. At the end of 1932 there were 210,900 tractors in the country, or about 1 tractor per 650 hectares of sown area.[62] It is true that mechanisation lagged somewhat behind the tempo of collectivisation, but the lag was not more than a few years. Nevertheless, the fact that a lag did exist jeopardised the success of the drive to collectivisation and threatened the economy of the country with collapse.

China's Five Year Plan does not visualise any large-scale mechanisation of agriculture. The first tractor factory—with an annual capacity of 15,000 tractors—will not be completed until 1959,[63] two years after the completion of the Five Year Plan. Thus it is intended to organise the whole of Chinese farming into producer co-operatives *before* any machinery is supplied to the countryside. In face of the chronic industrial backwardness of the country and the relative inability of agricultural machinery to raise output under Chinese conditions, the decision to go ahead with the co-operative organisation of farming without waiting for agricultural machinery was unavoidable. It is, however, a dangerous gamble.

[62] Baykov, *The Development of the Soviet Economic System, op. cit.*, p. 202.
[63] Li Fu-chun, *op. cit.*, p. 25.

PROSPECTS FOR COLLECTIVISATION OF CHINESE AGRICULTURE

Before embarking on a comparison of the prospects for 'collectivisation' in China with the results of collectivisation in Russia, it should be borne in mind that in Russia there was no great pressure of population on land whereas in China this factor is most compelling. Russia could therefore avert the catastrophe of a fall in agricultural output and productivity by ploughing up millions of acres of virgin land. China has much less scope for opening up virgin land, and where the possibility does exist, it is usually dependent on the prior implementation of elaborate irrigation and transport schemes; in other words, it is possible only after large investments of the country's scarce capital.

Again, collectivisation in Russia has brought a country that had been a granary for Western Europe to the position of scarcely being able to export grain at all. Rumania and Hungary, once important grain exporters, have had to resort to bread rationing. China has never been an exporter of grain; on the contrary, for more than two generations she has been a net importer. Any worsening of her present precarious grain balance would affect her more than the stagnation of agricultural production affected Russia and Eastern Europe. Any decline in the productivity of agriculture, or even its failure to keep pace with the increase in population could result in catastrophe in China, as the margin of output above the bare minimum is extremely small. In the past, the robbing of the peasants' meagre surpluses by landlords, usurers and militarists often caused famines which consumed millions of human lives. State capital accumulation at the expense of the peasantry could have similar results in the future. Moreover, the appetite of the social parasites of the past cannot compare with the insatiable needs of a State undertaking massive industrialisation.

There is an even more fundamental reason why the pattern of Soviet collectivisation could not be applied easily, or even perhaps at all, to China. In Russia, State control over the Machine Tractor Stations guarantees that a big portion of whatever the peasants produce will go into the State treasury to provide capital for industrialisation. In China the role of the machine tractor stations—even in the few places where they do exist—could not be as commanding, as intensive agriculture, especially garden cultivation is not, and could not be, as dependent upon mechanisation. The converse of this greater importance of human labour is that the will to work, care and zeal in production play a much greater role in China's agriculture than in Russia's. Forced deliveries, together with the emphasis on heavy industry, inevitably pour cold water on the peasant's desire to increase production: not only is he prevented from eating more but no consumer goods are offered to induce him to sell his surplus output. And without inducement, increased output from intensive agriculture is most unlikely.

The conclusion that the pattern of Russian collectivisation is likely to prove a false guide to China gains support from the economic history of the two countries. As pointed out elsewhere,[64] ever since Chinese agriculture became dependent on irrigation, serfdom gave place to a peasant economy based on private property. However exploited and oppressed the peasant may have been, it was not the whip which urged him to work. As against this, serfdom and the feudal whip were the salient features of rural society in Russia, with its extensive agriculture, for a thousand years. It will be much more difficult to mould the Chinese peasant who has not been a serf for millennia, into a kolkhoznik, than it was to mould the Russian. This is less a question of the difference in national character moulded by past rural socio-economic history than a basic difference in the rural economy of the two countries at present.

Meanwhile, in the immediate period ahead, Mao will tread carefully where complete collectivisation is concerned. And he will continue in this manner so long as Chinese agriculture is not mechanised at all. There are some factors which may, for a time, make it possible for him to avoid putting too much pressure on the peasantry. First, as there is already a tremendous urban population, running into some four score millions, the productivity of many of whom is extremely low (e.g., artisans, porters, pedlars, etc.), industrialisation can take great strides without significantly

[64] See pp. 83-4.

increasing the number of mouths to be fed in the towns. Secondly, Soviet economic aid may help to ease the pressure on the Chinese peasants. However, in the long run, the first factor must become exhausted, and the second prove insufficient for the needs of the waking giant of China. In the long run, Peking will have to tighten the belt of the Chinese peasantry considerably, and subordinate agriculture entirely to the needs of State capitalism.

It would be precipitate to conclude that the collectivisation of Chinese agriculture must inevitably end in failure. As the peasantry is incapable of moulding society and State, and as its amorphous mass is completely helpless *vis-a-vis* the centralised power, it is quite probable that an iron tyranny could carry out forced industrialisation and collectivisation whatever the sacrifice. And sacrifices there will certainly be, on a scale that will dwarf the sufferings of the Russian peasants. But this will not deter the new rulers of China from going along their chosen path.

CHAPTER IX

MAO AND THE PEASANTRY: HISTORICAL RETROSPECT

PAST PEASANT REVOLTS

Mao's rise to power on the crest of a peasant upheaval is not without precedent in China's long history. Hardly a generation has passed without a more or less widespread peasant revolt. Lack of space permits mention of only the most important of these. The first big recorded rising took place in 209 B.C. during the reign of the Second Emperor of the Ch'in dynasty. The whole of present-day Shantung and Kiangsu rose in arms, the Ch'in Empire was overthrown and the peasant leader Liu Pang took power (becoming emperor and establishing the Han dynasty). Again in A.D. 8 there was the mass peasant rebellion of the Red Eyebrows, so called from the way the rebels applied their war paint, which took hold over all northern China for many years. In A.D. 184 the rebellion of the Yellow Turbans shook the country. In A.D. 874 a peasant revolt broke out, which swept over most of the provinces of the Yellow, Yangtze, Huai and Pearl River Valleys in the course of ten years, gained hold of the capital, overthrew the T'ang dynasty and made the peasant leader emperor. (This rebellion collapsed after 27 years under the blows of the old dynasty.) In A.D. 1351, a peasant rebellion overthrew the Mongol Dynasty and replaced it with a new one, the Ming. 1628 bore witness to another big peasant rising which spread all over North China and, after a long struggle, led in 1644 to the downfall of the Ming dynasty. (This rebellion did not lead to the establishment of a new dynasty headed by a peasant leader, as was customary, but to the invasion of the Manchu into China proper.) Finally, there was the nearest relevant precursor of Mao's peasant movement—the Taiping Heavenly Kingdom.

The scale of the peasant revolts that fill the pages of Chinese history are without comparison elsewhere in the world.[1] Although not all the 25 dynasties chronicled in official histories of China rose on the crest of peasant rebellion, many did. In each case, the peasants overthrew the economic domination of the cities in which the State bureaucrats as well as the landlords, lived. Reforms aimed at lightening the burdens imposed on the peasants and often including land redistribution invariably followed. Sometimes the new leaders went so far as to propose a primitive sort of nationalisation of the land; others provided for the establishment of a rudimentary form of State capitalism. None of these ambitious reforms matured, however; they broke on the rock of the more or less static productive technique. The peasant wars which gave rise to them exhausted themselves, and the new emperor and his clique reintroduced the old social forms once again.

The Taiping rebellion followed the same tragic pattern. As the nearest relevant precursor of the Maoist revolt, it merits special attention.

The rebellion started in 1849 in a mountainous village in Kwangsi province. The peasant armies advanced northward from Kwangsi, fought in Hunan and Hupeh, brought most of the Yangtze River Valley under their sway and established their 'Heavenly Capital' in Nanking. Their forces then numbered as many as a million peasant-soldiers, who followed up previous successes with even greater victories until 17 provinces of the Empire—more than two-thirds of the country—were under their sway. They nearly, but not quite, succeeded in taking Peking, thus putting an end to the Manchu Empire. Their battles were so ardently fought that, it is believed, no fewer than twenty million lives were lost.

Hung Hsiu-ch'uan, the Heavenly King, declared that all land should be owned by those who cultivated it. All landlords' land was to be confiscated and reallocated in a general redistribution in which the land was to be divided into nine grades by quality and shared equally among all peasants according to need. The revolutionary government declared further:

[1] An investigator found records from local files of 67 peasant revolts within a period of some 180 years (1448–1627) in one small border region between Kiangsi and Fukien. (Shu-ching Lee, 'Agrarianism and Social Upheaval in China', *American Journal of Sociology*, Chicago, May, 1951.)

Having fields, let them cultivate them together; and when they get any rice, let them eat together; so also with regard to clothes and money let them use them in common, so that everyone may share and share alike, and everyone be equally well-fed and clothed.

The people were to be divided into groups of 25 households, each with its public granary to which the peasants would hand over their harvest after retaining an amount sufficient for their own maintenance. From this common granary relief was to be given to all who were, because of old age, infirmity or other disabilities, incapable of work; it was also to provide grants for marriages and funerals, as well as pay the salaries of government officials.[2] Equality of the sexes was proclaimed, and women actually held positions on equal terms with men in the administration and the army.

The amorphous mass of ignorant peasants could not raise a leadership of their own, and so the Taiping leaders were mainly intellectuals interspersed with some rich peasants, merchants, and even a few landlords.

Like all its predecessors, the Taiping rebellion did not lead to social equality. Privileges were quick to arise. The higher members of the hierarchy exploited their position to take more than an equal share of rice, meat, oil, etc., from the public granaries and storehouses.[3] They soon began to dress in rich and costly clothes, to wear gold and jewel-studded crowns and to live in luxurious palaces.[4] It was not long before such manifestations of privilege as the following were to be seen:

The sedan chair of the Heavenly King was carried by sixty-four porters and that of the East King by forty, and the latter's retinue was usually from several hundred to one thousand. Whenever he went out, all people in the streets had to kneel down at the sides of the road where he passed.[5]

[2] Hua Gan, *History of the Revolutionary Wars of the Taiping State* (Russian), Moscow, 1952, pp. 268–70.
[3] G. S. Kara-murza, *The Taipings* (Russian), Second Edition, Moscow, 1950, p. 86.
[4] For a description, see Lin-le, *Ti-ping Tien-kwoh, The History of the Ti-ping Revolution*, London, 1866, Volume I, pp. 243–4.
[5] Ssu-yü Teng, *New Light on the History of the Taiping Rebellion*, Cambridge, Mass., 1950, p. 123.

Very detailed ceremonial forms, ranks and titles were introduced to differentiate the upper levels of the hierarchy from the masses and distinguish between the members of the hierarchy itself. The Heavenly King with his sons and daughters headed the list; there followed another five kings, marquises, generalissimos and many others. Orders of precedence, modes of address, and all points of Oriental etiquette were reintroduced and strictly adhered to. [6]

Many historians consider that 'corruption was the fundamental cause of the failure of the Taipings. 'After Nanking was conquered, the leaders began to live extravagant, indolent and licentious lives, with a harem of women, contrary to the avowed platform of monogamy.' [7] This last was the crowning aspect of social inequality; moreover it was written into the law. A decree of 1861 regulated marriages as follows: high princes were allowed 11 wives, high ranking officers 3; middle ranking officers 2; other officers and rank and file 1. [8]

In time the leaders of the Taiping fell prey to jealousy and feuds. Blood flowed freely, almost all the chief leaders of the Taiping as well as scores of thousands of veterans were murdered. [9]

The available evidence suggests that the Taiping actually introduced the radical, egalitarian land law with which they had set out to change the face of the country in only a small portion of the area under their control. It is very doubtful whether their fate would have been any different to what it turned out to be, or that they would have done more than what former peasant revolts in China had succeeded in doing—merely resurrecting the old Chinese society—even if they had succeeded in overthrowing the Manchus and taking power over the whole country.

The peasantry proved itself capable of a mass revolutionary uprising which as such had a democratic character, but it proved incapable of democratic self-rule. They could be united only by an external force—an élite which rose above them and consequently dominated and exploited them. This inherent incapacity of the peasantry for self-rule makes their domination by an élite

---

[6] W. H. Medhurst, compiler, *Pamphlets Issued by the Chinese Insurgents at Nan-king*, Shanghai, 1853, pp. 51–3.

[7] Ssu-yü Teng, *op. cit.*, p. 71.

[8] Kara-Murza, *op. cit.*, p. 108.

[9] Hua Gan, *op. cit.*, pp. 171–5.

inevitable, but the élite need not be the same in every circumstance. The élite of the past—the Mandarinate of the Empire—mainly fulfilled the function of organising the country's large irrigation works. The present State bureaucracy, existing in a world of steel and electricity, embodies the urge of making China an industrial giant.

The lesson emerging from the Chinese peasant revolts is instructive. They foreshadow, embryonically, the Maoist peasant movement; its culmination in giving 'the land to the tiller' (land reform) as well as its negation of this in the expropriation of the peasantry (the so-called 'collectivisation of agriculture').

MAO NOT A PEASANT LEADER BUT AN EXPLOITER OF THE PEASANT REVOLT

The history of the Maoist Communist Party since its inception shows quite clearly that it was never a peasant party—that is, a party made up of peasants and representing their interests on the usual pattern—but an élite made up of ex-peasant army professionals and officials. The hundreds of thousands of CCP and PLA cadres lived under conditions which made them anything but typically narrow- and locally-minded individualists. Untrammelled with these typically peasant characteristics they were psychologically prepared to take power over a whole, and large, country. The fact that these cadres had for many years, stretching into decades, not worked on a small individual farm, but had obtained food through the 'supply system'—a centralised food allocation system—weakened or practically eliminated the basic peasant psychological traits which they had brought with them when they joined the Communist movement. The Communist Party was thus not a party made up of peasants, but a party of professional politicians and military activists. As Liu Shao-chi, the theoretician of the Party, second to Mao only, put it:

More than twenty years of civil war and national war have steeled our Party. Several hundreds of thousands of Party members have given up their respective occupations in society for a long time and become engaged in revolutionary military collective life and life-

and-death struggle . . . As a result . . . their sense of organisation and discipline strengthened.[10]

Again, the fact that the Party and army cadres had often to change their place of work and to move from one part of China to another, inevitably cut the Party member off from the village in which he was born and grew up, and from any real intimate identification with the peasantry. Thus, for instance, it was reported:

> . . . the data for 1943 show that in Taipei, of the 37 cadres of eight region Party committees there were only nine local cadres (or 26 per cent of the total) in comparison with 28 outside cadres (or 74 per cent of the total). Of the 37 cadres of county Party committees under the control of four region Party committees in Taiyueh only six (or 16 per cent) were natives of these counties, while 31 (or 84 per cent) were outsiders. In T'aihang, of the 18 cadres of five county Party committees under the control of the Sixth Region Committee only five (or 27 per cent) were natives and 13 (or 72 per cent) were outsiders.

Again:

> . . . according to reports from South Hopei, secretaries of region Party committees there had been transferred six times or more in seven years, with five times as the minimum; secretaries of county Party committees had been transferred five to 13 times.[11]

The connection between the CCP and the peasantry thus became very tenuous.

Careful scrutiny of the policies of the Communist Party over the many years of Mao's leadership shows that they were never identical with the interests of the peasantry as a whole, or of any of its strata. As a matter of fact the Party manœuvred between, but kept aloof from, the contending classes in the countryside—landlords and peasants—and the different strata of the peasantry. A cursory résumé of the history of the Party's agrarian policy brings

[10] Liu Shao-chi, *On the Party*, Report to the Seventh Congress of the CCP, delivered on May 14, 1945, Peking, 1951, p. 17.
[11] *Ibid.*, pp. 114–16.

this out clearly. A list of some of the sharp zigzags in this policy follows.

In December 1928 the Government of so-called Soviet China at Chingkangshan, on the Hunan-Kiangsi border, passed an agrarian law which provided for the nationalisation of all land: the Soviet Government became the owner of all land and distributed it among the peasants; private property in land was abolished, and its purchase and sale prohibited. This law alienated the mass of individualistic peasants, and it was therefore changed to expropriation of all landlords' land; rich peasants' land was expropriated except for a plot that could be tilled without hiring labour.[12]

After the destruction of the Soviets in South China, the Long March, the establishment of the Communist regime in Shensi in North-west China and the outbreak of the Sino-Japanese War, the agrarian policy turned full circle. On February 10, 1937, the Central Committee issued a statement which said: '. . . the policy of confiscating the land of the landlords will be discontinued . . .'[13] Instead a programme was announced providing for the reduction of rent and interest while guaranteeing landlords' property. Thus a *Decision of the Central Committee on Land Policy in the Anti-Japanese Base Areas*, passed by the Political Bureau on January 28, 1942, stated:

> In the areas where rent has not been reduced, rent should, in principle, be reduced by twenty-five per cent, i.e. a reduction of twenty-five per cent from the pre-war rate for rent . . . it should not uniformly be ruled that the landlord is to obtain no more than forty or sixty per cent, but there should be a twenty-five per cent reduction of the former percentage in rent. . . . In guerrilla areas or places near enemy (Japanese) strongholds, rent reduction may be less than twenty-five per cent.[14]

The Party would not identify itself either with landlords' or peasants' interests:

> . . . the policy of the Party is only to help the peasants in reducing feudal exploitation but not to liquidate feudal exploitation

[12] *Fundamental Laws of the Chinese Soviet Republic*, London, 1934, pp. 25–7.
[13] Mao Tse-tung, *Selected Works*, London, 1954, Volume I, p. 333.
[14] C. Brandt and associates, *A Documentary History of Chinese Communism*, London 1952, p. 282.

entirely, much less to attack the enlightened gentry who support democratic reforms. Therefore, after rent and interest rates are reduced, the collection of rent and interest are to be assured; and in addition to protecting the civil liberties, political, land and economic rights of the peasants, we must guarantee the landlords their civil liberties, political, land and economic rights . . .

In settling rural disputes, the working members of the Party and government should base themselves on the above basic principles and follow a policy of adjusting the interests of both sides. They should not take a one-sided stand either for the landlord or for the peasant.[15]

Speaking on the results expected from the law reducing rent, Liu Shao-chi, at the time Political Commissar of the New Fourth Army, declared in June 1941:

True, the income of the landlords will be a little decreased for the time being, and possibly their living standards will also be lowered. But this cannot be helped for the moment. Possibly also due to this reduction the anti-Japanese democratic movement will be viewed by them with dissatisfaction. But sooner or later rural production will increase, and the rent then received by the landlords may amount to even more than before the reduction . . .

At the same time we emphasise that we do not approve of rent reduction exceeding 25 per cent of the former rent . . .[16]

The Party's war-time programme for reducing rent and interest payments remained unaltered for about ten months after the war, except for one change of great importance in the North-east: land owned by the Japanese government or its officials or by the puppet government or its officials was confiscated and distributed among the peasants. On May 4, 1946, however, the CC, CCP, issued a directive calling for the purchase of portions of landlords' land, while leaving them a larger share than the average peasant. It warned especially against the encroachment upon the land of rich peasants. A draft law for government compulsory purchase of excess landlords' land in the Shensi-Kansu-Ninghsia Border Region, promulgated on December 21, 1946, set out in detail the

[15] *Ibid.*, pp. 278–9.
[16] L. K. Rosinger, *China's Crisis*, New York, 1945, pp. 207–8.

measures to be taken. The landlord was permitted to keep 50 per cent more land than the average middle peasant or, if he had been active in the war against Japan, 100 per cent more. The rest of his land had to be sold to the government for land bonds redeemable in ten years. Rich peasants' land was not to be touched. Landless and land-poor peasants would have to pay for the land—half the total compensation paid to the landlord—in instalments over ten years.[17] Similar measures were taken by Communist governments in other areas.

Later, under the pressure of civil war, when landlords and rich peasants inclined towards the Kuomintang and the Communist Party found it expedient to make its policies more attractive to the mass of the peasantry, its agrarian policy veered again to the left. In September 1947 an Agrarian Conference convened by the CC, CCP, passed a *Basic Programme of the Chinese Agrarian Law*, which became law on October 10, 1947. Its salient points are as follows:

1. All landlords' land was to be expropriated and divided equally among the poor peasants, the landlords getting the same amount of land; the surplus land of rich peasants was also to be taken over and distributed. All land to be distributed equally.

2. Landlords' animals, agricultural implements, houses, grain and other properties, together with the surplus animals, agricultural implements, houses, etc., of rich peasants, were to be confiscated and distributed equally among poor peasants, the previous owners getting no more than anybody else.

3. All standing debts were cancelled.[18]

The change in the military situation in 1948–9 and the entry of the PLA into areas in which the differentiation of the peasantry was more complex and diversified pushed agrarian policy once again very much to the right. In the period from April 1949 to June 1950, the policy adopted for all the new areas taken over by the PLA—East, Central, South, South-east and North-west China —was basically the same as the war-time one: rent was reduced by 25 per cent and was not to exceed 37·5 per cent of the crop.

[17] K. C. Chao, 'Chinese Land Policies', *Current History*, New York, June 1953.
[18] NCNA, North Shensi, October 13, 1947.

All debts had to be paid back with interest at 15–30 per cent per annum. If interest was double or more than double the principal, the debt was to be cancelled. Landlords' and rich peasants' commercial and industrial enterprises were to be protected. In a report to the Third Plenary Session of the Seventh Central Committee, Mao Tse-tung went so far as to say: '. . . there should be a change in our policy toward the rich peasants, a change from the policy of requisitioning the surplus land and property of the rich peasants, to one of preserving a rich peasant economy. . . .'[19]

Subsequent developments in the Party's agrarian policy have been described in the present part of this book.

From the short summary of the history of the Party's agrarian policy, it is obvious that the Party shifted from one section of the peasantry to another, now seeking the support of the poor peasants, now that of the rich, and at times even adapting itself to the landlords. No real peasant party, whatever stratum of the peasantry it represented, could change its line so quickly, so radically and so often. The Chinese Communist Party was certainly a movement of peasants, but it was not a peasant movement. It behaved like an élite, now moderate and mild, now baring its teeth and exhibiting its power.

It is almost superfluous to observe that since its rise to power, it has been impossible to identify the Party with the peasantry. Were the Party identified with the peasantry, it could never have instituted its current policies, aimed at the exploitation, oppression and eventual expropriation of this same peasantry.

Marxists considered it axiomatic that the peasantry must today follow the lead of either the working class or the bourgeoisie. As Lenin said:

The city cannot be equated to the village, the village cannot be equated to the city in the historical conditions of the present epoch. The city inevitably *leads the village*, the village inevitably *follows the city*. The only question is *which* of the urban classes will lead the villages.[20]

[19] NCNA, Peking, June 16, 1950.
[20] Lenin, 'The Year 1919', in *Works*, Russian, Volume XVI, p. 442, quoted in L. Trotsky, *The Third International After Lenin*, New York, 1936, p. 226.

And in every case of class conflict between the two main urban social classes—workers and capitalists—the peasantry has indeed followed one of them, or rather, some strata of the peasantry has followed the one, and some the other. The Russian Revolution highlighted this, as did the 1925–7 revolution in China. But history plays tricks. The mutual paralysis of the contending classes in the towns—the 1927 defeat of the workers who thereafter never rose again to be an independent socio-political force, and the continued impotence of the bourgeoisie, aggravated by the Japanese occupation of the key cities and by the rise of 'bureaucratic capitalism'[21]—turned the city into a political vacuum and scrambled the seemingly inexorable pattern. The peasantry had thus to find another leadership to replace the absent city leadership. It sought something more advanced, less narrow-minded and ignorant than it could produce itself; it found the Maoist élite.

Coming to power on the crest of a peasant revolt, the Maoist élite, like many of its predecessors in China's long history of peasant revolts, is bent upon exploiting the mass of the peasantry. Here the similarity with previous revolts ends. Born into a world of industrial giants and intent on quick industrialisation, the new élite does not limit itself to merely exploiting the peasantry. It is set upon its total expropriation.

[21] See pp. 188–90

PART THREE

THE TOWNS
UNDER MAO

CHAPTER X

THE STATE BECOMES OWNER OF INDUSTRIAL, TRADING AND BANKING ESTABLISHMENTS

FOREIGN CAPITAL

Foreign ownership of the most important sectors of the urban economy has greatly facilitated the establishment of State control over industry.

The infiltration of foreign capital proceeded almost without interruption since the turn of the century. Foreign investments rose from 787·9 million U.S. dollars in 1902 to 1,610·3 million in 1914, 3,242·5 million in 1931,[1] and 3,671·4 million in 1936.[2]

The share of foreign capital in different branches of China's production was (in 1933): coal, 39 per cent; pig iron, 82·5 per cent; iron castings, 52·2 per cent; electric power, 62·7 per cent; ship building, 48·2 per cent; cotton yarn, 29·1 per cent; cotton cloth, 61·5 per cent; cigarettes, 56·9 per cent.[3] Foreign capital is estimated to have formed 73·8 per cent of the total industrial capital of China (excluding Manchuria) in 1936.[4]

During the Sino-Japanese war, the Japanese Government and Japanese capitalists swallowed even more of the economy, either by way of open robbery or through new investments. They took over direct control of most of the communications, industries and public utilities; they forced many Chinese firms to take in Japanese 'partners'. Thus Japan came to control 63 per cent of North China's coal output and 62 per cent of other industrial production in the area.[5] She had an even greater hold in North-east China (Manchuria), where, in 1945, Japanese capital con-

---

[1] C. F. Remer, *Foreign Investments in China*, New York, 1933, p. 76.
[2] Wu Ch'eng-ming, 'Imperialist Enterprises in China and their Profits', CKKY, February 26, 1951; CB, 83.
[3] Wang Ching-yu, 'Why China could not be Industrialised', JMJP, May 21, 1953; CB, 272.
[4] Koh Tso-fan, *op. cit.*, pp. 27–8.
[5] Wang Ching-yu, *op. cit.*

trolled 99·8 per cent of all industrial capital.[6] In the country as a whole, the Japanese controlled 4,198,000 of the 5,356,000 spindles in the modern textile industry in 1941 (or 78·4 per cent, as against 44·5 per cent in 1937).[7] Whereas in 1902 Japanese capital totalled 1 million U.S. dollars, in 1914 it was 210·0 million; in 1931, 1,766·2 million, and in 1945 as much as 6,493·0 million.[8] In 1945 83·3 per cent of all foreign capital invested in China was Japanese. Britain trailed far behind with 9·8 per cent, the United States with 2·8 per cent, France with 2·6 per cent, Germany with 0·6 per cent, other countries with 0·9 per cent.[9] Japanese capital controlled thus nearly two-thirds of China's modern industry.

With the defeat of Japan, this vast economic empire stood ownerless.

'BUREAUCRATIC CAPITALISM'

The areas under Kuomintang control during the war were so backward and so far from the financial, commercial and industrial centres of the country that there was hardly sufficient private capital to satisfy even the meagre needs for industrial production in these parts. The State stepped in to fill the gap with the result that the major part of all industry in these areas was under its control. The State owned the following shares in the total capital of the main industrial branches: metallurgical industry, 90 per cent; power plants, 89 per cent; manufacturing of electrical machinery and appliances, 89 per cent; chemical industries, 75 per cent; machine-making industries (exclusive of electrical machinery), 73 per cent. The State's share in light industry was much smaller.[10] Production of such non-ferrous ores as wolfram, antimony, tin, mercury, copper and zinc, and of gasoline and kerosene oil was a complete State monopoly.

Under these conditions, the Kuomintang leaders made it plain that they had no intention of reverting to a private-property

[6] FEER, October 5, 1950.
[7] *Report of the United Kingdom Trade Mission to China, op. cit.*, pp. 122–3.
[8] Wu Ch'eng-ming, *op. cit.*
[9] *Ibid.*
[10] D. K. Lieu, *China's Economic Stabilisation and Reconstruction*, New Brunswick, 1948, p. 17.

industrial economy. Thus, Chiang Kai-shek wrote in *China's Destiny*, the political bible of the Kuomintang (in 1943):

> We must adopt a planned economy . . . it is imperative that we eventually accomplish the objective of 'transforming' [all] capital into state capital . . . [11]

The fact that Japanese property was virtually ownerless after the war made it possible for the Kuomintang vastly to enlarge on the theme of State ownership.

Before following developments in this sphere, a note of caution is necessary. State ownership under the Kuomintang is not to be identified with State ownership elsewhere in the world. One of its basic features is that many State-owned enterprises served in actual fact as a source of income for officials who shared in their profits. It was impossible to differentiate between government enterprises and those of high government officials acting in semi-official or purely private capacities. The State's higher military and political personnel looked upon State-owned enterprises as a kind of 'feudal' fief. A special term—'bureaucratic capitalism'[12] was coined to distinguish this type of State ownership.

After the Kuomintang Government had taken over Japanese industry, and handed it to State corporations, 'bureaucratic capitalism' covered 64 per cent of the electricity output of the country, 33 per cent of the coal output, nearly 70 per cent of tin, 45 per cent of cement, and 90 per cent of the sugar output in 1947.[13] It also had a dominant position in shipping, shipbuilding, civil aviation, etc. In addition, it had almost complete control over banking. At the end of 1946, State banks held 92 per cent of all bank deposits in China.[14] A State company, the China Textile Development Corporation, owned 49 per cent of all spindles, and 68 per cent of all looms in the country in 1946. It also accounted for 39 per cent of total cotton yarn production and 74 per cent of total cotton cloth production.[15] Another important State-owned

---

[11] Chiang Kai-shek, *China's Destiny*, London, 1947, p. 173.
[12] A. Nagano, *Development of Capitalism in China*, Tokyo, 1931, pp. 121–4.
[13] Boldyrev, *op. cit.*, p. 15.
[14] FEER, September 15, 1949.
[15] Wang Ching-yu, *op. cit.*

company, the China Petroleum Corporation, had monopoly rights in respect of all oil production and refining in China; it also had the right to decide the level of imports of oil products and to control their distribution.

Post-war conditions encouraged the growth of 'bureaucratic capitalism' as, amid prevailing scarcities, State-owned industry had access to sources of raw materials, foreign exchange and transport facilities controlled by UNRRA and the United States forces.

With the fall of the Kuomintang, Mao Tse-tung inherited a completely State-owned industrial complex in Manchuria, and a large State-owned sector in China proper.

STATE OWNERSHIP GROWS

Two factors combined to increase considerably the share of the State in industry, banking and trade after Mao's rise to power: first, the restoration of former Japanese-owned industry—especially heavy industry—which had suffered a greater decline than did the rest of industry in the aftermath of national and civil war; second, the fact that State industry grew at a faster tempo than private industry, following Government measures of taxation, control over raw materials, transport facilities, etc.

Share of State Ownership in Industry, Banking, Insurance and Trade
(percentage share)

	1952	1955
All industry	49·6[1]	63[5]
All modern industry	60[1]	
Modern heavy industry	80[1]	
Modern light industry	40[1]	
Banking	90[2]	100[6]
Insurance	97[3]	100[6]
Wholesale Trade (state and co-operative)	64[4]	95[5]
Retail trade (state and co-operative)	32[4]	82[5]
Foreign trade	90[6]	97 (1954)[7]

Sources:

[1] NCNA, Peking, September 30, 1953.
[2] *New China's Economic Achievements, 1949-1952, op. cit.*, p. 281.
[3] Boldyrev, *op. cit.*, p. 195.
[4] *Communiqué on National Economic, Cultural and Educational Rehabilitation and Development in 1952 (Revised)*, issued by the State Statistical Bureau, September 12, 1954.
[5] NCNA, Peking, June 14, 1956.
[6] Liu Shao-chi's Report to 8th CCP Congress, NCNA, Peking, September 16, 1956.
[7] NCNA, Peking, February 20, 1955.

The State's share in all industry rose from 33·9 per cent in 1949[16] to 63 per cent in 1955.

In addition to enterprises which are the property of the State, there are those owned in partnership by the State and private capitalists. Such enterprises accounted for 4·3 per cent of all industrial output in 1952[17] (6 per cent of modern industry[18]) rising to 16 per cent of modern industry in 1955.[19] Joint State-private banks accounted for 8–9 per cent of all loans and deposits in 1952.[20] Joint State-private trading firms accounted for 23 per cent of retail trade in 1955.[21]

The expropriation of foreign capital also helped to increase the State's share in industry, banking and trade. We have seen that foreign capital other than Japanese (and German) made up 16·1 per cent of all foreign capital in 1945. This became a target for attack, and it was soon crippled by an increasing volume of restrictions and punitive taxes. Foreign capitalists found themselves pouring money into China in order to keep their firms afloat instead of taking profits out of the country. It was estimated that about £375,000 a month was being sent from Britain and Hong Kong in 1950 to finance British firms in Shanghai. Losses were so heavy that share values declined to practically nothing. Thus British Ewo Cotton Mills stock depreciated by 92 per cent between May 24, 1948 and May 22, 1950, that of British Shanghai Docks by 91 per cent, and that of British Shanghai Lands by 80 per cent.[22] The outbreak of the Korean War aggravated their difficulties, and in the summer of 1952, British firms, following the lead given by American firms, decided to withdraw.[23]

Where the normal measures proved inadequate to close foreign firms, requisitioning was used. On December 28, 1950, the GAC issued a decree controlling American property and freezing American bank deposits in China.[24] On April 30, 1951, it

[16] NCNA, Peking, September 30, 1953.
[17] NCNA, Peking, September 30, 1953.
[18] NCNA, Peking, November 10, 1953.
[19] NCNA, Peking, June 14, 1956.
[20] *New China's Economic Achievements, 1949–1952, op. cit.,* p. 281.
[21] NCNA, Peking, November 19, 1955.
[22] *Financial Times,* London, May 31, 1950.
[23] See G. E. Mitchell, 'China and Britain, their Commercial and Industrial Relations', *Journal of the Royal Central Asia Asian Society,* July-October, 1952.
[24] NCNA, Shanghai, January 2, 1951.

requisitioned the properties of the British-owned Shell Company of China and proposed to purchase its entire oil stock.[25] On July 18, 1951, the PLA's Military Control Committee in Shanghai requisitioned all property belonging to the American Standard Vacuum, Caltex and Cathay Oil Companies, except for the premises of their general and branch offices, and proposed the purchase of all their oil stocks.[26] In April 1952, the British-American Tobacco Company ceased its activities in China, and transferred its assets to a Chinese firm, the Shanghai Tobacco Co.[27] In August 1952, the Shanghai Dockyards and Mollers Engineering and Shipbuilding Company were requisitioned.[28] In November 1952, four British firms in Shanghai (three public utilities—gas, tramway and water companies—and a shipping firm) were taken over by the Chinese authorities.[29] In November 1953, the Shanghai Municipal Government took over the French Tram and Power Company.[30]

MAO'S HONEYMOON WITH PRIVATE CHINESE CAPITALISTS

For the first few months after 'Liberation', the Chinese Government was very solicitous for private Chinese capitalists who reciprocated the interest. Their experience of the Kuomintang regime with its mushroom growth of bureaucratic State monopolies, led them to believe that the future could not be worse than the past.

Indeed, the private capitalist sector—Chinese as well as foreign—grew increasingly antagonistic to the Kuomintang and its operations during the last years of its rule. A. Morse, Chairman of the Hong Kong and Shanghai Banking Corporation, spoke bitterly at the Bank's annual meeting in Hong Kong on March 5, 1948, of 'the jungle growth of government monopolies and bureaucratic-controlled enterprises.'[31] Similarly, a conference of the China National Federation of Chambers of Commerce stated in a Manifesto:

[25] NCNA, Peking, May 1, 1951.
[26] NCNA, Peking, July 23, 1951.
[27] *The Times*, London, April 24, 1952.
[28] F. Moraes, *Report on Mao's China*, New York, 1953, p. 165.
[29] FEER, November 27, 1952.
[30] NCNA, Peking, November 10, 1953.
[31] *Financial Times*, March 8, 1949.

. . . our people have lost confidence in our government leaders who are only interested in their personal gain at the expense of public welfare. . . . We businessmen . . . stand firm and united in fighting against corruption and despotism.[32]

So tightly was private business squeezed by the state monopolies that on the eve of the entry of the Communist armies into Shanghai, a British capitalist economic weekly in Hong Kong could write:

The remaining foreigners in Shanghai are looking for an improvement when the Communist-appointed administration will assume control; as it has been for the last three-and-a-half years, life appeared to many as intolerable in chaotic Shanghai.[33]

After the entry of the PLA into Shanghai, the same paper again wrote:

At last, the hour of liberation struck for the citizens of Shanghai and a new page in the history of Shanghai opens. A great future lies before Shanghai, the commercial, financial and industrial centre of China. The oppressions and frustrations of the past shall now be forgotten . . . The nightmare is over.[34]

Mao was not niggardly with his promises to the capitalists. For more than twenty years he repeatedly stated (in the footsteps of Stalin) that the Chinese revolution was a 'bourgeois democratic revolution'.[35] In 1945 he said:

Because the target of the revolution is not the bourgeoisie in general, but imperialist and feudal oppression; the programme of the revolution is not to abolish private property, but to protect private property in general; the results of this revolution will clear the way for the development of capitalism . . .[36]

Foreign capital was also welcomed at that time:

[32] North China Daily News, November 23, 1948.
[33] FEER, February 9, 1949.
[34] FEER, June 1, 1949.
[35] See, for instance, Mao Tse-tung, Selected Works, London, 1954, Volume I, pp. 99 and 171.
[36] Mao Tse-tung, On Coalition Government, in Brandt, op. cit., p. 309.

We welcome foreign investments if such are beneficial to China's economy and are made in observance of China's laws . . . On this basis, [we] shall be able to absorb vast amounts of foreign investments.[37]

Liu Shao-chi reiterated the thought in an interview with foreign correspondents:

The Communist Party's programme for China at present is one of democratic capitalist development, based on state, private and co-operative enterprise . . .

The programme of the Chinese Communists is comparable to the political and economic concepts in the United States at the time of Jefferson and Lincoln.[38]

He promised that under Communist control private enterprise would be an integral part of the Chinese economy, and that many former Japanese enterprises would be turned over to private owners.[39] Chu Teh defined: 'Chinese Communism is democracy plus capital.'[40]

The authorities promised that after 'Liberation' the capitalists would be assisted by the Government. They would pay less taxes than hitherto; private property taken over by the Kuomintang would be returned to its former owners;[41] above all, the capitalists were promised aid in solving their labour problems. The theme of Communist propaganda was not the struggle of labour against capital, but class harmony and national unity. As Mao said in 1945:

Under the New Democratic system of government a policy of readjusting the relations between capital and labour will be adopted . . . both labour and capital [will] work jointly for the development of industrial production.[42]

[37] Mao Tse-tung, *On Coalition Government*, in Brandt, *op. cit.*, p. 312.
[38] NYT, December 5, 1945.
[39] R. Payne, *Journey to Red China*, London, 1947, p. 19.
[40] NCNA, North Shensi, June 10, 1948.
[41] See, for instance, the Communiqué entitled 'Liberated Areas Authorities Return Kuomintang Requisitioned Property to Owners', NCNA, North Shensi, August 27, 1948.
[42] Mao Tse-tung, *On Coalition Government*, in Brandt, *op. cit.*, p. 312.

The *Common Programme*, adopted as a substitute Constitution, on the foundation of the Chinese People's Republic, pursued the same idea:

> The basic principle for the economic construction of the People's Republic of China is to develop production and bring about a prosperous economy through the policies of taking into account both public and private interests, of benefiting both labour and capital . . . (Article 26).

In the same spirit the Central Committee of the Party, in its May Day slogans for 1950, included the following:

> Chinese workers in public and private enterprises! The development of production is our highest interest and task—exert your effort to develop production!
>
> Develop the correct attitude towards working discipline, raise working efficiency and encourage model workers in production!
>
> Resolutely carry out the policy of taking into account both public and private interests and of benefiting both labour and capital, welcome the national bourgeoisie in investing their capital in, and developing productive enterprises beneficial to the national welfare and the people's livelihood!
>
> Members of the Chinese working class! Consolidate your ranks and unite with the national bourgeoisie . . . [43]

The Communist authorities did not even claim to speak in the name of the working class, but rather as the arbiters between labour and capital. Accordingly General Chen Yi, Mayor of Shanghai, said on August 8, 1949:

> We do not deny there is a labour-capital issue in this city. But we want to put all the cards on the table and let everyone speak his mind on this issue in order to arrive at a solution. We believe that only we have the courage to approach this issue from the standpoint of both labour and capital. [44]

From general statements on class harmony, the Communist leaders proceeded to concrete measure of imposing discipline on

[43] NCNA, Peking, April 28, 1950.
[44] NYT, August 9, 1949.

the workers. On August 19, 1949, the Shanghai Military Commission promulgated the *Provisional Procedure for the Mediating and Settlement of Labour-Capital Disputes in Private Enterprises,* whose aim was the 'mediating and settling of labour-capital disputes in order to attain the goal of benefiting both labour and capital and developing production'. The workers were told that they 'must comply with factory administrative regulations and with the work orders of the capitalists. The capitalists alone have the right to hire and fire workers and employees'.[45]

Thus cajoled and pressed, the workers came to ask 'voluntarily' for cuts in their wages and for a lengthening of the working day. An NCNA communiqué remarked: 'There are many cases of workers voluntarily proposing wage cuts in Shanghai and other cities in order to get over temporary difficulties'.[46] Or, 'when the owner of the Hungchang Textile Factory decided to stop work for three months, workers found ways of helping him to keep the factory going . . . they agreed to accept cheaper food in order to reduce the factory's expenses. Encouraged by this co-operation, the owner decided to continue production . . .'[47] A report on conditions in Shanghai four months after 'Liberation' stated approvingly: 'In several cases workers have agreed to have their wages cut by 20–30 per cent and to raise their working time by 1–2 hours per day'.[48] A similar report came from Tientsin, twenty-one months after its 'liberation':

> Never before have there been such amicable relations and close co-operation between employer and employee as at present . . . in some factories workers have voluntarily suggested a reduction in wages to help their employers tide over difficulties.[49]

Under these favourable conditions the capitalists did well on the whole. Thus a report from North China said:

> The new regime has so far brought prosperous living conditions to all and sundry; the bankers and traders have no reason to

[45] For more particulars about these measures see pp. 213–4.
[46] NCNA, Peking, June 25, 1950.
[47] NCNA, Peking, September 14, 1949.
[48] FEER, September 15, 1949.
[49] FEER, October 5, 1950.

complain, and, in fact, no substantiated complaints are ever heard. Private trade is doing well and profits are high.[50]

A similar report came from Fukien in the South:

> There is everywhere optimism in evidence . . . there is genuine jubilation about the liberation of Foochow and the whole Fukien Province . . . Businessmen without exception enjoy now good trading conditions . . . [51]

A report made much later (September 18, 1952) stated:

> According to figures for eight major cities including Shanghai and Tientsin, the number of private industrial and commercial undertakings increased by 27 per cent in the two years ending December 1951. The total value of private industrial output has increased by some 70 per cent in the past three years.[52]

Similarly, in Mukden the value of the output of privately-owned factories and handicrafts was 5·8 times greater in 1952 than in 1949.[53] In Peking in 1951 there were only two private machine-making factories employing over 80 workers each, but in October 1953 there were 20 employing over 100 workers each.[54]

Many industrialists who had left the country, mainly for Hong Kong, to await developments, returned after 'Liberation'. Among them were Yung Erh-jen, owner of the Sung Sing Textile Mills (which employed over six thousand workers), of another five textile factories and a chain of flour mills; O. S. Lieu, a wealthy match, cement and wool manufacturer; Shen Pi-hua, Wang Kun-chung, wealthy industrialists and others.

Private capitalists must have amassed large profits since Mao's rise to power, if one is to judge from what the Communist administrators accepted as 'reasonable profits'. On June 24, 1952, Chen Yun, Vice-Premier and Chairman of the Committee of Financial and Economic Affairs, GAC, said in an address to the

[50] FEER, January 26, 1950.
[51] *Ibid.*
[52] NCNA, Peking, September 18, 1952.
[53] NCNA, Mukden, November 10, 1953.
[54] NCNA, Peking, October 9, 1955.

Conference of the All-China Federation of Industrial and Commercial Circles: 'Private factories will, according to concrete conditions, be guaranteed a profit of around 10, 20, or even up to 30 per cent on their capital, under conditions of normal and rational operation'.[55] That this rate of profit is high, even in China, where wages are extremely low, is made clear by an article in the Communist journal, *Chinese Industry*, which states that the average rate of profit in foreign-owned enterprise in China in 1934-8, was 15·3 per cent, and the rate of profit in 80 typical Chinese-owned industries was 13·7 per cent. It also quotes the following average rates of profit for the United States: 1909-14, 5·3 per cent and 1923-9, 6·2 per cent, and for Great Britain, 9·5 and 10·6 per cent respectively.[56]

The capitalists' mode of living accords with their big incomes. A British Labour M.P., Desmond Donnelly, reported a meeting with one of the richest capitalists in China:

> Over a pre-dinner cocktail, Mr. Yung, owner of the Sung Sing Spinning and Weaving Company, offered me a cigarette from his gold case. His diamond tie-pin sparkled as he leant forward.
>
> 'I own the largest group of spinning and weaving companies in Shanghai,' he explained. 'It has six factories and employs eighteen thousand workers.'
>
> I stared and then asked: 'And what are you doing in a Communist State?'
>
> 'Making money, at last,' was the suave self-confident answer.[57]

Yung's capital was estimated at the end of 1956 to be over JMP 60,000,000 (or about £9 million) and his income on it more than JMP 3 million (or about £450,000) a year.[57a] (Besides him there were another 68 millionaires in Communist China.)

A less sophisticated capitalist showed his appreciation of Mao's

---

[55] NCNA, Peking, June 24, 1952. And as a matter of fact it was estimated that the average rate of profit in private industry in China in 1951 was 29 per cent and in 1953 31 per cent. ('The Development of State Capitalism in China's Industry', TCKTTH, October 29, 1956.) Two years later, in 1955, with the strengthening of State control, the rate of profit declined to 19 per cent (*Ibid.*).

[56] Wu Ch'eng-ming, *op. cit.*

[57] D. Donnelly, 'The Communist Capitalist. What I Saw in Red China', *Daily Herald*, September 30, 1952.

[57a] *Ta Kung Pao*, Hongkong Communist daily, December 25, 1956.

promises of fat profits by hanging in the entrance to his store some modern slogans, in addition to the traditional ones which are presumed to bring luck. These read: 'After the Communist Armies are victorious, this store will begin to prosper', and 'After true Marxism is realised, this store will make great profits'.[58]

The Communists made a point of explaining that the prosperity of private industry was not an Indian Summer and that it would continue for a long time. A *People's Daily* editorial exclaimed: 'Our economic situation will continue to improve. Private industry and commerce will also have a more glorious future.'[59]

The State needed the aid of private industry in order to rehabilitate the economy. But its benevolent attitude was, in the event, no more than a temporary marriage of convenience, to last as long as it suited the regime. It was an uneasy relationship at best, a temporary and treacherous truce, in which there was never any doubt where the locus of power lay. Towards the end of the rehabilitation period (end of 1951), the State began to show the capitalists in no uncertain terms that they had no future as an independent class, that they could exist solely as agents of the State. The first major sign of this change in attitude was the Wu-fan ('5-anti') campaign with its five slogans against bribery, tax evasion, theft of State assets, cheating in labour and materials, and leakage of State economic secrets.

THE '5-ANTI'

The scope of the campaign was vast, covering private industry, commerce and even handicrafts. The *People's Daily* reported that in Shanghai alone, 163,400 private industrial and commercial establishments were investigated.[60] Po I-po, Minister of Finance and general manager of the campaign, stated that approximately 450,000 private establishments were investigated in the nine major cities of China (including Peking, Shanghai, Tientsin, Hankow, Canton and Mukden).[61]

According to the Communist press, the results of the campaign

[58] G. Peck, *Two Kinds of Time*, Boston, 1950, p. 715.
[59] JMJP, July 1, 1952; CB, 199.
[60] JMJP, April 3, 1952.
[61] PC, October 16, 1952.

proved that the overwhelming majority of capitalists were violators of the law. The following table[62] shows the seriousness of the situation at a glance.

City	Total No. of Enterprises (including handicrafts)	No. of Enterprises Seriously Violating the Law
Peking	50,000	45,000
Canton	40,221	34,590
Shanghai	163,000	138,550

In the North-East there were 49,175 cases of tax evasion by private capitalists in 1949, 117,360 cases in 1950, and 139,068 cases in 1951.[63] Po I-po stated that of the 450,000 private industrial and commercial establishments investigated in nine major cities '76 per cent were found guilty of various illegal transactions'.[64]

The State gained an immediate financial benefit from the campaign. It was no accident that the head of the Central Economy Inspection Committee was the Minister of Finance himself, Po I-po. There is no official Communist estimate of the total amount collected by the State, but an idea of its size may be gained from the fact that the private capitalists were accused of having illegal profits of JMP 50,000 million (2,500,000,000 U.S. dollars).[65] If the Government regained one-third of this sum, which is probably a conservative figure, it obtained JMP 17,000 million, or over 850 million U.S. dollars.[66] Other estimates give much higher figures. W. W. Rostow, for example, believes that the sum netted by the Government from the campaign was over 2 milliard U.S. dollars.[67]

That quite a large portion of the capitalists' property was taken by the State is clear. In December 1956 it was estimated that all the capital of private capitalists was only JMP 2,200 million, or some U.S. $900 million.[67a] Even if this were an understatement,

---

[62] Lo Yuan-chen, op. cit., p. 149.
[63] Ibid., p. 150.
[64] New China's Economic Achievements, op. cit., pp. 152–3.
[65] CCCP, April 17, 1952, quoted in S. Montell, 'The San-fan Wu-fan Movement in Communist China', Papers on China, Volume 8, February 1954.
[66] Ibid., pp. 163–4.
[67] Rostow, op. cit., p. 80.
[67a] Ta Kung Pao, Hongkong Communist daily, December 25, 1956.

there is no doubt that the fines paid by the capitalists during the '5-anti' campaign were heavy, if not crippling.

But the campaign was not undertaken merely for financial gain. Its main purpose was to 'educate' private capitalists to a 'correct' attitude towards the State. While only a small minority of the capitalists suffered severe punishment, all of them were shaken by months of incessant visits of inspection committees, mass meetings, demonstrations and other means of controlled mass pressure. At the end of the campaign they were left in no doubt that private enterprise is a dependent of the State.

The '5-anti' campaign, however, had some unplanned results, most unwelcome to Peking. Production in private industry fell immediately—by 34·06 per cent between January and February 1952.[68] The Government attempted to reverse the trend, by farming out orders to private industry, cutting the fines imposed on law-breaking capitalists, increasing State Bank loans, raising profit margins, and so forth, with the result that the situation improved rapidly, and by May output in private industry already exceeded the January level by 9·27 per cent, and in June by 25·48 per cent.[69] In many places, however, it took longer for private industry and commerce to regain the position existing prior to the '5-anti' campaign. Thus it was reported that primary product markets in various parts of Central-South China were still only 85 per cent as active in August 1952 as in the year before, and that the foreign trade of Canton had fallen by 30 per cent in value in the same period.[70] Liu Lan-t'ao, Chairman of the North China Administrative Committee, complained in August 1952 of the 'stagnancy of industrial production' in private enterprises.[71]

Practically all private industry had regained the level existing prior to the '5-anti' campaign and even surpassed it within a year. Yet the capitalists have never regained their complete self-confidence, as the State keeps them in their place, and incidentally ensures a constant flow of money from their pockets to its coffers by intermittently reintroducing small localised campaigns on the

[68] NCNA, Peking, August 3, 1952; SCMP, 389.
[69] *Ibid.*
[70] NFJP, October 28, 1952; CB, 226.
[71] JMJP, August 26, 1952; SCMP, 411.

pattern of '5-anti'. In September 1953 *Ta Kung Pao* accused Shanghai capitalists of falling under the spell of the five poisons:

> Results of check-ups recently conducted by the Tax Bureau revealed that 2,347 out of 2,758 business establishments have committed acts of evasion of tax . . . Still others made false entries for stock taken in. The ways for evasion of tax number as many as 70.[72]

Again, a few months later, the *People's Daily* wrote:

> In August and September 1953 the Tax Bureau of Shanghai checked up 1,368 industrial and commercial establishments, of which 1,126 or 81 per cent of the total number of establishments checked, were found to have evaded and omitted tax payments.[73]

On July 8, 1954, a *People's Daily* editorial complained of the widespread incidence of the five poisons,[74] and similar complaints continue to appear regularly in the press.

The background and immediate stimuli for the '5-anti' campaign were the threatening inflation, shortages, difficulties on the Korean War front, lack of funds to carry on the war and economic reconstruction at one and the same time. With the launching of the Five Year Plan the demand for funds grew greater, inflation threatened more menacingly, scarcities grew into famines, so that far more radical and permanent means of syphoning the funds of private enterprise into State-directed channels were found to be necessary.

PRIVATE INDUSTRY WORKS FOR STATE ORDERS

The first method by which the State makes sure that private industry follows the desired channel is by making it dependent on State orders. According to Yao Yi-lin, Vice-Minister of Commerce, orders placed by State companies with private factories in Shanghai between March and June 1952, and purchase of their manufactured goods constituted '80 per cent of the total

[72] TKP, September 1, 1953; SCMP, 647.
[73] JMJP, March 3, 1954; SCMP, 769.
[74] JMJP, July 8, 1954; SCMP, 852.

volume of business done by private factories'.[75] The situation in other cities was similar.

> Sixty-six per cent of the total output of private industry in Tientsin in the first six months of this year (1953) was produced under government contract.
>
> In . . . Canton, 64·8 per cent of the output of private industry in the fourth quarter of the year will be under government contract.
>
> In . . . Chungking . . . Government contracts account for over 60 per cent of the total output of private industry, including handicraft workshops.[76]

The share of state orders in the output of private industry in the whole of China rose from 12 per cent in 1949 to 29 per cent in 1950, 43 per cent in 1951, 56 per cent in 1952, 62 per cent in 1953, 79 per cent in 1954, and 82 per cent in 1955.[76a]

'STATE CAPITALISM'

Another means of tightening the State's control over private capital is the establishment of joint State-private enterprises, referred to as 'State-capitalist' enterprises. Private capitalists are inveigled into investing in State companies by lavish promises, such as, for instance, that of Li Wei-han, Vice-Chairman, GAC Committee of Financial and Economic Affairs, who said on September 2, 1954: 'Following the institution of public-private joint operation, profits of enterprises in general will be more than at the time of private operations', and this would 'enable private shareholders to earn more than at the time of private operations',[77]

Some supporting facts might be interesting in this connection:

> The public-private, jointly-operated Huahsin Textile Company at Tangshan built a cotton mill with 20,000 spindles, and better machines and safety facilities than in the old mill from its profits in 1953. The Textile Company plans to raise capital to build a new

[75] *New China's Economic Achievements, op. cit.*, pp. 230–1.
[76] PC, December 1, 1953.
[76a] 'The Development of State Capitalism in China's Industry', TCKTTH, October 29, 1956.
[77] NCNA, Peking, September 6, 1954; CB, 295.

mill with 50,000 spindles and 2,000 looms in the coming five years. Following its reorganisation, the Chunghsi Pharmacy in Shanghai increased its output of drugs in 1953 by six times over 1950 and reduced production costs by 50 per cent. Since 1951, it has changed itself from a losing concern into a profit-making concern, private shareholders received dividends and the concern set aside JMP 1,000,000,000 reserves each year for building a new plant.[78]

The case of the Min Sheng Steamship Company is quoted:

> Operating at a loss and carrying heavy debts for long in the past, this company was run at an average daily loss of JMP 140,000,000 right up to the time one month prior to its being placed under public-private management. But since it was changed into a public-private operated concern, the Company, instead of losing money, has made profits and shareholders have got dividends.
>
> Reversing the long-standing unbalanced position of receipts and expenditure the Company made a profit of JMP 12,000,000,000 in the short span of four months.[79]

Chien Jih-lin, General Manager of the Nanyang Brothers' Tobacco Company which had become a public-private joint enterprise quite early on, pointed out that during the preceding four years of its operation in its new form output had increased two and a half times, profits seven times, and productivity had nearly doubled.[80]

In view of the evidence, it seems odd that private capitalists show no enthusiasm at all for combining with the State in production. The main reason is the unequal distribution of profits between the partners. Profits may be high, but only a small proportion ends up in the pockets of the private shareholders. The *Provisional Regulations Governing Public-Private Jointly-Operated Industrial Enterprises*, adopted by the GAC on September 2, 1954, left it in no doubt that the profits of 'State-capitalist' enterprises were expected to flow by and large into the hands of the State and into accumulation. After payment of income tax, 'dividends for shareholders and remunerations to directors, managers and

[78] CNS, Peking, September 6, 1954; SCMP, 884.
[79] NCNA, Wuhan, October 4, 1953; SCMP, 665.
[80] TKP, June 16, 1954; SCMP, 842.

superintendents may take up around 25 per cent of the yearly amount of profits'.

> The balance left after payment of dividends and bonuses shall be set aside as reserve funds (Article 17).
>
> Reserve funds should be mainly used for developing production and should be invested by jointly-operated enterprises according to State plans either in their own enterprises, in other jointly-operated enterprises or in other private enterprises for public-private joint operation according to Article 2 of these Regulations (Article 18).[81]

A further reason for hesitancy on the part of private capital is that when a capitalist does enter into partnership with a State concern it is made quite plain to him that he is no more than a junior partner, or more correctly, an agent of the State. Thus the *Provisional Regulations* state explicitly:

> The Socialist sector of jointly-operated enterprises shall occupy the leading position but the legitimate rights and interests of private shares shall receive protection (Article 3).
>
> Jointly-operated enterprises should obey State plans (Article 4).
>
> Jointly-operated enterprises shall be under the leadership of the public party and operated and managed by representatives designated by competent organs of the People's Government in conjunction with the representatives of the private party (Article 9).
>
> Jointly-operated enterprises should observe the regulations of the competent organs of the People's Government in connection with production, operation, finance, labour, capital construction and safety and health (Article 15).[82]

It is therefore natural that many capitalists prefer to consume their capital rather than invest it in a State concern. The Communist press abounds with complaints about the many capitalists

---

[81] NCNA, Peking, September 6, 1954; SCMP, 884. Some fifteen months later (February 8, 1956) the State Council decided to fix the annual interest on private shares in jointly-operated enterprises at 5 per cent (NCNA, Peking, February 10, 1956). In 1956 it was planned that of the net profit of the State-private joint enterprises, only 11·4 per cent should be given to private owners (Chen Yun's Report to the National People's Congress, NCNA, Peking, June 30, 1956).

[82] NCNA, Peking, September 6, 1954; SCMP, 884.

who go to any lengths to get control of their capital in order to consume it. To take a couple of examples only:

> Many industrialists and merchants . . . have adopted such methods as obtaining dividends in advance or interests on stock in arrears, borrowing money from their enterprises, paying debts, and corrupting the employees and workers, in order to withdraw funds. Or they have used capital meant for production to purchase consumer goods, or indulged in feasting and drinking with wanton extravagance until their capital is exhausted . . .
>
> If the case is serious and endangers the national economy and the people's livelihood, they will receive punishment according to law. Their withdrawing of capital in order to buy consumer goods is an act showing their short-sightedness, misunderstanding, and stupidity and is an offence.[83]

A few months later the Tientsin *Ta Kung Pao* denounced capitalists who 'take the view that there "is no future for themselves", that the "good days will not last", and thus consider it far better to feast and spend lavishly, and adopt the attitude of "eating all up, spending all away, and selling all out".'[84]

The Peking Government is not deterred by any unwillingness on the part of private capitalists from transforming their firms into joint public private enterprises. On July 5, 1955, Li Fu-chun declared that the major part of private industry would be thus transformed by 1957. By then, he stated, the share of private industry proper would be no more than 12·2 per cent of the total value of the country's industrial output.[85] A few months later, however, the target was raised even higher, as was revealed at a session of the Executive Committee of the All-China Federation of Industry and Commerce—the organisation of private capitalists —where the immediate transformation of all industry was called for.[86] Following this lead, thousands of private capitalists 'applied' for 'partnership' with the State, with the result that 'all private industry and commerce in Peking, Tientsin, Shanghai,

[83] TKP, May 11, 1954; SCMP, 822.
[84] TKP, December 7, 1954; SCMP, 958.
[85] Li Fu-chun, *op. cit.*, p. 35.
[86] JMJP, November 25, 1955.

Canton, Wuhan, Shenyang, Sian and other major cities switched over to joint State-private operation in the 10 days between January 10 and 20th'.[87] Chen Shu-tung, Chairman of the All-China Federation of Industry and Commerce, could thus report with satisfaction on January 31, 1956: 'Most of China's big and medium cities had completed the change-over of private enterprise to joint operation and entered on Socialism.'[88] The *People's Daily* reported that 'in terms of output value, 92 per cent of China's private industrial establishments have come under joint State-private ownership'.[89]

THE FATE OF THE CAPITALISTS UNDER 'SOCIALISM'

Not only did the Communist Party promise handsome profits to the capitalists in the current and future stages of the New Democracy, but it was and is also liberal with reassurances as regards their welfare and status, and those of their children, under 'Socialism': then, it is promised, they will be the managers of Socialist society. As Liu Shao-chi put it in an address before a conference of Tientsin businessmen:

> You may be afraid of what will happen to you and your families when we develop from New Democracy to Socialism. But you need not really be afraid. If you do a really good job in developing your business, and train your children to be first-class technical experts, you will be the obvious people to put in charge of the nationalised enterprise and you may find that you earn more as managers of a socialised enterprise than as owners.[90]

Similarly Ch'ien Tuan-sheng, a political science professor, wrote in an article entitled 'If I Were a "Citizen Capitalist"' in the June 5, 1949 issue of the Peking *Progressive Daily*:

> . . . when the nation evolves from New Democracy to socialism, I too shall evolve from being a citizen capitalist to being a manager in the new socialistic industrial enterprise.[91]

[87] NCNA, Peking, January 21, 1956.
[88] NCNA, Peking, January 31, 1956.
[89] JMJP, June 20, 1956.
[90] Quoted by M. Lindsay in Van der Sprenkel, *op. cit.*, p. 139.
[91] Quoted by M. Bodde, *Peking Diary*, London, 1951, p. 196.

Shanghai Industry and Commerce struck the same chord:

> The bright future lying ahead of the capitalists is to become citizens of a Socialist social structure and cadres of a Socialist State.[92]

A big Tientsin industrialist declared: 'The Jen Li Company has opened two new factories since Liberation, and I expect to go into Socialism as the manager of all three, maybe of four or five, or even half-a-dozen by that time.'[93] If Socialism means all this to the capitalists, it is only natural that the *People's Daily* should announce that 'a number of capitalists and agents of capitalists have realised that a bright future for themselves and their children is inseparable from the might of the State and Socialist construction'.[94]

The image of 'Socialism' which the Communist leaders try to raise in the minds of industrialists and merchants has, as we have seen, nothing to do with egalitarianism. It is the image of a Managerial Society, or more correctly, of Bureaucratic State Capitalism. Those who had privileges in the past, will continue, as managers of industry and commerce, to have the same or even bigger advantages in the future.

[92] SKS, March 1955.
[93] CMR, January 1953.
[94] JMJP, August 10, 1955; SCMP, 1110.

CHAPTER XI

REGIMENTATION OF THE WORKING CLASS

THE WORKING CLASS PLAYS NO ROLE IN MAO'S RISE TO POWER

The urban working class did not play any role at all in Mao's rise to power. This fact greatly influenced the initial trends in Peking's labour policy.

The kernel of Mao's strategy was to rely on the peasantry as the bearer of the revolution. Thus, as early as February 1927, in his well-known *Report on an Investigation of the Peasant Movement in Hunan*, he wrote:

> To give credits where they are due, if we allot ten points to the accomplishments of the democratic revolution, then the achievements of the urban dwellers and the military units rate only three points, while the remaining seven points should go to the peasants in their rural revolution.[1]

Seeing that 'urban dwellers' presumably include some sections of the bourgeoisie and that 'military units'—those engaged in the Northern Expedition at the time—also take a share of the three points left over by the peasantry, the share of the proletariat in the revolution is according to Mao, scarcely more than residual.

Mao's strategy contradicted everything considered to be true by Marxists regarding the relations between the working class and the peasantry in a revolution. Lenin, for instance, declared unequivocally:

> There can be no doubt that all elements of the Party must strive toward the cities and industrial centres for only the industrial proletariat is capable of a resolute mass fight against absolutism.[2]

[1] Brandt, *op. cit.*, p. 83. This statement is deleted from recent editions of the *Report* and also from Mao's *Selected Works*.

[2] V. I. Lenin, 'The Workers Party and the Peasantry', *Works*, Fourth edition, Russian, Volume IV, p. 400.

Again he wrote:

> The city cannot be equated to the village, the village cannot be equated to the city in the historical conditions of the present epoch. The city inevitably *leads the village*, the village inevitably *follows the city*. The only question is *which* of the urban classes will lead the village?[3]

He vehemently rejected any notion that the Marxist Party should itself organise the peasantry:

> In our opinion, there should be no Social Democratic Peasant Committees. If they are Social Democratic, that means that they are not purely peasant committees; if they are peasant committees that means that they are not purely proletarian, nor Social Democratic committees.[4]

The same Marxist-Leninist line of argument was followed by the Chinese Communist Party leadership prior to Mao's taking control of the Party. For instance, it declared in August 1927:

> The major task of the Party is to *win over the majority of the working class*, to secure their active support for the vanguard of the proletariat, the Communist Party, and to induce them to believe in the Communist Party and consciously accept its leadership. Full attention should be paid to the labour movement, especially to industrial workers. Only thus can the leadership of the working class over the peasantry be strengthened.[5]

Mao's rise in the Chinese Communist Party coincided with a transformation in its social composition. Towards the end of 1926 at least 66 per cent of the membership were proletarians, another 22 per cent intellectuals and only 5 per cent peasants.[6] By November 1928, the percentage of workers had fallen by more than four-fifths, and an official report admitted that the Party 'did not

---

[3] Quoted in Trotsky, *The Third International After Lenin, op. cit.*, p. 226.
[4] V. I. Lenin, 'Attitude of the Social Democrats Toward the Peasantry', *Works*, Russian, Vol. IX, p. 214.
[5] Brandt, *op. cit.*, pp. 149–50.
[6] R. C. North, *Kuomintang and Chinese Communist Elites*, Stanford, 1952, p. 32.

have a single healthy Party nucleus among the industrial workers'.[7] It was admitted officially that workers comprised only 10 per cent of the Party in 1928, 3 per cent in 1929, 2·5 per cent in March 1930, 1·6 per cent in September of the same year, and virtually nothing at the end of the year.[8] From then and until Mao's final victory the Party had no industrial workers to speak of.

For a number of years the party was confined to insurgent peasant movements deep in the provinces of Central China where it established a Chinese Soviet Republic; later, after a military defeat in the Central provinces (1934), it moved to Northern Shensi, in the North-West. In both these areas there was practically no industrial working class to speak of. The peasant nature of the Party's social basis could not be better symbolised than in the 'capital', Yenan. This consisted of a cluster of small villages made up of caves dug in the loess cliffs and a population of 1,000 when Mao chose it as his residence and headquarters for the next twelve years. A Comintern organ was not exaggerating when it wrote that 'the Border Region is socially and economically one of the most backward regions of China'.[9] Chu Teh repeated: 'The regions under the direction of the Communists are the most backward economically in the whole country . . .'[10] Not one real town came under the control of the Communists until a couple of years before the establishment of the Chinese People's Republic.

Palpable evidence of the unimportance attached to worker elements in Communist Party strategy during the period of Mao's rise to power is the fact that the Party did not find it necessary to convene a National Congress of Trade Unions for 19 years after the one held in 1929. Further, it did not even seek workers' support, as witness its declaration that it did not intend to maintain any Party organisations in the Kuomintang controlled areas during the crucial years 1937–45.[11] When the Kuomintang Government in December 1937 decreed the death penalty for

[7] H. R. Isaacs, *The Tragedy of the Chinese Revolution*, London, 1938, p. 333.
[8] *Ibid.*, p. 394.
[9] *World News and Views*, April 22, 1939.
[10] S. Gelder, *The Chinese Communists*, London, 1946, p. 167.
[11] See Communist Manifesto published in Chungking on November 23, 1938, NYT, November 24, 1938.

workers who went on strike or even agitated for a strike while the war was in progress, a Communist Party spokesman told an interviewer that the Party was 'fully satisfied' with the Kuomintang's conduct of the war.[12] Even after the outbreak of civil war between the Communist Party and the Kuomintang, hardly any Communist Party organisations existed in the Kuomintang areas, which included all the industrial centres in the country.

The PLA's conquest of the towns exposed more than anything else the Communist Party's complete divorce from the industrial working class. On May 30, 1925, the Shanghai workers had focussed the attention of the world on themselves through a general strike which paralysed the city. These same workers reached an even more significant level of activity in March 1927, when, in a combined general strike and armed uprising, they seized the city, and then, on Communist Party instructions, handed it over to Chiang Kai-shek's army. No such proletarian uprising greeted the PLA.

In fact, the Communist leaders did their best to prevent any workers' uprisings in the towns on the eve of their being taken. Thus, before the fall of Tientsin and Peking, the commander of the front, General Lin Piao, issued a proclamation saying:

> The people are asked to maintain order and continue in their present occupations.
> Kuomintang officials or police personnel of provincial, city, county or other level of government institution; district, town, village or *pao chia* personnel . . . are enjoined to remain at their posts . . .[13]

At the time of the crossing of the Yangtze River, before the great cities of Central and South China (Shanghai, Hankow, Canton) fell to them, Mao and Chu Teh again issued a special proclamation stating among other things:

> It is hoped that workers and employees in all trades will continue to work and that business will operate as usual.
> . . . officials of the Kuomintang Central, Provincial, Municipal

---

[12] Isaacs, *op. cit.*, p. 456.
[13] NCNA, January 11, 1949.

or County Governments of various levels, or delegates of the 'National Assembly', members of the Legislative and Control Yuans or People's Political Council members, police personnel and heads of 'Pao Chia' organisations . . . are to stay at their posts, obey the orders of the PLA and People's Government.[14]

The working class obliged and remained inert. A report from Nanking on April 22, 1949, two days before the PLA occupied it, described the situation thus:

Nanking's populace is showing no signs of excitement. Curious crowds were seen this morning to gather at the river wall to watch the gun duel on the opposite side of the river.

Business is going on as usual. Some shops are closed, but it is due to lack of business. . . . Movie houses are still showing to packed houses.[15]

A month later a *New York Times* correspondent wrote from Shanghai: 'The Red troops began putting up posters in Chinese instructing the populace to be calm and assuring them they had nothing to fear.'[16] In Canton: 'After their entry the Communists made contact with the police station, and instructed the officers and men to remain at their posts to keep order.'[17]

After occupying the towns Mao followed a consistent policy of regimenting and atomising the working class, and subordinating it to State and Party.

NO RIGHT TO STRIKE

A few months after they took Shanghai, the Communist leaders found it necessary to have a policy for labour disputes. On August 19, 1949, the Shanghai Military Control Commission of the People's Liberation Army issued a *Provisional Procedure for the Mediating and Settlement of Labour-Capital Disputes in Private Enterprises.*[18] This was later copied, almost word for word, into the new

[14] NCNA, May 3, 1949.
[15] *North China Daily News*, April 23, 1949.
[16] NYT, May 25, 1949.
[17] *South China Morning Post*, October 17, 1949.
[18] NCNA, Shanghai, September 7, 1949.

Regulations Governing the Procedures for the Settlement of Labour Disputes (ratified by the GAC on November 16, 1950), applicable to the whole country.

The leitmotif of the *Regulations* is 'the principle of "equal regard for public and private interests, mutual benefits for both labour and capital, development of production, the thriving of the economy".' (Article 1.) The following three steps, and these only, are to be taken in labour disputes:

> The first step in the procedure for settling labour disputes shall be consultation between the two parties; the second step shall be mediation by the Labour Bureau [appointed by the Government], and the third step shall be arbitration by the arbitration committee established by the Labour Bureau. (Article 6).

Dotting i's and crossing t's the *Regulations* states:

> After a dispute has broken out, both parties, during the period of consultation, mediation or arbitration, shall maintain the status quo in production. The management should not resort to a lock-out, suspend payment of wages, cease providing meals or take any other measures which lower the workers' living conditions. Labour shall also maintain production and observe labour discipline. After arbitration by the Labour Bureau, even if one party disagrees and calls for settlement by the court, the two parties shall, nevertheless, abide by the arbitration award pending the verdict of the court.

To crown all, the decision of the People's Court is final and binding.[19]

This imposition of compulsory arbitration in place of freedom to strike completely contradicts the traditions of the Communist Party itself during the first decade or so of its existence, not to speak of the labour movement in other countries. On June 10, 1922, the Party issued *The First Manifesto of the CCP on the Current Situation* which included the demand: 'Freedom to strike.'[20] The *Manifesto of the Second National Congress of the CCP* (July 1922) also claimed 'the unlimited right to . . . strike'.[21] Similarly the Canton

[19] NCNA, Peking, November 25, 1950.
[20] Brandt, *op. cit.*, p. 63.
[21] *Ibid.*, p. 64.

Commune in December 1927 included in its programme 'the right to organise and strike'.[22] Four years later, in 1931, the Labour Code of the Chinese Soviet Republic again declared: 'The Soviets guarantee freedom of action to the trade unions. The unions shall have the right to declare strikes and to lead them . . .' (Article 59).[23]

While the 1950 *Regulations* can find no support in the traditions of the labour movement or of the Chinese Communist Party, they can find an exact replica in the labour policy of the Kuomintang. The Kuomintang Government in June 1928, decreed an *Act Concerning the Settlement of Labour Disputes* which prohibited strikes and imposed compulsory arbitration.[24] In October 1942, the Kuomintang Government passed the *Regulations Governing Labour Policy in Time of Emergency*, which again prohibited strikes.[25] The Labour Programme adopted on May 17, 1945, stated: 'Labour unions . . . shall use arbitration and mediation to settle disputes between labour and capital.'[26]

LABOUR DISCIPLINE CODE

Prohibition of strikes and the imposition of compulsory arbitration are insufficient by themselves to guarantee that the workers, collectively or individually, will be disciplined. The worker can resort to other means of defence: absenteeism, coming late to work, the go-slow, deliberately producing shoddy goods, damaging equipment, and so on. To close these loopholes, the Peking Government repeatedly issued regulations, admonishing the workers to abide by labour discipline. The *Outline of Labour Regulations for State-Operated Enterprises*, issued on May 6, 1954, states:

Late arrival or early departure without good reason, or playing around or sitting idle during working hours shall be subject to proper punishment or dismissal, as the case may require (Article 17).

If due to non-observance of working procedures or irresponsibility,

[22] Isaacs, *op. cit.*, p. 365.
[23] *Fundamental Laws of the Chinese Soviet Republic, op. cit.*, pp. 62–3.
[24] A. B. Wagner, *Labour Legislation in China*, Peking, 1938, pp. 227–9.
[25] N. Wales, *The Chinese Labor Movement*, New York, 1945, p. 108.
[26] *China Handbook, 1937–1945*, New York, 1947, p. 51.

rejects are turned out or the tools and equipment are damaged, the worker or staff member shall be held responsible for part or whole payment of compensation for the material loss as conditions may require, whether he is punished or not. The amount of compensation shall be decided by the management and deducted from his wages until it is completely paid up, but the maximum amount to be deducted each time must not exceed 30 per cent of his actual monthly wages. If he corrects his error immediately and this is proved by concrete facts, the amount of compensation may be reduced, as the case may be (Article 21).

Workers and staff members breaching labour discipline shall be subject to the following disciplinary action by the management, as conditions may warrant:

(1) To be served warning.
(2) To be given demerit.
(3) to be given a major demerit.
(4) To be transferred to work with lower pay, or to be demoted (either in grade or in post) (Article 15).[27]

To ensure that management does not cover up breaches of labour discipline, the *Outline* stipulates:

Except for cases of a complicated nature which the management cannot dispose of in time with good reason, penalty shall be meted out to the responsible administrative personnel who fail to carry out the sanctions within the time limit (Article 18).

THE LABOUR BOOK

To strengthen labour discipline, a Labour Book was introduced by the Ministry of Labour. This has to be shown to the director of an enterprise whenever a worker takes on a job. The *Outline of Labour Regulations for State-Operated Enterprises*, mentioned above, states:

Workers and staff members applying for employment should submit to the management of an enterprise papers certifying their past record issued by the office where they previously worked, or a certificate issued by the labour office of the local people's government.

[27] JMJP, July 14, 1954; SCMP, 859.

If the applicant has had no previous experience, he should produce a certificate issued by a government organ of the *chu* where he resides, or identity papers issued by his school. No employment can be given without any of the above papers (Article 1).[28]

Obviously, a worker cannot get a new job under these conditions unless he carries a satisfactory certificate from his old employer. The Labour Book helps the Ministry of Labour to keep firm control over the employment and movement of workers.

And firm this control certainly is. The need for a permit to leave a place of work was dramatically highlighted in a case of arson at the Matien Coal Mine in Hunan in July 1954, in which 44 workers were killed. The *China Youth Journal* gave the following explanation for the crime of Liang Chung-shu, a miner:

In July this year, he heard that the wages were higher at a certain coal mine in Kwangtung and wanted to go over there. In order to realise his mean and selfish end, he resorted to the venomous measure of arson, thinking that once the mine was destroyed, the workers would have no work to do and no dormitories to stay in and he would be free to apply for a transfer.[29]

THE JUDICIARY INTERVENES

Law, to be effective, must be supported by the power to execute it. The Labour Bureaus, which have semi-judicial functions, and the People's Courts, play a role in this connection. Two other institutions have been created specifically to deal with breaches of labour discipline—industrial tribunals and workers' courts. The Second All-China Judiciary Conference convened in Peking in April 1953 resolved 'to carry out the gradual and selective establishment of special tribunals in industrial and mining districts and along railway lines and waterways',[30] for the preservation of labour discipline. Steps were soon taken to put this resolution into effect: 'The regional people's courts under the Supreme People's Court have established or are setting up 22 special tribunals in

[28] JMJP, July 14, 1954; SCMP, 859.
[29] CKCNP, December 2, 1954; SCMP, 947.
[30] NCNA, Peking, May 12, 1953; SCMP, 573.

factory and mine districts and along railway lines.'[31] These
courts appear to be very busy. One report states that the Tientsin
Railway Special Court dealt with 61 cases involving breach of
labour discipline in two months.[32]

Workers' courts in factories are 'elected' from among the
workers and employees of the plant.

> The candidates should be named by the broad workers and staff
> members. . . . The general practice is to have the candidates
> named jointly by the Party organ, the management, the trade union
> and the Youth League. After consideration and discussion by the
> workers and staff members, election can be held by ballot or show
> of hands at a meeting of workers and staff members or a workers'
> and staff members' representative meeting.[33]

The courts are 'set-up . . . under the active assistance and guidance
of the local people's court.'[34]

> It is charged with the responsibility of settling labour and pro-
> duction discipline cases found among the workers and staff members
> (after such cases have been handed over or agreed upon by the
> management or leadership), such as breach of labour discipline,
> delinquency of duty, minor cases of theft, and disputes among the
> workers and staff members. The measures of education and sanction
> to be given by the court are generally: criticism before the public,
> admission of error and apology, warning, suggestion to the manage-
> ment of the production enterprise for demerit, reduction of salary,
> demotion, suspension or dismissal.[35]

WORKERS VIOLATE LABOUR DISCIPLINE

Despite the law, judiciary and police, and the trade unions
(which also play an important role in disciplining the workers),[36]
workers' performance is disappointing to Peking. Again and again

[31] NCNA, Peking, September 3, 1953; SCMP, 648.
[32] NCNA, Tientsin, February 15, 1954.
[33] 'Explaining the Workers' Court in Production Enterprises', JMJP, February
18, 1954; SCMP, 754.
[34] Ibid.
[35] Ibid.
[36] See p. 233-50.

widespread breaches of all laws and regulations by 'anarchist' workers are reported. The *People's Daily* of July 8, 1953, listed some of these:

> The state of slackened labour discipline is more common now than before, as manifest in the following aspects:
>
> *First*, the rate of absenteeism, sick leave and leave of absence increased while the attendance rate decreased. Statistics of Tientsin's 99 state-operated and local state-operated units revealed that in January and February this year, a total of 196,149 working days, equal to 4,251 workers absent from work for two months, were lost due to absenteeism on the part of workers. In some factories, the rate of absence was as high as 30 per cent . . .
>
> *Second*, the workers arrived late. . . . At the end of the day, they did not wait until the working hours were finished before they went to wash their hands and waited to leave. During the working hours, they fooled around and kept themselves idle or worked at a low speed.
>
> *Third*, the workers did not observe the factory regulations, the working rules, the safety measures and violated the working procedures . . .
>
> *Fourth*, the workers took little care of their tools and machines and wasted much raw material . . .
>
> *Fifth*, a large number of defective pieces and rejects were produced, due to no attention being paid to the quality of products. Preoccupied with the desire to fulfil the target, some workers paid little attention to the quality of their products and sought to deceive the inspectors by masquerading the defective pieces and rejects as good pieces.[37]

Details to substantiate this over-all picture can be supplied from many localities. Indeed there is such a wealth of examples that it would be well to limit the evidence to reports covering the space of a couple of months. The *Daily Worker* of June 5, 1953, dealt with absenteeism in Shanghai factories:

> The attendance rate of workers of the No. 15 Mill of the state-operated Shanghai Cotton Mills is very low. In April, of the 643 workers of the fine yarn workshop, 117 asked for leave of absence.

[37] JMJP, July 8, 1953; SCMP, 631.

Many of the workers on leave of absence did so to play around . . .
According to statistics, about 20 per cent of the sick leave was taken
on false pretences. [38]

NCNA gives another report:

The relaxation of labour discipline finds its expression mainly in
asking for sick leave while the workers are not sick, asking for leave
of absence under false pretences, and asking for absence from duty
for no valid reasons . . . A small part of the workers in some of
the factories even resorted to all sorts of irregular means to get a
sick-leave slip from the doctor. They pretended to be afflicted with
headache, abdominal pain and general malaise, which are difficult
to diagnose, or even take some hot pepper and hot water before
they go to the clinic for their temperature to be taken. [39]

A similar report came from Peking. A *Daily Worker* article entitled
'Slack Labour Discipline in Peking's Factories and Mines', said:

Of the 18 local state-operated and municipal enterprises of the
city, only 10 maintained a 90-per cent attendance record of workers
during the past three months. The 5th Flour Mill of Peking in the
first quarter of the year showed an average attendance record of
only 73·5 per cent. The local state-operated enterprises of the city
showed a total leave of absence of 355,816 working hours or 44,477
working days in the first quarter of the year. Of this 28·9 per cent
represents leave of absence for personal affairs or for no reason at
all. The situation is also serious in state-operated factories and mines
where the attendance rate of workers is low. For instance, the
workers' attendance rate for April at Ch'eng Tzu Mine in the western
suburb of Peking was 89 per cent, while the lowest rate for a certain
month reached only 76 per cent. In the Railway Workshop at
Changhsintien, a total of 10,514 working days were lost through
leave of absence by workers in the first quarter of the year. For the
working days lost, repair of 12 locomotives might have been completed. [40]

The same sad story was repeated in a NCNA communiqué
describing conditions in Chungking factories:

[38] KJJP, June 5, 1953; SCMP, 605.
[39] NCNA, Shanghai, July 16, 1953; SCMP, 631.
[40] KJJP, June 14, 1953; SCMP, 606.

In general, violations include reporting for work late and leaving early, asking for leave of absence without sufficient justification, or even being absent without obtaining leave. For instance, statistics for No. 610 Factory for the month of April show that workers who applied for incidental or sick leave, or were absent without leave, numbered 1,063 (leave of absence for child-birth, weddings and funerals excluded). In all, 5,084 workdays were lost. Many of those who obtained leave did not need it.

Some workers intimidated doctors into signing medical certificates for sick leave although they were not sick, and spent the time away from work seeking pleasure. Others have habitually been late for work, or have often taken time off to play during working hours. [41]

In Tientsin the situation was no better.

The state of slackness of labour discipline is rather serious in some of the state-operated factories in Tientsin. . . . According to statistics of 99 state-operated and local state-operated units in Tientsin, a total number of 196,000 working days, equal to 4,200 workers' absence from duty for two months, was lost during January and February alone. The situation is comparatively more serious in the Second Factory of the Tientsin State-operated Cotton Mill where during the first quarter of the year 30,540 working days, equal to 985 workers leaving production for the whole month of March, were lost. [42]

A few months later, a *People's Daily* editorial of December 13, 1953, wrote the following:

According to the statistics of the 92 factories of the First Ministry of Machine Building Industry of the CPG for the first half of the year, the workers' idleness or absence from work amounted to a total of over 1,300,000 workdays, equal to 8,800 persons laying off for 6 months. [43]

As an example of the triumph of 'Communist education' the *Daily Worker* made the following report: 'In the Shansi Coal Mine

[41] NCNA, Chungking, June 26, 1953; SCMP, 631.
[42] KJJP, June 3, 1953; SCMP, 605.
[43] JMJP, December 13, 1953; SCMP, 709.

the attendance rate for May was 80 per cent, but following education on labour discipline it went up to 85 per cent.'[44]

Another accusation levelled at workers is that they conduct
'go-slow strikes'. The *People's Daily* repeatedly urges workers to
'combat go-slow strikes and negligence of duties in State organs
and production enterprises',[45] to struggle against workers who
'stage go-slow strikes',[46] against 'counter-revolutionaries' who
'organise go-slow strikes';[47] it complains of 'a large number of
cases involving counter-revolutionary sabotage, corruption and
theft, delinquency of duty and go-slow strikes causing tremendous
losses to State property'.[48] In all probability, 'go-slow strikes' in
most instances cover cases of workers who simply cannot keep
pace with 'model workers', the Chinese Stakhanovites. But
possibly, in some cases at least, there is a little fire behind the
smoke. Go-slow strikes are certainly in the tradition of the Chinese
labour movement, and during the 'thirties were its most prevalent
form of struggle.[49]

Accusations for violating labour discipline are numberless. The
violators are frequently called 'anarchists', the causes for
'anarchism' being given as 'bourgeois predilection for indolence,
pleasure, selfishness, bourgeois individualism and liberal laxity.'[50]
But sometimes the attack unwittingly reveals the major real
causes for slackness—poor health, the difficulty of the work, bad
housing, too many meetings which tire the workers, and so on.
These causes were brought out by the National Committee of the
All-China Textile Workers' Trade Union when proposing measures to combat absenteeism:

> To strengthen health work in summer, as sickness has been the
> biggest reason for absence. Special attention should be given to the
> hygiene of the masses, especially their problem of food, so as to
> minimise gastro-intestinal diseases.

[44] KJJP, August 5, 1953; SCMP, 637.
[45] JMJP, March 30, 1954.
[46] JMJP, June 6, 1954.
[47] JMJP, August 20, 1954.
[48] NCNA, Peking, September 8, 1954.
[49] See W. E. Gourlay, '"Yellow" Unionism in Shanghai: A Study of Kuomintang
Technique in Labour Control, 1927–1937', *Papers on China*, Volume 7, February 1953.
[50] JMJP, July 8, 1953; SCMP, 608.

To improve labour conditions by checking up the ventilation facilities. . . .

To reduce the rate of thread-breaking so as to reduce the fatigue of workers, as this has a direct bearing on the attendance rate of workers. . . .

To reduce the number of meetings as much as possible. Too many meetings for too long a duration have taxed the workers' energy too much and badly affected their health. Spare time should be scientifically distributed and the duration of meetings shortened and strictly restricted to assure the workers their rest.

. . . Poor dormitory conditions depriving the workers of enough rest has been one of the causes for sickness.[51]

Another important fact emerges from the descriptions of labour indiscipline: in many cases even the cadres prove unequal to the task of egging on the workers. There are Party members who 'choose to wink at acts of violation' of labour discipline, justifying their action by the thought that they are 'protecting the interests of the working class'.[52] The *People's Daily* complained:

The leadership cadres in some of our departments and enterprises have cherished an erroneous conception of the problem of labour discipline, considering that strict implementation of discipline is a 'capitalist way of management', a 'warlord's style of work', or 'commandism'. Therefore they consciously or unconsciously adopt a compromising attitude towards acts of breach of labour discipline, nor do they take any drastic action against them.[53]

The same paper repeats the theme some weeks later:

Some Party committees and branches . . . take little heed of the state of labour discipline of their units. . . . They have never . . . urged the management to deal drastically with acts of breach of labour discipline.[54]

[51] KJJP, June 4, 1953; SCMP, 605.
[52] KJJP, June 14, 1953; SCMP, 606.
[53] JMJP, October 22, 1954; SCMP, 922.
[54] JMJP, November 16, 1954; SCMP, 939.

CHAPTER XII

INCREASING INEQUALITIES AMONG WORKERS; STAKHANOVISM

The whip is a severely limited weapon for imposing labour discipline. Carelessness on the part of workers can be very costly, especially in modern industry with its delicate machinery. Absenteeism keeps expensive machinery still. A high labour turn-over means time and money lost in training newcomers. The attitude of workers to production in modern industry is therefore a factor of prime importance for efficiency. To cudgel workers is consequently quite insufficient. It might well be dangerous, for behind a façade of obedience a worker can carry on the old Chinese tradition of passive obstruction and evasion of government decrees, demands and prohibitions. He has to be motivated to work by self-interest as well. The carrot must accompany the knout.

The cheapest means of harnessing self-interest to production is the piece-work system, which uses big wage differences to sharpen the rivalry between workers. The acutest form of such competition is Stakhanovism.

While a large modern industrial plant undoubtedly acts as a powerful objective factor in integrating the workers as a class, employers have at their disposal a number of effective methods of disrupting this unity. The piece-work system is one of the most important. The same threat of hunger which can impel workers to unite against their employers, may also be made to stir up a fight for survival amongst the workers themselves.

A regime that resorted to piecework on a large scale was the Nazis'. They were very insistent on spreading the system for the following reason:

> The preponderance of the performance wage brings the problem of wage differentials into the forefront of social policy. It is essential that this problem be understood not as an economic question but as the *crucial political problem of mass control.* . . . Wage differentiation

is the very essence of National Socialist wage policy . . . the wage policy is consciously aimed at mass manipulation. [1]

The Russian leaders and Mao use piecework for the same purpose. But here its socio-political purpose is intertwined with the economic purpose of keeping the worker on his toes, and getting the maximum labour out of him. [2] To fulfil this role, the wage system must make the differentials between workers of different skills as wide as possible. Li Li-san, at the time Minister of Labour, stated curtly: 'We oppose egalitarianism in wage payments. . . .' [3] The differentials that existed under Kuomintang rule were insufficient for Communist purposes, as Li I-ch'ing, Deputy Chairman, Finance and Economic Committee, Central-South MAC, made clear:

> The multi-grade wage system of KMT rule was confusing and the difference between the grades rather small. This resulted in serious egalitarianism and affected the working morale and labour ardour of the workers and staff members. [4]

In point of fact the wage differentials in Kuomintang China were tremendous. For instance, a male worker's average monthly wage in cotton spinning in 1928 was 15·16 Chinese dollars, while that of the average printer was 44·75 Chinese dollars. The differences would show up even more if the wages of an unskilled labourer in the spinning industry were compared with those of a highly skilled printer.

All historical experience testifies that the fewer the workers' rights and the more downtrodden they are, the greater are the wage differentials, and especially between skilled and unskilled workers. [5]

Returning to the attack on egalitarianism, the *Yangtze Daily* opposes all the factors in the wage system which work towards

---

[1] F. Neumann, *Behemoth*, London, 1942, p. 353. My emphasis.
[2] For an elaborate analysis of the piece-work system in Russia, see T. Cliff, *Stalinist Russia. A Marxist Analysis*, London, 1955, pp. 8–11.
[3] Li Li-san, 'The Labour Movement in China', PC, January 16, 1950.
[4] CCJP, September 29, 1952; SCMP, 466.
[5] This is clearly illustrated by the following table comparing the wages of skilled

equality and urges the necessity 'of overcoming any considerations as to length of services, family burdens, labour attitude, political manifestations, or any such points which should not be mixed up with skill when the technical standard is fixed for wage-grading.'[6]

These principles pervade all the wage scales issued by the Communist authorities. These are not issued uniformly for the whole country. Each of the six administrative regions into which the country was divided between 1949 and 1953 issued its own wage scale, but as they were not very different from each other, a description of one—that of Central-South China—will serve as an illustration for all.

The wage system for Central-South China was embodied in the *Provisional Regulations Concerning Wages in State-operated Factories, Mines and Communications Enterprises*, promulgated by the Central-South MAC on August 16, 1952.[7] Its first aim was, 'in accordance with the technical complexity existing in various industries, to facilitate the promotion of the piecework system and encourage the workers' technical progress as well as to overcome the serious egalitarianism in wages . . .' (Article 2). All branches of industry were divided into eight groups, beginning with coal mining, iron and steel, non-ferrous mining, and ending with match and tobacco

---

and unskilled workers between the two world wars in an economically advanced country like Britain and a backward one like Rumania:

Skilled Wages as Percentage of Unskilled

	Pattern Makers	Fitters and Turners	Iron Moulders	Plumbers	Electricians	Brick-layers	Carpenters	Painters
Britain	131	127	130	147	152	147	147	146
Rumania	200	210	252	300	182	265	223	275

(Clark, *Conditions of Economic Progress*, Second Edition, *op. cit.*, p. 460). Or to take another example: '. . . a locomotive engineer of ordinary length of service and rating receives 3·3 times the wages of an unskilled man of ordinary length of service in Spain, while in New Zealand the ratio is only 1·2' (*ibid.*, p. 461).

The history of the workers' movement in Russia shows that whenever it was powerful, differences in wages diminished. Thus, for instance, during the 1905 revolution, while the wages of skilled workers in St. Petersburg metal industry rose by only 12 per cent, those of apprentices rose by 22 per cent, and of unskilled workers by 18 per cent, thus diminishing the differential between skilled and unskilled workers and apprentices (F. Semonov and Associates, *The Proletariat in the Revolution of 1905–1907* (Russian), Moscow-Leningrad, 1930, p. 32).

[6] CCJP, August 17, 1952; SCMP, 414.
[7] *Ibid.*

production. Additional groups covered non-industrial occupations such as transport and communications. Within each group five categories of wages were to be established 'in accordance with the relative importance of various enterprises of the same industry in the national economy, the conditions of technical equipment, their scales and levels of production, and with due regard to the prevailing wage level . . .' (Article 4). After deciding to which of the five categories an enterprise belonged, individual wages in it were to be determined according to a table containing 7–8 grades. This did not cover general labourers and apprentices, who came under the following regulation: 'For general labourers, servants and apprentices in various individual enterprises, one to three categories of wage standards are prescribed and each category is further classified into certain grades.' 'Managing personnel, technicians and skilled workers who possess high technical knowledge and experience' were also not covered. The different industries issued a detailed wage table accompanying these regulations.

The *Regulations* contained a chapter entitled 'Disguised Wages'.

By disguised wages are meant the five kinds of allowances given in various establishments to workers and employees for housing, water supply, electricity, coal and rice (including allowances for meals) (Article 25).

These were to be abolished (Article 26) as they inclined to lessen actual wage differences and ease the pressure to work harder.

We have seen that piecework is probably the greatest factor in increasing wage differentials and counteracting the natural egalitarianism of the factory. Needless to say, its wholesale introduction directly contradicts the Communist Party's objection in principle to it in former years. For instance, in January 1925, the *Fourth Manifesto of the CCP on the Current Situation* called for the 'abolition of the piece-work system'.[8] Today, however, the piece-work system reaches a culmination in the so-called 'patriotic emulation campaign'. Already in 1950, the first year after Mao's coming to power, over 683,000 workers took part in emulation

[8] Brandt, *op. cit.*, p. 76.

campaigns. The number rose to 2,380,000 in 1951 and 2,820,000 in 1952; in 1953 80 per cent of all workers and employees took part.[9] Peasants also take part in 'patriotic emulation campaigns', and they are prevalent even in forced labour-camps.[10]

After instituting the piecework system, the first task is to fix the norm, or labour quota. One way of doing this was suggested by the *Labour Law* of the Chinese Soviet Republic issued in 1931, which stated:

> Piece-work rates must be based on the average work performed per day and the average daily wage (calculated according to the time required in the given branch of industry to produce the given article) (Article 33).

This method, quite acceptable to workers where they are free to organise in defence of their interests, is not good enough for Peking, as it does not make the workers hustle nearly enough. The average output of an average worker is therefore discarded as the norm. The Chinese Communist propaganda organ *Study* which explains that this norm is unsatisfactory, goes on to say that even output that lies somewhere between that of an average worker and a 'model worker' is not good enough, but that the output of 'model workers' alone should be taken as the norm.[11] This method of fixing the norm finds the Kuomintang method badly wanting. No wonder Li I-ch'ing bluntly attacked the Kuomintang for the fact that 'the quota set was too old and low, the unit value extraordinarily high'.[12]

Norms, once established, are not permanent. They remain in force for only a limited time, otherwise they would lose their value as an incentive. But the limited time is not too short either, because if it changed too often it would rouse opposition, and have a negative effect on workers' morale. The Communist leaders, therefore, prefer a periodic change in the norms more frequent than would be tolerated by workers with free trade unions, but not frequent enough to make the norms fluid. This need was

[9] JMJP, April 1, 1955.
[10] JMJP, May 1, 1955.
[11] Chi Yun, 'What is National Economic Plan?', HH, October 1, 1952.
[12] CCJP, September 29, 1952; SCMP, 466.

emphasised by Kao Kang, Chairman of the North-east People's Government, when he said:

> The question of norms should be solved in accordance with the norms policy stipulated by the State, and no arbitrary and frequent revision of norms is permitted as it will affect workers' production morale.[13]

On the other hand, the above-quoted *Regulations* on wages in the Central-South region stipulated that the norm could be changed as frequently as once every 'half a year' (Article 21).

'Conservatism' in fixing norms should also be avoided. Thus, at an East China Conference of Local Industries the main speaker, Tan Chen-lin, Third Secretary of the CCP's East China Bureau, stated that

> some comrades are afraid of discussing with the workers the elevation of existing norms for they consider existing norms very high already. Such a conservative view of norms is not the Marxist view. Norms always go forward. Norms which are advanced today may possibly become backward ones tomorrow. Our existing norms are a long way behind the Soviet norms.[14]

It is not surprising that with norms fixed so high many workers do not manage to fulfil them. For instance, the average output of plasterers in Liaoning Province in 1954 was 60–80 per cent of the norm fixed.[15]

Some four years after the August 1952 *Regulations*, however, it was found that the wages system was still inadequate. Thus, for instance, *Ta Kung Pao*, of May 22, 1956, in an editorial entitled, 'The Important Significance of Wage Reform', stated:

> As things stand now, egalitarianism, lack of uniformity, as well as other irrational phenomena, are much in evidence in the wages system. Wage differentials are not noticeably great. . . . There is

[13] NCNA, Mukden, June 17, 1952; SCMP, 357.
[14] NCNA, Shanghai, December 14, 1953; SCMP, 711.
[15] JMJP, September 26, 1955.

also very little difference in wages between piece-work and time-work systems. . . . The piece-work system has been extended too slowly and within too small a scope.[15a]

On June 16, 1956, the State Council passed a *Decision on the Reform of Wage Structure.*[15b] This tried to put an end to all remnants of egalitarianism, to increase wage differences, and to strengthen the piece-work system, so as to make workers hustle. The *Decision* states:

There shall be abolished the wage unit system and the commodity prices subsidy system. There shall be enforced the system of wage scales expressed directly in money. . . .

There shall be improved the system of wage grades. . . . There shall be appropriately increased the differences between the wage scales for high-grade workers and those for low-grade workers . . . and higher scales for piece-work than for time-work, so as to overcome egalitarianism in wage payment.

All work which can be calculated on piece rates shall in 1957 be fully, or mostly, brought into this system. . . .

At the same time there shall be established and perfected the system of periodical (generally annual) examination and revision of norms to ensure that the norm has a scientific foundation and comparatively advanced levels.

The title 'labour model' is conferred on the most successful workers in the emulation campaign. 'Labour models' are given material and psychological rewards which include cash bonuses, free vacations in rest houses and sanatoria, priority on housing lists, medals, write-ups and photos in the papers, invitations to be guests of honour at public receptions, personal greetings from top Government and Party leaders, and so on.

Only a small minority of workers makes the grade. At the end of 1954, only 374,340 out of some four million workers and employees in factories and mines were 'labour models'.[16] After making the grade, the 'labour model' dare not rest on his laurels.

[15a] TKP, May 22, 1956; SCMP 1314.
[15b] NCNA, Peking, July 4, 1956; SCMP 1327.
[16] JMJP, April 29, 1955; CB, 363.

Of 65 women model workers in agriculture in the province of Sinkiang in 1951, only 17 received the same recognition in 1952.[17]

Workers are often tempted into falsifying their production achievements by their desire to become 'labour models'. The *People's Daily*, for instance, reported serious falsifications of labour records by Li Yung-lu, a Communist Vice-Chairman of the Peking Committee of the National Railway Workers' Trade Union, and Hsi Neng-an, a Communist chief of the Locomotive Engineering Section of the Peking office of the Tientsin Railway Administration in an attempt to get the title of 'specially meritorious labour model'.[18] A few weeks later the *People's Daily* found it necessary to devote a long article to the subject.[19] But despite the admonition, the practice did not cease. And so on January 27, 1954, the Executive Committee of ACFTU issued a *Directive Concerning the Further Development of Emulation Drives in State-operated Industrial and Mining Enterprises* which warns: 'The criminal act of false declaration of merit to steal honour should be opposed. . . .'[20]

Sometimes the records announced are simply fantastic. For instance, a miner 'labour model', Chao Wen-hsin, is reported to have cut 243 tons of coal in 7 hours 20 minutes on March 19, 1951.[21] A fellow miner is said to have done even better and cut 254 tons of coal in one day.[22] This far surpasses even the output of the man who gave the name to the movement—Alexei Stakhanov, a coal miner who on August 31, 1935, cut 102 tons of coal in six hours. And these astonishing results are obtained in country where the average output of coal per man-day is less than half a ton! (It is true that coal cutting is merely one job in the mining process, but nevertheless the above paradox remains.) In all probability the record-breakers who cut 243 and 254 tons of coal in a day were helped by a number of assistants, had a specially chosen face to work with specially prepared tools, and other

[17] Ho Yen-lin, 'Give Model Workers Time to Labour', HCKFN, July 9, 1953.
[18] JMJP, July 19, 1952; SCMP, 386.
[19] JMJP, August 8, 1952; SCMP, 397.
[20] JMJP, April 11, 1954. Similar cases are reported by NCNA, Peking, February 7 and 27, 1953, and JMJP, March 24, 1953.
[21] PC, April 1, 1951.
[22] CR, March–April, 1952.

advantages—all facts not mentioned in order not to detract from the achievements.

However, even labour emulation has some unhealthy features from Peking's standpoint. Record-breaking might mean harm to precious machines, can make for the production of shoddy goods, and lead to serious accidents. It tends to degenerate to simple shock work, an unwished for consummation recognised by the leaders. Lai Jo-yu, Chairman of the ACFTU, complained of this when he said:

> Labour emulation is taken as a means of shock work: labour emulation is not organised in ordinary time, and it is only organised when tasks are urgent or cannot be completed. Moreover, labour emulation is simply regarded as an increase in shifts and working hours. Thus it is not well understood that labour emulation should be a regular mode of labour.

Moreover, shock work had detrimental results, as Lai Jo-yu pointed out:

> Increasing shifts and working hours to finish jobs through shock work impaired workers' health, caused deterioration of the quality of products, and incurred payment of additional wages, thus wasting manpower, resources and money.[23]

Sometimes the emulation drives are pursued only for a short time and in honour of national occasions. This, too, is not to Peking's satisfaction. Thus a *People's Daily* editorial complained of enterprises which 'only mobilise the workers for such a drive once a year around May Day or the National Day'.[24]

All in all, however, there is no doubt that labour emulation is a powerful accelerator of production. It is more effective than all disciplinary legislation in chaining the workers to production, in drawing the last ounce of energy out of them, and in keeping them a disunited, amorphous mass.

[23] Lai Jo-yu's speech to the National People's Congress, NCNA, Peking, July 21, 1955.
[24] JMJP, May 29, 1955; SCMP, 1063.

CHAPTER XIII

THE ROLE OF THE TRADE UNIONS

THE AIM OF THE TRADE UNIONS TO BOOST PRODUCTION

In appealing to the personal interests of the workers through their fear of the law or their desire for material improvement, the Communist leaders further the atomisation of the working class. But in order to transmit their appeals, they must have the workers organised in some manner. This difficulty is solved by means of the unions which serve as an organisation for the workers while at the same time they are deprived of all independent power and initiative. Their role is that of a conveyor belt, transmitting the will of the rulers to the workers.

The Communist leaders do not conceal the fact that the main function of the trade unions is to boost production. Thus Li Li-san, Minister of Labour and Vice-President of the ACFL, declared that the struggle for increased production is 'the most fundamental task of the Chinese trade unions'.[1] Similarly an ACFL Report on work in the year May 1, 1949–May 1, 1950, stated: 'The direction marked out for trade-union work is production.'[2] Lai Jo-yu, present chairman of ACFTU, declared: 'The paramount, constant work of trade unions in a people's State is to rally and guide all the workers, technicians and employees in patriotic emulation consciously and actively to work for the growth of production.'[3] To ensure that the trade unions pay sufficient attention to production, 'attached to each trade union is a production department, and once a measure beneficial to the cause of production is devised, it is immediately popularised all over the country.'[4]

This motif of production also runs through arrangements which elsewhere serve to defend workers' interests, namely collective agreements. In China the aim of the 'collective agreements'

[1] Li Li-san, 'The Labour Movement in China', PC, January 16, 1950.
[2] CKKJ, May 1, 1950; CB, 24.
[3] NCNA, Peking, May 14, 1953.
[4] CKKJ, May 1, 1950; CB, 24.

made out between the factory director and the Chairman of the trade union, is above all to increase production. An article in the *Daily Worker* dealing with the subject begins with the following sentence: 'Collective agreements are the best means for organising all employees and workers to launch labour emulation campaigns and for ensuring the overall and balanced fulfilment and overfulfilment of the State plan.' The article highlights this motif in its list of the main provisions to be included in 'collective agreements':

(1) After discussion by the masses, various targets in the factory's production plan should be included in the collective agreement as the total objective for the common struggle of all workers, engineering and technical personnel, and employees.

(2) The main problems which must be solved in order to fulfil the total objective of the agreement should be pointed out, and provisions should be made for the various practicable demands of workshops, sections, and departments for solving these problems and for the implementation of technical measures.

(3) Provision should be made for the propagation of various kinds of advanced experience.

(4) Measures should be put in hand for strengthening labour discipline.[5]

It is only natural that when the trade unions, and with them their instrument, 'collective agreements', are harnessed to boosting production, too much attention to workers' welfare—'economism'—becomes a target of abuse. Thus Li Li-san insisted on the necessity

. . . of correcting the workers' persistent habit of occupying themselves exclusively with their own interests without taking into account the general interests. . . . Of correcting the error of workers who in their own narrow interests make exaggerated, inadmissible demands.[6]

Likewise, the annual report of the ACFL on May 1, 1950, emphasised: 'The idea of engaging in production merely for

[5] KJJP, October 18, 1953; SCMP, 705.
[6] Documentation Francaise, *La Situation Interieure de la Chine*, Volume II, p. 37.

welfare's sake must be given up.'[7] Time and again the press rebukes workers for being selfish and interested only in their own welfare. Thus workers of the Woosung Machine Factory in Shanghai were told that they 'spoke merely from the standpoint of individual welfare and did not sufficiently recognise that the State must accumulate capital to strengthen its defence and develop its industry.'[8]

But it seems that Li Li-san and the other trade-union leaders did not go far enough in subordinating welfare to production, as a couple of years later they themselves were criticised for 'economist deviation'. Lai Jo-yu stated in his report to the Seventh Congress of ACFTU (May 1953): 'It should be pointed out . . . that the leadership of the All-China Federation of Trade Unions . . . has committed mistakes of economist and syndicalist tendencies.'[9] How was this 'economism' of the national leadership of the trade unions expressed? Mainly in excessive demands for workers' welfare: 'In the matter of welfare and living conditions of the workers, account is not taken of actual possibilities and needs.'[10] Lai Jo-yu underlined the pressing need: 'The immediate and sectional interests of the working class must be subordinated to the long-term and over-all interests of the state, that is, the interests of the state led by the working class.'[11] Of course it is the State, that is, the Communist leadership, that decides what are the 'long-term and over-all interests' of the working class!

But workers are not easily immunised against 'economism'. Life proves to them daily that they get only part of what they produce. Take, for instance, the information contained in a *People's Daily* editorial entitled 'Workers Struggle for the Realisation of Socialist Industrialisation':

In 1952, the workers of State-operated enterprises produced a yearly average value of JMP 100,000,000 *per capita*. Of this, except for JMP 500,000 as the average monthly wage for each worker, 94 per cent directly represented capital created for the State.[12]

[7] CKKJ, May 1, 1950; CB, 24.
[8] CFJP, June 25, 1952; SCMP, 375.
[9] *The Seventh All-China Congress of Trade Unions*, Peking, 1953, p. 52.
[10] *Ibid.*, p. 66.
[11] *Ibid.*, p. 54.
[12] JMJP, December 13, 1953; SCMP, 709.

Even if these figures are exaggerated, both as regards wages and even more as regards productivity, they show clearly how extreme the exploitation of the workers is. What wonder that some workers

> do not see clearly the relation between the interests of the individuals and the interests of the State, between temporary interests and permanent interests, and, regardless of the financial ability of the State, demand too high wages, amenities and living conditions.[13]

Are they to blame for not understanding that it is necessary to make 'the interests of individuals subordinate to those of the State and temporary interests to permanant interests . . .'?[14]

Doubts about the absence of exploitation in state industry occupy workers' thoughts. Even in Woosung Machine Factory in Shanghai, which gained high praise for its political education, workers seemed dissatisfied on this score.

> We once posed such a subject: 'Does exploitation still exist in our Woosung Factory?' The various opinions expressed in the discussion showed that there was much confusion in the workers' appreciation of this matter. Quite a number of persons were of the opinion that exploitation still existed . . . Some spoke merely from the standpoint of individual welfare . . .[15]

Workers, 'misunderstanding the nature of our State-operated enterprises' could go so far as to

> compare the relationship between the working-class and the State-operated enterprises with that between the working-class under the Kuomintang reactionary rule and the capitalist enterprises. The State-operated enterprises have been viewed as the same as the capitalist enterprises. The raising of material and cultural life of the workers has been placed in opposition to the development of production. . . . Evidently this is utterly erroneous.[16]

[13] JMJP, December 13, 1953; SCMP, 709.
[14] *Ibid.*
[15] CFJP, June 25, 1952; SCMP, 375.
[16] JMJP, February 7, 1953; SCMP, 516.

'Evidently' to the *People's Daily*, but not, it seems, to the workers! But when the ACFL does such things as praise the Wusan Factory for raising productivity in 1952 by 447 per cent, but average wages by only 77 per cent,[17] is it to be wondered at that workers think that brutal exploitation gets commendation and that they themselves should resist exploitation! Li I-chi'ing, in a report on wage reform in the Central-South region, stated in so many words that exploitation was to continue: 'The increase in wage scale must follow the increase in labour productivity and the former must be slow and lower than the latter . . .'[18]

THE COMMUNIST PARTY AND THE TRADE UNIONS

The Communist leaders make no effort to disguise the complete subordination of the trade unions to the Party. Thus a *People's Daily* editorial says:

> The Communist Party is the highest organisational form of the working-class, while the trade union is the mass organisation of the working-class, and must, under the centralised leadership of the Communist Party, serve as a bridge between the Party and the working-class.[19]

Elaborating the theme, Lai Jo-yu, Chairman of ACFTU, wrote:

> How should union organisations carry out Party policies and decisions?
> That union organisations must work under the leadership of the Communist Party is an unalterable principle. 'Not a single important decision is arrived at by the mass organisations of the proletariat without guiding directions from the Party.' (Stalin, *On the Problems of Leninism*) . . . the union's function is to strive to attain the objective pointed out by the Party, to carry out the Party's policies and decisions.[20]

The question of how a trade-union official should act in the event of conflict between the instructions of the trade-union

[17] NCNA, Peking, January 3, 1953; SCMP, 488.
[18] CCJP, September 29, 1952; SCMP, 466.
[19] NCNA, Peking, February 7, 1953; SCMP, 516.
[20] KJJP, December 18, 1954; SCMP, 1024.

leadership and those of the Party is on the whole irrelevant to conditions in China where the whole apparatus of the trade unions from top to bottom is Communist-dominated. But sometimes small disagreements do occur. Lai Jo-yu commented on the correct attitude to take in such a case. Describing the position prior to the defeat of Li Li-san's 'economist' leadership of the All-China Federation of Trade Unions, that is, prior to his own ascendancy, he said:

> . . . trade unions in various localities, under the correct leadership of the local Communist Party organisations, did not accept much of the incorrect advice from the All-China Federation of Trade Unions.[21]

The moral is clear. It is the duty of trade-union officials who are members of the Communist Party to carry out Party instructions in their union work even when they clash with the instructions of the higher bodies of the union.

Communist domination of the unions is abundantly clear from the fact that the Chairman, two of the three Vice-Chairmen and all the eight members of the Central Secretariat of the ACFTU are CCP members. It is even more clearly shown in the manner of appointment of this leadership. Take, for instance, the case of Lai Jo-yu, the present chairman. He has no roots in the Chinese Labour movement, and was not prominent in it until a short time before his 'election' to his present position. He was not on the 53-man Executive Committee elected by the Sixth Congress of the ACFL at Harbin in August 1948, nor was his name on the list of officials of major trade unions attending the Congress. It is doubtful whether he was even present. The first time his name appeared in a Communist source was in *Tu Pao Shou Tse, 1950* (*Handbook for Newspaper Reading, 1950*), issued by the Hankow *Yangtze Daily*. Here he was listed as one of the 31 members of the people's Government Council of Shansi Province as well as the Deputy Secretary of the Shansi Bureau of the Party. There is no mention of him as a trade-union leader.[22] Indeed, Shansi has

---

[21] *The Seventh All-China Congress of Trade Unions, op. cit.*, p. 53.
[22] K. C. Chao, *The Mass Organisations in Communist China*, Cambridge, Mass., 1953, p. 17, mimeographed.

hardly a single industrial town. 'Then at the end of September 1952, Lai wrote an article on "The Chinese Working Class on the Eve of Large-Scale Economic Reconstruction" to celebrate the third anniversary of the People's Republic of China. This shows Lai had replaced Li Li-san as the spokesman of the ACFL. By the end of January 1953, Lai had succeeded in becoming one of the six men elected to the then Standing Committee of the ACFL at the second Plenum of the Sixth Executive Committee of the ACFL. . . . At the Seventh Congress of the ACFTU, Lai delivered the keynote speech on May 3, 1953, to the Congress, entitled "Struggle for the Task of Accomplishing the Industrial Construction of the Nation".'[23] He was immediately elected Chairman of the new Executive Committee of the ACFTU. In this manner a person practically unknown to the workers and with no past trade-union activity to his credit, was quickly pushed to the top position in the ACFTU by the skilful manipulation of the Party leaders.

Chu Hsueh-fan, one of the Vice-Chairmen of the ACFTU (and Minister of Posts and Telecommunications) also has an interesting history. After Chiang Kai-shek liquidated the Communists in 1927, Chu threw in his lot with him and remained one of the top leaders of the legal Kuomintang unions up to 1945. When he attended the inaugural meeting of the World Federation of Trade Unions (1945) as a representative of the Kuomintang's Chinese Association of Labour, the Communists branded him a 'reactionary' and head of the opium-smuggling racket in China. That, however, did not deter the Communist leaders of today from raising him to his present position.

With the trade unions absolutely dependent on the Party, it is not to be wondered at that the trade-union cadres often show a complete lack of initiative, wait for all decisions to be taken by the Party, and completely obliterate the difference between the trade unions and the Party. This is most unwelcome to the Communist leadership, as it limits the effectiveness of the trade unions as *mass* organisations, as conveyor belts connecting the millions of workers with the Party, and as it hampers the mobilisation of the workers for the tasks set them from above. Time and again trade-union

[23] *Ibid* pp. 17–18.

cadres are chastised for obfuscating the difference between Party and unions. Thus, for instance, at a meeting of the Shanghai Federation of Trade Unions held in January 1955 it was said that

> Certain bottom-grade organs of trade unions definitely do not prosecute their programmes of work under the leadership of the Party independently but place reliance on the Party in almost everything. If the secretary of the Party branch happens to be away the chairman of the trade union will refuse to make any decisions at all. In the event of urgent affairs when the public must see the chairman of the trade union he will generally answer them with the evasive reply that he must seek first the views of the Secretary of the Party committee. [24]

An article dealing with the question of the correct relations between Party and trade unions, makes it clear that while basic decisions on policy and personnel of the trade unions should be left to the Party, small day-to-day issues should be decided by the trade unions themselves.

> . . . the leadership role played by the Party over trade-union organs is to acquaint the proletariat with the targets of the liberation movement, to reach decisions on the important political and organisational topics of the trade-union organs, to guide the latter in their ideological and educational work, and not to indulge excessively in interference with the daily routine of unions of workers or to take undue interest in their petty affairs. Governed by the foregoing principles, the selection of leading cadres of trade-union organs should without doubt proceed under the leadership and supervision of the Party. [25]

ALIENATION OF THE TRADE UNIONS FROM THE WORKERS

Communist trade-union policy faces the predicament that the trade-union cadres, by over-emphasising production, will alienate the workers, which would undermine their own efficiency in trans-

[24] Liu Tzu-chiu, 'On Problems of Party Leadership over Trade Union Organs', HH, October 2, 1955; ECMM, 14.
[25] *Ibid.*

mitting the will of the central leadership to the working class. The Communist leaders insist, therefore, that a certain, if subordinate role, should be played by the unions in looking after workers' welfare. They repeatedly warn against too great an identification of trade unions with factory and mine management, against the complete neglect of workers' welfare in the interests of production, and so forth. Thus, an ACFL *Report on Work in the Year May 1, 1949–May 1, 1950*, criticised trade-union cadres for paying 'too little attention to the workers' life'.

> Under conditions materially possible, what should and could be done yet remains undone. Productivity is demanded of workers but not accompanied by encouragement. Thus trade unions become more and more isolated from the masses.[26]

Similarly, Teng Tzu-hui, Vice-Chairman of the South-Central MAC, harangued the trade-union bureaucrats in these terms:

> Many of the factory trade unions have recently adopted the position of the capitalists, issuing the same slogans, speaking the same language, acting like them. The unions defend management, and certain workers in the State enterprises reproach them for concealing the truth from them. I believe they are right. The members of the unions in the private enterprises have overstepped our principles of concessions to the capitalists. They have served as their mouthpieces by asking the workers to accept a lowering of their living standards even in circumstances where this was useless. In certain factories the capitalists could have accepted the demands of the workers, but the union proceeded to convince them to withdraw these demands. In this way they aroused their discontent and were accused by them of being 'lackeys' of the capitalists. For example, in the coal mines of Ta Hye the workers, when they learned of the dismissal of the union chairman, were as joyful as if they had learned of the liberation of Taiwan or of a rise in wages . . .

Teng Tzu-hui goes on to say:

> In the State enterprises, the position of the trade-union cadres must not be confued with that of the administration, which too

[26] CKKJ, May 1, 1950; CB, 24.

readily supports the interests of the management at the expense of the workers and has too greatly increased the severity of working conditions. Numerous laws have been passed which place the workers at a disadvantage. When that occurs, the unions must listen to the workers and then negotiate with the factory for a revision of the programme. They must above all represent the workers, formulate their demands and even apply to the courts in order to gain their objective of defending the workers. This method of acting will favour the development of production and will avoid strikes or work stoppages.[27]

The editor of the *Daily Worker* criticised trade-union practice in a like manner:

. . . the union became isolated from the masses. . . . Certain unions of the state enterprises have behaved like servants of the administration and have been deaf to the demands of the workers.[28]

Despite criticism things were no better more than two years later.

In primary trade-union organisations and among basic-level cadres, cases of bureaucratism, commandism and breaching of law and discipline are also numerous. Major expressions of such a state of affairs are: (1) unconcern for the difficulties faced by the masses in production and living, refusal to listen to the voices and views of the masses, and refusal to discuss, study and report to Party committees and superior trade unions the views of the masses; (2) lack of proper democratic life and democratic style of work, particularly lack of criticism and self-criticism. For a long time trade unions do not carry out re-election, members' general meetings or congresses are not held, members are not told of trade-union work and members' criticism and suggestions with regard to trade-union work are not heard; (3) a number of trade unions in private enterprises have not been reformed or not thoroughly reformed, while a small number of trade unions are still usurped by running dogs of capitalists, who oppress the workers and violate law and discipline at will.[29]

[27] CKKJ, August 4, 1950.
[28] CKKJ, November 15, 1950.
[29] KJJP, February 26, 1953; SCMP, 530.

Again, according to Hsu Chih-chen, General Secretary and Chief of the Organisation Department of ACFTU:

> Some of our trade-union organisations have long ceased to call membership meetings or congresses and to make reports on their work and their expenditure to them. They neither hold timely re-elections nor carry out criticism and self-criticism, especially criticism from below. As a result, these trade-union organisations have become alienated from the masses, thereby hampering supervision from below. These conditions have given impetus to the growth of bureaucratism, commandism and violation of regulations in the trade-union organisations.[30]

Still later, Lai Jo-yu took issue with the bureaucrats, urging them not to neglect worker's welfare on condition that it cost the State little.

> If we were really concerned for the welfare of the masses, it should have been possible for us to render more services to them provided that we did not increase Government expenditure. Strengthening our work in this field will definitely not result in weakening the production of the masses, but it is necessary for promoting labour emulation campaigns more extensively and intensively.[31]

A much-boosted enterprise is the First Automobile Factory now in construction. NCNA wrote of its trade-union work:

> The Company's trade union has never set up any trade-union committee, nor has it established any preparatory committee. . . . All the work of the trade union has been based on individual leadership. The chairman of the trade union makes the decision and there is no collective leadership, with the result that the trade union has seriously estranged itself from the masses.[32]

The First Automobile Factory has many counterparts, as the NCNA message goes on to recount:

> . . . similar conditions of a varying degree exist under different forms in the trade-union organisations of other comparatively large

[30] *The Seventh All-China Congress of Trade Unions*, op. cit., p. 95.
[31] KJJP, December 18, 1954; SCMP, 1024.
[32] NCNA, Peking, March 20, 1955; SCMP, 1024.

factories and mines, especially some of the newly built and enlarged factories and mines.[33]

Although trade-union cadres are expected to impose labour discipline, the Communist leaders are not happy when the cadres prove too zealous. One particular aspect that came in for criticism concerned the grant of sick-leave certificates to workers. Doctors have no power to issue sick-leave certificates. It is up to the trade-union officials to decide whether or not to endorse the doctor's advice. In this they are sometimes too harsh. A letter to a Communist paper telling of conditions in a textile mill in Shanghai describes the procedure for issuing certificates:

> Before issuing a sick-leave certificate, the doctors have to refer the matter to the Labour Insurance Committee of the Trade Union, or to obtain the consent of the Trade Union Section attached to the shop. However, when such a matter is referred to the Labour Insurance Committee, it does not treat it properly enough. For instance, after a doctor has certified for sick leave, the certificate has yet to be endorsed by the secretary of Labour Insurance, and Trade Union Section Chief and the Labour Insurance Committee, and to be discussed and passed by the Trade Union Section. Moreover, the duration of sick leaves cannot exceed three days at a time, after which another doctor's certificate will have to be obtained and approved by the Trade Union Section.

All this is approved of, but the trade-union officials sometimes go too far in worrying the sick. The letter goes on:

> Trade Union cadres would, in feigned courtesy, visit them to find out whether they were really sick or merely feigning sickness. When discovering a bottle of medicine not yet completely finished by a patient, they would criticise the patient for abusing labour insurance . . .[34]

The *Daily Worker* also has some unhappy reports:

> . . . the trade-union work and the administrative work is not clearly demarcated. At present, the administrative cadres are mostly concurrently members of the trade-union committees and the working

[33] NCNA, Peking, March 20, 1955; SOMP, 1024.
[34] CFJP, June 7, 1952; SCMP, 374.

committees. In the case of Factory One of the Peking Machine Works, the production and wages committee consists of 11 members, of whom one is chief of the workshop, 3 are foremen and 3 are chiefs of sections. The members of the iron-casting workshop committee of the factory are mostly administrative personnel and none of them take part in production. The same situation was found in the Mukden Machine Works' Factory Three before the working order of the trade union there was overhauled. The chairmen of the factory's statistical committee and housing committee are also chiefs of the administrative division and section respectively . . . Besides, due to the key administrative cadres being generally kept rather busy, it is difficult for them to find the time to take up the trade-union work, as a result of which there often is nobody to look after the trade-union work. [35]

In order that the reader might not draw the erroneous conclusion that the trade unions should be conducted as bodies separate from the management of industry, the *Daily Worker* hastens to add:

Of course, this does not mean that administrative leadership cadres should not take part in the trade union work, nor does it mean that the trade union should not absorb administrative cadres. The trade union committee can absorb, apart from the activists in general, administrative leadership cadres for participation in the committee.

To preach collaboration between trade unions and management in the interests of production on the one hand, and the separation of the trade union leadership from management in the interests of mass manipulation on the other is certainly easier than to practise them. Consequently the trade union leaders are constantly being reproved for blurring the boundary line between themselves and management. Thus, on August 10, 1955, the Executive Committee of ACFTU resolved that 'full-time cadres of trade union basic-level organisations should be separated from business personnel'. [36]

[35] KJJP, February 9, 1954; SCMP, 763.
[36] NCNA, Peking, August 10, 1955.

One expression of the integration of trade unions and management, despite the warnings uttered against their identification, is the presence of large contingents of management personnel among the delegates to trade union conferences and congresses. Thus, for instance, at the Seventh All-China Congress of Trade Unions (May 1953), of the 813 delegates, hundreds were 'technicians, engineers and managers in State-owned industry'.[37] In places where the role of the trade union is to defend workers from their employers, no real trade unionist would agree to employers' delegates being present *en masse* with full voting rights at a trade union congress. But in China things are different. As Liu Ning-i, First Vice-Chairman of ACFTU said:

> Factory directors and managers . . . are persons who have been commissioned by the State to represent it in running a unit of the people's economy . . . They too are entitled to trade union membership.[38]

Imagine officials of the nationalised industries in Britain taking part in the deliberations and decisions of the trade unions! Or, even more to the point, delegates of the British Electricity Authority participating in and influencing the policy of the Communist-dominated Electrical Trades Union!

True to the same pattern, the individual unions in China convene common congresses with foremen's organisations. Describing one such combined conference—that of the foremen of State-owned textile mills and of the National Textile Workers' Trade Union (held February 25–March 5, 1954) the NCNA said:

> The conference decided that the tasks of the textile industry during 1954 should consist of the following: Further strengthening of technical guidance, popularisation of advanced experience and launching of labour emulations which should evolve round the further strengthening of the planned management and the implementation of operation plans; systematic institution and implementation of the superintendent responsibility system, regional management and responsibility system, and further improvement of labour organisation; training of large numbers of cadres; strengthening of overhead cost control, gradual implementation of business

[37] Chang Yin-sing, 'Workers Take Stock', CR, July–August 1953.
[38] Liu Ning-i, 'What Chinese Trade Unions Do', CR, May–June 1953.

accounting system and elevation of the level of industrial management in order to develop production, raise the quality of products, practice rigid economy, lower production cost and raise productivity of labour; fulfilment and overfulment of the 1954 State plans. [39]

Nothing about workers' welfare!

These conferences must be particularly unpalatable to workers, as they stress the principle of 'one-man management' and with it the increase in foreman's powers, without the workers gaining one iota of control. A conference of superintendents of factories and mines was convened in February 1954 by the Bureau of Steel and Iron Industry of the Ministry of Heavy Industry. The NCNA reported:

. . . the conference considered that it is necessary to set up the single leadership system for the administrative leaderships at all levels, enabling the whole body of workers to obey a specific administrative leader (i.e., factory superintendent, director of workshop and foreman), and demanding that administrative leaderships at all levels assume full responsibility within the scope of their jurisdiction. [40]

Likewise, the *People's Daily* wrote:

The basic-level administrative cadres (mainly the foremen) are directly responsible for leadership of the workers. They are most closely related to the workers and directly supervise their work. The order of the factory chief and the workshop chief must be transmitted by them to the workers. So they have a heavy responsibility to perform towards the consolidation of labour discipline. [41]

Thus while workers can exercise no control over foremen, they have nevertheless to swallow their presence at trade union congresses!

PLETHORA OF BUREAUCRACY IN THE TRADE UNIONS

Between 1922 and 1929 five national trade union congresses were held. But after the Fifth Congress in 1929, 19 years passed

[39] NCNA, Peking, March 10, 1954; SCMP, 767.
[40] NCNA, Peking, February 14, 1954; SCMP, 749.
[41] JMJP, November 16, 1954; SCMP, 939.

without another. The next congress, in Harbin in August 1948, drew up a constitution providing for an All-China trade union congress once every two years. However, another five years passed before the next congress took place (in May 1953). At Harbin sanction was given for less frequent conventions; they were to take place once every four years (Article 14).[42] The constitution failed to stipulate how often the Executive Committee of the All-China Federation of Trade Unions should meet. The result is that power resides in the Secretariat, a group of eight persons.

A similar concentration of power is to be seen in the individual unions and their branches. Thus the new constitution stipulates that the National Congress of each union shall be convened once in three years (Article 19).[43] Congresses of provincial trade union councils as well as trades councils in those cities under the direct control of the Central Government (Peking, Tientsin and Shanghai) and provincial congresses of the unions shall be convened every two years. Congresses of other cities and city-wide congresses of unions shall be convened annually (Article 23).[44] General meetings of workers in a plant or of their representatives shall be convened every year or half-year (Article 28).[45] These stipulations result in real authority being vested in the secretaries of the respective organisations.

The Congresses that are convened so infrequently generally last only a short time and invariably turn into mere platforms for the leadership to announce their policies, for which they are loudly—and of course unanimously—applauded. The following excerpt from a report by C. T. Daru, an Indian Socialist trade union leader, specially invited to attend the Seventh Congress, gives an impression of its character:

> The Congress of the ACFTU was remarkable for its monotony. It is difficult to say what substantial business it transacted or what deliberations it made. . . . The speeches of the Chinese labour delegates . . . were all cast in a uniform pattern and if you heard one you could predict all others in advance . . . Every time a speaker referred to the name of 'Chairman Mao' all the delegates

[42] *The Seventh All-China Congress of Trade Unions*, op. cit., p. 133.
[43] *Ibid.*, p. 134.
[44] *Ibid.*, p. 136.
[45] *Ibid.*, p. 138.

THE ROLE OF THE TRADE UNIONS

including the members of the presidium had to stand up as a mark of respect . . .[46]

The ordinary workers were hardly represented at this Congress at all. As has already been mentioned, of the 813 delegates present, hundreds were 'technicians, engineers and managers in State-owned industry'.[47] Another couple of hundred were 'labour models'.[48] There were also many permanent paid trade union officials. Little room was left for ordinary workers.

In view of the virtual absence of workers' representation at what is supposed to be the summit of the trade union movement—its national congress—and with trade unions bending their main efforts to production, playing the role of watchdogs for the employer-state, and largely neglecting workers' welfare, it is not to be wondered at that the workers at the bench are quite apathetic, and the trade union branch becomes a monopoly of paid officials. Of these there are plenty: at the end of 1953 there were 31,563 full-time trade union officials 'in the basic union organs'.[49] Their salaries eat up a large proportion of union funds. Of the total expenditure of JMP 686·2 milliard by trade unions in 1951 and 1952, 337·8 milliard was spent on administration.[50]

The way union funds are spent intensely annoys the workers. As a *Workers of China* editorial in January 1951 had to admit:

The broad masses of [union] members often see that money they pay as dues is either sunk in the bank without anything done for them or spent carelessly by union officials without any detailed accounting. Some [union cadres] even squandered the fund for personal enjoyment or absconded. They [the members] say that 'union, union, we pay dues and get nothing'. They regarded some unions as not different from those organised by the reactionary Kuomintang in the past—that is, collecting money from the members and doing nothing for them. Some of them refused to pay membership fees any more and requested withdrawal from the union. Some even man-handled the union cadres and threw away the sign

[46] C. T. Daru, 'Report on Red China', *The Radical Humanist*, Calcutta, October 4, 1953.
[47] Chang Yin-sing, 'Workers Take Stock', CR, July–August 1953.
[48] *Ibid.*
[49] NCNA, Peking, April 30, 1954.
[50] Chao, *Mass Organisations, etc., op. cit.*, p. 49.

249

of the union. Thus, it resulted in the alienation of union organisation from the masses . . .[51]

Lack of democratic control in the unions smooths the path for widespread embezzlement by union officials, for the taking of bribes for services to the employers, and for similar corruption. The *Daily Worker* describes the results of a check-up of trade union branches:

> According to an investigation into 173 basic-level trade union organs and 45 trade union organisers in private enterprise in 6 *chu* of Tientsin, problems are found to exist in 126 units, 7 basic-level organs have completely deteriorated in quality, and part of the committee members of 21 basic-level organs and 19 organisers have changed completely. 75 trade union cadres are found to have either been bought over or sent in by the bourgeois class, 110 failed to draw a clear class line of demarcation, 11 showed bad style of work, and 152 are of dubious class status.[52]

A month later the *Daily Worker* returned to the same subject in an editorial, saying:

> To give another instance, in the 16th cadres' training class conducted by the Canton Federation of Trade Unions, there are 202 students, all of them cadres from the basic trade union organs of the various processing factories, with 52 trade union chairmen, and 122 members of trade union committees. . . . Statistics reveal that of the 202 cadres, 179 have helped capitalists to deceive the state; 21 abetted in cases of substitution of good material with inferior material and failure to fulfil the contract; 111 failed to report even when they discovered the substitution; 17 assisted capitalists to compete with State economy to grab the market; and 3 helped capitalists to deceive the tax organs.[53]

A month later the *Daily Worker* wrote again: 'According to statistics of 39 provincial and municipal trade unions from January 1954 to the end of February 1955, cases of corruption and theft of trade union funds amounted to over 2,700 . . .'[54]

[51] Chao, *Mass Organisations, etc., op. cit.*, p. 53.
[52] KJJP, February 6, 1955; SCMP, 994.
[53] KJJP, March 11, 1955; SCMP, 1013.
[54] KJJP, April 23, 1955.

CHAPTER XIV

URBAN WORKERS' LIVING STANDARDS

WAGES

A study of current wage levels is extremely difficult, especially if the level of real wages or a comparison with pre-war levels is aimed at. There are many figures on current nominal wages in individual factories in China, and even general comparisons of wage levels as percentages of 1949, but there are *no* comparisons with pre-war standards. 1949 was an exceptionally bad year and cannot serve as a yardstick for measuring general tendencies in workers' living standards.

We shall begin with what there is to hand—some data about nominal wages of urban workers under Mao. A *People's Daily* editorial dealing with construction work, reported that in building the First Automobile Plant 'labour remained idle from time to time, totalling 740,000 man-days in the past two years, and wasting JMP 450,000 in wages'.[1] This makes the average wage of a building worker in this plant JMP 0·6 per day (new currency) or about JMP 180 per year of 300 days' work. The *Daily Worker* wrote: '. . . in the Anshan Steel and Iron Company extra shifts and extra time accounted for over 1,050,000 extra man-days for which JMP 1,150,000 had to be paid in wages.'[2] The wage per day therefore averaged JMP 1 (new currency). This includes overtime pay which is higher than normal. In connection with the two cases just cited, it should be borne in mind that wages in the North-East are considerably higher than elsewhere in China. A report in the *People's Daily* on the Salt Administration in Chekiang Province stated that as a result of reorganisation, personnel was cut by 121 and 'the amount of wages saved each year exceeded JMP 60,500'.[3] This makes the average annual wage of an employee in the Salt Administration about JMP 500 (new currency). 'The monthly income of a stevedore in Chungking averaged over

[1] JMJP, April 27, 1955.   [2] KJJP, May 27, 1955; SCMP, 1076.
[3] JMJP, May 10, 1955.

JMP 500,000.'[4] This is equivalent to JMP 50 (new currency) a month, or about JMP 2 a day. In an article entitled 'Workers' Rising Living Standards', two samples of the budgets of highly-skilled, presumably prosperous, workers from the North-East are given. One tells of a blast-furnace worker, Chiang Tze-chi, who earned JMP 353,800 (old currency); the other of a foreman in the Anshan Iron and Steel Plant who earned JMP 379,400 a month (old currency).[5] This is JMP 1·3–1·5 per day (new currency). On March 18, 1953, Peking Radio told of a successful worker full of 'productive zeal', one 'Chang Hui, a worker in the Military Uniform Factory in Peking', who 'was now earning JMP 300,000 in a fortnight'.[6] This is JMP 150,000 (old currency) a week, JMP 15 (new currency), or about JMP 25 a day.

There are a number of methods of calculating the *average* nominal wage. One figure is obtained from a report on wage reform in the Central-South Region made by Li I-ch'ing, Vice-Chairman of the Financial and Economic Committee, Central-South MAC, which states that a worker's minimum wage was fixed at 100 *fen* (wage units) and the maximum at 386 *fen* with an average of 218·52 *fen* a month.[7] The *fen*, or wage unit, is based on the price of a basket of commodities sold by State trading companies and co-operatives. The contents of the baskets vary according to local consumption habits. When the system was introduced in April 1952, a *fen* in East China, for instance, represented the value of 0·88 lb. of rice, 0·22 ft. of white cloth, 0·06 lb. of vegetable oil, 0·02 lb. of salt, and 2·2 lb. of coal or 2·75 lb. of firewood. The value of the wage unit is announced at 5-day intervals by the People's Bank. On September 8, 1952, the money rates for one wage unit were JMP 2,551 in Shanghai, 2,268 in Peking, 2,796 in Canton and 2,040 in Mukden. The wage unit system has been adopted by State industry and by many private enterprises. An average of 218·52 *fen* is therefore some JMP 400,000–500,000 (old currency) a month or JMP 40–50 (new currency) a month.

[4] NCNA, Peking, April 28, 1953; SCMP, 561.
[5] PC, February 16, 1952.
[6] NCNA, Peking, March 19, 1953.
[7] CCJP, September 29, 1952; SCMP, 466.

A very similar result is reached by another method of calculation. Referring to the quota of National Economic Bonds (1955) issued by the State Council to be distributed among workers and employees, the *People's Daily* said:

> If the number of workers in 1953 is taken for calculation, they are required to take up only a little more than JMP 70,000 per head on an average. Calculating on the basis of data obtained from 19 provinces in 1954, the quota works out to be less than 1·4 per cent of their annual wages on the average.[8]

From this it is easy to calculate that the average income—wages and salaries—is about JMP 5,000,000 (old currency) or JMP 500 (new currency) per annum. In all probability the *People's Daily* inclined to understate the burden of the bonds, to make it appear that they make up a smaller percentage of the wages bill than is really the case. Average income is therefore in all probability somewhat lower.

A third method of calculation leads to practically the same result. Seeing that every member of the trade unions has to give dues equal to 1 per cent of his wage or salary, and as the total income of the unions from dues in 1952 was JMP 37,940 million,[9] the total wage and salary bill of trade union members was JMP 3,794,000 million. In August 1952 there were 8,100,000 members of trade unions.[10] Hence the average monthly wage or salary per trade union member was JMP 470,000 (old currency), or JMP 47 (new currency).

All these calculations lead to the same conclusion—that the average wage and salary is JMP 40–50 per month (new currency).[11] Included in this average are the salaries of technicians, managers, etc., and the wages of 'model workers' and foremen. If they are taken out, the average for ordinary workers would drop considerably below JMP 40–50 per month, probably to about 25–30

[8] JMJP, January 9, 1955; SCMP, 975.
[9] Chao, *Mass Organisations, etc., op. cit.,* p. 49.
[10] NCNA, Peking, September 29, 1952.
[11] An extreme case of low wages was quoted by a *People's Daily* editorial which dealt with grain speculators. It mentioned that these merchants 'hired children and women at the rate of JMP 2,000 to JMP 3,000' (old currency) per day, or JMP 0·2–0·3 (new currency), to help them make flour out of grain (JMJP, November 19, 1953).

per month, or about JMP 1 per day. The nominal value of the JMP, according to the official rate of exchange, is 2s. 11d. The average wage and salary, therefore, is about 117s.–146s. a month, or for ordinary industrial workers, 73s.–88s. a month.

Apprentices get much less even than this. In Hupeh Province, for example,

> as remunerations (besides food) to a new apprentice, an allowance equivalent to 10–15 prevailing wage units in general cases (with an allowance higher or lower than this rate in the case of some trades where different conditions prevail) shall be given each month during the first year of apprenticeship, such allowances shall be gradually raised according to progress of technique and production during the second and third years of apprenticeship. Other amenities shall be given according to old practices.[12]

10–15 wage units are equivalent to JMP 2·5–3·8 or the mighty sum of 7s.–10s. 6d. a month—for a 10–12-hour day!

Pre-war wages, according to different estimates were as follows:

Pre-war Nominal Wages of Urban Workers (*in yuan*)

	Average Monthly Wage	Average Daily Wage	Source
Shanghai (1925) male workers	20		W. Ayres, 'Shanghai Labour and the May 30th Movement', *Papers on China*, Volume 5, May 1951.
Shanghai (1928) male, industry	21		H. D. Lamson, quoted in Lowe Chuan-hua, *Facing Labour Issues in China*, London, 1934, pp. 16–17.
Shanghai (1930) male, cotton workers	15·57		R. H. Tawney, *Land and Labour in China*, 2nd ed., London, 1937, p. 146.
Wusih (1929)		0·4–0·5	*Ibid.*, p. 147.
Hankow (1929)		0·36–0·65	*Ibid.*
Peking (1920's): servant	12		S. D. Gamble, *How Chinese Families Live in Peiping*, New York, 1933, p. 317.
rickshaw-puller	12		
carpenter	14		
post office sorters and clerks	20–35		

[12] JMJP, April 23, 1953; SCMP, 566.

In 1925 the yuan was equivalent to about 2s. (0·50 U.S. dollars); in 1929–33 it averaged 1s. 2d. (0·29 U.S. dollars). The average monthly wage of male workers in industry in Shanghai was thus equal to about £2 0s. 0d. (10 U.S. dollars) in 1925–28, and declined to £1 4s. 0d.–£1 8s. 0d. (6–7 U.S. dollars) in the 1930's, while wages elsewhere were markedly lower. At present the average wage throughout China is JMP 25–30 a month, which, at the current official rate of exchange is £4–5 (11–13 U.S. dollars). This is much above the 1920's and early 1930's level of nominal wages, but the rise is *not* greater than the decline in the value of of the U.S. dollar or the pound sterling expressed in goods, as prices have practically tripled since then. This rough calculation suggests that real wages expressed in dollars or pounds of constant value, have probably not changed much one way or the other since more than thirty years ago.

A lack of statistical data on the cost of living renders it impossible to make a meaningful comparison between real wages today and those prevailing before the war. However, a comparison of available prices of some everyday necessities shows that prices changed in the same direction and more or less to the same extent as nominal wages:

| | | Retail Prices in Shanghai in 1932 and 1952 | | |
Commodity	Unit	1932 yuan	June 1952 JMP	1952 price/1932 price
Rice	Catty	0·096–0·103	1,500–1,560	some 15,000
Pork	,,	0·307–0·370	6,000	17,000–20,000
Chicken	,,	0·451	7,400	16,500
Salt	,,	0·071	1,250	17,500
Kerosene	,,	0·143	5,150	36,000
Coal	Picul	1·700	28,200	16,000
Cigarettes	Ten	0·051	1,250–1,750	25,000–34,000
Soap	Piece	0·065	1,900–2,300	29,000–35,000

Sources: for 1932: 'Cost of Living Figures for Shanghai in 1932', CEJ, April 1933. For 1952: CMR, August 1952.

The average monthly wage of workers in Shanghai rose during the same period from 15·57 yuan in 1930 to some JMP 250,000–300,000 in 1952, that is some 16,000–20,000 times.[12a]

[12a] A very similar conclusion regarding the real wages of Chinese workers at present was arrived at through a different method of analysis by Yuan-li Wu, in his book, *An Economic Survey of Communist China*, New York, 1956, p. 447.

Wu's study, which is the most recent economic analysis of Mao's China, unfortunately reached me only after the present book was in print, so that it could not benefit from this important work.

In considering workers' wages, account should be taken of the large number of deductions made from them. First there is 'voluntary' buying of State bonds. 'Incomplete statistics up to mid-March (1954) show that the entire workers and staff members of the nation have subscribed a total of JMP 1,762,833,000,000 worth of construction bonds.'[13] Then there are special donations. The most important to date was in aid of the Korean war. Railwaymen, for instance, 'donated JMP 41,200,000,000, equivalent to 27 fighter planes'.[14] This donation is equal to about JMP 8 per head (new currency), or about a week's wages. Then there is the 'voluntary savings'. For example, in 'the city-wide patriotic savings drive' in Taiyuan, Shansi Province, from January to March 1952, workers put down 4 per cent of their wages as savings deposits. The NCNA, reporting this, finds this a most unsatisfactory achievement.

> The average savings potential of each working person constituted approximately 20 per cent of his income, yet his actual amount of savings represented only one-fifth of his savings potential.[15]

Then again, fines for failure in production cut into workers' pay packets. Thus, for instance, in November 1955, in the 6th Shop of the 443rd Factory under the First Ministry of Machine Building, 68·4 per cent of the workers were fined for such misdemeanours.[15a] Forty per cent of all the workers in the motor transport units in nine municipalities and *hsien* in Heilungkiang, including Harbin, were fined in March 1956.[15b]

The fate of the traditionally substantial New Year Bonus, now abolished without compensation, is also a source of lament to the workers. The Communist Government attacked this bonus vigorously. The Economic and Financial Committee, GAC, issued a *Directive on Year-End Double Pay and Bonus in Public and Private Enterprises* on December 8, 1951. This provided that:

> 1. No year-end double pay or bonus shall be paid by all public enterprises that originally had no such practice.

[13] JMJP, March 25, 1954. In 1956 workers were to buy 53 per cent more bonds and in 1957 (plan) 59 per cent more. (JMJP, December 31, 1956).
[14] JMJP, June 29, 1952.
[15] NCNA, Peking, June 14, 1952; SCMP, 358.
[15a] KJJP, May 18, 1956.
[15b] *Ibid.*

2. All public enterprises that formerly paid year-end bonus not exceeding half a month's pay shall continue the practice.

3. All public enterprises that formerly paid year-end double pay or bonus exceeding half a month's wages, shall pay half a month's wages, the amount over and above shall be cut to one-half but in no case should the total amount (including the half-month's wages mentioned above) exceed two months' pay. The bonus may be paid out in instalments.

All Ministries, administrations and banks under the Central People's Government shall make no year-end double pay (or similar payment) as from 1951, irrespective of whether there has been such practice before or not.[16]

The same decree also announced that the payment of New Year Bonus in all private and joint State-private enterprises would cease from 1952.

The real value of wages depends very much on the number of persons they have to sustain. In 1931 it was stated that in Shanghai 'the average earnings of husbands are sufficient only to support themselves and their wives, but no children, unless the family income is supplemented from other sources, most commonly the labour of the wife and the children'.[17] A survey conducted in 1929–30 among Shanghai working-class families showed the average number of employed persons per family to have been 2·06.[18] Under the Communist Government no departure has been made from this tradition that the wages of one person suffice to support only himself and one other person, and not a whole family. The Sixth Trade Union Congress held in Harbin in August 1948 made no bones about it. It was 'decided that the minimum wage of an ordinary worker should be sufficient for the maintenance of two persons including the worker'.[19]

It would be interesting to make a comparison of wages in State and private industry, but for lack of sufficient statistical data, such a task cannot be accomplished satisfactorily. At the same time, many press items make it clear that the State figures

[16] NCNA, Peking, December 8, 1951.
[17] H. D. Lamson, 'The People's Livelihood as Revealed by Family Budget Studies', CEJ, May 1931.
[18] E. M. Hinder, *Social and Industrial Problems of Shanghai*, New York, 1942, p. 44.
[19] Li Li-san, 'The Labour Movement in China', PC, January 16, 1950.

I

compare badly with private industry. The Shanghai *Liberation Daily*, for instance, complains that skilled workers were being lured away from State industry by private industry, and ends with the lament: 'Employees and workers accepted new offers chiefly because they wanted better wages and welfare provisions.'[20] Again, an NCNA communiqué accusing many Shanghai workers of a 'simple economic viewpoint', of being interested only in higher wages, quoted the case of a plane operator at the Hutung Ship Building Factory, Yuan Ah-hsiang, who 'often asked leave of absence, sometimes for a period of over 10 days, in order to work outside to receive higher wages . . .'[21] The Tientsin *Ta Kung Pao* reported a case of private industrialists who 'hijacked' workers from State industry and were brought before the Shanghai People's Court for it. The following quotation concerns one of them:

> Profiteer Tsou Shu-tang, proprietor of the Chunghua Auto Repair Shop, hijacked 7 technical workers during June and July 1953 from the state-operated East China Auto Repair and Assembling Plant, the Repair and Construction Plant of Shanghai Public Communications Company, and the Tien Pao Lu Factory of Shanghai Hardware Trade Union, and employed these technical workers for four months when he accepted excessive orders for profiteering. When his action was discovered, he moved his workshop and arranged for the workers to enter the workshop from the back door . . . He was sentenced to 3 years' imprisonment.[22]

The 'hijacking' was done, presumably, by paying higher wages. The *People's Daily* also joined in the general complaint.

> Some workers are often absent from work, causing serious losses to the enterprises and hampering production plans . . . The reason why they lay off their work . . . is because they can make more than they receive from the factory. From this it is clear that they have been corroded by capitalist thought.[23]

[20] CFJP, October 11, 1951.
[21] NCNA, Shanghai, July 16, 1953.
[22] TKP, June 1, 1954; SCMP, 826.
[23] JMJP, November 16, 1954; SCMP, 939.

Liu Tao-sheng, Secretary of the Central Committee of NDYL, attacked capitalists for attracting workers away from State industry by paying higher wages:

> In private enterprises, lawless capitalists are trying to disintegrate the working class by bribing and enticing their workers with higher wages, increased welfare benefits and various corrupt bourgeois ways of living.[24]

The Tientsin *Ta Kung Pao* returned to the attack on private capitalists for their 'raising of salaries and wages'.[25] The trade union paper, the *Daily Worker*, is also unhappy because workers are paid too well in private industry:

> By means of paying higher wages and extra bonus, they [the nefarious capitalists] split workers from the government and trade unions and drag away technical personnel and workers from state-operated enterprises.[26]

Understandably enough, when private enterprises are turned into joint State-private enterprises, the workers are not enthusiastic about the change. Thus we find the Tientsin *Ta Kung Pao* arguing in an editorial:

> . . . the workers and staff members of a few private enterprises . . . entertain the fear that after they embark upon the path of state capitalism, especially public-private joint operation, their wages will be cut and their amenities reduced.[27]

Likewise the *People's Daily* wrote: 'Some senior staff members and even workers worry that after reorganisation, their wages, amenities and duties will be readjusted.' But the paper hastened to allay their fears: 'As a matter of fact there is no cause for undue worry. The State is always concerned about the conditions of workers and staff members.'[28] Again a *People's Daily* editorial said:

[24] CKCN, November 1, 1954; SCMP, 944.
[25] TKP, December 7, 1954.
[26] KJJP, February 6, 1955; SCMP, 994.
[27] TKP, December 22, 1954; SCMP, 963.
[28] JMJP, March 3, 1954; SCMP, 769.

There are some office employees and workers of private enterprises who, receiving higher wages and better amenities in private enterprises, are afraid of reduction in wages and amenities and afraid of the rigorous labour discipline after the private enterprises have come under joint operation. Consequently, their attitude is not active enough towards joint public-private operation. These office employees and workers mainly lack the collective idea of the working class; they cannot see the collective and long-range interests of the working class for their immediate and insignificant interests.[29]

Where partnership is a fact, it seems that the representatives of the State are harder nuts to crack where wages are concerned than those of the private side. Hence we find the Tientsin *Ta Kung Pao* chastising representatives of the private side in joint public-private enterprises who 'sow discord between representatives of the public side and the workers' saying: 'I agree to a wage increase but the superintendent [referring to the representative of the public side] does not agree', and 'joint operation has commenced but your wages have been reduced'.[30]

Even more important than the level of wages is the relation between wages and labour productivity. In Mao's China, the latter rises considerably while wages lag far behind. Thus, the Minister of Labour, Ma Wen-jui, had to admit in a speech to the National People's Congress:

The labour productivity of industrial enterprises in the whole country was raised by 15 per cent in 1954, but average wages were increased only by 2·3 per cent. In 1955, labour productivity was raised by 10 per cent, but average wages increased only by 0·6 per cent, while in some enterprises real wages actually registered a decline.[31]

However hard the lot of the workers may be, it is easier than that of the peasants whose living standards fall far short of the urban workers. A *People's Daily* editorial refers to peasants who 'take the erroneous view that the job of the workers is light, their

[29] JMJP, January 17, 1956.
[30] TKP, February 20, 1955; SCMP, 999.
[31] NCNA, Peking, June 29, 1956.

wages are too high and their life is too good'. The editorial con-
jures up excuses for the workers. One of them is:

> The value of production by workers is several times greater than
> the value of production by peasants, and the earnings of the workers,
> while being higher than those of the peasants, are only equivalent
> to a small portion of the value created by them, which is not the case
> with the peasants.[32]

You see, peasant, the worker is exploited even more than you are,
so why grumble? In order to avoid the growth of peasant jealousy,
especially during the spring festival when many workers 'spend
their holidays in the country while many peasants go to cities and
factories to visit their sons and daughters', the editorial advises
the workers not to flaunt their higher living standards too much:

> The best thing to do is to rouse workers who intend returning
> home for the holidays to draw up, after discussions, disciplinary
> rules that they will observe during their stay in the countryside,
> such as, no insult to the peasants, no quarrels with the peasants, no
> gambling, no superstitious activities, no gluttonous eating and
> drinking, no land purchase, no loans, no hoarding of grain, no
> speculative business, observance of government law and rural order,
> etc.[33]

The fact that workers' standards are considerably higher than
that of the peasants is of great importance for the regime. Raw
peasants, newly arrived in the towns, do not compare their wages
with those obtaining in other countries, nor with those of Chinese
workers in the past. The main thing for them is that the new life
in town is better than the old. They are more or less content with
their new lot. This contentment of hundreds of thousands of
peasants who migrate annually into the towns becomes a source
of social stability to the regime.

FOOD RATIONING IN TOWNS

One very important factor affecting workers' standards besides
wages and prices is the availability of goods. In Chinese conditions

[32] NCNA, Peking, January 11, 1954; SCMP, 730.
[33] Ibid.

the most important foodstuff is grain. It is rationed in all towns at present.

As already noted,[34] the state monopoly of the grain trade was established on November 19, 1953. By the end of January 1954, grain rationing systems had been set up in 13 municipalities, 156 medium-size towns, all county seats and many market towns, with a total population of some 60 million people.[35] To unify the rationing system, the State Council promulgated *Provisional Measures for Fixed Supply of Grain in Towns* on August 25, 1955. This provided for a monthly ration that should not, on an average, exceed the following amounts:[36]

	Rice Growing Area Catties	Wheat Growing Area Catties
Workers on particularly heavy physical labour	50	55
Workers on moderately heavy physical labour	40	44
Workers on light physical labour	32	35
Employees	28	31
University and middle school students	32	35
General residents and children over 10 years	25	$27\frac{1}{2}$
Children aged 6–10 years	20	22
Children aged 3–6 years	13	14
Children under 3 years	7	8

Grain cards are needed for the purchase of all grain products like flour, vermicelli, noodles and cakes.

These rations are extremely small. They do not even reach those prevailing in Moscow in the blackest days of the war.[37] Compare it with what Vice-Premier Teng Tzu-hui declared in 1953 to be necessary: 'Each person would on an average need 850 catties of grain,'[38] or about 71 catties a month. The rations fixed in 1955 signify a decline in urban consumption levels. Thus in 1954

[34] See pp. 132–3.
[35] NCNA, Peking, February 28, 1954.
[36] NCNA, Peking, August 25, 1955.
[37] In December 1942 the monthly bread and groats ration for heavy workers in Moscow was the equivalent of some 52 *catties*; for ordinary workers, 40; employees, 33; dependants, 26; children under 12, 26·4 (Calculated from L. Volin, *Survey of Soviet Russian Agriculture*, Washington, 1951, p. 175). It is true that from 1 lb. of flour more than a pound of bread can be made. In Britain 280 lb. of flour (or 350 lb. of wheat) yields 378 lb. of the present 'national loaves' made of flour of 80 per cent extraction. Nevertheless, the ration is extremely meagre.
[38] Teng Tzu-hui, Speech to Second National Congress of NDYL, July 2, 1953, NCNA, Peking, July 2, 1953.

the average consumption of grain in towns was 590 catties per head,[39] or 49 catties a month.

However, these facts did not deter a group of nutrition experts dealing with grain rationing from drawing very consoling conclusions. The head of the Department of Nutrition, Yang En-fu, said that 'from the nutrition viewpoint, the measure of fixed supply of grain is both scientific and practical as the different rations supplied to the people according to their different age groups and the different types of labour they are engaged in will provide them the necessary calories'.[40] Again, Research Fellow Ching Ta-hsun 'indicated that the Chinese people habitually eat too much cereal food . . . The enforcement of the measure of fixed supply of grain will work in favour of the improvement of the people's eating habits and will contribute to their good health'.[41]

The deficiency in the grain ration for townspeople is aggravated by the fact that there is very little other food. The average quantity of edible oils distributed per month in Peking was 'not more than 10 ounces per person. The quantity is even smaller in many other towns'.[42] The consumption of meat, milk, eggs and sugar is extremely small, indeed practically negligible even in normal times.[43] And things are not improving. The *People's Daily* of December 14, 1956, described the pork supply situation in Peking in the following terms:

> The residents in the city of Peking are queueing to buy pork in an orderly manner these days as they did in the past, but they feel that it is now more difficult to buy it than ever. Anyone who wants to buy a little pork has to brave the biting cold wind to join on to a queue at 4 or 5 o'clock in the morning, but after queueing, one cannot always get it. The masses are very much dissatisfied with this situation.[43a]

The position is worse, of course, in places outside the capital.

[39] JMJP, November 3, 1955.
[40] NCNA, Peking, August 31, 1955.
[41] *Ibid.*
[42] NCNA, Peking, September 23, 1954. This is about 280 grams. In Moscow in December 1942 the monthly fat ration for different categories of people was: heavy workers, 800 grams; ordinary workers, 800; employees, 400; dependants, 200; children under 12, 400. (Volin *op. cit.*).
[43] See p. 27.
[43a] JMJP, December 14, 1956; SCMP 1451.

HOUSING IN THE TOWNS

One heritage weighing heavily on the Chinese people is the terrible housing conditions in the towns. Numerous surveys have dealt with the subject. A study of 230 working families in Shanghai in 1927–8 found that 62·6 per cent of the families occupied one room per family, and 33·5 per cent two rooms.[44] Another study made in Peking showed that 113 of the families surveyed lived in 134 rooms, an average of 1·2 rooms per family; 4 families had 7 persons per room; and the average was 3·4 persons per room; 9 families had 1 room per person.[45] A study of the housing conditions of 61 workers in Tangku showed that the average number of rooms per family was 1·72; the average number of persons per room, 2·67.[46] (It should be borne in mind that the usual room in town has an extremely small area. The average being about eight feet by eight or nine feet.)[47]

A fuller and more vivid conception than can be garnered from figures is to be gained from the following description of housing conditions in Shanghai:

> Housing development where the bulk of the Chinese population lives consists of row after row of two-storeyed houses, the rows separated by alleyways . . . each floor ten to twelve feet in height. The width of the house is usually eleven to twelve feet, and the depth varies from twenty-four to forty feet. The house itself originally contains a single front room downstairs and a kitchen behind, with two rooms above. By the construction of horizontal and perpendicular partitions, however, spaces are provided for additional families. A principal tenant rents the house from a landlord, and by subdivisions produces what Chinese call *pai ke hsiang*—a dovecote, with cubby holes in each of which a family lives.
>
> The typical Shanghai 'Chinese house' is entered from the small courtyard in the front. One steps into the main downstairs room which is often the residence of the principal tenant, who may cut

[44] Simon Yang and L. K. Tiao, *A Study of the Standard of Living of Working Families in Shanghai*, Peiping, 1931, p. 60.
[45] S. D. Gamble, 'Peiping Family Budgets', *The Annals of the American Academy of Political and Social Science*, Philadelphia, November 1930.
[46] Lin Sung-ho, *Factory Workers in Tangku*, Peiping, 1928, p. 81.
[47] S. D. Gamble, *How Chinese Families Live in Peiping*, op. cit., p. 129.

off a narrow passageway to provide the other tenants with access to their own quarters, or may permit his own room to be the passageway. As a rule, he builds a vertical partition toward the back of the room, thus making a second room which lacks a window. This room in turn may have a horizontal partition, creating an upper space, access to which can be obtained half-way up the stairway. This dark loft may be the only home that many a family knows. The kitchen, at the rear of the house, may or may not be used for its original purpose; more likely it is the residence of yet another family, while portable coal-briquette stoves are placed anywhere for cooking purposes. In the same way the upper front room may have both vertical and horizontal partitions, making spaces for other families; and the room above the kitchen will have yet another household.[48]

In addition to the millions living in such slums, there are twenty or more million who live in sampans and junks on the maze of canals and waterways.[48a] Every waterside town and village has a colony of sampans and junks. A quarter of the population of Canton lives in such houses. No similar instance of such a large population afloat exists anywhere else in the world.

The situation has not improved with the passing of the years. During the war against Japan and the civil war thereafter, hardly any new houses were built and old houses fell to pieces; at the same time the urban population increased enormously. In April 1951 the Communist Vice-Mayor of Shanghai gave the following sombre information:

In the whole of Shanghai there were about 300,000 houses in 1937. At that time the population of Shanghai was 3,000,000. Now there are only 246,000 houses left, a reduction of about one-sixth. The population has actually increased by 2,000,000.[49]

G. F. Winfield, summing up the situation, did not exaggerate when he said: 'Well over 90 per cent of the people of China need to be rehoused.'[50]

[48] Hinder, *op. cit.*, pp. 83-4.
[48a] O. M. Green in *The Scotsman*, December 1, 1951.
[49] *Shanghai News*, April 29, 1951.
[50] Winfield, *op. cit.*, p. 90.

Since Mao's rise to power, a great building programme has been carried out. Nevertheless it is a mere drop in the ocean of need, especially as building certainly does not keep pace with the growth of the urban population. Thus in Mao's best year for housing construction, 1954, living quarters with a total floor space of 13 million square metres were built.[51] In the three years, 1953–55, a total of 30 million square metres were built.[51a] To see the inadequacy of this achievement it should be compared with building the United Kingdom where the *whole* population is only half China's *urban* population, and where slum clearance scarcely exists as a problem when thought of in Chinese terms. In the years 1953–55, some 100 million square metres of housing were built in the United Kingdom.[52] China's current housing effort is barely enough to keep pace with the increase in the urban population, let alone provide accommodation for each family. Thus, for instance, a *People's Daily* editorial wrote:

> The Yumen Mining Affairs Bureau has over the past years stepped up housing construction 3·96 fold but, during the corresponding period, the number of workers has increased by 11·6 times, with the result that housing is not enough to go round. In Shenyang, newly built workers' quarters during 1949–55 covered an area of 1,500,000 square metres, registering a 31·2 per cent boost in 1955 over 1949. During the same period, however, the number of workers in Shenyang rose by 217 per cent, with the result that housing congestion was further aggravated.[53]

The living space built is far from commodious by any standard. According to a Report made on February 12, 1953, by Po I-po, Minister of Finance, '217,500 rooms were built to accommodate about 1 million people' in 1952,[54] that is, nearly five persons per room!

One important improvement, however, has been achieved by the new regime. The network of water and sewerage pipes and

[51] NCNA, Peking, September 22, 1955.
[51a] JMJP, June 26, 1956.
[52] Calculated from Ministry of Housing and Local Government, *The Cost of House Building*, London, 1952, p. 3, and General Statistical Office, *Annual Abstract of Statistics*, London, 1956, p. 61.
[53] JMJP, June 26, 1956; SCMP, 1331.
[54] NCNA, Peking, February 20, 1953.

electricity, introduced into the large cities of China during the 1920's and 30's but limited to small areas in them, is now being spread to cover wide areas in the large cities[55] and has also begun to penetrate the smaller ones.

After the Five Year Plan started meeting increased difficulties, especially in 1955, house-building was curtailed and reduced in quality. On June 24, 1955, a high official of the Ministry of Building explained a few of the measures taken to cut down building costs:

> In the past, the inside and outside walls of the lower two floors or flats in Peking were put at 37 millimetres on each side while the upper two floors were set at 24 millimetres. The new preliminary blueprints have set the thickness of all the outside walls at 24 millimetres, thus cutting down building costs by JMP 6·06 per square metre.

Other measures include:

> . . . thinning of the floors, the use of substitutes for wall partitions and flooring, limiting each storey to three metres in height, adoption of public lavatories, kitchens and baths in place of private ones as well as economising on construction materials and fixtures.[56]

Walls less than an inch thick!

In defending the cut in building standards, the Communist leaders used the argument that this would bring about a cut in rent, and unwittingly revealed that present rents are often beyond the means of the workers. Thus Lai Jo-yu told the National People's Congress that housing standards had to be cut, as

> . . . the standard of some factory living quarters is too high and house rental is beyond the means of workers, who thus cannot afford to occupy the living quarters. Thus a situation has been brought about in which on the one hand a housing shortage is particularly

[55] Thus, for instance, while in 1949 only 30 per cent of the population of Peking were supplied with piped water, now 97 per cent are said to be so supplied (NCNA, Peking, August 23, 1956).
[56] NCNA, Peking, June 24, 1955.

felt in industrial cities, and, on the other, living quarters are available but are beyond the means of worker masses.[57]

Again,

> The dormitories of the First Automobile Plant, and of the Tsitsihar Locomotives and Wagons Plant, because of their high costs, call for monthly rentals ranging from more than JMP 10 to JMP 40 for a room, and the workers are reluctant to move into them.[58]

The Minister of Finance, Li Hsien-nien, complained:

> The dormitories newly built for workers of the Tsitsihar Locomotives and Wagons Factory were beyond the means of workers because rental on each flat ranged from JMP 18 to 41 per month, or two to six times higher than the old dormitories.[59]

This is certainly a high rent, making up from 25 to 100 per cent of the average wage. Compare it with what India's Premier, Nehru, was told on visiting a State cotton mill in Peking: 'A worker pays less than 1 per cent of his total earnings in rent'![60]

Reports such as the following sometimes reach the press, corroborating this picture of appalling urban housing conditions:

> Taiyuan has become an important heavy industry centre in North China. In the past two years, the population of the city has grown from 240,000 to 500,000. There are 40,000 industrial workers in Taiyuan. Housing conditions of workers is deplorable. It is rather a common phenomenon that over 20 workers are crowded in one small room. One room, formerly a toilet, is now accommodating six workers. In one coal mine outside Taiyuan, 250 worker-families are housed in 123 rooms. In one room (10 by 10 feet) are housed 3 worker-families. Most of the houses are leaking. When there is heavy rain outside there is also heavy rain inside the houses; when the rain outside stops, rain still continues within.[61]

[57] NCNA, Peking, July 21, 1955.
[58] JMJP, June 19, 1955; SCMP, 1076.
[59] NCNA, Peking, July 9, 1955; CB, 336.
[60] NCNA, Peking, October 23, 1954.
[61] HHJP, January 12, 1952, quoted in FEER, October 30, 1952.

Compare this grim reality with some of the highly-exaggerated claims. Lai Jo-yu had the temerity to write on September 17, 1952:

It is planned . . . to completely solve the problem of living quarters for workers and staff within 3–5 years, with initial steps already taken this year.[62]

The President of the India-China Friendship Association went even further, declaring that the housing question was already solved:

. . . in Canton, as in the rest of China today, there is no housing problem . . . Everyone can easily get a house according to his needs.[63]

LENGTH OF WORKDAY, HOLIDAYS AND WORKING CONDITIONS

Another factor affecting workers' living standards is the length of the workday and of holidays. Since taking power, Mao has on the whole preserved the same conditions as existed previously under Kuomintang rule.

In 1946 a sample survey of working conditions in 240 factories in Shanghai employing 92,971 workers showed that the average working day was 9·94 hours. However, hours varied considerably from industry to industry. The longest day—11·93 hours—was in the paper manufacturing industry, the shortest—7 hours—in telephone companies. In Chungking the modal average was 9 hours, found in 20 out of 68 factories; the longest working day was 12 hours, in 3 factories; 13 factories worked 11 hours a day and 12 worked 8 hours.[64] Similar conditions obtained in industry in other cities, although on the whole the working day was 1–3 hours longer than in Shanghai.

The same survey, dealing with rest days, states that of the 240 Shanghai factories, 3 had no rest days, 76 had two days a month,

[62] NCNA, Peking, September 17, 1952; SCMP, 420.
[63] Sundarlal, *China Today*, Allahabad, 1952, p. 26.
[64] Ta Chen, 'The Labour Policy of the Chinese Government and its Reactions on Industry and Labour', *International Labour Review*, January 1949.

and 131 had 4 days. Public utilities had 4 days. Three factories had no annual holidays, 165 had 5–10 days, and 46 had 11–15 days. 188 paid wages for rest days and 205 paid wages for annual holidays, while 28 did not pay wages on rest days, and 21 did not pay wages on annual holidays.[65] On the whole, as regards holidays, Shanghai workers had considerably better conditions than workers elsewhere in China.

On coming to power, the Communists avoided shortening the working day. The *Common Programme* stated:

> For the present period, an eight- to ten-hour day should in general be enforced in publicly- and privately-operated enterprises, but under special circumstances this matter may be dealt with at discretion (Article 32).

There is no mention of rest days and holidays in the *Common Programme*. The *Trade Union Law* (of June 29, 1950) made no mention of the working day nor the number and frequency of rest days and holidays.

The authorities actually lengthened the working day for a certain time, but they soon found that too long a day had a deleterious effect on the quantity, as well as the quality, of output. In addition, since equipment is much more precious than human labour in China, full employment of machines through a multiple-shift system is more economic than an excessive lengthening of the working day. Furthermore, serious unemployment in the towns urged against long hours. And so, on August 3, 1952, the GAC issued a *Decision on the Labour Employment Problem*, stating:

> For the sake of safeguarding the health of the workers and employees, raising labour productivity, and enlarging the size of employment, the system of working 8–10 hours per day should be strictly observed in a systematic and planned manner. All comparatively larger public and private factories, mines, and communications or transportation enterprises should practise the 8-hour system where possible. The one-shift a day system can be changed into two or three-shift system where circumstances as to raw materials, marketing, and technical conditions allow. State-operated shops or

[65] Ta Chen, 'The Labour Policy of the Chinese Government and its Reactions on Industry and Labour', *International Labour Review*, January 1949.

co-operatives in industrial or mining districts or large or medium cities should also follow the 8-hour system. The working hours for those engaged in work harmful to health should even be shortened to less than 8 hours. Extra-hour and extra-shift practices should be strictly prohibited in all private and public enterprises.[66]

To underline the importance of the maximum utilisation of industrial equipment, the Ministry of Textile Industry issued a directive *Concerning the Present Situation of the Textile Industry and the Arrangements for Future Work*, an extract from which reads:

At present, except for a few individual places where factory equipment has not yet been brought into full play, the 3-shift production system has been put into practice in all the State-operated factories, and the utilisation rate in 1953 will reach 95·4 per cent.[67]

As a result it was reported in 1953 that 'most State-owned industries and mines . . . enforce an 8-hour working day. Moreover, workers are now entitled to a day off per week'.[68]

This puts China in a position similar to that of neighbouring countries as regards the length of the working day. In Hong Kong 'Broadly speaking an 8-hour day and a 48-hour week is worked by Government, by European and by some Chinese concerns'.[69] Similarly in Burma, 'hours of work in factories have been reduced from 54 to 44 a week and from ten to eight a day'. In India 'no adult workers in factories may work for more than 9 hours per day of 48 hours per week'.[70] The Indian *Factories Act, 1948*, provides that workers in non-power-using factories employing 20 or more workers and power-using factories employing 10 or more, should get one day a week holiday (without pay) and an annual holiday with pay of 1 day for every 20 days worked for adults and 1 day for every 15 days worked for youths, i.e., 12–16 days paid holiday a year. The same provisions were applied to workers on large

[66] NCNA, Peking, August 3, 1952; SCMP, 388.
[67] TKP, December 24, 1953; SCMP, 733.
[68] Chiang Tao, Vice-Director of the Department of Labour Protection, ACFTU, 'Safety in Industry', PC, July 1, 1953.
[69] FEER, August 6, 1953.
[70] ILO, *Problems of Labour and Social Welfare in Southern and Eastern Asia*, New York, 1950, p. 17, mimeographed.

plantations (tea, coffee, rubber and cinchona plantations of 25 acres or more employing at least 30 workers) by the *Plantations Labour Act, 1951*. Indian miners, according to the *Mines Act, 1952*, are entitled to a weekly unpaid holiday of 1 day and an annual paid holiday of 14 days for the small number of miners paid a monthly salary, or 7 days for other miners.[71] China's labour laws thus lag behind those of India, or, for that matter, of Japan.[72] (In all these countries, however, the laws are scarcely observed.

Experience in the West has shown that the shortening of the working day is not only necessary for industrial workers but can also be beneficial to the employers.[73] Nevertheless in China, when industrial managements get into difficulties over fulfilment of the Plan, they manage to get round the 8–10 hour working day limit by overtime or extra shifts. The prevalence of such practices led the North-East People's Government on May 7, 1952, to promulgate *Provisional Regulations Governing the Restriction of Extra Shifts and Extra Hours in Factories and Mines*. This stated:

For extra shifts and extra hours . . . the maximum overtime must not exceed two hours per day, and the working hours of extra shifts must not exceed the hours of a normal workday. Extra shifts or extra hours must not be imposed for more than four times consecutively and the total extra shifts and extra hours must not exceed 48 hours per month.

. . . In case extra shifts and extra hours exceed the limit of 48 hours, reports should be made to the local labour administration for approval. . . .

[71] 'Important Labour Laws at a Glance', *Indian Labour Gazette*, August 1955, published by Ministry of Labour, Government of India.

[72] A report on Japan in 1950 stated: 'A basic 8-hour day and 48-hour week were established, with extra pay for night work. Six days' paid vacation annually was guaranteed after one year of service, with more for longer service'. (M. S. Farley, *Aspects of Japan's Labor Problems*, New York, 1950, p. 58.)

[73] Thus, for instance, it was shown in Britain during the First World War that in a 12-hour day, workers in munitions industry did not produce more than in a 10-hour day. (*The Times*, London, June 9, 1940.) Similarly, the manager of a large factory in Germany found to his cost during the Second World War that the prolongation of the working week to 60 instead of 48 hours was accompanied by a decline of the portion of the day spent productively from 84 to 70 per cent, so that notwithstanding the lengthening of the working week by 12 hours, the time spent productively rose only by 2 hours. This was because absenteeism rose from 4 to 11 per cent, and production of bad quality goods rose from 3 per cent of the whole output to 8 per cent. (*Reichsarbeitsblatt*, May 27, 1944, quoted in E. Varga, *Changes in Capitalist Economy after the Second World War* (Russian), Moscow, 1946, pp. 111, 113.)

It is further stipulated by the North-east People's Government that the practice of the following among productive workers is strictly prohibited:

To work 24 hours consecutively with an off period of 24 hours to follow;

To work 12 hours consecutively with an off period of 12 hours to follow;

To work 16 hours consecutively in the three 8-hour shifts system before the rest period. The workers are also not allowed to work consecutively for over 12 hours before the major rest period.

. . . Juvenile workers under 14 years of age, female workers more than six months pregnant and female workers with unweaned babies under four months will not be allowed to work extra hours.[74]

48 extra hours a month, on top of the 8–10 working hours a day, is no small addition. But to make matters worse, when the pressure from above to fulfil the production plan grows, managers of industry very often stretch the working day beyond its legal limits. Thus the GAC Committee for People's Supervision, in a circular dealing with labour accidents, issued on September 18, 1952, stated:

An analysis of part of the cases recently disposed of by this Committee and other committees for people's supervision of the different localities reveals that the desire of over-stressing the completion of work on the part of the leadership personnel of certain factories and mines is the main factor leading to injury and death. Under the slogans of 'accomplishing the production mission' and 'implementing the economic accounting system', they demand an unlimited stretch of labour of the workers, extend their working hours, and encourage them to 'throw themselves into the boiling water and burning flame' [meaning any sacrifice possible]. For instance, the brick factory of Ma Chia Kou, Kailan, failing to keep up its production previously, mobilised its workers to pull bricks out of the hot kiln heated to 130 degrees Centigrade in order to fulfil its contract in time to avoid a fine. . . . The result was that 41 out of the 43 workers sustained injury through burns, some even turning out to be fatal cases . . .

[74] KJJP, May 29, 1952; SCMP, 361.

Again:

> In some factories, additional shifts and extra hours to fulfil the production norms have not only seriously affected the workers' health but caused injuries and deaths. For instance, the Taiyuan Machine Factory extended working hours without any restriction. In normal times, the workers work 12 hours a day, with double shift at times. Worker Yang Chung-k'uei of the factory lost his life on July 25 after he worked a double shift up to 16 hours when, due to overwork, he failed to co-operate with the worker controlling the switch and died of electric shock.[75]

Similarly the *People's Daily* reported that

> railway workers in Shichiachuang on the Peking–Hankow line usually work up to 24 hours consecutively. In September 1951, thirty-six workers worked for over 24 hours at a stretch; eleven worked for 27 hours at a stretch; three worked for 30 hours at a stretch; and one worked for over 39 hours at a stretch.

The one who worked more than 39 hours without stopping was decorated as a 'labour model'.[76] Similarly, it was reported that in the private Kung Chun Bedcover and Garment Factory in Wuhan, the prolongation of the working day and addition of shifts brought the average working day up to 17 hours. This resulted in 330 out of 1,882 workers employed becoming ill.[77] Again, in the Shanghai Weaving Factory No. 7, the working day averaged 15 hours, to the jeopardy of the workers' health; one 'labour model', Ku Chin-shan worked so hard and for so long sleeping only five hours a night, that she verged on collapse.[78] It was reported that 'many workers collapsed through sheer fatigue' at the Anshan Steel Works.[79] More than two and a half years later the Peking *Daily Worker* described conditions in the Anshan Steel Works thus:

[75] NCNA, Peking, September 17, 1952; SCMP, 446.
[76] FEER, October 30, 1952.
[77] CCJP, October 27, 1951.
[78] JMJP, August 14, 1953.
[79] JMJP, September 18, 1953.

The team leaders and the foreman forced workers to work extra shifts or hours. During a week in April, some workers in this outfit worked as long as 35 hours at a stretch; others, 17 hours.[80]

Lai Jo-yu, corroborating what has been said, made an all-out attack on the evil for the harm it does the State:

There has been no limit to the prolongation of working hours, individual workers have worked continuously for 72 hours through additional shifts and working hours. In order to fulfil their tasks, individual factories have required their workers to work on Sundays for a period of ten months. On the surface, this unlimited increase of labour intensity has resulted in accomplishment of production plans but actually it has brought about damage to the State in varying degrees. As a result of exhaustion, sickness and casualties have been serious. There are quite a few cases in which, owing to exhaustion, workers have fainted, vomitted blood or even died. In individual factories, increased shifts and working hours reached 260,000 hours, but the number of hours lost due to sick-leave amounted to 220,000, the two almost cancelling each other out. Moreover, owing to shock-work, the quality of products has failed to reach the planned targets. The huge expenditure for increased shifts and working hours has increased the cost of production. For example, according to 1954 statistics for a certain industry, this expenditure alone amounted to over JMP 10,000 million. Such a serious situation must arouse the attention of those concerned.[81]

Whatever limit to the working day does exist applies only to the 3 or so million workers in modern industry. It does not cover workshops and not fully mechanised factories which employ some 20 million workers.[82] There is no law that covers the working day of these workers or that provides for their holidays. Only apprentices get some legal protection, and this again not through a unified law covering the whole country, but only through various laws enacted by different provincial governments. Thus in Hupeh the law for apprentices provides:

[80] KJJP, May 27, 1955; SCMP, 1076.
[81] KJJP, February 20, 1955; SCMP, 1024.
[82] JMJP, July 13, 1954.

Working hours shall generally not exceed 10 hours per day in the case of handicraft shops and factories operating partly with machinery, and not exceed 12 hours in the case of small and independent workshops.

. . . Off days and old and new holidays shall temporarily be set at 45 to 70 days in a year to be determined by the various trades through consultations in the light of concrete conditions. Wages to be paid for the fixed holidays—3 days for the Spring Festival, 1 day for the New Year, 2 days for the National Day, 1 day for May Day; for other fixed holidays old custom shall be followed.[83]

The long working day, together with the intensity of labour in the 'patriotic emulation campaigns' necessarily lead to a neglect of safety precautions and to a high incidence of industrial injury. A *Circular on Disposal of Serious Cases of Injury and Death Caused by Negligence of Production Safety in Certain State-operated Factories and Mines* issued by the GAC on September 17, 1952, pinpointed the responsibility:

One factor responsible for the accidents is that some leadership cadres in factories and mines have their work ill planned, and when time becomes short for the task to be completed, they start rushing workers blindly by extra shifts and extra working hours in disregard of the safety of the workers.[84]

Statistics on labour accidents are very patchy. But the impression is gained that the situation on the whole is not improving. Thus, in the North-east, the industrially most advanced area of China, 'the number of accidents in the power industry increased 13·5 per cent in 1952 over 1951 and cases of injury in coal mines increased by 20 per cent in 1952 compared with the previous year'.[85] Between January 1950 and January 1952 Shanghai trade unions published statistics of industrial accidents entailing hospital treatment, i.e., excluding cases treated at the factories or by private physicians.

[83] JMJP, April 23, 1953.
[84] A. W. Shurcliff, 'The Control of Industrial Labour in Communist China', *Monthly Labour Review*, Washington, August 1953.
[85] Chao, *Mass Organisations, op. cit.,* p. 155.

	Deaths in Hospitals	Patients	Accidents Causing Disabilities
January 1950	92	550	8
April 1950	70	625	7
July 1950	130	700	15
October 1950	132	550	18
January 1951	105	700	12
April 1951	118	600	14
July 1951	170	800	23
October 1951	255	2,050	77
January 1952	260	1,700	65

Source: R. L. Walker, 'The Working Class in Communist China', *The Radical Humanist*, Calcutta, August 30, 1953.

Note the rapid rise in the two years. No wonder the authorities decided to stop publishing these statistics.

The *People's Daily* provided a glimpse of developments in 1953:

> During the first half of the year, accidents were not only not reduced, but were actually more serious compared with the same period in 1952. Particularly in the North-east and North China regions, accidents in the State-owned coal mines greatly increased.[86]

The same paper wrote nine months later:

> According to statistics of the five CPG Ministries of Industries, a total of over 2·3 million man-days, equal to 7,000 men remaining idle for a whole year, were lost through suspension of work, due to accidents, in a period of 10 months last year. The loss to production under such conditions is inconceivable.[87]

A letter to the Shanghai *Liberation Daily* complained:

> In transport departments, many accidents have been caused as a result of over-burdening the workers. The carrying of excessively heavy loads has caused the workers to vomit blood, to complain of aching bones, to suffer injuries from falls, and to hurt their spines.[88]

Not only are the workers the victims of industrial accidents but, to add insult to injury, they are often accused by management of being responsible for them. Thus the *Daily Worker* complained:

[86] JMJP, September 1, 1953.
[87] JMJP, June 6, 1954; SCMP, 829.
[88] CFJP, June 22, 1954; SCMP, 893.

277

. . . the management of some enterprises often shifts the responsibility for injury and accidents to the workers, and even blames the already unfortunately injured. The causes for the accidents are often described as due to 'breach of work procedures', 'carelessness of workers' and 'workers being too clumsy'. In this way, the real reasons leading to various accidents are obscured. For instance, the grinder of the 'chlorine trough' in Workshop 52 of the Mukden Chemical Works has no safety equipment. The workers had pointed this out but the workshop took no action, with the result that an accident occurred where a worker had his fingers cut off. Analysing the causes of the accident, the man in charge of the workshop put it: 'Carelessness on the part of workers.' Out of 66 accidents that happened in the forging and rolling workshop of the Mukden Heavy Machine Works, 65 have been ascribed to the 'carelessness of workers'. With the wrong analysis came the deviation of purely punishing the workers, as was witnessed in the case of the Mukden Chemical Works stated above, where the worker who had lost his fingers was fined one month's bonus and made to criticise himself before the public.

In many instances, when a serious loss is caused to the enterprise due to an accident, the worker responsible is sent to the people's court to be punished as a criminal, but nothing is done to locate the responsibility on the part of the management and to mete out the necessary punishment according to law.[89]

Some time later Lai Jo-yu spoke on the same theme:

A few enterprises even held struggle meetings against workers who were injured while performing public duties, demanding that the workers confess how they were injured and allowing them to give only subjective and not objective causes. A number of trade union cadres not only overlooked and raised no objection to such practice but even took part in it.

. . . production accidents are frequent in many enterprises . . . some units, instead of investigating and analysing the causes of accidents, frequently shifted the blame to the workers and penalised workers without checking up the responsibility of the leadership, without rectifying matters.[90]

[89] KJJP, January 21, 1955; SCMP, 986.
[90] Lai Jo-yu, Report to Executive Committee of ACFTU, August 5–10, 1955, NCNA, Peking, August 30, 1955.

With the inordinate enthusiasm for 'socialist construction', labour conditions are overlooked; workers are exhorted to exert themselves, and attention to their health is disregarded. Thus in Kaifeng:

> With the end of exploitation, even those carriers thought lazy in the past have become diligent. 'Carry more and walk faster!' has become the slogan. The production plan which the carriers adopted as part of their patriotic compact stipulates that each man pulls 500 *catties* of goods per load, but everywhere this plan is being over-fulfilled. In the station district, for example, one popular carrier transports 1,200 *catties* each load, while Fu Tu-heng and Kuo Sien have broken their former records by each pulling 1,650 *catties* per load. An average of 900 *catties* per load is now being pulled by each carrier.[91]

It is relevant to note here that even with the usual load to carry, porters' 'work is extremely debilitating. At the age of forty the people are usually old and broken and their average life expectancy remains far below that of the peasants'.[92] No wonder labour accidents are very numerous among transport workers!

The same exertions are demanded of female workers. Women work in mines, often on the heaviest work in the pit, and the Communist authorities in China describe this as a great achievement. China is not the only country in Asia where women are employed in the mines. In India in 1950 women formed 20·5 per cent of the total labour force in mining. In Japan, in October 1952, 10·9 per cent of the labour force in mining were women.[93] India was not very proud of her showing, and in 1952 passed a Mines Act that banned the employment of women in mines.[94] The Chinese Soviet Republic itself, in its *Labour Code* of 1931 prohibited women from working in mines and foundries, and in other heavy work (Article 35).[95] Today, however, besides working in the mines, women work in the building industry, as stevedores, railroad builders, and so on. The *China Monthly Review* boasted of

[91] CMR, February 1952.
[92] Quoted by Wittfogel, *op. cit.*, p. 690.
[93] 'Women's Employment in Asian Countries', *International Labour Review*, September 1953.
[94] *Indian Labour Gazette*, New Delhi, August, 1955.
[95] *Fundamental Laws of the Chinese Soviet Republic*, *op. cit.*, p. 58.

the way women participate in the Huai River water conservancy project:

> Describing her work here Li Su-ying [a 25-year-old woman] said: 'We found many new ways of speeding up work. Work that had taken 20 days we did in four.' She led in carrying light railway track, in showing the other girls what they could do. They went bare-legged into the icy river to do jobs men did not want to do.[96]

SOCIAL INSURANCE

Labour Insurance Regulations were promulgated on February 27, 1951, and revised on January 2, 1953. A description of their main aspect follows. The Regulations cover workers and employees in the following enterprises:

> A. State, private, or co-operative-owned factories and mines as well as those jointly operated by public and private capital, employing 100 or more workers and staff members, and their subsidiary organs.
> B. Railways, water transport, post and telecommunications and their subsidiary organs.
> C. Capital construction units of factories, mines, and transportation enterprises.
> D. State-owned building companies (Article 2).[97]

Among the enterprises covered by the above article there may be exceptions.

> Enterprises within the scope of the present Regulations which, due to special financial stringencies, find it difficult to continue operations or which have not yet formally opened business operations, may temporarily put off the carrying out of the present Regulations after agreement has been reached through consultation between the managements or the owners of the enterprises and the primary trade union committees and after approval of the labour administration organ of the local people's government has been obtained (Article 6).[98]

[96] CMR, November-December 1952.
[97] *Labour Insurance Regulations of the People's Republic of China*, Peking, 1953, p. 6.
[98] *Ibid.*, p. 7.

Up to the end of 1955, the total number of workers covered by labour insurance was about 5,700,000 (or about 13 million with their families).[99] Thus some 2 per cent of the population benefits from social insurance.

To assess the significance of the Chinese *Labour Insurance Regulations* it might be compared with India's *Employees' State Insurance Act, 1948.*

	India[100]	*China*
Coverage	Factories of 20 workers and over.	Factories of 100 workers and over.
Workers' contributions	About 2½ per cent of wages.	None (Article 7).
Sickness benefit.	58 per cent of average wage (first two days of sick leave unpaid).	60–100 per cent of wages for first six months of sick leave and 40–60 per cent later (Article 13B).
Disablement benefit	50 per cent of wage for total period of disablement and free medical treatment.	60–75 per cent of wages if injured at work (Article 12).
Pension to family of deceased workers	Widow, 30 per cent of wage; each son until age 15 and daughter until marriage, 20 per cent, on condition total does not exceed 50 per cent of wage.	If the worker died of sickness or injury sustained at work, 25–50 per cent of wage of the deceased to continue until the dependants no longer have status of dependants. In addition a lump sum equivalent to 3 months' wages (Article 14A). If worker did not die from injury or sickness sustained at work: a pension equal to 6–12 months' wages to his family plus a funeral benefit equivalent to 2 months' wages (Article 14B).
Maternity benefit	50 per cent of average wage payable for 12 weeks.	100 per cent of average wage payable for 7 weeks (Article 16A).
Old Age pensions	None (The Employees' Provident Funds Act, 1952, provides for an old age pension in the form of a lump sum, a fairly small benefit difficult to compare with that in China).	At age of 60, 50–70 per cent of former wage if retired or 10–20 per cent of wage if 'the interest of the enterprise calls for his staying on at the job' (Article 15A).
Medical treatment	Free of charge.	Free medical treatment except for cost of expensive medicines, travelling expenses to hospital and meals at the hospital (Article 13A).
	Families of insured workers are not covered.	Families of insured workers are covered (Article 13E).

[99] JMJP, May 2, 1956.
[100] B. M. L. Moorthy, *Social Security in India*, Bombay, 1954.

This comparison shows India's provisions to be more progressive than China's in some respects, while in others the position is reversed. In both countries social insurance provisions are quite modest.

A specific feature of labour insurance, not to be found in any but the Communist-controlled countries, is the special privileges conferred on 'model workers'. The *Regulations* provide them with the following benefits:

A. The cost of expensive medicines, travelling expenses involved, and meals at the hospital during treatment for sickness or injury not sustained at work shall be borne by the management or owner of the enterprise concerned.

B. When undergoing medical treatment for sickness or injury not sustained at work, wages are to be paid in full during the first six months.

Relief benefit for sickness, for injury or disablement not sustained at work shall be at a rate equivalent to 60 per cent of the wages of the person concerned. Invalid pension for disablement sustained at work shall be equivalent to the full amount of the wages of the person concerned.

Allowances for disablement sustained while at work shall be at a rate equivalent to the difference between the wages received prior to the disablement and the wages received after resuming work. In the case of death being incurred while at work the lineal dependants shall receive a relief benefit equivalent to 30–60 per cent of the wages of the person concerned. Old-age pensions upon retirement shall be 60–80 per cent of the wages of the person concerned. Old-age pensions for persons continuing to work beyond the age limit shall be 20–30 per cent of the wages of the person concerned. Provisions for dealing with such matters are set forth in Detailed Rules for Carrying Out the Labour Insurance Regulations of the People's Republic of China.

C. The right to priority in receiving benefits from the communal labour insurance establishments (Article 19).

Taking the privileges endowed on 'labour models' in conjunction with statistics for rest-homes and sanatoria, it is clear that they are practically the only workers deriving any benefit at all from these much-publicised institutions. Statistics compiled at the end of 1955 reveal that there were a total of 57,700 beds in sanatoria and rest homes.[101] Assuming that the average length of stay at these institutions is one week, only a tiny minority of the working class could get to them. *People's China* of December 16, 1954, said:

'In the past three years, over 800,000 workers and employees have been to rest homes or sanatoria.'[102] As there were 223,000 'labour models' in April 1953,[103] and as it is quite certain that many high officials also holiday at the sanatoria and rest homes, the number of over 800,000 visitors in three years leaves little place for ordinary workers and employees, even if only those (numbering with their families over 10 million in 1953) covered by Labour Insurance are included. In face of this, it is certainly ironical to read that 'holidays at rest homes are becoming a regular feature in the lives of the industrial workers of Shanghai'.[104]

EDUCATION

Undoubtedly one of the greatest achievements of Mao's regime is the rapid extension of education.

The number of pupils in primary schools in China rose as follows: 1909–10, 1·5 million; 1929–30, 8·8 million; 1936, 21·4 million; 1949–50, 24 million; 1955–6, 53·1 million.[105] Practically all children in towns now attend primary schools. Some urban workers' children may manage to get to secondary schools, and some might even reach University. The highest pre-Liberation record of pupils in secondary schools was 1,878,523; the 1955–6 total of 4,473,000 leaves this far behind.[106] Again, the highest pre-Liberation record of students in universities was 155,036; in 1955–6 there were 292,000.[107] In addition, workers have opportunities for learning in evening schools; in 1952 as many as 2,700,000 workers were enrolled in evening classes.[108]

[101] NCNA, Peking, June 14, 1956.
[102] PC, December 16, 1954, p. 5.
[103] NCNA, Peking, April 24, 1953.
[104] NCNA, Shanghai, April 30, 1954.
[105] NCNA, Peking, June 14, 1956.
[106] *Ibid.*
[107] *Ibid.*
[108] JMCY, October, 1952.

These figures are certainly impressive. Even so, the number of pupils in schools in China is still smaller, relatively to the population, than in India. In India in 1949–50 there were 43,247,872[109] pupils in all schools (primary, secondary and higher), that is, 75 per cent of the number of pupils in China in 1955–6, while the population of India was only 60 per cent of that of China. In June 1956, the Chinese Minister of Education, Chang Hsi-jo, reported that 'only a little more than 52 per cent of children of school age have been admitted to schools'.[110]

As a general rise in educational-technical standards is a concomitant of industrial civilisation, there is no doubt that Mao's China is sure to achieve high educational-technical levels in the future.

[109] *Statistical Abstract, India, 1951–52*, Calcutta, 1953, pp. 75, 164.
[110] NCNA, Peking, June 20, 1956. Even of those admitted to school a great many leave after a short time. In 1955, 5,100,000 primary school pupils and 150,000 middle school students left. (*Ibid.*)

CHAPTER XV

SOME GENERALISATIONS ON PEKING'S LABOUR POLICY

Peking's labour policy faces a dilemma. With the emphasis on heavy industry there cannot be a substantial rise in workers' living standards, even at the cost of the peasants. The mass of the peasantry is too poor to provide the resources needed for industrialisation as well as an appreciable improvement in the industrial workers' conditions. At the same time the rulers in Peking need to bring the Chinese workers to raise their productive efficiency and increase their production enthusiasm, very important factors for the success of the industrialisation drive. And in order to achieve this their living standards have to be raised.

To extricate themselves entirely from this quandary is impossible. But it is possible to alleviate the situation by raising workers' standards a little, at the cost of the peasantry, or by merely improving urban workers' standards in comparison with those of rural workers. In the latter case, very little need be done in practice. For peasants newly arrived in town, urbanisation itself appears as—and is—an amelioration of their living conditions and an enlargement of their horizon. It is only after years or even decades, after these peasants have been well-baked by the industrial machine, that these factors will wear off.

This dilemma facing labour policy might be met in yet another way: by promoting certain individuals and sections of the working class above the rest through bribes of one sort or another or even through incorporating them into the lower echelons of the bureaucracy itself. But this weapon too will in time prove to be double-edged. The newly created privileged social stratum, the Stakhanovites, foremen, and so on, will become so estranged from the broad masses that they will serve only to incense the workers even more against the regime. But of course this is a long-term process. So long as millions of peasants keep moving into the towns to become industrial workers and hundreds of thousands of unskilled workers become skilled workers, while tens of thousands of the latter become 'model workers', foremen, managers; in other words, so long as the escalator of social advance moves quickly, and there is no crush, the Peking Government can, by and large, subordinate the consumption of the people to the needs of capital accumulation without losing its dynamism: the striving of workers to increase output, and the acceptance, although perhaps without great enthusiasm, of Peking's policies. In these conditions the fierce struggle for personal advancement leads to the atomisation of society and prevents the integration of any dissident groups.

Peking's labour policy is to prevent the workers from putting forward demands for immediate benefit which might threaten to block the path for economic progress chosen by the rulers. Simultaneously, it aims at, and succeeds in, avoiding a head-on collision with the industrial proletariat by the use of the dual techniques of mass persuasion and pressure; keeping control of state and economy firmly in the hands of an élite who alone is qualified to chart the necessary path and to judge where the proletariat's real interests lie. This policy might succeed for a time, for years, even for decades, but its very success must eventually narrow its own field of manœuvre. Sooner or later Peking will break on the horns of its labour policy dilemma.

CHAPTER XVI

FORCED LABOUR

FORCED LABOUR IN ANCIENT CHINA

The Chinese rulers are much more candid than their Soviet tutors when it comes to the question of forced labour camps. Probably this is due to the absence of a democratic humanitarian tradition in China, which was not the case in Russia and because, unlike Stalin, Mao did not have to fight against the Socialists' abhorrence of prison labour. Indeed, the history of forced labour in China is practically as old as that of the Empire.

Forced labour and mass corvée have created great monuments to their memory. There is the Great Wall, a magnificent structure which runs for 1,600 miles over mountains and valleys, averaging 25 feet in height, 13 feet in width at the top, and with guard towers every hundred yards or so. Tradition has it that over a million people perished in its construction and were buried in its mass. Another monument to slave labour and corvée is the Grand Canal. Dug 2,000 years ago, it is 1,290 miles long and 40 yards in width; compared with it the Suez and Panama Canals are water-filled ditches. According to a work written in A.D. 629, the Emperor Yang Ti mobilized 7 million people in A.D. 605, to work on the canal. Professor Wittfogel, quoting this figure,[1] referred to it as somewhat fantastic. According to 'The History of the Sui Dynasty' (*Sui Shu*), Emperor Yang, the second Emperor of this dynasty, mobilized more than a million people for work on the Grand Canal. A similar number were put to work on the Great Wall. The same Emperor mobilized about two million people 'every month' for the construction of the new eastern capital, which included the building of a new imperial palace.[1a]

---

[1] Wittfogel, *op. cit.*, pp. 128–9.
[1a] This information was kindly proffered to the author by Professor Wittfogel in a private letter.

THE EXTENT OF FORCED LABOUR IN MAO'S CHINA

It is impossible to give even a rough estimate of the number of people in slave camps in China. But there are many indications that it runs into millions. For instance, in a Report made by Teng Tzu-hui (Vice-Chairman, Central-South MAC) on November 21, 1951, it was stated that in the Central-South Region between November 1950 and November 1951 'there were inactivated a total of 460,000 native bandits. . . . With the inclusion of the achievements in the operations in the winter of 1949, the total number of native bandits inactivated in the region was 1,150,000. . . .' Only a minority of these 'inactivated bandits' were executed, the majority being condemned to forced labour. As the Report goes on to say, 'among the criminals arrested in the Central-South Region, only 28 per cent were executed, about 2 per cent had their death sentence stayed for two years, 50 per cent were made to undergo reform through labour service while serving their sentences, while the remaining 20 per cent were handed to the masses for surveillance and reform.'[2] Again, in a *Report on the Work of the Kwangtung Provincial Government during the Past Ten Months* given by Ku Ta-ts'un, its Vice-Chairman, on September 15, 1951, it was stated that in this short period a total of 89,701 counter-revolutionaries were arrested: of these 28,332 were executed, while 'those whose crimes were punishable by death but who did not incur the intense hatred of the public were sentenced to death but had their execution delayed for two years during which time they were made to undertake forced labour to give them a chance to reform themselves'.[3] If some 60,000 people are condemned to slave labour in only one of China's twenty-seven provinces in a matter of ten months, the size of the slave labour force in the country as a whole must be huge. There is some corroboration from other sources. It was reported from East China on November 19, 1951, that 'in the course of the last two years, armed forces in East China inactivated a total of more than 225,000 bandits'.[4] An article written in September 1951 entitled

[2] CCJP, December 13, 1951; CB, 157.
[3] NFJP, September 18, 1951; CB, 124.
[4] CFJP, November 27, 1951; CB, 160.

'Great Achievements of the People's Republic of China During the Past Two Years' has this to say:

> Apart from annihilating the Kuomintang troops, the People's Liberation Army also has wiped out more than one million bandits in the past two years. Banditry, a legacy of the Kuomintang days, has been in the main eliminated and social order established all over the country.[5]

A year later the Minister of Finance, Po I-po, stated:

> In the past three years, we have liquidated more than two million bandits; counter-revolutionaries and secret agents have also been put under custody and control.[6]

'INMATES OF FORCED LABOUR CAMPS, DO NOT WANT TO LEAVE THEM'

One feature specific to Mao's China is that the law makes no pretence of assuring those undergoing 'labour service for reform' freedom to leave the camp on the expiry of their sentences. Thus the *Regulations Governing Labour Service for Reform of the People's Republic of China* decreed on August 26, 1954, stated:

> When an important counter-revolutionary criminal or habitual robber or habitual thief, during the period of labour service for reform fails to engage actively in labour service, frequently violates prison regulations, and is actually proved to have failed in getting reformed, so that there is the possibility of his continuing to endanger social security after his release, on the approach of the expiry of his sentence, the organ enforcing labour service for reform may submit views to the competent people's security organ for examination, and with the handing down of the judgment according to law by the local people's court, he may be required to continue labour service for reform (Article 72).[7]

Nor are only 'unreformed criminals' condemned to a prolongation of their prison terms after the expiry of their sentences. The

[5] NCNA, Peking, September 24, 1951; CB, 120.
[6] *New China's Economic Achievements*, etc., *op. cit.*, p. 152.
[7] NCNA, Peking, September 7, 1954; CB, 293.

*Provisional Measures for Dealing with the Release of Criminals Under-
going Labour Service for Reform on the Expiry of their Sentences, and for
Placing them in Employment* of August 26, 1954, provides for the prolongation of detention in three cases:

(1) When the criminal voluntarily desires to remain in the corps
for employment and his services are needed for production therein;

(2) When the criminal has no home to return to, and no job to
to take up;

(3) When the criminal undertakes labour service for reform in a
place extensive in area and sparse in population, so that on the
expiry of his term there is need for him to participate in the local
settlement measures and build his home there (Article 2).[8]

The Minister of Public Security, Lo Jui-ching, commenting on
this, said:

With the enforcement [of these Measures] not only will certain
criminals be relieved of anxiety for employment on the expiry of
their sentence, but the State will also have its difficulties reduced
in dealing with the unemployment problem.

In point of fact, during the past few years, some of the organs
enforcing labour service for reform have been carrying out such
measures. The Ching Ho Farm in Peking during the past four
years has released 5,384 criminals on the expiry of their sentences
and after performing labour service for reform, and 1,455 of them
voluntarily elected to remain at the Farm, being 27 per cent of all
those released.[9]

Similarly, an article entitled 'Reform Criminals into New Men',
in the *People's Daily* of October 6, 1954, stated:

Criminals after completing their term of corrective labour have
requested in large numbers to remain in the original units for production. Corrective labour organs in different areas have mostly
approved the spontaneous applications of such criminals on the
completion of their prison terms to remain with the units for production.[10]

[8] NCNA, Peking, September 7, 1954; CB, 293.
[9] *Ibid.*
[10] JMJP, October 6, 1954; SCMP, 927.

One can imagine how difficult life must be outside prison if people prefer to remain in.

ECONOMIC IMPORTANCE OF FORCED LABOUR

Regulations Governing Labour Service for Reform of the People's Republic of China state:

> Production in labour service for reform shall serve the interests of national construction, and be included in the State's production-construction general plans (Article 30).[11]

The *Regulations* make it quite clear that forced labour exists in all branches of the economy. It states:

> Production of labour service for reform shall be subject to the unified leadership of the committees of financial and economic affairs of the People's Governments of different levels, and also to concrete guidance by the relevant agricultural-forestry, industrial, financial, communications, water conservancy, and commercial departments (Article 31).

Already some years earlier the Minister of Public Security, Lo Jui-ching, had unashamedly pointed out the value to the Government of forced labour: 'forced labour . . . is possessed of the greatest political and economic significance . . . Compulsory labour will produce wealth for the Government.'[12] Proof of this can frequently be gleaned from the press. For instance, the *People's Daily* in an editorial, mentioned with satisfaction:

> According to statistical returns from different areas, of the criminals in confinement throughout the country, more than 83 per cent have participated in agricultural and industrial production, or have been organised into various engineering corps for the felling of timber, construction of buildings, restoration and construction of conservancy works and the building of railways and highways.[13]

[11] NCNA, Peking, September 7, 1954.
[12] JMJP, October 11, 1951.
[13] JMJP, September 7, 1954; CB, 293.

The *People's Daily* even went so far as to claim that the forced labour camps are 'the vanguard of Socialist production in the countryside'.[14]

Prisoners are employed in forced labour even before they are proved guilty. As Lo Jui-ching stated: 'Criminals awaiting judgment, capable of participating in labour service, shall also be made to do so.'[15]

Note, by the way, that even prior to judgment, an arrested person is called, and treated as, a criminal!

To ensure that prisoners show the required enthusiasm for production, they are tempted with the same carrot as workers outside.

The *Regulations Governing Labour Service for Reform of the People's Republic of China* stipulates: 'Production competition may be launched among criminals, to raise production efficiency and to promote the active zeal of criminals in labour service for reform.'[16] This, as well as some other features of the *Regulations*, are copied from Soviet precedents, and Lo Jui-ching was therefore giving credit where credit was due, when he stated that in drafting the *Regulations*, 'assistance was received from Soviet legal experts'.[17]

[14] JMJP, April 1, 1955; SCMP, 1027.
[15] NCNA, Peking, September 7, 1954; CB, 293.
[16] *Ibid.*
[17] *Ibid.*

CHAPTER XVII

BUREAUCRATIC MISMANAGEMENT—A CANCER EATING INTO CHINA'S ECONOMY

INTRODUCTION

Under competitive capitalism based upon private ownership of the means of production, the market determines the prices of factors of production as well as of the commodities produced. The individual capitalist must operate an accurate accounting system, lest he pay the penalty of financial loss; or, after a grave miscalculation, even bankruptcy. In a statified economy, where most of the prices are determined administratively, and where the income of the plant manager has no direct relation to the real economic situation of his plant, accurate accounting becomes even more necessary, as the manager of a plant can conceal the defects of the enterprise for a long time should it become necessary. He is not subject to the market law, neither directly nor immediately. Without accurate accountancy any distortion in one enterprise can be assimilated as an element in the calculations of other enterprises, and so on cumulatively. The Government may punish the manager who fails, but the failure comes to light only after the damage is done.

The extremely harsh administrative punishments (demotion, imprisonment, etc.) tend to boomerang and defeat their purpose. For they encourage the dissembling manager, and provide an even more powerful incentive for such managers to plot with other officials of the administration. The same ruthless quality of the retribution engenders a high degree of circumspection, not to say timidity, in any manager faced with the need to take a risk or make a decision. There is consequently a marked tendency throughout the managerial side of Chinese industry to 'pass the buck' and to increase, *ad nauseam*, the number of unproductive officials. Again, the managers are sharply conscious of the unequivocally administrative nature of the sanctions hanging over them, and, therefore, of the great extent to which their own fate depends upon the arbitrary decisions derived automatically from a current general policy which can be and is frequently superseded overnight by one of an entirely different character.

Finally, it is a commonplace that the complexity and diversity of a modern industrial economy necessitate the maximum degree of local autonomy and initiative and the widest field of managerial discretion. But this is a state of things in direct conflict with extremes of bureaucratic rule.

The Chinese Communist press abounds in accusations of grave bureaucratic mismanagement directed against factory and mine managers, heads of State trading companies, State financial officials, and so on. These accusations clearly reveal the gravity of the situation. In the space available no more than a few examples can be cited.

MISMANAGEMENT IN INDUSTRY AND MINING

A common complaint against management in industry is its over-staffing with administrative personnel. A *People's Daily* editorial wrote about local State-owned industries:

> . . . many enterprises are huge in structural organisation with too many administrative personnel and high expenditure for non-productive purposes. According to returns from 195 local State-operated plants in Shantung, administrative personnel account for less than 10 per cent of the total number of staff members and workers only in the case of 7 plants; 10–20 per cent in the case of 50 plants; and 20–50 per cent in the case of 138 plants.[1]

Referring to the same question, the *People's Daily* pointed to the position in the mines:

> At present, a relatively important problem confronting the organisation of labour in State coal mines is this: the proportion of administrative staff is excessively large and the distribution of personnel extremely irrational. In 1953, the administrative staff in State coal mines constituted on an average about 32 per cent of the production personnel—over 50 per cent in some individual units

[1] JMJP, March 11, 1954; SCMP, 777.

—thus causing numerous instances of staff redundancy within the enterprises.[2]

Li Fu-chun pointed to other examples of overstaffing:

> There are . . . many enterprises with an excess of non-productive personnel and many inflated departments and divisions. Take the Penhsi Iron and Steel Works for instance, which is far from being an isolated case. Workers form only 56 per cent of the total personnel of the company, while administrative personnel constitute one quarter. According to the findings of the Peking Municipal Committee of the Chinese Communist Party, the Shihchingshan Iron and Steel Works, the Shihchingshan Power Plant and the Chingho Woollen Textile Mill can reduce their staff by more than 3,600 men, which is one quarter of the total number of workers and staff of these three units.[3]

Another common accusation against industrial management is inattention to the quality of output, due to the overpowering urge to fulfil targets, thus gaining praise and avoiding punishment. For instance, the Tientsin *Ta Kung Pao* told the following tale of woe:

> Of the 13 principal products manufactured by the State-operated Mukden Medical Appliances Factory, 9 were below the standard quality during the first quarter of the current year, and the State-operated sales departments had to return the goods to the factory. For clamps alone, 72·69 per cent of the finished products had to be made over again. The standard of quality of preparations for injection made by the State-operated Shanghai Drug Factory has also deteriorated steadily, compared to last year and the year before. Due to the poor quality of its products during April and May this year, the State-operated Canton Paper Factory had its products returned, thus affecting the completion of the production plan. . . . The bicycle tyres produced by some rubber factories showed serious defects in that the tracks are not prominent enough and holes are often present.[4]

[2] JMJP, August 29, 1954; SCMP, 915.
[3] Li Fu-chun, *op. cit.*, p. 110.
[4] TKP, July 20, 1954; SCMP, 863.

MAO'S CHINA

A complaint against No. 8 Rubber Factory:

> Defective pieces have been allowed to pass freely by each hand, and rubber shoes with holes as large as a bean have been glibly passed for packing and shipment out of the factory as approved finished products to the market.[5]

Then there is the Changsha Machine Plant where the managers 'blindly chased after quantity to the neglect of quality with the result that 57 per cent of the water pumps produced in the first half of 1954 were found to be inferior and sub-standard products'.[6]

The following is typical of a long list of complaints of this nature made by Li Fu-chun:

> . . . take, for example, the Dairen Factory and Mine Car Plant, one of the enterprises under the First Ministry of Machine-building Industry: 90 per cent of the 322 50-ton open wagons produced by that plant in the first quarter of the year had to be done over again because they did not come up to design specifications. The Shenyang Second Machine Tool Plant is an extreme case. All the 380 drilling machines produced by the plant had to be done over again because violation of the regular procedure for trial manufacture resulted in failure of the finished products to meet design specifications. Rejected parts alone caused a loss of JMP 1,200,000. Consequently, from September 1954 to the first quarter of this year, the plant failed to turn out any finished products. Forty per cent of the ploughshares produced were rejects because their curves did not follow specifications and their metal parts were not of the required hardness after heat treatment.[7]

State factories resort to deception to cover up the bad quality of their products and increase their profits. Thus a *People's Daily* editorial writes:

> For profit-making purposes, some enterprises went to the extent of nonfulfilment of contract, replacing goods of good quality by those of inferior quality, raising the cost of products, and building their 'profit' on the loss of brother enterprises and the masses.

[5] TKP, July 20, 1954; SCMP, 863.
[6] JMJP, December 13, 1954; SCMP, 959.
[7] Li Fu-chun, *op. cit.*, pp. 108–9.

296

For instance, the iron pipes supplied by the Hsuanhua Machine Works to the capital construction department were rejects which leaked. But the factory . . . had the holes covered over and then sold them as good products. Some of the State-operated cotton textile factories of Shanghai have for long used various means of deception to sell their poor-quality cloth as good-quality products. Other enterprises, to increase their production value and make greater profits, do not produce the kinds of articles as specified by the State, but blindly turn out products of higher value and less labour but often unwanted by society. For instance, certain State-operated pharmaceutical factories of Shanghai, neglecting the production of low-valued but widely demanded products, devote themselves to producing preparations of high price and small demand. Some tool factories do not turn out small tools of low cost but large tools of high cost.[8]

Another item in the accusations levelled against industrial managements is that in order to achieve their targets they alternate fits of overactivity with periods of slackness, to the detriment of output, equipment and the workers' health. The *People's Daily* gave illuminating percentage figures of such fluctuations: 'Some factories and mines fulfilled 10 per cent of plans during January, 360 per cent in March, 14 per cent in April and 249 per cent in June.'[9]

Again, industrial managements are accused of callously wasting precious materials, a particularly grievous fault in such a poor country. Thus, from the Kailan coal mines comes this sad tale:

In purchasing and requisitioning supplies the Supply Department and other units of the Kailan Coal Mine are characterised by irresponsibility, chaotic system, blind purchases and improper storage, with the result that huge quantities of supplies are accumulated and damaged. The supplies (not shown on books) scattered about and left under nobody's care total 4,000 to 5,000 items and are valued at JMP 85,000,000,000 according to preliminary estimates.

The Supply Department, not knowing that 5 tons of spring steel was in stock, foolishly purchased 20 tons of spring steel last year, a quantity sufficient to cover 60 years' requirements of the Kailan

[8] JMJP, March 30, 1955; SCMP, 1027.
[9] JMJP, August 18, 1953; SCMP, 639.

Coal Mine which needs only one third of a ton per annum. Further, ignorant of the stock position the Supply Department purchased quantities of carbon brushes which are sufficient for 20 years' requirement.

The storage of supplies is also characterised by lack of responsibility with the result that large quantities of supplies are damaged. Cables worth JMP 50,000,000,000 are placed in a broken mat-shed and exposed to the elements. If they are kept in such a state for long they will certainly be completely ruined. Abandoned in the 'scrap iron yard' are 500-volt ampere transformers and parts of 500 h.p. electric hoisting machines. Seamless steel tubings and 5 tons of '·5' steel plates, which have been abandoned in the scrap iron yard and long exposed to the elements are covered with rust. Four tons of iron plates long kept in the open have rusted to such an extent that they can hardly be distinguished from mud.[10]

To cover up such waste, factory managers often resort to the simple device of overstating the quantity of materials needed for the work in hand. Thus, for instance, 'the Shanghai Steamship Engine Plant set the plant norm of metals consumed for the casting of moulds for axles at 1,722 kilograms, but actually only 777 kilograms were needed'.[11] Again, 'the Shanyang Second Machine Tool Plant in its plans for casting provided for 35 per cent of waste in cuttings, but actually only 21 per cent was required'.[12]

One further disease from which management suffers, is the lack of an adequate tie-in between different industries and plants. This causes different industries to develop disproportionately, creating overproduction in some and underproduction in others. To quote some examples from the *People's Daily*:

> The production of 'rotating-furnace' steel in the Tangshan Steel Plant, for instance, has increased day by day and the amount of pig iron of low phosphorus content needed for production has exceeded the figure in the original plan by one-third. The said plant did not give the problem sufficient thought while making production plans. The amount of pig iron it has ordered is thus not enough

[10] JMJP, July 24, 1953; SCMP, 624.
[11] JMJP, August 20, 1955; SCMP, 1142.
[12] *Ibid.*

for its needs, and the stock available is not adequate. Nor has the said plant been able promptly to take delivery of the materials it ordered. So the production of 'rotating-furnace' steel had to stop while waiting for raw materials to arrive. The Liu-li-ho Cement Factory at Peking has often had to suspend the production of cement because of its failure to realise that there is not enough gypsum (one of the raw materials for making cement). The Taiyuan Machine Factory has accepted many orders for coal-crushing machines, but neglected roller bearings and ball bearings. None of the coal-crushing machines it has made, therefore, can be turned to productive account because of the lack of roller bearings and ball bearings.[13]

MISMANAGEMENT IN CAPITAL CONSTRUCTION

The tale of mismanagement in industry is repeated in capital construction. One of its main scourges is the overstocking of materials. The *People's Daily* gives some instances:

Not a few capital construction units blindly purchased and distributed materials without regard to actual requirements and did not adequately keep and use them, thus resulting in their overstocking, waste and loss. This practice cannot be tolerated. For example, JMP 30,500,000,000 worth of machinery and equipment was purchased by the State-operated No. 5 Cotton Spinning Factory in Shensi Province before capital-construction designs were definitely decided upon, and consequently this machinery and equipment was uselessly accumulated. Some capital-construction units have purchased materials without previous planning, and so materials have often been duplicated or bought in excess. When materials were purchased severally in Peking and Chungking for the Chungking Municipal Electrical and Engineering Corporation this year, over JMP 790,000,000 worth of machinery was duplicated and there was an excess of over JMP 2,100,000,000 worth of equipment and materials, owing to lack of co-ordination.[14]

A few further examples of the inflated allocation of materials follow:

By providing labour and materials liberally the three construction companies under the Wuhan Building Construction Bureau made

[13] JMJP, November 4, 1952; SCMP, 461.
[14] JMJP, August 20, 1953; SCMP, 654.

out of materials alone JMP 19,300,000,000 profits or 35·49 per cent of the total issue of materials during the first half of 1953. Of the profit made by some work sites under the South-west Bureau of Building Construction, 27·8 per cent was accounted for by over-estimate of building cost. A construction group under the North-west Bureau of Building Construction, which undertook the project of building the Military Outfit Plant, provided bricks for walls without making allowance for windows and doors, as a result of which it saved bricks required for the project. In undertaking a project for building a warehouse for the Petroleum Co. at the cost of JMP 1,300,000,000 the 1st Construction Company of the Central-South Bureau of Building Construction made JMP 900,000,000 profits, or 69·6 per cent of the total building cost.[15]

Mismanagement results in very low utilisation of scarce and precious construction machines. Thus, for instance, a *People's Daily* editorial said:

Of the 12 kinds of principal machines commonly used by the department of building construction, more than 40 per cent was not used at all during 1954. During the first half of 1954, utilisation of each earth excavator by each shift reached only 39·4 per cent in the North-east region.[16]

Another waste is the excessive construction of buildings of a non-productive nature, such as office buildings, auditoria, and the like. Thus Li Fu-chun's *Report on the Five-Year Plan* states:

In the past few years, there has been widespread and serious extravagance and waste in the building of non-productive projects.

According to figures of the State Statistical Bureau, 21·6 per cent of the total investment of the six industrial ministries of the Central People's Government in 1953 and 1954 was non-productive invest-ment. In the First Five Year Plan of the Soviet Union, however, non-productive investment in the industrial departments com-prised only 14·5 per cent of total investment. Non-productive in-vestment formed 24·3 per cent of this country's capital construction investment in 1954.[17]

[15] JMJP, May 17, 1954; SCMP, 825.
[16] JMJP, January 27, 1955; SCMP, 984.
[17] Li Fu-chun, *op. cit.*, p. 104.

To round off the picture of mismanagement in construction, we can do no better than quote at length a report on one key construction project.

Waste of materials is an important aspect of the waste characterising the No. 360 Project. In the first place, materials are piled up. Due to a hurried start of construction, no plans were drawn up for organisational measures of construction, and materials were purchased aimlessly; in consequence, materials purchased were not according to the specifications required for the project and quantities of rolled steel and timber were put away after arrival when they were found unfit for use. According to preliminary estimates, JMP 14,400,000,000 funds are tied up on this account.

Due to the lack of a correct budget and quota, and the lack of a sound delivery and return system, materials were used wastefully. Preliminary estimates place such waste at JMP 1,800,000,000 (actual wastes must be higher than this). For instance, structural steel aimlessly cut amounted to 143 tons. Loss of timber was also serious. Good pines were used for making tool cases and work sheds. Workers' families and kitchens used timber over 1 metre long as firewood, or for making furniture. Cement was also wasted due to lack of technical control and failure to grasp the compounding ratios. Between April 10 and the end of May alone, 481 tons of cement were wasted.

When the No. 360 Project was inspected, over 40 wooden sheds were found on the work site. Nobody knows what these sheds were built for and not even officials of the work site could tell when these wooden sheds were built, who built them, who approved the building, where the materials were procured and what was their purpose.

The work site bought from the China Communications and Electric Supplies Company JMP 140,000,000 worth of electric supplies. Payment was made but no delivery was taken of the supplies. It was several months afterwards when the seller discovered this mass of electric supplies while taking stock, and the seller urged the Engineering Company to take the supplies away.

The No. 360 work site was in disorder with sand everywhere and nail-studded moulds strewn here and there blocking the ways. Posters announcing 'beware of upturned nails' were posted everywhere, but that did not prevent the feet of workers being pierced. At one time, nails were used up and no money was available to buy nails, which worried the director of the work site who did not know what to do. Later a man who happened to inspect the work site and godowns collected 13 barrels of nails in no time.

The surprisingly low productivity of labour at No. 360 work site considerably increased the engineering cost, thus causing huge waste . . . when productivity of labour reached its lowest mark at the work site, the labour productivity of steel structure workers and mould workers reached only 15 per cent of the norm, and that of reinforced concrete workers reached only 40 per cent of the norm, while that of bricklayers reached only 5 per cent of the norm.

More extravagant was the purchase of furniture and fixtures for the Plant Construction Office. 28 sets of sofas and 33 carpets including one high-grade carpet costing JMP 14,360,000 and velvet plush-upholstered sofas costing JMP 5,900,000 were bought. More cars and radio sets were bought than were required and furniture in general was of high grade. Furniture alone cost JMP 4,000,000,000. For one thing, more than 100 desks were surplus.[18]

MISMANAGEMENT IN TRADE

Trade follows the same pattern of mismanagement. Po I-po, Minister of Finance, complained in a speech on January 6, 1953, that the Ministry of Commerce

has done very little work, and we may say, very bad work in serving the consumers, in studying people's concrete requirements according to regions, in shortening the period of capital turnover, in reducing trading charges and in cutting miscellaneous expenses.[19]

One result of mismanagement in trade is the amassing of unmarketable goods, especially serious in poverty-stricken China. In an article entitled 'Unmarketable Merchandise Accumulates in State Trading Departments', the *People's Daily* writes:

At present dead stock and goods of inferior quality occupy 20–31 per cent of the entire circulating capital of the State trading departments.

Recently the Ministry of Commerce of the Central People's Government made key-point investigations in provinces and cities

18 JMJP, August 7, 1954; SCMP, 887.
19 NCNA, Peking, January 13, 1953; SCMP, 492.

of the conditions of accumulation of unmarketable goods in State corporations. . . . In these corporations, dead stocks and inferior goods total 157 items, tying up approximately JMP 4,000,000,000,000 in capital. . . . If JMP 4,000,000,000,000 were used to buy steel rails, it could complete a railway track 4,400 kilometres long. If the money were used to develop the textile industry it could equip 17 up-to-date textile mills each having 50,000 spindles and an appropriate number of looms. If the money were used to buy aeroplanes, it would be enough for 2,266 fighters. If it were used to buy guns, 4,444 cannons or 5,000 anti-tank aircraft guns could be bought. This shows only a portion of dead stocks and tied-up capital in State trading departments.[20]

Again:

Poor management and arbitrary shipment of goods in various State trading enterprises have not only increased incidental losses and wasted money in transport, but also caused the accumulation of unmarketable goods. Before finding out whether paper was required in Chekiang, the China General Goods Corporation ordered shipments to be sent there, so that paper stocks estimated at JMP 44,700,000,000 have been accumulated. The China Ramie Corporation sent 2,500 tons of ramie in April 1952 from East China to Tientsin, where they were supposed to be exported. One thousand tons were found not to conform to specifications. After re-processing, they were still unexportable, although 300 tons (estimated at JMP 3,100,000,000) had been lost during re-processing. They were not marketable in North China and so had to be shipped back to East China. The South-west Branch of the China Industrial Materials Corporation, without investigating local requirements, blindly ordered large quantities of steel from its head office in 1951. At present it has accumulated about 8,000 tons of steel, estimated at JMP 80,000,000,000–120,000,000,000. These steel materials have found no buyers for over a year.[21]

The managements of marketing and supply co-operatives are not more efficient than those of the State trading companies. The Tientsin *Ta Kung Pao* reported:

[20] JMJP, January 29, 1953; SCMP, 510.
[21] TKP, September 28, 1953; SCMP, 671.

Losses were generally prevalent. In the first quarter, basic co-operatives in rural villages throughout the country, after closing their accounts for their supply business, showed losses instead of profits. Four out of the five provincial co-operatives in East China suffered losses.

The superstructure of co-operatives at various levels is gigantic, and many of their personnel redundant. The proportion of administrative staff is too big. Efficiency has thus become low and the pay-roll large.[22]

Another issue of *Ta Kung Pao* painted the following picture of mismanagement in co-operative trading organisations:

Last April, the All-China Federation of Co-operatives sent several working teams to inspect the warehouses of the No. 1 Wholesale Bureau's wholesale centres at Shanghai, Hankow, Mukden and Sian and its South-west Marketing Department's warehouses. . . . According to preliminary statistics, of the total amount of commodities in the warehouses of the four wholesale centres, 22·8 per cent constituted overstocking.

The fact that accounts have not corresponded with transactions is also serious. For example, the South-west Marketing Department discovered that in the case of 14 items accounts were not in agreement with the transactions. With regard to nine of these 26 items, there were goods but no entries in the accounts. In respect of four items, there were entries in the accounts and no goods in the warehouse. . . . Of thirteen other items . . . there were 11,300 dozen more in stock than shown in the accounts.

The safe-keeping of commodities in the warehouses has been in extreme disorder . . . The warehouses have been terribly dirty, dust has been very thick, and waste paper has covered the whole floor. Dust was flying when commodities were received or despatched. Besides, commodities were often not packed, urns not covered and packages not sealed, thus turning white cloth into grey cloth, white paper into black paper, and brown sugar into mud. Various commodities were all covered with a thick layer of dust. . . . In the Chunghua warehouse in Fuhsing, more than ten barrels of lard were not sealed and the lard was tainted. More than 30 barrels were leaking so that the barrels themselves got rotten and wormy.

[22] TKP, September 28, 1953; SCMP. 671.

In the Huachung warehouse, 18 of the 61 barrels of honey stored were leaking and two of them became sour.

Moreover, commodities were not classified but stored in disorder, and many commodities of the same kind were scattered in several places. In the warehouse of the Shanghai wholesale centre, sugar barrels were carelessly stacked on a pile of paper: loose papers were scattered all over the floor so that transport workers just walked on them. No one worried about this way of spoiling things. In the warehouse of the Hankow wholesale centre, cotton yarn, cotton cloth and cement were put together, thus becoming a mixture of an unknown kind.

As large quantities of commodities were 'compressed, thrust aside, piled up and added to', the commodities last stored in the warehouses were first taken out. The commodities first stored were compressed by large piles of other goods and could not be moved, so that they deteriorated and became unsaleable because of being stored too long. In the Taiho warehouse of the South-west Marketing Department, 19,940 umbrellas were stored so long that they got stuck and could not be opened. In the warehouse of the Shanghai wholesale centre, over 3,000 bolts of blue cloth faded completely because of being compressed for too long a time.[23]

IN CONCLUSION

In every case of mismanagement, whether by an individual manager, a Minister directing an industry or the State Planning Commission directing the whole economy, the discrepancies are overcome and the gaps filled by the strict methods of government dictation. Totalitarian, bureaucratic-political dictatorship helps to overcome the results of bad planning and management, which in fact have their origins in this self-same bureaucratic set-up. Therefore, the mismanagement corroding China's national economy (as well as the economy of Russia and her East-European satellites) does not preclude very substantial, nay stupendous, achievements. The price being paid by the people for these achievements as well as for the bureaucratic mismanagement and waste is quite another question.

[23] TKP, August 5, 1953; SCMP, 640.

CHAPTER XVIII

THE NEW PRIVILEGED

Where there are pariahs there are privileged. Actually China's poverty and the quick industrialisation leave very little leeway for luxuries even for the rulers. And so, in comparison with the upper classes in the West, the standard of living of the new ruling class in China—the State, Party and Army bureaucracy, the factory managers, technicians, and the like—is extremely low. It is not inconsiderable, however, in comparison with that of the ordinary workers and peasants in the country. Nor is this all. Present privileges are only small beginnings. With the increasing industrialisation of the country, the sources from which to feed the appetites of the ruling class will be greater, and with eating, the appetite itself will grow. One element in this rise of standards is the fact that industrialisation will depend more and more on the efficiency of the managers, technicians etc., and their wishes will have to be heeded. Again, to the extent that industrialisation demands the tightening of the masses' belt, the guardians of the process of forced national savings and accumulation, will become ever more powerful. While guarding their ward, they will not forget themselves.

This functional relationship between the productivity of their society and the privileges of the Maoist bureaucracy is shown clearly in the development of the latter over the last two decades. During the anti-Japanese war, differences in the standard of living of rank-and-file soldiers and commanders in Mao's army were very small. The following pay scale operated in the Eighth Route Army:[1]

Commander of Army	$5·00 a month
Regimental Commander	$4·00 a month
Lower officers	$3·00 a month
Rank and file	$2·00 a month

In the other Communist army—the New Fourth Army—pay ranged from $1·50 to $5·00 a month.[2] There were some differ-

[1] I. Epstein, *The People's War*, London, 1939, p. 76.
[2] *Ibid.*, p. 266.

ences between the rations of commanders and high government officials and those of ordinary soldiers: only the former ever had eggs, for instance.[3] In addition, commanders and high government officials had the services of orderlies; they alone were entitled to the use of a horse. The 'luxuries' were indeed very simple, but in the midst of general poverty, even a small piece of meat, or nourishing soup, can be a great attraction. Nevertheless, poor as these 'luxuries' were, not a little friction arose among officials and commanders on their account. Testimony for this is to be found in a speech by Liu Shao-chi in 1941:

> . . . some of you quarrelled or struggled with each other about orderlies, horses, food, clothing, medical treatment, promotion, etc. . . . Why don't they give me an orderly or a horse? Why don't they give me medical treatment? Why don't they promote me? Why don't they give me good food and clothing?
> . . . Take another example. In East Anhwei, government personnel were given a small salary.[4] So some comrades asked to be sent to work in the government organisations, with the aim that they might get a salary. When they were not allowed to go they launched a struggle under the slogan of opposing government personnel having salaries.[5]

During the anti-Japanese war, however, privilege did not have good soil to nourish on. For a certain time after Mao's victory too the urgent need for economy prevented any great increase in luxuries. In 1950, three-quarters of the State employees, numbering 9 million, were still on the 'supply system', by which they were supplied with their daily necessities and a little spending money equal to 20 *catties* of millet a month. Under this system administration costs were kept to a minimum of 70 *catties* of millet per employee per month.[6] Although the 'supply system' did not mean complete equality, differences were not very large. Shortly after military victory, it was replaced progressively by a salary

[3] C. and W. Band, *Dragon Fangs*, London, 1948, p. 233.
[4] At the time of the Anti-Japanese War Government personnel in the Communist Areas were provided with all daily necessities. Except for some pocket money, they had no salaries.
[5] Liu Shao-chi, *On Inner-Party Struggle*, Peking, n.d., pp. 42–4.
[6] Yang P'ei-hsin, 'Price, Finance and State Bonds', HCS, January 29, 1950.

system, so that by the end of 1952 the transfer of all state officials from the 'supply system' to the salary system was practically complete.[7]

Salaries showed a wide range. The lowest-paid officials were the rural cadres. A Directive of the Central-South MAC of June 13, 1951, fixed rural government cadres' salaries thus:

> The *ts'un* chief, the chairman and the secretary of the Peasants' Associations will each receive a monthly allowance of 100–150 *catties* of rice (or wheat in wheat-producing areas). Monthly allowances for the commander of the People's Militia will be half this amount.[8]

At the same time, in the rural areas of Hunan, the salary of a headmaster of a primary school was 220–300 *catties* of rice per month; of primary-school teachers, 150–280 *catties*; and of other primary-school employees, 140–180 *catties*.[9]

Passing from the countryside to the towns, and going to the other end of the scale:

> Technicians and engineers get up to 1,700 *catties* per month. Those with very special qualifications sometimes get 30 per cent more as an allowance. In the case of a few experts and specialists, their salaries are fixed by the government.
>
> The salary of professors in universities are the same as those of engineers and technicians in factories. They are generally 1,000 to 1,500 *catties* of rice per month. In colleges and schools the salaries of teachers generally range between 800 and 1,200 *catties* of food grains per month.[10]
>
> Cabinet Ministers get a salary of 22,000 *catties* of millet per month.[11]

B. Shastri, leader of the Indian Praja Socialist Party, visiting China in 1953 as a guest of ACFTU, described his shock when he learnt 'of the disparity between the wages of the average worker

[7] Boldyrev, *op. cit.*, p. 76.
[8] CCJP, June 19, 1951; CB, 131.
[9] Chao, *Source Materials*, etc., *op. cit.*, III, p. 34.
[10] Sundarlal, *op. cit.*, pp. 127–8.
[11] *Ibid.*, p. 62.

and the salary of a manager': workers were paid 50–60 wage units per month, while a factory manager received 2,750 wage units.[12]

Despite differences amongst the officials, collectively they enjoy a standard of living far above that of workers, and much further above that of peasants. One index of this is the consumption of cloth, which, although not a luxury, is very scarce in China. A *People's Daily* editorial gives the following information:

According to a survey conducted by the Tsinan Municipality, *per capita* consumption of cotton cloth during 1953 was 94·19 feet in the case of cadres of municipal organs, 92 feet in the case of industrial and commercial capitalists, 64·8 feet in the case of workers, and 39·58 feet in the case of other city dwellers. In the case of peasants of many areas, actual consumption of cotton cloth each year . . . was only 10–20 feet and, in some cases, only 5 feet . . .[13]

The bureaucrats sometimes strive for more than is economically possible. This was mentioned in a speech of Kao Kang, given to a North-East Top Level Party Members' and Cadres' Conference on August 31, 1951:

Certain of our organisations and leadership cadres have been heavily imbued with the spirit of bureaucracy. They care very much about outward appearance. For instance, one can see a growing number of American or British-made motor cars in the streets of Mukden, and the sending of gifts or invitations to banquets is also increasingly seen. It would seem that they would not be able to go to the office if not riding in an American or British-made motor car, that short of gift-sending one could not show the friendship formed during the revolution, and that if a meeting were held without a banquet, it would not show the success of the meeting.[14]

Again, Li Fan-fu, Deputy Director, Department of Propaganda, South China Sub-Bureau of the Central Committee, CCP, stated:

[12] B. Shastri, 'Red China: Workers' Paradise', *Thought*, New Delhi, November 7, 1953.
[13] NCNA, Peking, September 17, 1954; SCMP, 894.
[14] TPJP, December 1, 1951; CB, 163.

One cadre insisted he would buy only Western-style furniture and his family of four was served by 12 servants including a doorman, table waiter and guards. Their food consisted of expensive delicacies and five meals were served daily. The cadre even wanted to buy an American-made radio costing H.K. $3,500 and used the best kind of tea selling at over JMP 200,000 a *catty*. His way of life was in every way patterned after that of the bourgeoisie.[15]

The bureaucrats, it seems, also try to keep a distance between themselves and ordinary mortals. Although the existence of servants and orderlies is accepted as a matter of course and does not need justification, when cadres begin to think that they should be debarred from Party membership, and say 'only cadres can enter the Party, and there is no chance for orderlies to become Party members, no matter how long they have served as such'—then, according to Ou Meng-chueh (Vice-Director of the Organisation Department, South China Sub-Bureau of the Central Committee, CCP), who quotes these words, they go just a little too far, and deserve to be reprimanded.[16]

Differences in income between the bureaucracy and the mass of the people in China are much smaller than in Russia. We do not yet hear of factory managers earning 100 times more than workers.[17] But there is no doubt that the differences are growing much faster in China than they did in Russia. They are today much greater than they were in Russia ten years after the Revolution. During the NEP period (1921–8), a unified scale of wages was in existence,

which contained seventeen grades ranging from apprentices to the top specialists, and which gave the most highly-skilled worker three and a half times as much as the lowest-paid unskilled worker. Specialists could earn a maximum of eight times as much as the unskilled worker. (This did not apply to Party members, who had a special scale of maximum wages, much below that of non-Party specialists.) . . .

15 NFJP, June 14, 1952; SCMP, 376.
16 NFJP, September 2, 1952; SCMP, 413.
17 A great deal of material on income differences in Russia is to be found in Cliff, *op. cit.*, pp. 53–68.

In industry, the average wage of workers in March 1926 was 58·64 chervonets roubles, while a factory manager received 187·90 chervonets roubles if he was a Party member, and 309·50 chervonets roubles if he was not a Party member.

There were some factors, however, which mitigated these differences until the introduction of the First Five Year Plan. First of all, no member of the Communist Party was allowed to earn more than a skilled worker. This provision was of great importance, as the majority of the directors of enterprises, departments of industry, etc., were Party members. In 1928, 71·4 per cent of the personnel of the managing boards of the trusts were Party members, as were 84·4 per cent on the boards of the syndicates, and 89·3 per cent on those of individual enterprises.[18]

Unlike the Russian Communist Party, whose traditions of egalitarianism survived for years after the Party took power, the Chinese Party, even before seizing power, was deriding egalitarianism.[19]

As the general level of productivity and culture is much lower in China than it was in Russia, there is no doubt that inequality will continue to grow much more quickly in the former than it did in the latter.

THE MAOIST ÉLITE AND THE BUREAUCRACY OF THE ANCIENT CHINESE EMPIRE

The Maoist bureaucracy, despite some innovations, is carrying on a very old tradition, that of the Mandarinate of the Chinese Empire. A comparison of the two bureaucracies is of value, as it puts the present one in the right historical perspective.

The material basis for the centralised bureaucracy of the Empire was the large-scale irrigation works. As Marx put it:

This prime necessity of an economical and common use of water . . . necessitated, in the Orient where civilisation was too low, and the territorial extent too vast to call into life voluntary association, the interference of the centralised power of government. Hence an

[18] Cliff, *ibid.*, pp. 55–6.
[19] See article 'The Incompatibility of Socialism and Egalitarianism', JMJP, September 14, 1952; SCMP, 427.

economic function devolved upon all Asiatic governments; the function of providing public works.[20]

Wittfogel formulated the same idea thus: Irrigation is 'everywhere in China an indispensable condition for intensive agriculture, on the basis of which Chinese agrarian society was constructed, just as the industrial society of modern capitalism has been constructed on the basis of coal and iron'.[21] Significantly, an historian who lived just after Ssu-ma Ch'ien had managed to unite the whole country (220 B.C.), attributed this success to the development of irrigation in the Ching River Valley and particularly to the digging of the Chengkuo Canal which was opened in 246 B.C., i.e., 26 years before Ssu-ma Ch'ien unified the country.

Like the Maoist bureaucracy, that of the Empire found itself in permanent conflict with the basic classes of society, and primarily the peasants. The primary function of the Mandarinate was the construction of public works. But there was an unavoidable connection between the development of irrigation to increase yields and the digging of canals to transfer much of it to State granaries, and increasing exploitation and mass misery. Hence 'the great unpopularity of Han Wu Ti and Sui Yang Ti, both very energetic and enterprising monarchs, whose achievements in the field of public-works development, including canal building and promotion of irrigation, resulted in public discontent and financial disaster in the one case and loss of the empire in the other'.[22]

Not only was the State bureaucracy in conflict with the peasants from whom it drew taxes and whom it conscripted for public works, but it also came up against the private landowners who tried to seize the greater share of the surplus product produced by the peasants for themselves. This struggle was waged, *inter alia*, around the repeated attempts of the State to destroy or at least limit large land ownership.[23]

[20] K. Marx, 'The British Rule in India', *New York Daily Tribune*, June 25, 1853. Marx, *Selected Works*, Vol. II, London, 1942, p. 652.
[21] Wittfogel, *Wirtschaft*, etc., *op. cit.*, p. 229.
[22] Ch'ao-ting Chi, *Key Economic Areas in Chinese History*, London, 1936, p. 122.
[23] See Wittfogel, *Wirtschaft*, etc., *op. cit.*, p. 385ff.

Again the State bureaucracy was in constant conflict with another class of society, the merchants. Roads and canals were developed in order to transfer land rent to State granaries. A certain measure of monetary development also became necessary to achieve this centralisation of taxation. On this basis there arose a powerful class of merchants, and one of the main themes of Chinese history soon became the struggle of the Central State to hold this class in check, by heavy taxation of merchants' profits, by seizure of their property, and so forth.[24] To the same end, the State again and again tried to establish monopoly control over the production, or at least the sale, of many articles; in the case of at least two of the most important articles in agrarian China, salt and iron, it was successful.[25] One result of this struggle against the merchants, was that merchant (and artisan) guilds in China were never as strong as their equivalents in Europe.[26] Similarly, the city-state was never known in China.[27]

The State was not as successful in establishing a monopoly over the peasants' surplus product. It never managed to bring its struggle against landlords and merchants to a victorious conclusion, as its own officials were implicated in private landlordism. The merchants indulged in buying land from impoverished peasants (whom the State 'emancipated' from feudalism in order to be able the better to tax them) on a large scale and created a class of town-dwelling merchant-landlords not very different from the State officials who held land in a private capacity and the remnants of the old feudal gentry.

There were countervailing factors, however, that worked against the centralisation of economic power in the hands of a few landlords, as was the case in feudal Europe, or merchant magnates, as was the case during the Renaissance in certain advanced Western cities. The permanent struggle waged by the centralised State against the individual landlord (and merchant) and the constant buying and selling of land inhibited both land ownership by single families through many generations and the appearance

---

[24] See Wittfogel, *Wirtschaft, etc., op. cit.*, p. 708ff.
[25] *Ibid.*, p. 722ff.
[26] *Ibid.*, pp. 509–10, 571–3, 713–19.
[27] *Ibid.*, p. 572.

of large landed properties, such as were featured in feudal Europe. Again, the landlords of the Chinese Empire were much less powerful politically than the landlords of feudal Europe. The landlords of Oriental society did not usually live in country manors but in walled towns. While the landlords or gentry of feudal Europe were warriors and judges, each of them being thus the political sovereign of his domain, nothing of the sort existed in Oriental society. There the maintenance of order and the dispensation of justice were concentrated in the hands of the State bureaucracy.

The bureaucracy of the Empire was recruited from different classes of society, yet it stood alone as a distinct corporate body. State positions were nominally non-hereditary, although in point of fact they were really open only to children of landlords, merchants and high bureaucrats, who alone had the facilities to prepare for the state examinations. (The difficulty of Chinese writing was a guarantee of this class monopoly.) To secure the unity of the bureaucratic centralised State, an examination system was introduced; regular and frequent shifting of officials from one locality to another also prevented the crystallisation of local enclaves of vested interests in opposition to the central government. A similar function was fulfilled by the Censorate.[28] In an interesting sidelight, Wittfogel points to the appointment of eunuchs to high political posts as one of the methods used to prevent the inheritance of high State posts.

To sum up, Oriental society had an autocratic State bureaucracy which concentrated in its hands the management of a decisive sphere of the economy and which was at permanent war with the centrifugal forces of individual ownership. It was an archetype of totalitarianism long before the term was coined.

The common characteristics of Oriental society and Bureaucratic State Capitalism—whether of Stalinist Russia or Maoist China—come so readily to mind, that it is no accident that the leadership of the Communist Party of Russia, as well as that of China, make every effort to suppress Marx's concept of the Oriental society which he explicitly described as a special kind of society in which a tyrannical state is chief entrepreneur,

28 See p. 371.

oppressing and exploiting the people. Instead they substitute the term feudalism or slavery.[29]

The numerous common features of the old Oriental society and of Mao's China should not, however, blot out the big differences. While the old autocratic State managed the irrigation system—which was a key sphere of contemporary economic life—it left the greater part of production proper in the hands of private persons.[30] The Maoist State manages the key sectors of industry, banking and trading, and is bent on enlarging its control to the management of all production and distribution both in industry and agriculture. From the fact that in Oriental Society the State did not manage all the economic processes, it follows inevitably that in certain segments of social life, even though they be secondary—such as village communities and artisan guilds—rudimentary and limited forms of self-government did exist.[31] With Mao's bureaucratic management of the whole economy, the Party and State bureaucracy will squeeze out all such elements and assume totalitarian control over all aspects of life. Working towards the same end is the fact that the means of communication in the twentieth century are much more advanced than those available to the Confucian Mandarinate. Now, for the first time in Chinese history, the totalitarianism inherent in Oriental society can come to complete fruition.

[29] For the reaction in Russia against Marx's concept of Oriental society, see Wittfogel, 'The Influence of Leninism-Stalinism on China', *Annals of the American Academy of Political and Social Sciences*, September 1951; Wittfogel, 'Russia and Asia', *World Politics*, July 1950; L. Krader, 'Soviet Oriental Studies—1940–48', FES, July 28, 1948.

Sometimes Soviet writers do mention the basic characteristics of Chinese society —the nonexistence of serfdom, the freedom to buy and sell land, the high development of money economy, etc.—but are nevertheless careful to call this feudalism. For a glaring example, see E. Varga, *Basic Problems of Economics and Politics of Imperialism* (Russian), Moscow, 1953, pp. 389–91. Varga goes so far as to quote Wittfogel's *Wirtschaft und Gesellschaft Chinas*.

[30] Although it is true that ancient China had large-scale State-directed mining such as existed in seventeenth- and eighteenth-century Europe, and also large-scale handicraft manufacturing (Wittfogel, *Wirtschaft*, etc., op. cit., p. 508), these were exceptions.

[31] Wittfogel, 'Oriental Despotism', *Soziologus*, Berlin, No. 2, 1953.

PART FOUR

THE STATE

CHAPTER XIX

INTRODUCTION

A totalitarian state invades every pore of society, controls every action of its citizens, tries to mould their every thought and feeling. It uses both violence and propaganda in extreme forms to make them amenable to control from above. By regimenting their leisure time, the state tries to rob them of time and freedom to think for themselves; by keeping them continuously active, according to plans and in channels decided upon from above, it ensures that this activity will not be spontaneous, a result of people's own independent thoughts, but a mere incorporation into the state machine. For all this, the unity and fusion of State and Party are necessary. Heading both must be the Leader.

As a bureaucratised society tends to empty all social relations of their personal element, to make them anonymous abstractions, the Leader, with superhuman attributes, must fill the gap and become the unifying link between people, Party and State. Besides, adulation and semi-worship of the Leader serve as an opiate for the citizen who can neither account for nor remedy his helplessness and misery.

In modern China the State is not only 'special bodies of armed men, prisons, etc.' (in Marxist terminology), but also, as in ancient China, an organiser of social production. It is the great builder, and as such, easily becomes an object for state fetishism.

But the state as an organiser of social production becomes responsible for all failures in production, for poverty, for economic exploitation; it becomes the natural butt for all discontent, vocal and otherwise, the focus of every social protest.

In order to mitigate this effect, the state highlights its social and industrial achievements while simultaneously carrying out punitive swoops among lower executives and individual bureaucrats whom it uses as public scapegoats and showpieces in its purges.

This finding of scapegoats—'self-criticism'—serves not only as a device to deflect popular criticism from Peking on to the individual bureaucrat but also to prevent the bureaucracy from being too inefficient. It also gives the masses the feeling of 'active political participation' and thus tries to bridge the gulf between the democratic pretensions of the regime and its autocratic nature.

Police terror and the absence of competing propaganda agencies allow a complete divorce of propaganda from truth. But, on the other hand, the exposure of the smallest lie from the propaganda machine, the smallest weakness in the state, can cause a disillusionment, entirely disproportionate by objective standards, to the carefully fostered belief in the state, its future and potency. Hence the need for an 'iron curtain', or a 'bamboo curtain', to prevent the smallest chink of light from coming in from the outside, and hence also the need for the constant repetition of Communist propaganda. But the very repetition of propaganda reveals its limitations as an anodyne. Propaganda wears thin where it clashes repeatedly with observation and where its slogans have to change at an increasing rate. Hence the need to compound propaganda—defined by one historian as 'violence committed against the soul'—with police terror—violence committed against the body.

Mao's State-Party may be approached from the summit, moving downwards to where the bureaucratic machine contacts and engulfs the mass of the people, or alternatively from the bottom going upwards towards the summit of the hierarchy. The peculiar characteristics of Mao's totalitarian regime as distinct from other bureaucratic state structures which leave some leeway for people's independent activities is best revealed in the latter approach, which we shall adopt.

CHAPTER XX

POLICE CONTROL OF POPULATION

URBAN SECURITY ORGANISATIONS

The mass of the people is incorporated into the bureaucratic police machine through the Security Committees. Their activities were regularised by the *Provisional Regulations Governing Organisation of Security Committees* decreed by the Ministry of Public Security on August 10, 1952. Provision was made for security committees in every factory, enterprise, school and street in the cities, and in every *hsiang* (administrative village) in the countryside (Article 3).[1]

Security committees were promptly established, and proliferated so rapidly that the Minister of Public Security, Lo Jui-ching, could speak of the existence of 'millions of security organisations' a short time after the decree was published.[2]

These *Provisional Regulations* were replaced two years later by three sets of new regulations: First, *Organic Regulations of Urban Inhabitants' Committees*; secondly, *Organic Regulations of Urban Street Offices*; and thirdly, *Organic Regulations of Public Security Sub-stations*. All three were adopted by the Standing Committee of the National People's Congress on December 31, 1954. The first of these defined the task of Urban Inhabitants' Committees thus:

(1) Undertake public welfare work for inhabitants;
(2) Reflect views and demand of inhabitants to local people's councils or their deputed organs;
(3) Mobilise inhabitants to respond to Government calls and observe laws;
(4) Direct mass security work;
(5) Mediate over disputes among inhabitants (Article 2).

The integration of social welfare and police-political control makes the committees more efficient as implements of totalitarian control.

[1] NCNA, Peking, August 10, 1952; CB, 216.
[2] NCNA, Peking, September 27, 1952; CB, 218.

Each committee was set up under the guidance and control of its municipality. To secure centralised control Article 9 provides that:

> Public and miscellaneous expense for inhabitants' committees and living allowance for members of inhabitants' committees shall be allocated under centralised plans by the people's councils of provinces and municipalities directly under the Central People's Government according to scales to be separately fixed by the Ministry of the Interior.[3]

The main aim of the second set of regulations is clearly to make the urban street offices serve as agents of the Security Police:

> The area under the jurisdiction of street offices should generally correspond to the area under the jurisdiction of public security sub-stations,

which cover 100–600 households (Article 3).

The offices employ quite a number of full-time officials:

> A street office shall have 3 to 7 full-time cadres (Article 5).

The finances of these offices are also under central government control (Article 7).[4]

The third set of regulations, relating to public security sub-stations, states that these are to be established not only in municipalities, but in all *hsien*. Here again the functions of political-police control are combined with those of social welfare. The character of these sub-stations is given in Article 1:

> Public security sub-stations are the organs of municipal and *hsien* public security bureaux deputed to take charge of security work.

Article 2 elucidates their tasks:

> Public security sub-stations shall carry out the following tasks:
> (1) Ensure enforcement of laws on public security and social order;

---

[3] NCNA, Peking, December 31, 1954; CB, 310.
[4] *Ibid.*

(2) Suppress sabotage activities or *flagrante delicto* of counter-revolutionaries;

(3) Prevent and curb activities of bandits and other criminals;

(4) Place counter-revolutionaries and other criminals under surveillance according to law;

(5) Control the census;

(6) Exercise control over theatres, cinemas, hotels, chop carvers and radio suppliers as well as explosives, inflammable articles and other dangerous articles;

(7) Guard the scene of important criminal cases and assist the relevant department in breaking the cases;

(8) Direct the work of security committees;

(9) Conduct propaganda among inhabitants concerning elevation of revolutionary vigilance, observance of law, observance of public order and respect to public morality;

(10) Take an active part and assist in welfare work for inhabitants. [5]

The Security Committees are not innovations. They were preceded by a similar institution, the *pao chia*, which has a history of thousands of years. Emperor Shang Yang, in about 350 B.C., following up still earlier practice, introduced a law by which the population was grouped into units of five or ten families. When a member of one family committed a crime, the other nine families were to inform the authorities about it, failing which they were collectively punishable. R. Lee, writing about the *pao chia* system, explained its function thus:

The principal functions of the *pao-chia* encompassed practically all the things that a village government could be asked to perform. It was responsible for the preservation of local peace and order, which included the apprehension of criminals, settlement of disputes, maintenance of a village police and self-defence system and, more significantly, the supervision of individual conduct according to orthodox moral and ethical precepts. Its tax-collecting, labour-conscripting and census-taking duties made it an important appendage of the official bureaucracy. It also acted as machinery through which long-term governmental policy, such as the promotion of agricultural production and universal military training of the country populace, could be effectuated. [6]

[5] NCNA, Peking, December 31, 1954; CB, 310.
[6] R. Lee, 'The Pao-chia System', *Papers on China*, Volume 3, May 1949.

In some periods the authorities insisted that each *pao chia* should put a card bearing the name, age, sex, kinship status and occupation of the members of the family on the front door of each house.

The *pao chia* was, all in all, an almost perfect surveillance system, with neighbour spying upon neighbour and relative spying upon relative. Only Mao, with better means of communication at his disposal, has improved on it.

INTERNAL PASSPORTS

The Constitution of the People's Republic of China states:

> Citizens of the People's Republic of China have freedom of residence and change of residence (Article 90).

Notwithstanding these fine phrases, the Communist authorities issued regulations controlling all movement within the country a short time after coming to power. Unified Regulations were issued in July, 1951.

Starting with the towns, the Ministry of State Security issued *Provisional Regulations Governing Urban Population*, which states:

> The control over residents shall be uniformly carried out by the People's Public Security Organs (Article 4).
>
> Any change in the members of the household should be properly reported by the head of the household concerned who should proceed to the local public security organ with his census record:
>
> 1. *To move out :*
> All those who move out should first notify the public security organ of change of residence, cancel the census record of the old place of abode, and apply for change-of-residence permit (change of residence within the jurisdictional area of the same public security organ does not require a permit).
>
> 2. *To move in :*
> All those who move in should report to the local public security organ to enter his name in the census record within three days of arrival (Article 5).

Visitors staying for three days and more, should be reported to the public security sub-station (Article 6).

Census records should be kept by all households and faithfully entered for checking. Hospitals should have census records as well as records of in-patients; arrival and departure of patients should be regularly reported (Article 7). [7]

To leave no loophole open in urban areas, the Ministry of State Security issued *Provisional Rules for Control of Hotels and Lodging Houses* a couple of weeks later, which states, amongst other things:

All lodging houses and hotels must provide passengers' registration books, and correctly fill in the particulars and submit them daily to the People's Public Security Organ for scrutiny (Article 8).

Those who in accordance with provisions of the rules make report and denunciation leading to arrest of important criminals or to breaking of bandit and secret service cases may be given honorary or material rewards according to the circumstances of the case. [8]

But these laws controlling the movement of population in the towns were found to be insufficient. The grain crisis created a very tense atmosphere in the countryside and Peking felt constrained to take precautions by controlling the movements of the rural population also. So on June 9, 1955, the State Council issued a *Directive Concerning Establishment of Permanent System for Registration of Persons*, which closely follows the *Provisional Regulations Governing Urban Population*, quoted above.

To tighten supervision, not only has the citizen to register his place of residence but also his place of work:

Registration of persons for organs, organisations, schools, and enterprises: In places where there are public security stations, the registration is to be handled by the public security stations. In villages and in towns where there are no public security stations, the registration is to be handled by the *hsiang* or *chen* people's councils. The organs, organisations, schools and enterprises concerned should also designate special personnel to assist in the registration. [9]

[7] NCNA, Peking, July 16, 1951.
[8] NCNA, Peking, August 4, 1951.
[9] NCNA, Peking, July 2, 1955.

To secondary-school pupils, the Ministry of Education addresses this warning, in its *Rules of Conduct for Middle School Students*:

> Always have your student identity card with you and see that you do not lose it (Article 18).[10]

STRUGGLE AGAINST 'COUNTER-REVOLUTIONARIES'

On February 21, 1951, Peking decreed the *Regulations of the People's Republic of China for Punishment of Counter-Revolutionaries.* These prescribed extremely harsh punishments for a long list of crimes, many of them vaguely defined. Thus Article 10 of the *Regulations* states:

> Any of the following provocative and instigating acts with counter-revolutionary purpose shall be punished by prison terms of more than three years; serious cases shall be punished by death sentence or life imprisonment:
>
> (*a*) Instigating the masses to resist and sabotage the collection of grains and taxes, labour service, military service or implementation of other administrative decrees of the People's Government.
>
> (*b*) Alienating and splitting the solidarity between the government and the nationalities, democratic classes, democratic parties and groups and people's bodies.
>
> (*c*) Conducting counter-revolutionary propaganda and agitation, fabricating and spreading rumours.[11]

It is clear from sub-Article (a) that every opposition, in whatever form, to any decree of the government, and from sub-Article (b) that any opposition to the Communist Party or any of its policies, is to be considered a counter-revolutionary act, and to be punished with all the rigour of the law.

Penalties were made retroactive—an unprecedented innovation.

To cow the people and sink the purport of the *Regulations* deep into their consciousness, their promulgation was followed by much-publicised mass accusation meetings and executions involving the death of tens of thousands and the participation of millions—a

[10] KMJP, June 18, 1955; SCMP, 1094.
[11] NCNA, Peking, February 21, 1951.

vast, specifically Chinese operation without parallel in the history of Russia or the Russian European satellites. Masses were brought to open courts, usually held in big fields (in Shanghai it was held in the huge stadium where dog races were formerly run). The proceedings were broadcast from morning till night. Powerful loudspeakers at every street corner bellowed the shouts of the crowds and the screams of the accused, some of whom were stoned or beaten to death, while the blare was heard all day: 'Kill! Kill!'[12]

At the end of the campaign, the Minister of State Security, Lo Jui-ching, wrote proudly:

> According to the Public Security Bureau of Peking, a total of 29,626 mass (accusation) meetings were held in Peking with an aggregate attendance figure of more than 3,379,000. In the period ranging from March to July, 21,400 mass meetings were held in Tientsin with an aggregate attendance figure of 2,200,000. . . . According to incomplete figures covering the eight administrative areas and four municipalities of Hopei, 653 trial and accusation meetings had been held with more than 3,900,000 people attending . . . more than 60 per cent of the population of the Central-South region, more than 70 per cent of the population of Fukien Province, and more than 80 per cent of the population of Nanking have all been subjected to this education.[13]

DENOUNCING RELATIVES

In fighting 'counter-revolutionaries' Peking tries to break the bond between father and son, or brother and sister, calling for denunciation of counter-revolutionary relatives. *New China News Agency* reported from the North-East:

> During the denunciation movement, many instances had occurred of counter-revolutionaries being denounced by their family members

---

[12] NYHT, October 1, 1951.

[13] JMJP, October 11, 1951. And the campaign against 'counter-revolutionaries' does not let up for a moment. Thus, for instance, over 3,000 'counter-revolutionaries' surrendered to the security authorities in Shanghai during January–October 1955. (CFJP, December 29, 1955). Again, on December 31, 1956, Lu Wei-liang, deputy chief prosecutor of the Kwangtung Province, reported that in this province alone during the past year (1956) 2,103 counter-revolutionaries had given themselves up to the authorities (*Wen Hui Pao*, Hongkong Communist daily, January 5, 1957).

and relatives. According to statistics of public security organs in nine cities, denunciation letters of this kind had reached several thousand. Kao Hui-ming, a woman worker of a certain factory in Chinchow of Liaohsi Province, denounced her husband Liu Kuang-chih, who was chief of the reactionary religious sect called 'Lan Chi Tan', and she herself led the public security personnel to put culprit Liu under arrest. Liu Ching-chih, proprietor of a smithy at Hsikang district in Port Arthur-Dairen municipality, denounced his counter-revolutionary cousin named Liu Jui-shih, who had escaped from Shantung Province to his house. Li Chih-feng, a girl student of a certain school at Tsitsihar, denounced her counter-revolutionary father Li Tieh-ping, who had just escaped to the North-East from Chengchow in Honan Province.[14]

The *China Youth Journal* published an open letter by a student called Lu Ch'eng-hsu accusing her father of being an agent of Chiang Kai-shek. The letter opens with these words:

Lu Hsu,
When I write out this stinking name of yours, I feel ashamed and intolerably insulted.
In the past I looked upon you as my father, but now I have seen your true face; you are a cannibal with your teeth bared in madness and your paws whipping about in the air.

It ends with these:

Now, I am a member of the New Democratic Youth League, and you are the people's enemy, forever unpardonable. Between us there is nothing in common now. I would rather be a daughter of the people than the slave of a special agent. It is our sworn principle that we will never co-exist with our enemy. So no matter where you hide yourself, we will get you in the end. You just wait and see.[15]

Similarly, when a former Kuomintang military commander was arrested in Canton, his daughter, a member of NDYL, published a biting denunciation: 'In the interests of the people, I demand that he be put to death, to set an example of what happens to all enemies of the people.'

[14] NCNA, Mukden, June 4, 1951.   [15] CKCNP, May 8, 1951.

A man accused in Shanghai of aiding Chiang Kai-shek was executed after his three daughters demanded the death penalty. In celebration of International Children's Day in Nanking on June 1, 1951, a number of model children were selected, one of whom was a twelve-year-old boy who had exposed his father as a counter-revolutionary and demanded his execution. To his mother he said: 'What is there to mourn in the death of a counter-revolutionary?'[16]

During the '5-anti' and '3-anti' campaigns citizens were again called upon to denounce the members of their families. Thus one article appealed to women saying :

Sisters, if your own father, brother, husband or child has committed any of the above-mentioned crimes, you must rid yourselves of any scruples and courageously prevail on them to confess or you must report them. You must not be afraid to 'wash your dirty linen in public' and you must not fear that your relatives will suffer punishment or that your family economy will be affected. Everybody must understand that it is a glorious thing to induce your own relatives to confess or to report your own relations, the only shameful thing is to protect them.[17]

Another incident during the '3-anti' campaign tells of a sixteen-year-old girl, also a member of NDYL, shouting at her father, accused of corrupt practices, in a public trial: 'I hereby declare to you that I no longer recognise him as my father. . . . I completely support the punishment administered to him by the People's Government.'[18]

The Shanghai *Liberation Daily* wrote in praise of people who denounced their relatives:

With a sense of responsibility towards the Fatherland, many readers reported their observations of suspicious acts amongst friends without loss of time; some exposed counter-revolutionary conduct on the part of their relatives. This shows that the political consciousness of the masses is being continuously raised . . .

[16] The above two examples are quoted by Theodore Hsi-en Chen, 'The Marxist Remoulding of Chinese Society', *American Journal of Sociology*, January 1953.

[17] 'All Sisters of China Vigorously Join the "San Fan" and "Wu Fan" Movement!' SSST, February 25, 1952; CCPR, 14.

[18] Theodore Hsi-en Chen, *op. cit.*

We have promptly forwarded these letters to the departments concerned for investigation and attention.[19]

More recently the *China Youth Daily* appealed:

. . . every youth should look at things about him and see if there are any suspicious persons whose background is not clear and if there are any counter-revolutionary activities and then report (verbally or in written form) to the public security organ or Party organisation and, if necessary, give help to arrest the enemies . . .

Some youths are irresolute lest denunciations of relatives, friends and acquaintances should hurt their feelings and harmony . . . He who is a counter-revolutionary is our enemy, with whom it is out of the question to talk of feelings and harmony. Pending his confession, we cannot pardon him. For a NDYL member not to denounce a counter-revolutionary known to him means protection of counter-revolution.[20]

The same issue of the paper commended We Kuo-chu, a student who, on receiving a letter asking for financial help from his 'counter-revolutionary father' who had run away from a forced labour camp, went to the police and helped them recapture him.[21]

A similar 'act of glory' was performed a week later by one Yang K'e-kuei who denounced his brother Yang Pao-jen as a counter-revolutionary.[22] One Lou Shiao-ai 'prosecuted his counter-revolutionary father, uncle and brother'.[23]

Anyone who does not heed the call to denounce father or brother is liable to heavy punishment. Thus NCNA reported:

The People's Court of Kwang Chi *hsien* in Hupeh Province recently sentenced Lan Jang-li to five years' imprisonment for shielding his counter-revolutionary father, Lan Hua-fan, over a long period.[24]

[19] CFJP, June 22, 1954; SCMP, 893.
[20] 'Let Everybody Denounce Counter-Revolutionaries', CKCNP, August 6, 1955; SCMP, 1110.
[21] *Ibid.*
[22] NCNA, Tientsin, September 13, 1955; SCMP, 1140.
[23] CKCNP, September 6, 1955; SCMP, 1130.
[24] NCNA, Wuhan, August 27, 1955.

CHAPTER XXI

PROPAGANDA

The Communist bureaucracy uses many propaganda devices—newspapers, magazines, books, pictorial booklets (Chinese comic books), radio, mass meetings and demonstrations, mobile cinemas, mobile dramatic units, plays and songs, people's reading rooms, lantern-slide shows, newspaper reading groups, and the Yangko dance.

The Constitution says that 'Citizens of the People's Republic of China have freedom of speech, freedom of the press, freedom of assembly, freedom of association, freedom of procession and freedom of demonstration' (Article 87). But how is this translated into life?

The *Provisional Regulations Governing the Control of Book and Periodical Publishing, Printing and Distribution Trades*, promulgated on August 16, 1952, makes it clear that only what is approved of by the Communist authorities can be published:

> Those enterprises that print books or periodicals . . . shall not undertake the printing of books or periodicals which violate the Common Programme of the Chinese People's Consultative Conference or the decrees of the Government:
>
> Before delivery they shall send to the local organs in charge of publication administration one copy each of the books or periodicals printed.[1]

Broadcasting is well developed. In February 1953 there were 71 broadcasting stations and 20,519 radio-diffusion exchanges.[2] These latter transmit programmes through wired speakers directly into homes and public places without the programmes ever going on the air. The Government is not only expanding the radio-diffusion exchange system, so that the people hear only what Government officials intend they should, but the law also inter-

---

[1] NCNA, Peking, August 18, 1952; SCMP, 409.
[2] CNS, April 7, 1953; CCPR, 41.

venes to ensure that no-one uses any other kind of receiver and so preserves the Government's monopoly of broadcasting. In August 1951 *Provisional Regulations for Control of Radio Equipment* were promulgated, to be replaced on July 23, 1955, by *Regulations Governing Radio Equipment*. These put under State control all radio receivers, as well as all radio parts. No-one is allowed to buy or repair any radio without 'a permit from the local public security station'.[3]

Total control over the means of communication facilitates the dissemination of any propaganda lie the authorities might wish to put over. During the Korean War, for example, Peking tried to minimise the danger of the A-bomb. *Cartoon Monthly*, a Shanghai publication with a nation-wide circulation, printed a cartoon in its December 1950 issue entitled 'Why the Atom Bomb Cannot Win a War'. The reason given was that 'an atom bomb is only as powerful as an ordinary 3,000 lb. bomb'—less, mark, than the ordinary 2-ton bomb! A cartoon alongside showed frantic Americans preventing an American flyer from dropping the atom bomb, above the caption: 'The atom bomb is too expensive for large-scale production.'[4]

The monopoly of propaganda makes it possible to give a wholly distorted picture of the world outside China. Thus, a *Southern Daily* supplement entitled 'Look, This is the American Way of Life' described conditions in the United States in these terms:

Ten states in the United States were suffering from serious floods but nobody cared. At least 20 million people were homeless.

In New York, the biggest city in the United States, the south-east district is the home of the labouring masses. Housing conditions in this district may be divided generally into the following four kinds:

(A) Living quarters, train style. In such quarters, 5 or 6 families live on the same floor. Those living in the middle rooms, which are without windows, never see sunlight or breathe fresh air the whole year round. As regards the two families living in the front and back rooms, you can be sure that the capitalists would press them for more rent. The stairs of houses of this category are so rotten and dangerous to walk on that we dared not go up.

[3] JMJP, July 26, 1955.
[4] E. Hunter, *Brain-Washing in Red China*, New York, 1951, pp. 223, 226.

(B) Warm bed. The labouring people who cannot afford to live in quarters mentioned above, are obliged to sleep in rented beds. But the exploiting capitalists, who leave no stone unturned, rent one bed to three persons separately, giving each eight hours to sleep in it. Such beds, always occupied, are called 'warm beds'. The rental is, if I remember correctly, 25 cents for an eight-hour sleep.

(C) Hallways. The way to solve the question of sleep for those labouring people who cannot even afford to rent a 'warm bed' is to rent space in the hallways of hotels with 'warm beds'. The cruel capitalists will not let people sleep on the floor of such hallways free.

(D) Piles of old newspapers. According to a social welfare worker of the slum districts, those who have no money to rent space in a passage usually pile newspapers in a street corner and dig in for warmth. In warm weather they sleep on benches in the park, subject to constant interference by policemen.[5]

The State monopoly of propaganda also serves the leadership in another way. To cover itself, and above all Mao, from suspicion of human error, the propaganda machine uses the censor's scissors to bring the past into line with the present. Above all, the past of Mao himself must not deviate. In a moment of indiscretion, a Shanghai daily published a speech by Chou En-lai in which he said: 'A man cannot be completely faultless, and even Mao Tse-tung cannot be considered faultless. Even Mao had to leave out complete portions of his works while compiling the *Selected Works of Mao Tse-tung*.'[6] Three weeks later the paper ate its words, and corrected the statement as follows: 'Chou pointed out that it is difficult to achieve perfection. Even within the Communist Party of China only Chairman Mao, Comrade Liu Shao-chi and a few other leaders have achieved the stage of perfection.'[7] The censor's work is indeed heavy. If one took the trouble to compare articles and speeches in Mao's *Selected Works* with earlier versions of the same, innumerable censor's gems would come to light.

One of the props of the propaganda monopoly is the law on State secrets. The *Provisional Regulations for the Preservation of State Secrets* promulgated by the GAC on June 8, 1951, includes as State secrets such things as the State financial plans and budgets,

---

[5] NFJP, December 7–9, 1950; CB, 55.
[6] *Ta Kung Pao*, Shanghai, August 22, 1949.
[7] *Ibid.*, September 10, 1949.

State economic plans, and 'secrets concerning scientific inventions and discoveries, culture, education, hygiene and medicine'.[8] Indeed, there are very few items of news that cannot be classified as secret, if the State so desires. And the penalty for divulging them is very harsh.

One distinguishing feature of totalitarian propaganda making it fundamentally different from propaganda carried out by any other bureaucratic machine, is the reliance it places on the people as active broadcasters of propaganda, as participating spokes in the great propaganda wheel. This is achieved above all in huge campaigns that follow upon the heels of one another and keep the people in a state of permanent tension. In these campaigns the masses are activated 'spontaneously'. Since the inauguration of the People's Republic of China, the main campaigns have been Land Reform, which began in the New Liberated Areas in 1949 and approached completion in 1952; the Suppression of Counter-revolutionaries campaign which occupied the best part of 1951 and extended into 1952; the Resist America—Aid Korea movement inaugurated in 1951 and eclipsed only after the '3-anti' and '5-anti' movements were in full blast (end of 1951—middle of 1952); and the Production Increase and Economic Campaigns preceding and succeeding the '3-anti' and '5-anti' campaigns.

Besides mass meetings, demonstrations and the like the regime relies on the Agitators—another important institution—to 'activate' the masses. The agitators take an active part in such mass propaganda organisations as announcers' centres, blackboard bulletins, newspaper reading teams, and amateur dramatic clubs. But above all, their job is to explain the policies of the Party and State in every factory and shop and to every citizen in his home.

The recruitment of Agitators is carefully planned. Thus, for instance, quantitative stipulations laid down for Southern Kiangsu are:

> In industrial and mining enterprises, Agitators may be developed to five per cent of the number of workers and employees, but the maximum number is not to exceed ten per cent. If possible, Agitators

[8] NCNA, Peking, June 10, 1951.

should be available in every workshop and in every unit. In rural districts, it is demanded that generally Agitators should be increased to one per cent of the rural population. Those in middle schools and above may be increased to about five per cent of the entire number of persons in the schools. [9]

The Communist leaders emphasise personal oral agitation which brings the Party into more direct and intimate contact with the masses. The Agitators serve as its mouthpiece and its 'eyes and ears' among the people. They are the guarantee that the Party's propaganda will get across, for in conditions of illiteracy and general poverty many people are beyond the reach of newspapers and radio; even those within their reach may be unwilling to make use of them. But the Agitator's oral propaganda cannot be avoided. The Agitator also ensures a wide circulation for the newspapers, by daily reading aloud from them, as this is one of his main duties. Finally, the local Agitator, more than any other medium of communication, can concentrate on just those elements of propaganda the Party wishes to emphasise at any given time in any locality and among any particular group of people. This is of benefit as it allows a high degree of differentiation in the content of propaganda. [10]

REGIMENTATION OF LEISURE

The regimentation of leisure is necessary if the people are to be prevented from thinking 'wrong thoughts' and taught the 'right thoughts'. This is very strenuously pursued by the authorities. For example, in the Woosoong Machine Factory in Shanghai, praised by the *Liberation Daily* for its organisation of political education, so much time was taken up by this activity that it was found necessary to restrict it. The time-table for political study in this factory makes interesting reading:

Mondays: The shift began in the morning. Political lessons were given between 8 and 9 o'clock in the morning.

[9] CFJP, August 18, 1952; SCMP, 415.
[10] For a very good analysis of the role of oral agitation in the Communist regime, see A. Inkeles, *Public Opinion in Soviet Russia*, Cambridge, Mass., 1951, pp. 121–31.

Tuesdays: Discussions on political subjects were held in the morning for one hour.

Thursdays and Fridays: One hour each in the morning were spent on meetings at which the '3-anti', the Democratic Unity Drive, Examination of Patriotic Pacts, etc., would proceed.

To make sure that the workers learnt well, 'all the staff of employees and workers in the factory, including cooks, participated in tests arranged for them'.[11]

The higher authorities drew up a 24-hour time-table for cadres. A Communist paper reported:

The People's Government of Tientsin Municipality has announced its autumn schedule for all subordinate organs effective from September 15, as follows:[12]

6.00 a.m.	Get up
6.30–7.00 a.m.	Breakfast
7.00–9.00 a.m.	Study
9.00–12.00	Working hours
12.00–2.00 p.m.	Lunch time
2.00–6.00 p.m.	Working hours
6.00–6.30 p.m.	Dinner time
7.00–9.00 p.m.	Spare-time activities
10.00 p.m.	Go to bed

Regimentation of leisure, has, however, some negative results from the standpoint of the regime. It is liable to swallow up too much of the workers' or students' time, to the detriment of their health, production, studies, and so on. Thus the *Yangtze Daily* complained about political propaganda in factories in Wuhan:

There have been too many meetings, which left little time for the workers to rest. In certain units, meetings of one and a half hours' duration were held even after the workers came off night duty before they could go home, reducing them to extreme fatigue.[13]

[11] CFJP, June 25, 1952; SCMP, 225.
[12] *Chin Pu Jih Pao*, Tientsin, September 14, 1951.
[13] CCJP, August 15, 1952; SCMP, 408.

Peasants' meetings are often so numerous that production is affected, and the Central Committee of the Party is constrained repeatedly to pass resolutions limiting their number. Some idea of their frequency may be gained from an announcement that in the South-west during the spring ploughing season, 'In a number of areas mass meetings were reduced from 20–30 in the past to 3–4 times each month now.'[14]

A *People's Daily* editorial entitled, 'Teachers should not be Indiscriminately Drafted for Social Duties', complained:

> The serious phenomenon of the indiscriminate drafting of teachers to take part in social duties has been universally found to exist in all localities, and is especially serious in the small cities and rural districts. There, numerous teachers have been forced to interrupt their teaching to take part in the prevailing focal tasks, shock tasks, and other social duties outside their schools, or even requested to work in various organs for long periods without being able to return to their schools. An adverse influence has thus been exerted on the completion of pedagogic plans, the political and professional studies of the teachers, the qualitative and quantitative improvement of teaching and the long-term plan of the training of personnel for the country.[15]

Numerous examples followed. To take one, from the town of Sian:

> Shih Yu-ch'in, principal of the Provincial Girls' School (middle school) holds as many as 8 concurrent jobs; Fan Hsi-min, principal of the Peikuan Primary School, holds 11 concurrent jobs, while the principal of the Kan-er-tu Primary School has to spend at least 35 hours a week on outside work. With too many duties, some principals and teachers have too many meetings to attend and therefore understand too little of the conditions of their schools. They even seldom have the chance to see their pupils. The principal of Chunghsin Primary School of Anyang, Honan, in the 40 days from the end of September to the first part of November 1952, spent 21 days attending meetings.[16]

[14] JMJP, May 27, 1953; SCMP, 583.
[15] NCNA, Peking, March 17, 1953; SCMP, 537.
[16] JMJP, March 17, 1953; SCMP, 540.

At an NDYL School Work Conference, in April 1953, it was stated:

> The state of confusion in schools has not been corrected. Too many student organisations have been set up, and the students have to attend too many meetings. There are too many activities that hinder study.[17]

The same sad situation exists in the field of scientists' work. A *People's Daily* editorial, entitled 'Ensure that Scientific Workers Concentrate their Efforts on Professional Activities', says:

> Many of our scientists, professors, medical doctors and other scientific workers have for long been unable to concentrate on pedagogical and scientific research work. Social duties have taken much of their time. Some heads of departments and pedagogical research offices of institutes of higher learning have to spend about 30 per cent of their time the year round for participation in social duties. The situation is serious where part of our scientific workers are occupied by too many concurrent jobs. In individual instances, a medical doctor takes 22 jobs concurrently, a scientist 13 jobs and a professor 5 to 10 or even 18 jobs. More or less similar conditions exist in the institutes of higher learning in all large cities.[18]

It must not be concluded that the Communist leaders want only a small portion—that is, small as recognised in other countries—of the people's time to be devoted to politics. On the contrary, the *People's Daily* commended the universities for their correspondence courses which stipulate that of a total of 1,080 hours, '420 hours will be used for political lessons, constituting 39 per cent of the total hours'.[19]

Another negative effect of the incessant blast of propaganda derives from its very repetitiveness. It is liable to get so boring that even many cadres do not bother to pay attention to it. That this is the case was borne out by an examination of the political

17 JMJP, April 21, 1953; SCMP, 563.
18 JMJP, February 27, 1955; SCMP, 1003.
19 JMJP, December 20, 1952.

knowledge of government officials in Peking carried out in June 1952. It was a test in current affairs, based on facts published many times in the daily papers. Nevertheless a great many of the officials failed the test abysmally, showing appalling ignorance. Some probing into the reasons uncovered the following:

The results of the investigation covering a total of 28 organisations including the 13 units under the Municipal Government, the Organisation Department of the Municipal Committee, the United Front Department, the Municipal Federation of Trade Unions, the Public Security Bureau, the District Committee of the 5th Ward, and the 10 units under the District Offices of the 2nd and 8th Wards were as follows:

There were in the 13 units under the Municipal Government a total of 7,772 employees capable of reading newspapers who subscribed to a total of 1,286 copies of newspapers (an average of 6 persons per copy). Of them, 1,943 persons or 25 per cent were reading the newspapers seriously and regularly, 4,587 persons or 59 per cent just glanced over the papers (reading only the headlines or items of interest to them), while 1,242 persons or 16 per cent seldom or never read any newspapers.

A similar position existed in other branches of the Peking administration.

46 of the 86 persons in the Labour Bureau, including the seven persons who had had experience of '5-anti' work in inspection teams were unable to answer in full what were the five poisons . . . One of the questions set by the Labour Bureau in its test was 'What are the people's democracies in East Europe?' Of the 86 candidates only 6 could give a correct answer. The answers given by 14 persons were all wrong, while 30 persons stated that they knew nothing of the subject. A deputy section chief and a team leader gave 'Indonesia, Vietnam, Korea and Japan' as an answer. A Party Agitator quoted India, Sweden, Holland and Yugoslavia, while some even cited China, Iran, Denmark, Belgium and Chile.[20]

[20] Propaganda Department of the CCP Peking Committee, 'Strengthen the Leadership in Newspaper-Reading Work among the Government Employees', JMJP, July 6, 1952.

EVERYTHING SUBORDINATED TO THE STATE

Even the most intimate feelings of the individual are not beyond the arm of the State and its propaganda machine. Time and again the press, especially that directed towards the youth, calls for the subordination of love to State needs. The journal *China Youth*, for example, complained that many youths exaggerate the importance of, and refuse 'to place love in a secondary position' in their lives. They thus ignore 'the slogan of our broad youth: "All for the Motherland" and "All for Socialism".' How can a young man feel deeply the need of a girl's love when Big Brother needs him?

> The way part of our youth now devote themselves to love and throw themselves into a frenzy of love-making is quite incompatible with the great era in which we live. . . . Our leader Chairman Mao Tse-tung expects the entire people to work hard and the entire youth to be 'good in health, good at study and good at work.' The great call of Chairman Mao Tse-tung and the sense of sacred duty of defending and building our fatherland combine to make all our youth work all the harder with a strong will and a full spirit. During this period, if some of our youth take too much interest in love and devote too much of their time and energy to this problem, it would be detrimental to the national interests.[21]

Other emotions are also not to be tolerated. A language teacher, Ch'en Fang-wen was reproved for deviating from the general line on literature by not discouraging writings which were sad and affected the pupils' devotion to Party and state aims:

> Under the charge of Ch'en Fang-wen, a number of youthful and impressionable students were ideologically poisoned. This was reflected in the work done by these students. One of them, a girl, wrote a composition entitled 'An Unforgettable Incident', in which she recalled memories of one of her cousins with whom she once fell in love and who later died of cholera. The composition was full of decadent ideas and melancholy thoughts. Ch'en Fang-wen approved the work immensely, and wrote at the end of the paper: 'A deeply moving work which demonstrates your ability to write.'

[21] CKCN, April 1, 1955; SCMP, 1052.

Again:

> Another student, a married woman, wrote a composition entitled 'My Thoughts', in which she wrote about her child at home who kept engaging her thoughts. Such thoughts naturally prevented her from devoting herself whole-heartedly to her studies. Instead of correcting her fault Ch'en Fang-wen taunted her for not having expressed her sadness well. [22]

The mother should not think of her son, but of the Party!

Marriage too is not the intimate affair of two individuals, but a bond that must be subordinated to the State. Thus a *People's Daily* editorial, explaining why people should aim at happiness in marriage, wrote:

> . . . it must be realised that by causing other people to suffer from one's own incorrect acts, one not only injures the other party, but also injures the State and the people as a whole. For such improper acts, during a specified period of time and to a definite extent, will influence the normal feelings of certain people and the work entrusted such people by the State and the people. Here the character and morals of an individual assume political significance. To consider marriage and family problems merely as individual problems of private life is unilateral and incorrect. [23]

Hence 'model workers', when they marry, should take into account, as a first consideration, the production needs of the State. As an example to follow, this instance was given:

> Liu Pao-ling, a worker in the weaving room, hoped that she would find a husband who worked in heavy industry. Two years ago, at a social evening organised by the Youth League members and young workers of the mill and the Shanghai Steam Turbine Works, she made the acquaintance of Tang Chien, a lathe-operator. They enjoyed each others' company and began to write to each other. Last year, they became man and wife. [24]

[22] JMCY, July 1954; SCMP, 917.
[23] JMJP, March 8, 1955; SCMP, 1006.
[24] 'Woman Textile Workers—Then and Now', PC, June 16, 1954.

Unfortunately there are deviationists from the correct line on marriage. Some army officers were rebuked as follows:

> Among some comrades there now emerges a tendency to be separated from politics. . . . Some officers even go to the extent, when solving their marriage problems, of disregarding political conditions, seeking mates blindly, with the result that opportunities are afforded the counter-revolutionaries.[25]

If such intimate aspects of life must be subordinated to the State, it stands to reason that all other aspects of life must also be. It is thus not surprising to read that 'school education must be linked closely with and made to serve politics'.[26] Or again, 'academic research must be made to serve politics'.[27]

[25] JMJP, August 1, 1955; SCMP, 1106.
[26] KMJP, October 20, 1955.
[27] JMJP, October 14, 1954.

CHAPTER XXII

'ELECTIONS'

One of the most important mass activities dictated by the bureaucratic propaganda machine is the 'elections' to State bodies.

Immediately after 'Liberation', the Communist leaders did not bother to make any pretence at elections. To give their rule a semblance of constitutional legality, however, they convened the People's Political Consultative Conference on September 21, 1949. This, consisting of 662 hand-picked delegates from 45 organisations, fathered the *Common Program* and the *Organic Law of the Central People's Government*. The administration of the Liberated Areas was left to Military Control Commissions, one for each of the six regions into which the 28 provinces were grouped. The Military Control Commissions also controlled the municipal administrations, and Commission chairmen in important cities like Shanghai and Nanking were simultaneously mayors of their respective municipalities.

A step away from total military rule was taken when the GAC adopted, on December 2, 1949, *Regulations for the Organisation of the Conferences of Representatives of All Circles in Various Provinces, Municipalities and Hsien*. These 'All Circles Conferences' were formed of *selected* delegates from different organisations, political, social and military. Their decisions had to be ratified by the Peking Government, which on occasion proved difficult. The Shanghai 'All Circles Conference', for instance, was refused permission to elect a mayor and deputy mayor in November 1949 because 'the organisational power and the political consciousness of the Shanghai masses were not up to the required standards'.[1] (In October 1950, the Shanghai 'All Circles Conference' was at last permitted to elect a mayor and four deputy mayors; but, *mirabile dictu*, Chen I, the mayor in office, who was the military commander, was elected).

[1] CFJP, December 14, 1949.

About a year after 'Liberation', elections were permitted to a People's Representative Conference, at village, district, county, municipal, provincial, regional and national levels, to produce administrative organs—the People's Government—at their respective levels.

Elections are free, but all candidates must support the programme put forward by the Communist Party. The *General Regulations Governing the Organisation of Conferences of Representatives of the People at Hsiang Level*, adopted by the GAC on December 8, 1950, stated:

> Delegates to the Conference of Representatives of the people of the *hsiang* may be elected from among persons irrespective of nationality, class status, sex, and religious belief, as long as they are opposed to imperialism, feudalism and bureaucratic-capitalism, and support the Common Programme . . . (Article 3).[2]

Even when all the candidates support the same programme, Peking still does not approve of a contest between them. Accordingly a single-list system of candidature is operated. Describing such elections in Shanghai a participant writes: 'Those who were brought up in the old tradition [of Western democracy] might wonder at the fact that the number of names appearing on the ballot equals that of the number to be elected.' He goes on to say: 'This is a great contrast to the practice of old democracy in which an individual voter is faced with a hodge-podge of candidates and often the voter does not really know enough about the candidates to make an intelligent choice.'[3]

What about the secret ballot? Liu Shao-chi, in an address to the Third People's Representative Conference on February 28, 1951, said that elections 'by popular vote and secret ballot' were undesirable 'formalism' that would 'cause the people trouble, impede their active spirit and is incapable of improving the actual representative character of the people's representative conferences, or of improving the democratic quality of the people's regime . . .' He added:

[2] HHYP, February 1951; CB, 144.
[3] Chen Ren-bing, 'The People's Representatives' Conferences', CMR, December 1950.

Secret balloting takes place only in colleges, where the voters are all literate and are experienced in voting. Elsewhere the voting takes place by a show of hands after the list of candidates has been discussed. [4]

There are a number of other interesting 'democratic' elements in the elections to People's Representative Conferences, but for the sake of brevity, we shall pass straight on to the Election Law and practice of the administrative organs prevailing today, namely the All-China People's Congress and Local People's Congresses at all levels.

The Election Law was promulgated by the Central People's Government on March 1, 1953. Its salient features are that the lower administrative organs—people's congresses of *hsiangs*, towns and the like—are to be elected directly by the citizens, while those at a higher level are to be elected by the lower organs (Article 3), and that elections to the lower administrative organs 'may be conducted by a show of hands or by secret ballot', while 'elections to a people's congress of and above the county level shall be conducted by secret ballot' (Article 55). [5]

The explanation that the open ballot elections at lower levels are dictated by the illiteracy of the people does not hold water, as comparison with municipal and general elections in other countries which suffer from widespread illiteracy, such as India, Nigeria, Gold Coast, Indonesia, will show. It is precisely where Party and police control is least secure—in elections at the lower levels—that the authorities fear the secret ballot.

The question of a single list of candidates is not dealt with by the Law itself. But an official commentary on the Law by Vice-Premier Teng Hsiao-ping, makes it quite clear that one list is intended:

. . . joint nomination by the Communist Party of China, the various democratic parties and the various people's organisations in fact should be, and can be, the main form for submitting lists of candidates for election as delegates to the people's congresses. [6]

[4] PC, April 16, 1951.
[5] *The Electoral Law of the People's Republic of China*, Peking, 1953, Article 55.
[6] Teng Hsiao-ping, 'An Explanation to the Election Law', NCNA, Peking, February 12, 1953.

The manner of nomination to be adopted was laid down by the Central Election Committee in a *Directive on Election Work at Basic Level* issued on April 3, 1953. It states that the local election committee, chaired by an appointee of higher level authorities, is to decide who is to be included in the list of candidates.

> The election committees should, on the basis of the results of the collective study of the discussions by the elector teams and according to the views of the majority of electors, put forward official lists of candidates,

who are to be chosen as follows:

> The election committees may, in general cases, hold consultations with the representatives of CCP organisations and people's bodies for the nomination of candidates.

To make assurance double sure, the *Directive* instructs:

> The number of candidates for delegates nominated by the election committee and proposed to the election meeting should generally be the same as the number of delegates to be elected, that is to say, the same number of candidates should be nominated as the number of delegates that will be elected by the electoral district in question.[7]

So much for electoral theory. Now to electoral practice. The selection of candidates to the National People's Congress, the so-called parliament of China, took place as follows, according to a *New China News Agency* message of July 6, 1954:

> Lists of candidates for the National People's Congress were discussed and unanimously approved yesterday at the 56th (enlarged) session of the Standing Committee of the National Committee of the Chinese People's Political Consultative Conference. They will be submitted to the people's congresses at provincial and municipal levels throughout the country, and will form part of the candidates' lists which the various congresses will choose for the election of deputies to the National People's Congress.

[7] NCNA, Peking, April 7, 1953; SCMP, 551.

After this, every Provincial People's Congress naturally did what was expected of it and voted practically unanimously for the candidates nominated by the supreme State body.

In the election of 564 deputies to the Peking Municipal People's Congress,

> the candidates jointly named by the CCP, democratic parties and groups, and people's bodies, have been elected by majority votes as deputies to the Peking People's Congress. Sixty-seven per cent of the deputies have been elected by full votes, while the rest got 1–2 votes less than the others. [8]

The election by the Peking Municipal People's Congress of deputies to the National People's Congress took place as follows:

> Due to the full democratic consultations before the voting, the votes garnered by the elected deputies were very concentrated: 9 received 100 per cent of the votes (539 votes); 19 received one vote less than the full vote; 3 received 2 less; 2 received 3 less; while even the lowest one received only 4 less than the full vote. [9]

Even greater uniformity was shown in the election of 46 deputies to the National People's Congress by the Kwangtung Provincial People's Congress: 'The result of the voting showed that there was no invalid vote. All the 46 elected deputies were returned on from 99 to 100 per cent of the votes cast.'[10]

The fact that China goes through the ritual of 'elections' at all is primarily a reflection of the strength of the democratic idea which they embody. It is the homage paid by vice to virtue. In addition they give the people a feeling of participation in political life, take the edge off popular opposition to the State, and at the same time serve as a medium for political indoctrination.

[8] NCNA, Peking, August 10, 1954; SCMP, 873.
[9] NCNA, Peking, August 22, 1954; CB, 290.
[10] *Ta Kung Pao*, Hong Kong, Communist Daily, August 14, 1954; CB, 289.

CHAPTER XXIII

THE PARTY

PARTY STRUCTURE

Since the Chinese Communist Party is a State Party, an analysis
of its structure and functioning naturally forms part of an analysis
of the State machine.

It is the biggest Communist Party in the world. At the end of
June 1956 it had over 10·7 million members.[1] It is a monolithic
and totalitarian organisation. It is true that its Constitution provides for 'democratic centralism', but under the prevailing conception, it has very little democracy and very much centralism.
Liu Shao-chi showed this clearly when he said:

> Party members who disagree with the Party's leading body or
> any Party organisation should submit their views and criticisms to
> the appropriate Party organisation and should not talk about it
> casually among the masses. . . . Party members or Party committees
> of a lower level who disagree with a Party committee of a higher
> level, may bring the issue to the Party committee of a higher level,
> or ask it to call a meeting to study the matter, or should refer the
> matter to a Party committee of a still higher level, but they should
> not talk about it casually or inform Party Committees of a still lower
> level about the matter.[2]

Liu Shao-chi repeated the thought in a speech to the seventh
Party Congress (May 14, 1945):

> No responsible Party leader, including members of the Central
> Committee, should publicise their views on national issues without
> the Central Committee's approval. They may discuss their views at
> the meetings of local Party committees and make suggestions to the
> Central Committee. But it is impermissible for them to make public,
> either inside or outside the Party, views not yet made known by the
> Central Committee or to circulate and disseminate these views among

[1] NCNA, Peking, September 13, 1956.
[2] Liu Shao-chi, *On Inner-Party Struggle, op. cit.*, pp. 66–7.

348

other local Party committees. The reason is that should such views or decisions conflict with those of the Central Committee, it would leave a very bad impression in the Party and among the people, or before our enemy.[3]

Thus differences should not be aired as 'it would leave a very bad impression'! Democracy indeed!

'Democratic centralism' can be democratic only on condition that Party members have the right to elect the members of Party bodies and to form minority groups which nominate candidates of their own. Nothing of the sort is permitted in the CCP.

The leaders adopt a cavalier attitude towards the Party Constitution. Take the question of convening Party Congresses. Up to the 1945 Congress, the Constitution had provided for the convention of a National Congress annually (Article 35); the 1945 Constitution changed this to once in three years (Article 29). But not the slightest attention was paid to either of these Articles in fact, and Party Congresses were held very infrequently:

1st Congress	July 1921 (Shanghai)
2nd ,,	May 1922 (Hangchow)
3rd ,,	June 1923 (Canton)
4th ,,	January 1925 (Shanghai)
5th ,,	April 1927 (Wuhan)
6th ,,	July–September 1928 (Moscow)
7th ,,	April–June 1945 (Yenan)
8th ,,	September 1956 (Peking)

Seventeen years passed between the Sixth and Seventh Party Congresses, and eleven between the Seventh and Eighth.

Nevertheless the *People's Daily* has the effrontery to print an article entitled 'The Party Congress is the Foundation of Democracy within the Party', and which goes on to say that Party Congresses

have the right to examine and ratify reports of Party committees, discuss and decide on important problems of the Party, and elect the leadership organs of the Party at the respective levels—the

[3] Liu Shao-chi, *On the Party, op. cit.,* p. 99.

Party committees. This shows that the system of Party congresses provides the foundation for the promotion of democracy within the Party, the development of criticism and self-criticism. It is also the important guarantee for the thorough implementation of the system of democratic centralism and the principle of collective leadership in the Party. [4]

Actually the long lapse of time between Party Congresses has not affected the efficiency of its leadership: decisions have been made, new members co-opted to the Central Committee, and so on.

The leadership is somewhat less unscrupulous about the convention of a smaller body, the Central Committee. But even in this case, the Party Constitution is far from being the guiding light it is supposed to be. Article 33 of the 1945 Party Constitution provides that regular sessions of the Central Committee should take place every six months (instead of three months, as the old Constitution stipulated). But, in fact, it met only seven times in the eleven years since 1945.

Lower Party bodies are subordinate to the Central Committee and its organs, the Politbureau and the Secretariat. According to the 1945 Party Constitution, the Central Committee has the power to veto the election of secretaries of the local, municipal and district Party committees (Articles 40 and 48). This, taken together with the provision of a long interval—two years—between the convocation of provincial, regional, county, city and sub-district Party congresses (Articles 40 and 47), [4a] increases the power of the higher Party committees over local ones and over the Party rank and file, while at the same time it enhances the dependence of local Party committees on the higher bodies.

As the intervals between Party Congresses and also between Central Committee plenary sessions are so great, the central bodies that sit more or less permanently—the Political Bureau and

[4] JMJP, April 28, 1955; SCMP, 1040. The Party Constitution adopted by the Eighth Congress of the Chinese Communist Party (September, 1956) provided for a more infrequent convention of Party Congresses—once in five years (Article 31).

[4a] The Party Constitution adopted by the Eighth Congress of the Party (September, 1956) stipulates that Party Congresses for provinces, autonomous regions and municipalities directly under Peking's control should be convened once in three years (Article 38).

the Central Secretariat—gain in status and importance. Article 34 of the 1945 Constitution states:[5]

> The Central Political Bureau shall be the central leading body of the Party and direct all the work of the Party during the intervals between the plenary sessions of the Central Committee.
> The Central Secretariat shall attend to the daily work of the Central Committee according to the decisions of the Central Political Bureau.

To bring the concentration of power to the highest pitch, the 1945 Constitution states:

> The Chairman of the Central Committee shall be concurrently the Chairman of the Central Political Bureau and of the Central Secretariat.

This post of Chairman did not exist in the 1928 Party Constitution.

PARTY CONTROL COMMITTEES

As the Party is the leading body in the country, it invests its members with certain material and psychological privileges. But as a 'deviation' of Party members is much more dangerous to the regime than a deviation among the general public, Party members find themselves more severely disciplined and under much sharper scrutiny than other people. In addition to carrying an internal passport, a labour book, and to being under the supervision of the State, urban or rural security committees like others, Party members are in duty bound first to spy on one another, and secondly to bear the brunt of special Party bodies of control.

The first duty was clearly stated by Liu Shao-chi:

> When Party members discover any other Party member doing something wrong and acting in a manner detrimental to the interests of the Party they must report such activities to the appropriate

[5] Liu Shao-chi, On the Party, op. cit., p. 165.

Party organisation and should not attempt to cover up the matter or attempt to mutually shield one another. [6]

The control of Party members is undertaken by Control Commissions whose method of election and function were defined in the 1954 Constitution thus:

> The Central Control Commission shall be elected by the Central Committee in plenary session. The control commission of a lower Party organisation shall be elected by the said lower Party committee in plenary session and shall be submitted to its superior Party organisation for approval (Article 57).
>
> The functions and powers of the central and lower commissions shall be to take or annul disciplinary measures against Party members and to deal with Party members' complaints (Article 58).
>
> The control commissions at all levels shall function under the direction of the Party committees at the corresponding levels (Article 59). [7]

After some years in power and with the strain of industrialisation beginning to tell, Peking found it inconvenient to have the control commissions under the direction of the Party committees of the same level, as it hampered centralised control. And so a Party Conference (in March 1955) revised the position, disconnecting the control commissions from such direction. The resolution states:

> The central and local party control committees shall have the right to check on violations by Party organisations of a lower level of the Party Constitution and discipline and state laws and decrees, and to suggest to the Party committees of the same level how to deal with the cases. [8]

Although expulsion from the Party is as terrible as was excommunication from the Church in the Middle Ages, the control commissions may use even harsher penalties, through State and police action. As the Conference Resolution stated:

Liu Shao-chi, *On Inner-Party Struggle, op. cit.*, p. 67.
Liu Shao-chi, *On the Party, op. cit.*, p. 179.
NCNA, Peking, April 4, 1955.

The central and local control committees of the Party should work in close co-ordination with the procuratorial organs of the State and the control organs of the Government at every level, so as to give full and effective display to the role of the supervisory organs of the party and the State.[9]

THE PARTY AND OTHER MASS ORGANISATIONS

Although the Communist Party is very large, its total membership represents only $1\frac{1}{2}$ per cent of the population. The rest of the population are mobilised and directed through other mass organisations under its control. Practically every person in China participates in, or is affected by, at least one of the mass organisations, such as the All-China Federation of Trade Unions with 12,450,000 members at the end of 1954;[10] the All-China Federation of Democratic Youth which in 1953 had 18 million members;[11] the New Democratic Youth League with 20 million members in September 1956;[12] the Young Pioneers with 30 million members at the beginning of 1957;[13] the All-China Students' Federation having, at the beginning of 1953, 3,290,000 members;[14] the All-China Federation of Democratic Women, with 76 million members early in 1953;[15] the Sino-Soviet Friendship Association, with 58 million members at the beginning of 1953;[16] and the Peasant Associations with more than 100 million members.

In many instances people are members of a number of organisations. Many organisations also join others *en bloc*. For example, the Army (PLA) and all the Federations of Industry and Commerce (the organisations of private industrialists and merchants) belong *en bloc* to the Sino-Soviet Friendship Association. Again, the NDYL is an affiliated member of the ACFDY.

Communist Party members in these organisations are supposed to work under Party directive, and carry out Party instructions,

[9] NCNA, Peking, April 4, 1955.
[10] NCNA, Peking, April 25, 1955.
[11] JMJP, August 16, 1953; SCMP, 997.
[12] NCNA, Peking, September 24, 1956.
[13] NCNA, Peking, February 5, 1957.
[14] Chao, *Mass Organisations, etc., op. cit.,* p. 123.
[15] *Ibid.,* p. 88.
[16] *Ibid.,* p. 123.

even if they conflict with the higher bodies of these other organisations. In this connection the Communist Party Constitution stipulates:

> In the leading body of a government agency, trade union, peasant association, co-operative society or any other mass organisation, where there are three or more Party members holding responsible positions, a Party fraction shall be formed. The task of a Party fraction shall be to guide the Party members in the leading body of the said organisation, to strengthen the influence of the Party and to carry out the policy of the Party (Article 60).
>
> The Party fractions in non-Party organisations shall be placed under the leadership of the Party committees at the corresponding levels and carry out the decisions of the said committees.
>
> The Party committees at all levels may ask the responsible members of important Party fractions to attend their meetings (Article 62).[17]

Thus, high or low, a Communist Party member in another organisation is duty bound to carry out Party instructions.[18]

These mass organisations are completely controlled by Party Cadres. We have seen this already in the case of the ACFTU. The situation in some of the other organisations can be reviewed cursorily.

The Constitution of the NDYL opens with an unambiguous sentence: 'The NDYL of China is a mass organisation of progressive youths, led by the Chinese Communist Party and is also the lieutenant and reserve force of the Party.' To secure tight control by the Party, provincial, municipal and *hsien* committees of the NDYL are directed to work under the Party Committees of the same level (Article 20, NDYL Constitution). The Secretary of a NDYL Committee above the *hsien* level must be a member of the Party (Article 22, NDYL Constitution). An editorial in *China Youth Journal* stated a known fact: 'NDYL cadres . . . are in general members of the Communist Party . . .'[19]

[17] Liu Shao-chi, *On the Party, op. cit.*, pp. 181–2.
[18] One case in which the head of the ACFTU, Lai Jo-yu, openly approved the obedience of Communist Party trade union cadres towards the Party leadership when it clashed with the trade union leadership, has already been mentioned. See pp. 238.
[19] CKCNP, April 7, 1955; SCMP, 1035.

The ACFDY is under Party and NDYL control. Its basic aim, according to a Manifesto of its First Congress, is

> to unite under the great leadership of Mao Tse-tung, all democratic youths who are opposed to imperialism, feudalism and bureaucratic capitalism, irrespective of their class, party, political belief, religious conviction, race, occupation and sex. [20]

Its chairman, Liao Ch'eng-chih, is also a member—second in command—of the Central Secretariat of the NDYL. (This youth leader, born in 1908, is now 49 years old. Another Vice-Chairman, Sha Chien-li, born in 1903, is now 54 years old!) Both the Federation's First Vice-Chairman, Liu Tao-sheng, and its Fourth Vice-Chairman, Ch'u Tan-liang, are on the Secretariat of the NDYL.

The Young Pioneers, an organisation for children aged 9 to 15, is under the direct guidance of the NDYL.

The Communist Party also controls all the other numerous organisations, big and small. To pick out one example, a Communist, Burhan, is the Chairman of the Islam Association of China; another Communist, Liu Ko-p'ing, is chairman of the Association for Moslem Culture.

Thus, while each mass organisation has its own field of operation, it works towards the same goals as all other organisations. Consequently, when a major campaign is launched, all the mass organisations are easily mobilised to attend the same meetings, join the same parades, and shout the same slogans.

THE COMMUNIST PARTY AND OTHER 'PARTIES'

Officially there are other legal parties in China besides the Communist Party: the Revolutionary Committee of the Kuomintang, the China Democratic League, the China Democratic National Construction Association, the China Association for Promoting Democracy, the Chinese Peasants' and Workers' Democratic Party, the China Chih Kung Tang, the Chiu San

---

[20] Chao, *Mass Organisations, etc., op. cit.,* p. 120.

Society and Taiwan Democratic Self-Government League. It is, however, fruitless to search for any difference in programme between these parties and the Communist Party. They all religiously repeat that they 'accept the leadership of the Chinese Communist Party'. A joint declaration of all the non-Communist parties in May 1950, declared:

> We, the democratic parties of China, are unconditionally united under the leadership of the great Communist Party and Chairman Mao Tse-tung for the building of an independent, free, democratic, united and prosperous China. To achieve this, we pledge ourselves to carry out fully all [the Communist Party's May Day] slogans.[21]

Similarly, the China Democratic National Construction Association, the party of the national capitalists, defined itself in its Constitution thus:

> A democratic party of the Chinese People's Democratic United Front, which takes as its programme the general principles of the Regulations of the Chinese People's Political Consultative Conference and, under the guidance of the Communist Party of China and in pursuance of the demand of the general task of the State in the transition period, seeks to unite and educate the national bourgeoisie of China to enthusiastically accept Socialist transformation and persistently struggle against internal and external enemies, in the endeavour to build a Socialist society.[22]

The Communist Party decides on the programme and policy of the other parties, and plans their organisational activities. Thus, for instance, an official announcement instructed each party. from which class it was to recruit its members:

> Those principally eligible for new membership of the various democratic parties are:
> For the Revolutionary Committee of the Kuomintang; Kuomintang members who at present still occupy Government positions and those who have done distinguished service in their work or

[21] NCNA, Peking, May 4, 1950.
[22] TKP, April 14, 1955; CB, 327.

in resisting American aggression and helping Korea or in land reform.

For the China Democratic League; Petty bourgeois intelligentsia, particularly educational and cultural workers, college students, technicians, practitioners, Government employees and patriotic and democratic overseas Chinese.

For the China Democratic National Reconstruction Association; National industrialists and merchants.

For the China Peasants' and Workers' Democratic Party; Government employees, specialists and technicians.

For the China Association for Promoting Democracy; Progressive intelligentsia, practitioners and administrative workers.

The Chiu San Society will admit new members mainly from among progressive workers in cultural, educational and scientific fields.[23]

In many cases members of the Communist Party are key people in the non-Communist parties. For example, Nan Han-chen, formerly Governor of the People's Bank of China and now Chairman of the International Trade Promotion Committee, is a member of the Communist Party and at the same time Vice-Chairman of the China Democratic National Construction Association.

THE PARTY AND THE STATE ADMINISTRATION

On September 23, 1951, Vice-Premier Tung Pi-wu defined the correct relationship between the Party and the State administration:

(1) The Party should issue proper directives to the administrative authority machineries on the nature of the tasks to be carried out and the proper course to follow in their implementation; (2) through the administrative authority machineries and their subsidiary departments, the policy of the Party should be enforced, while the operations of these machineries should be supervised; and (3) the Party should select and promote loyal and capable cadres (Party members or non-members of the Party) for work in the administrative authority machineries.

[23] NCNA, Peking, January 25, 1951.

In fact,

> All the laws and orders issued by the Central People's Government have been in keeping with the decisions of the Party, and many important documents and proclamations had first been drafted by the Party (there has not been a single document which had not been prepared or at least considered first by the Party), the drafts being then brought before the National Committee of the CPPCC, or its Standing Committee for discussion, after which it was passed on to the Central People's Government Council or the Government Administration Council for further discussion and adoption.

But *complete* identification of Party and State has serious disadvantages. Each deficiency of the State administration is bound to be put at the door of the Party, and all criticism of the State administration will concentrate on the Party. Hence Tung Pi-wu tried to draw some boundary between State and Party:

> But the Party does not directly control the affairs of State, and it is incorrect to say that the Party and the State's administration are one and the same thing. . . . That is to say, the Party assumes leadership in the administrative authority of the State, but it does not issue orders directly to the machineries exercising the administrative authority of the State.[24]

In fact, the Party plays safe, and puts its bureaucrats at the head of the State bureaucracy. The key ministries are tightly controlled by Communist Party officials. The most important, those directly related to political power, are headed almost entirely by Communists. The Minister of the Interior and three of the four Vice-Ministers are members of the Communist Party. So are the Minister of State Security and seven of his eight Vice-Ministers, the Minister of Defence and three of his seven Vice-Ministers, the Minister of Foreign Affairs and four of his five Vice-Ministers, the Minister of Finance and five of his six Vice-Ministers, the Minister of Foreign Trade and five of his eight Vice-Ministers. Other ministries (such as the Ministries of Food, the Textile Industry, Light Industry, Water Conservancy) have non-Communist Ministers, but Communist Vice-Ministers.

[24] JMJP, January 30, 1952; CB, 162.

PARTY TUTELAGE

Before Mao's rise to power, China had been totalitarian for centuries. It had been ruled by an élite, the Confucian mandarins who formed a scholar-official class. In Mao's China the Party perpetuates these traditions of tutelage.

The Mandarinate's *pao chia* system[25] and the *Censorate*[26] both have close parallels in Communist China. Other traditional devices for persuasion and coercion are also followed up today. For example, the 'rulers of Imperial China were concerned about the songs the people sang as they worked, and royal commissions for the inspection and reform of mores would solemnly report on the tone of popular ditties and suggest measures for reform'.[27] The Communist Government picks up where the Mandarinate left off and then goes much further in controlling songs, folk dances and all other aspects of popular culture. But it is much more efficient in this respect than the Mandarinate, and can marshal far better techniques. Besides, where the new rulers seek *absolute* conformity the old left a good deal of private life outside its control.

Another difference between the Communist Party and the Mandarinate is that the former pays lip service to the 'withering away of the State and Party', when its dictatorship will give way to a sovereign people, while the latter considered its rule to be eternal. Of course, it is up to the guardians of the people to decide when the people qualify for sovereignty.

[25] See pp. 323–4.
[26] See p. 371.
[27] A. F. Wright, 'The Chinese Monolith, Past and Present', *Problems of Communism*, Washington, July–August, 1955.

CHAPTER XXIV

CONCENTRATION OF STATE POWER

Communist China is controlled by three bureaucracies—the Party, the civil State administration, and the army—with separate chains of command, but unified in the same persons at key points. This integration is shown very clearly in the person of Mao. He is Chairman of the Party (i.e., Chairman of the Central Committee, of the Political Bureau, and of the Central Secretariat). He is also Chairman of the People's Republic of China with the following powers, as defined by the Constitution:

> The Chairman of the People's Republic of China, in accordance with decisions of the National People's Congress or the Standing Committee of the National People's Congress, promulgates laws and decrees; appoints or removes the Premier, Vice-Premiers, Ministers, heads of Commissions and the Secretary-General of the State Council; appoints or removes the Vice-Chairman and members of the Council of National Defence; confers State orders, medals and titles of honour; proclaims general amnesties and grants pardons, proclaims martial law; proclaims a state of war; and orders mobilisation (Article 40).

As head of the State, Mao also automatically heads the third bureaucracy, that of the Army. The Constitution says:

> The Chairman of the People's Republic of China commands the armed forces of the country, and is Chairman of the Council of National Defence (Article 42).

Similarly, Liu Shao-chi, First Secretary of the Party (and thus second to Mao in the Party hierarchy), is also Chairman of the Standing Committee of the National People's Congress (the highest civilian State body) and was for five years Vice-Chairman of the Council of National Defence. Likewise, Chou En-lai is a member of the Political Bureau of the Party, Premier of China, and was for five years Vice-Chairman of the Council of National Defence.

There is one feature of the relations between the three bureaucracies in China which distinguishes her not only from Western capitalist countries, but also from Russia, namely, the unique position of the army bureaucracy. It is headed by a Council of National Defence. Before 1954, the Council of National Defence, then called the People's Revolutionary Military Council, stood higher than any ministry in the administrative hierarchy, including both the Ministry of Foreign Affairs and of the Interior. It was on a par with the Government Administrative Council, i.e., with the 'Cabinet', headed by the Premier, Chou En-lai. The only body higher than it was the Central People's Government Council headed by Mao. Even in Russia the Army is under the Ministry of Defence, which is formally, at least, no more than an equal among all the Ministries and is under the authority of the Prime Minister. The same rule applies to Britain, France and the U.S.A. The senior position of the People's Revolutionary Military Council enabled the military 'to play a much more important political role in Communist China than it does in the Soviet Union'.[1] To add to its unique position, the *Constitution* states that while the Standing Committee of the National People's Congress has power 'to supervise the work of the State Council (i.e., the Council of Ministers), the Supreme People's Court and the Supreme Procurator's Office' and 'to appoint and remove their personnel' (Article 31), it has no power whatever over the Council of National Defence. Notwithstanding this article, however, the military seems to have somewhat less power now than before the adoption of the Constitution in September 1954. For the first time a Ministry of Defence has been added to the State Council, with the same status as all other ministries. (The People's Revolutionary Military Council was not abolished, but changed its name to the National Defence Council). Its appearance as a member of the 'cabinet' signifies some decline in the influence of the military in civil government. Another pointer in the same direction is the fact that a number of key Party and

[1] S. B. Thomas, *Government and Administration in Communist China*, New York, 1953, pp. 33–41, mimeographed.

Government leaders who were members of the People's Revolutionary Military Council do not sit on the new body: both Liu Shao-chi and Chou En-lai were vice-chairmen of the former but are now not even members of the latter. This does not mean that the military has lost its extreme importance in the State administration; it continues to be headed by Mao, and not by the seemingly natural head, the Commander-in-Chief of the Army. In this connection it should be remembered that Mao is neither chairman nor even a member of the State Council or of any other State administrative body. In addition, it is noteworthy that among the Vice-Premiers there are four leading generals; also that General Chu Teh is the Vice-Chairman of the People's Republic of China, and hence Mao's Deputy.

The tie-in of the three bureaucracies shows itself in every rung of the administrative ladder. When China was divided into six Regional Administrative Areas (1949–53) each of the chairmen of the Military and Administrative Councils appointed by the Central People's Government Council in Peking was concurrently chairman of the Area Sub-Bureau of the Central Committee, CCP, Commander of the corresponding PLA Military Area, and a member of the Central People's Government Council. Thus there were only about twenty people altogether running the civil administration and army in the centre and in the six administrative areas.

There is naturally less tie-in among the lower rungs of the three bureaucracies. Too close a tie-in here might indeed have worked towards the dispersal of power, but not towards its centralisation.

Just below the Central Government in the civil administration stand the provinces, at present 23 in number (till their dissolution the six regional governments occupied an intermediate position between the provinces and the Central Government). Below the province stands the government of the *hsien* (county), numbering 2,082 in 1956, or about 80–90 per province. Then comes the *chu* (district), and lastly the *hsiang* (administrative village consisting usually of a few villages), numbering 220,000 in 1956. In addition there are autonomous regions, and three municipalities—Peking, Shanghai and Tientsin—which are under the direct control of the Central Government, thus being in a similar administrative position to the provinces; other municipalities (166 in 1956) which have a similar administrative position to the *hsien*; and, lastly, small towns (5,000 in 1956) which have a similar position to the *hsiang*.[1a]

The Central Government exercises tight control over the lower governments. The *Organic Law of the Central People's Government of the People's Republic of China* adopted on September 29, 1949, provides that the Central People's Government shall have the authority for 'appointment or removal, or confirmation of the appointment or removal . . . of chairmen, vice-chairmen and chief administrative personnel of people's governments in various major administrative areas, provinces and municipalities' (Article 7).[2] The GAC also has the right of annulling or revising the decisions and orders of the Committees, Ministries, Commissions, Academies, Administrations, and governments of all levels, which do not conform to the laws and decrees of the State and of the decisions and orders of the Government Administration Council; 'directing the work of local people's governments throughout the country'; 'appointing or removing, or confirming the appointment or removal of the chief administrative personnel of county and municipal level and above, not included in Article 7, Section 9, b' (Article 15).[3] Articles 18 and 25 give a long list of ministries with absolutely centralised control, including all economic ministries, the Ministry of Public Security, People's Procurator General's Office, etc., etc., leaving very little room for local administration.

When the *Constitution* was drafted in 1954, it left this administrative set-up intact.

The absence of local self-government does not mean the absence of an active local administration. The election of People's Congresses at *chu* and *hsiang* level together with the right to criticise lower officials—so-called 'grass-root' democracy—are of great value to Peking: they help combat inefficiency and corruption among local officials and provide a safety valve for popular dissatisfaction; instead of the regime as a whole being made the

[1a] SSST, October 25, 1956.
[2] *The Important Documents of the First Plenary Session of the Chinese People's Political Consultative Conference*, Peking, 1949, p. 32.
[3] *Ibid.*, pp. 34-5.

butt of criticism, local scapegoats are found. Above all, it gives the masses the feeling of active participation in running the country, a kind of substitute democracy.

In this description of the administrative set-up, no mention has been made of China's 'parliament', namely the National People's Congress, and its predecessor, the Chinese People's Political Consultative Conference. This oversight is not accidental, as the 'parliament' has practically only a ceremonial value. According to the *Common Programme* (1949) the Chinese People's Consultative Conference was the supreme legislative authority in the country. But it met only once, in September 1949, when it sat for 12 days and 'elected' the Central People's Government Council. Its National Committee which by law is supposed to meet once in six months [4] held four sessions in five years. The merely ceremonial nature of the National People's Congress is clearly shown by the fact that its deliberations on the State Budget—one of its main tasks—takes place many months *after* its measures are already operating. Thus, for instance, the annual budget of 1956, effective from the 1st of January of that year, was announced to the National People's Congress by the Minister of Finance, Li Hsien-nien, on June 15. [5] Similarly the State budget for 1955, effective from January 1 of that year, was 'deliberated' by the National People's Congress and 'decided' upon seven months later on July 30, 1955. [6]

PEKING'S CENTRALISM VERSUS NATIONAL SELF-DETERMINATION

China is a land of many nationalities. According to the census of population taken on June 30, 1953, 35 million people, or 6·06 per cent of the population belonged to minority nationalities. [7] Many of them differ widely in history, language and culture from China's majority nationality, the Han.

[4] *The Organic Law of the Chinese People's Political Consultative Conference*, Article 14; ibid., p. 27.
[5] NCNA, Peking, June 15, 1956.
[6] NCNA, Peking, July 30, 1955. The 1954 budget was 'approved' on June 17, 1954.
[7] Among the minority nationalities of more than 1 million people Mongols numbered 1,462,956 (of whom about 800,000 lived in Inner Mongolia), Hui people 3,559,350, Tibetans 2,775,622, Uighurs 3,640,125, Miaos 2,511,339, Yis 3,254,269, Chuangs 6,611,455, Puyis 1,247,883, Koreans 1,120,405, Manchus 2,418,931. Other minorities totalled 6,718,025 (NCNA, Peking, November 1, 1954).

The same pattern of centralised control as practised in local affairs is shown in Peking's attitude towards the minority nationalities.

In the past the Chinese Communist Party recognised the right of all nationalities to self-determination, including their right to secede from China and build independent states. The *Constitution of the Chinese Soviet Republic* (November 7, 1931) includes the following:

> The Soviet Government in China recognises the right of self-determination of the national minorities in China, their right to complete separation from China, and to the formation of an independent state for each national minority. All Mongolians, Tibetans Miao, Yao, Koreans and others living on the territory of China, shall enjoy the full right to self-determination, i.e., they may either join the Chinese Soviet State or secede from it and form their own State as they may prefer.[8]

The democratic right of self-determination, including secession, traditional to all Marxists, and included even in the Stalin Constitution of the U.S.S.R., entirely disappeared from Chinese pronouncements when Mao came to power. The *Common Programme* (1949) merely states:

> All nationalities in the People's Republic of China shall have equal rights and duties (Article 9).
> Regional autonomy shall be exercised in areas where national minorities are concentrated (Article 51).
> All national minorities shall have freedom to develop their dialects and languages, to preserve or reform their traditions, customs and religious beliefs (Article 53).

Not a word about the right of self-determination! Crossing its t's the *Constitution* states:

> The People's Republic of China is a unified, multi-national state.
> . . . National autonomous areas are inalienable parts of the People's Republic of China (Article 3).

[8] *Fundamental Laws of the Chinese Soviet Republic, op. cit.,* p. 22.

The *General Programme of the People's Republic of China for the Implementation of Regional Autonomy for Nationalities* rejected self-determination when it laid down that:

> The autonomous organ of each national autonomous region is a local government led by the people's government of the next higher level, under the unified leadership of the Central People's Government (Article 2).

When the instrument through which all policies are carried out is the highly centralised Communist Party, national self-expression is empty of all content. The same applies in the sphere of economics.

National autonomy or self-government has very little meaning unless there is economic autonomy. But nothing is further from the minds of the rulers in Peking. As the *General Programme* states:

> The autonomous organ of a national autonomous region may, subject to the unified financial control of the State, administer the region's finances within a sphere prescribed by the Central People's Government and the local people's governments above its level (Article 19).

With control over the Communist Party, the military, civil administration, the mass organisations, over press, radio, book publishing and other media of communication so centralised, the minorities in autonomous areas are free to shout the same slogans as everyone else—using their own language.

Peking's centralisation has developed the concept of Han leadership over the other nationalities. As in the Soviet Union, where the only nationality called 'great', 'leading', 'elder brother', and the like, is the Great Russian, so in China the Han alone have all the attributes of greatness. Accordingly at a Conference of the Preparatory Work Committee of the Tung Nationality Autonomous Region in West Kwangsi (held November 6–10, 1952) the Vice-Chairman of the CPG Commission of Nationalities Affairs, Liu Ko-p'ing, said: 'The Tung compatriots should achieve a better unity with the Han Chinese, and meekly study from the Han Chinese.'[9]

[9] CNS, Nanning, November 18, 1952; SCMP, 455.

CONTROL OVER THE CADRES

Marx taught that the first act of the Socialist revolution is the smashing of the old State machine inherited from capitalism—the State bureaucracy, army, judiciary, etc. Mao Tse-tung taught the opposite: the need to retain the old personnel, however tainted they were. That is why 'the public functionaries left by the Kuomintang reactionary regime were retained *in toto* by the People's Government at the time of the take-over . . .'[10]

As a matter of fact practically all the judicial personnel of Communist China were taken from the old regime. Thus, Shih Liang, Minister of Justice, in a *Report on Reorganisation of People's Courts* made on August 13, 1952, stated:

Of the 104 judges in Shanghai People's Court, retained judicial personnel number 80; of the 120 judges in Tientsin People's Court, retained judicial personnel number 97; of the 26 judges in 8 *chu* people's courts in Mukden, retained judicial personnel number 23; of the 16 judges in Central-South Branch of the Supreme People's Court, 13 are retained judicial personnel. In some areas that were liberated late, the people's courts are basically the old ones. . . . According to the statistics of Wuhan Municipal People's Court, Canton Municipal People's Court, Kwangtung Provincial People's Court, Kiangsi Provincial People's Court, and all peoples' courts in Kwangsi Province, elements of reactionary parties and groups and special service agents constitute 64 per cent of the total number of retained judicial personnel. Elements of reactionary parties and groups and special service agents constitute 83 per cent of the total number of retained judicial personnel in Taiyuan Municipal People's Court.[11]

The Minister of Finance stated that 'over 90 per cent of the tax collectors are former personnel of the Kuomintang regime'.[12] Even many former Kuomintang generals have been retained in high administrative positions. Thus, among the 97 members of the National Defence Council, there are thirty former Kuomintang

[10] NCNA, Peking, August 3, 1952; SCMP, 388.
[11] NCNA, Peking, August 22, 1952.
[12] *New China's Economic Achievements, op. cit.*, p. 81.

Generals: four Vice-Chairmen (Chang Chih-chung, Lung Yün, Ch'eng Ch'ien, Fu Tso-yi) and 26 members.

Among the retained Kuomintang personnel are people with most offensive histories. To quote a few cases. Marshal Li Chi-sen, notorious as the butcher of the Canton Commune in 1927, was Vice-Chairman of the People's Republic of China, Deputy to Mao Tse-tung, from 1949 to 1954. General Ch'eng Ch'ien, old-time Hunan warlord and Kuomintang satrap, who conducted mass slaughter of workers in Wuhan and peasants in Hunan Province in 1927, became Vice-Chairman of the National Defence Council, Deputy to Mao Tse-tung. Chiang Lan, supporter of the military dictator, Yuan Shih-kai, in 1914, became Vice-Chairman of the People's Government, deputy to Chou En-lai. General Liu Wen-hui, who formerly played a major role in suppressing the Soviet movement in Szechwan, became a member of the National Committee of the People's Consultative Council. General Wu Hua-wen, puppet general under the Japanese, and once prominent in the fight against the Communists, became the Commander of the 35th People's Liberation Army. There are scores of Kuomintang generals, notorious for their leading roles in the Bandit (Communist) Suppression drive, who are sitting today among the Deputies to the National People's Congress. On December 27, 1948, NCNA published 'A List of the Most Notorious Leading War Criminals', including the following persons who today are *persona grata* in Peking: General Fu Tso-yi, then Commander-in-Chief, North China: Wang Wen-hao, former Kuomintang Premier; General Cheng-Ch'ien, Governor of Hunan. 'All of these . . . are notorious for their heinous crimes and every democratic Chinese agrees that they should receive just punishment.'[13] Just punishment indeed! General Fu Tso-yi is now Minister of Water Conservancy, Deputy to the National People's Congress, as well as Vice-Chairman of the National Defence Council; Wang Wen-hao is a Deputy to the Chinese Political Consultative Conference; Ch'eng Ch'ien, besides being a Vice-Chairman of the National Defence Council, is also a deputy to the National People's Congress. Yeh Kung-chao and Li Jung-yuan, former Premiers of the Pei-yang warlords' regime, are also deputies to the same august

[13] NCNA, North Shensi, December 27, 1948.

body. Their tainted past did not deter Vice-Premier Li Wei-han from saying of the members of the Chinese Political Consultative Conference: 'All have, in different degrees, a splendid fighting history behind them.'[14]

This mass recruitment of former Kuomintang officials is one source of weakness to Peking. It enhances the possibility of demoralisation and 'deviation' among its functionaries. Even were this not so, however, many other sources of demoralisation exist.

We have seen the measures of police control over the general population and the Party rank and file used by the Peking Government. No less vital is the control over Government and Party officials, the cadres. This demands special measures. As State ownership of industry, banking, trade, cultural and other institutions increases, the number and importance of Government cadres rises tremendously.[15] The same applies to other officials, above all those of the Party, whose importance grows with the stiffening of Party control over all economic, political and cultural life. In face of the general poverty, widespread illiteracy and the lack of a really active democratic life, the temptations and opportunities for corruption of the cadres are very great, as is the danger that they may lose their zeal through red tape, and drift into general inefficiency. Furthermore, local cadres will tend to find a way out of performing the extremely arduous tasks delegated them from the Centre by simply cheating Peking. The possibility of 'deviations' is inherent in this situation.

Whatever the reason, whether because of contamination by demoralised ex-Kuomintang personnel, or because it is rife with new opportunities, Mao's regime is continually dogged by the repeated corruption of large sections of its officialdom. Although Mao's bureaucracy, compared with that of the Kuomintang period, is purity itself, whatever corruption still exists cannot be tolerated, as a planned economy is wholly dependent upon the efficiency of its bureaucracy.

[14] NCNA, Peking, June 29, 1951; CB 89.

[15] At the time of the founding of the People's Republic of China on October 1, 1949, apart from the military services, the number of government cadres was about 720,000, while by September 20, 1952, it had risen to 2,750,000 (NCNA, Peking, September 30, 1952).

A number of campaigns have been launched to fight corruption amongst officials. The most prominent of these was the '3-anti' movement lasting from October 1951 to July 1952. The range of the campaign was vast. According to a report of An Tzu-wen, who directed it,

> In all organs at the *hsien* level and above throughout the country, a total of 3,836,000 persons participated in the '3-anti' movement. There were uncovered more than 105,000 persons guilty of corruption charges involving sums of more than JMP 10,000,000 each, the number being 2·7 per cent of all personnel taking part in the movement. Others guilty of less serious cases of curruption were exposed and educated in the course of the movement.[16]

Lesser crimes were committed by a large number of officials. Po I-po reported on October 1, 1952, that 4·5 per cent of the Government personnel had been punished.[17] Probably this was an intentional understatement designed to assure the people *after* the campaign that corruption was not as widespread as they had inclined to believe from press reports.

At the same time as the '3-anti' campaign was in force, a purge of corrupt elements among Party cadres and ranks took place. An Tzu-wen wrote:

> In party organs which have undergone the process of this reorganisation, an average of 90 per cent of the members have been found to satisfy the conditions of membership, and only about 10 per cent of them have failed to qualify. Among this 10 per cent, from 3 to 5 per cent were bad elements and they have been dismissed from the Party. From 5 to 7 per cent were those, who, after education, personally admitted that they did not qualify for membership and were prepared to withdraw from the Party voluntarily as well as those who lost their qualifications through passiveness and backwardness and were persuaded to leave the Party.[18]

3–5 per cent 'bad elements' in a party of about 6 million members is 180,000–300,000!

[16] NCNA, Peking, February 9, 1953; CB, 251.
[17] JMJP, October 1, 1952.
[18] NCNA, Peking, February 9, 1953; CB, 251.

To establish the purge in Government, industry, trade and other departments as a permanent institution, People's Supervision Committees and Denunciation Reception Rooms were created. The Supervision Committees had been introduced as early as 1949 by the *Organic Law of the Central People's Government of the People's Republic of China*, which stated that Supervision Committees 'shall be responsible for supervision over the execution of duties by government institutions, and public functionaries' (Article 18).[19]

Denunciation Reception Rooms, where anyone can drop accusations into 'opinion boxes', were first introduced on a large scale during the '3-anti' and '5-anti' campaigns.

The idea behind the '3-anti' campaign and the permanent purge (besides, of course, finding scapegoats), is not so much to punish corrupt functionaries or to get rid of the old personnel, as to frighten them, to cow them into submission. With this achieved, the People's Supervision Committees active, and People's Denunciation Reception rooms everywhere waiting for callers, the totalitarian control of the State bureaucracy by its chiefs and masters is complete.

As with so many present-day Chinese institutions, these organs of control over State officials are not innovations but successors to earlier Chinese practices. During the Empire the Censorate ('eyes and ears') officials were the instrument of central supervision over provincial officials. Their job was to check, without fear or favour, the work of all State officials—in theory even of the Emperor himself. In actual fact their main work was to expose any deviation of local officials from the imperial will.[20] The comparison should not be pushed too far, however, for where the Emperor had only some thousands of officials to supervise, Mao has millions.

---

[19] *Important Documents of First Plenary Session of Chinese People's Political Consultative Conference, op. cit.*, p. 37.
[20] Brief summaries of the history of the Censorate in H. Wist, *Das Chinesische Zensorat*, Hamburg, 1932, and R. L. Walker, 'The Control System of the Chinese Government', *Far Eastern Quarterly*, November, 1947.

CRITICISM AND SELF-CRITICISM—WEAPON OF CENTRAL GOVERNMENT CONTROL

An important institution in the political life of China, as well as in that of other Communist countries, is 'criticism and self-criticism'. Criticism from below is supplemented by decrees, instructions and orders from higher Party and State bodies. It encourages the mass of the people to participate in the supervision of the lower echelons of the bureaucracy.

Criticism, however, must confine itself to within very definite limits. It must not apply to Party policies nor high officials. In practice the bulk of it comes from the authorities themselves, and the masses are activated only after the green light has been shown. Criticism from below is thus an adjunct of criticism from above; it does not deal with basic issues, but is restricted to minor, mainly procedural matters.

Criticism from below gives the masses the feeling that they are not left altogether without protection from the bureaucrats. It serves as a channel of communication between the people and the top leadership; hostile feelings are directed against local petty bureaucrats exclusively.

However, criticism, from below cannot divert popular antagonism from Peking completely. When local officials are criticised for the scarcity of consumer goods, for example, and the scarcity continues despite the criticism, it cannot take long before it dawns on people that it is not the local bureaucrats that are responsible, but the policies of the Central Government. In the long run, frustration at the ineffectiveness of public criticism cannot but alienate the people from the regime. For a time, however, criticism from below can serve to keep the lower bureaucrats from 'deviations', to strengthen the bureaucratic machine and to increase popular support for the regime.

Popular criticism from below, synchronised with criticism from above, reach their climax in big purges of Communist leaders, a phenomenon already some decades old in Russia, of a few years' standing in Eastern Europe, and now appearing in China.

NEW CAMPAIGN AGAINST COUNTER-REVOLUTIONARIES

Following the general dearth of resources, which came to a head in the 1955 grain crisis, a new campaign against counter-revolutionaries was launched. This time the victims were not remnants of the old society, but members of the new bureaucracy; they were not members of its lower ranks, but top bureaucrats. As with Russia during her Five Year Plans, so China during hers must, it seems, sacrifice her own leaders on the altar of the god of industrialisation.

The first to travel the road to Golgotha was Kao Kang. Kao Kang had a long history in the Communist movement of China. He was a native of Shensi Province, led guerrilla forces there and established a Shensi Soviet prior to the arrival of the main Chinese Communist forces in the North-west late in 1935. He then rose quickly in the Communist hierarchy till in 1949 he was secretary of the North-east Bureau of the CCP, and headed the North-east People's Government that was established in August 1949. He was also one of six Vice-Chairmen of the Central People's Government and a member of the Political Bureau (one of nine); Chairman of the State Planning Commission, Central People's Government; Chairman, People's Economic Planning Committee, North-east People's Government; Secretary of the North-east Bureau of the CCP; Vice-Chairman of the People's Revolutionary Military Council; Commander as well as political Commissar of the North-east Military District; member of the Committee for the Drafting of the Constitution. In 1954 he was accused of a counter-revolutionary plot.

Accused of conspiracy with Kao Kang was Jao Shu-shih, also a top Party and Government leader. He was a member of the Central Committee, CCP; First Secretary of the East China Bureau of the CCP; Chairman of the East China People's Government; member of the Central People's Government Council; member of the People's Revolutionary Military Council; Political Commissar of the East China Military District; Director of the Organisation Department of the Central Committee.

It is probably not an accident that the two most prominent scapegoats held responsible for the difficulties in which the Five

Year Plan became involved were the chiefs of the two most important industrial regions of China—the North-east (Manchuria) and East China. Kao Kang committed suicide, and Jao Shu-shih was executed. Other officials suffered a similar fate.

The blood of Kao Kang and Jao Shu-shih had scarcely dried, when a new large-scale purge began. It started with the denunciation of Hu Feng, a distinguished literary critic and author, and his fellow *literati*. Up to the time of his arrest Hu Feng was a Deputy to the National People's Congress; a member of the Executive Committee of the Union of Chinese writers; a member of the editorial committee of *People's Literature*; a member of the National Committee of the All-China Federation of Literary and Art Circles. Many other *literati* were denounced too. Originally they were accused of deviation from 'Socialist realism': the accusation against one was that he complained of the failure of novelists to draw real characters; another was accused of grumbling that all Communist heroes were described as immaculate; a third wrote a novel about life in the countryside which was too lifelike to conform to 'Socialist realism'.

But then, like a rolling snowball, the accusations against the group gathered weight. The *People's Daily* described the 'Hu Feng clique' as 'imperialist and Kuomintang secret agents, reactionary army officers, Trotskyites, revolutionary renegades and apostatic surrendered personnel'.[21] For good measure charges of murder and rape have also been put at the door of some of the members of the 'clique'. The 'clique', we are told, succeeded in gaining positions of influence in practically all social, political and cultural organisations:

> According to present available material, the Hu Feng factionists have infiltrated into some of our government organs, military organs, educational organs, cultural and publishing organs, newspapers and economic organs. They have also infiltrated into the leadership organs of certain trade unions, NDYL organisations and organisations of the masses.
>
> They have also infiltrated into the Chinese Communist Party with some taking up posts of considerable importance.[22]

[21] JMJP, June 10, 1955.
[22] *Ibid.*

That the number of these people is not small is clear from a statement in the same editorial:

> The great majority of our revolutionary ranks (over 90 per cent) are good people. Only a very small number are covert counter-revolutionaries and bad characters.

If only half of the ten per cent of 'bad elements' of the Party were 'counter-revolutionaries', their number would exceed 450,000! What a reserve army for a purge!

The mass organisations were mobilised to wipe out the 'Hu Feng clique'. The NDYL, the All-China Federation of Democratic Youth, the All-China Federation of Students, the Revolutionary Committee of the Kuomintang, the China Democratic Construction Association, the Chiu San Society, the Democratic League, the Chih Kung Tang, the All-China Federation of Industry and Commerce, every trade union, every college, the Chinese Academy of Sciences, etc., etc.—in short, all political, economic, social and cultural organisations were mobilised to hold mass denunciation meetings.

The Communist leaders do not nourish hopes that in time the plague of 'counter-revolutionaries' will recede. Thus, Shih Liang, Minister of Justice, stated on July 29, 1955:

> The greater the victory of Socialist construction, the greater is the defeat of the enemy who is bound to carry on all sorts of sabotage against our national construction in his attempt to avert extinction. This is borne out by the number of criminal cases of undermining economic construction. For instance, the number of cases of undermining economic construction dealt with in Hopei during 1954 was 160 per cent higher than in 1953: of these, cases of sabotage by counter-revolutionaries were 165 per cent higher than in 1953 and cases of sabotage by law-breaking capitalists and other criminals were 106 per cent higher than 1953. Cases of counter-revolutionary sabotage of economic construction as dealt with in Shansi during the first quarter of this year increased two-fold compared with the corresponding period of 1953 and cases of undermining agricultural producer co-operatives also increased two-fold. Cases of sabotage that broke out in Kweichow during the first quarter of 1955 were

13 per cent higher than the fourth quarter of 1954: of these, cases of murder rose by 27·4 per cent and cases of arson rose by 90 per cent.

Again:

> From January 1954 to May this year, the people's courts of all levels in China dealt with 364,604 cases (figures for Sinkiang and individual areas of other provinces for the current year are lacking) involving counter-revolutionaries and economic construction. This figure accounted for 30·92 per cent of the total number of criminal cases during the corresponding period.[23]

The greater the burden of forced industrialisation and the greater the disparity between the promises and the fulfilments of the regime, the thinner wears its propaganda and the more urgent becomes the need for compounding propaganda with violence to keep the people in a state of permanent tension. Peasant unrest under the impact of compulsory State purchases, the need to explain away economic setbacks as the result of 'sabotage', and the need to spur the people on to almost superhuman efforts—all this causes Peking to unleash wave after wave of spy-hunting. The first act in the drama is already behind us. Vyshinsky can rest assured that his work lives after him.

[23] Shih Liang, Minister of Justice, speech to National People's Congress, NCNA, Peking, July 29, 1955; CB, 349.

CHAPTER XXV

THE LEADER

Chinese Communist ideology sees the leader as the link between State, Party, Army and people. But he is much more than the supreme legislator, administrator and commander. The leader of a totalitarian State-Party where no individual is out of his reach, nor any activity, thought or feeling beyond his empire, is omniscient and omnipotent, almost divine. The people's feeling of awe towards him is not only, or mainly, imposed by the idolatrous propaganda of his henchmen, but reflects the whole social set-up. As so often during periods of profound economic and social upheaval which result in misery, anxiety and a feeling of helplessness amongst the masses, people embrace quite irrational superstitions, including adulation of a Saviour.

The Chinese people, and especially the peasants, cannot yet grasp the real causes of their misery. Local officials seem to blame, not the distant Leader. And in their destitution and degradation they pray to the Leader-Saviour to shield them from the encroachments of the local functionary and to deliver them from misery.

One verse of the 'Internationale' says, 'We want no condescending Saviour, no God, no Caesar or Tribune . . .' but this applies to a democratic, conscious, self-mobilised collective of workers, who build a society on the basis of the freely-given material and intellectual contributions of millions of people. In such a society economic and cultural power has too collective a character to permit only one figure among ciphers. Such a society is poles apart from one built on blind masses, cowed, manipulated and goaded by a totalitarian bureaucratic machine.

The leader cult is rooted in yet another aspect of Chinese Communist rule. The regime needs the purge—the selection of scapegoats to account for national or local difficulties. The person who singles out its victims and chooses their successors in office must himself be beyond its reach. He has also to be the arbiter between different sections of the bureaucracy. With power to confer life and death and himself being outside the scope of the purge, the picture of the Man-God is complete.

There is no need to look far for precedents for such a leader cult in the history of China. The cult of Sun Yat-sen is a fairly recent example. The 1924 Kuomintang Constitution (written by Borodin, Moscow's Supreme Adviser in China) made Sun Yat-sen President of the Party for life (Article 21); stated that 'members should follow the direction of the President' (Article 22); that the President should have the power to veto resolutions of the National Congress (Article 25); and that his voice should be decisive in the Central Executive Committee (Article 26), which was the highest authority between Congresses.[1] After Sun's death in 1925, weekly Sun Yat-sen memorial meetings were made compulsory in offices, factories, schools and barracks, at which everyone had to bow three times before his portrait, his 'will' was read, and three minutes silence observed thereafter. To cap the worship of Sun Yat-sen, his body was embalmed, like one of the ancient Pharaohs, and kept in a magnificent marble mausoleum, rivalling the tombs of China's greatest emperors.

However, the cult of Sun Yat-sen pales before that of Mao. Mao's power is not only incomparably greater than Sun's, but greater even than that of the mightiest of China's emperors. It is impossible to quote more than a few of the typically idolatrous utterances made by Party leaders, Ministers, University professors, authors, poets, workers and peasants. Mao is commonly called Chiu Hsing—the Saving Star. A selection of popular dance songs published in 1944 included the following two songs:

> The sun rises, a point of red,
> The people's saving star is Mao Tse-tung.
> In order to improve our lot
> He has initiated a great production movement.

The second song:

> The East is red, the sun rises;
> China has produced a Mao Tse-tung.
> He plans a way of life for the people;
> He is the people's great saving star.[2]

[1] A. N. Holcombe, *The Chinese Revolution*, Cambridge, Mass., 1930, pp. 356–70.
[2] Quoted by C. Moy, 'Communist China's Use of the Yang-ko', *Papers on China*, Volume 6, March 1952.

A children's book includes the following rhyme:

> Mao Tse-tung is like the sun:
> He is brighter than the sun.
> Little brother, little sister,
> Everyone clap hands, come and sing. [3]

Not to be outdone, Wa-ch-mu-chi, Governor of the Yi Nationality Autonomous *chou* in Lianshen (Sikang) sang the following hymn of praise at the National People's Congress: 'The sun shines only in the day, the moon shines only at night. Only Chairman Mao is the sun that never sets.'[4] Practically the same words were used about another Leader—Stalin—in another country of supreme superlatives: 'I would have compared him to the shining moon, but the moon shines at midnight, not at noon. I would have compared him to the brilliant sun, but the sun radiates at noon, not at midnight.'[5]

Portraits of Mao hang everywhere. Five storeys high, they adorn Shanghai and other cities. Trains carry portraits of Mao over the boilers. In many peasant houses his picture replaces the former kitchen god, and a kind of grace is said before meals by the household: 'Thank Chairman Mao for our good food.'[6] His pictures occupy the tiny household shrines where formerly clay images were kept. A report of the Peking Municipal People's Government quotes a peasant approvingly:

> Formerly we worshipped Kuan Kung who was said to be omnipotent. Where is his omnipotence? Whom shall we worship? To my mind, we should worship Chairman Mao.[7]

Special obeisance is made to Mao at all public meetings. A description of a mass trial ran:

> The meeting opened with the singing of the national anthem . . . Then everybody took off their hats and bowed to the national flag and to the portrait of Chairman Mao.[8]

[3] J. Belden, *China Shakes the World*, London, 1952, p. 121.
[4] NCNA, Peking, July 26, 1955.
[5] *Znamya*, Soviet Authors' Union Monthly, October 1946.
[6] Van der Sprenkel, *op. cit.*, p. 33.
[7] *General Report of Peking Municipal People's Government on Agrarian Reform in Peking Suburban Areas*, approved by GAC on November 21, 1950; CB, No. 72, p. 9.
[8] Hsiao Ch'ien, *op, cit.*, p. 72.

At another meeting, aping the high-mightiness of former land-lords and rulers, Mao's picture and the pictures of other Communist leaders were carried on sedan chairs after the singing of the national anthem, and again 'everybody bowed to the national flag and the picture of Chairman Mao', just as they had formerly done to the landlord as he was carried by.[9] Another meeting 'began with a moment of silent bowing before a large portrait of Mao Tse-tung mounted on the stage'.[10]

Maoism has turned a complete circle. The throne of Huang Ti is filled again.

[9] *Ibid.*
[10] Bodde, *op. cit.*, p. 214.

PART FIVE

CHINA AND
RUSSIA

Deputy Foreign Minister, replied on July 13, that since Stalin and Molotov were just leaving for Potsdam no answer could be given until their return to Moscow.

As the United States Strategic Bombing Survey, *Japan's Struggle to End the War*, rightly stated:

> Based on a detailed investigation of all the facts and supported by the testimony of the surviving Japanese leaders involved, it is the Survey's opinion that certainly prior to 31 December 1945, and in all probability prior to 1 November 1945, Japan would have surrendered even if the atomic bombs had not been dropped, even if Russia had not entered the war, and even if no invasion had been planned or contemplated.[8]

STALIN ASKS A HIGH PRICE FOR ENTERING THE PACIFIC WAR

In February 1945, some months before the final collapse of Japan, Roosevelt, Stalin and Churchill met at Yalta largely to discuss operations in the Far East. On February 10, Molotov, Russian Foreign Minister, presented Harriman, U.S. Ambassador in Moscow, with a memorandum called 'Draft of Marshal Stalin's political conditions for Russia's entry in the war against Japan', which read:

> The leaders of the three Great Powers—the Soviet Union, the United States of America, and Great Britain—have agreed that in two or three months after Germany has surrendered and the war in Europe has ended the Soviet Union shall enter into the war against Japan on the side of the Allies on condition that:
>
> (1) The status quo in Outer Mongolia (the Mongolian People's Republic) should be preserved:
>
> (2) The former rights of Russia violated by the treacherous attack of Japan in 1904 should be restored, viz:
>
> (a) The southern part of Sakhalin as well as all the islands adjacent to this part of Sakhalin should be restored to the Soviet Union,
>
> (b) Possession of Port Arthur and Dairen on lease should be restored,

[8] U.S. Strategic Bombing Survey, *Japan's Struggle to End the War*, Washington, 1946, p. 13.

(c) The rights possessed by Russia before the Russo-Japanese War to the operation of the Chinese-Eastern Railroad and the South-Manchurian Railroad providing an outlet to Dairen should be restored on the understanding that China should continue to possess full sovereignty in Manchuria:

(3) The Kurile Islands should be handed over to the Soviet Union.

The Heads of the three Great Powers have agreed that these claims of the Soviet Union should be unquestionably satisfied after Japan has been defeated.

For its part the Soviet Union expresses its willingness to conclude with the National Government of China a pact of friendship and alliance between the U.S.S.R. and China in order to render assistance to China with its armed forces for the purpose of liberating China from the Japanese yoke.[9]

The core of Stalin's demands affecting China was control over Port Arthur and Dairen, the Chinese Eastern Railroad and the South Manchurian Railroad. These railroads had always been the key to control over China and an approach to the Pacific Ocean.

Back in 1892, Witte, Tsarist Minister of Finance and driving spirit behind the construction of the Chinese Eastern Railroad, had argued that this railway would give Russia 'control over the entire movement of international commerce in Pacific waters'.[10] Another aspect was emphasised by P. M. Romanov, friend of Witte, who stated that the construction of railways from Russia to Port Arthur or Dairen 'would place Peking absolutely at our mercy'.[11]

Russia acquired the right to build the Chinese Eastern Railroad in 1896, the naval base of Port Arthur and the right to build the South Manchurian Railroad in 1898. The Chinese Eastern Railroad was opened to traffic in 1903. The Russo-Japanese War of 1904–5, however, resulted in Russia's exclusion from Southern Manchuria and the transference to Japan of the leased territory of Liaotung (in which Port Arthur and Dairen are situated) and that part of the Chinese Eastern Railroad which runs from Port Arthur to Changchun. Russia retained the main line and the

[9] H. Feis, *The China Tangle*, Princeton, 1953, pp. 244–5.
[10] B. A. Romanov, *Russia in Manchuria, 1892–1906*, Ann Arbor, 1952, p. 2.
[11] *Ibid.*, p. 115.

branch line running from Harbin to Changchun. After the 1917 Revolution, Russia relinquished her imperialist rights in China. On July 25, 1919, Karakhan, Soviet envoy to China, issued the following statement:

> The Soviet Government returns to the Chinese people, without any compensation, the Chinese Eastern Railway, and all the mining, timber, gold, and other concessions seized by Russian generals, merchants and capitalists . . . [12]

The intention was not acted upon, however. Years later, on March 12, 1935, Russia sold the Chinese Eastern Railroad to Manchukuo, that is, to Japan.

Concerning this vital artery a Chinese historian has written:

> In the world history of railway building, no line of communication by rail has involved more international controversies, caused more intense international rivalry and proved more tragic in its results than the Chinese Eastern Railway. [13]

At Yalta Stalin was set on regaining control for Russia of this strategic link and of the two ports of Dairen and Port Arthur, thus retrieving the concessions wrung from China by Tsarist Russia.

However, he did not have it all his own way. Accordingly, after some haggling, he agreed (1) that the Manchurian railways would not be a completely Russian enterprise, but a common Sino-Soviet enterprise, (2) that while Port Arthur would be a Russian naval base, Dairen would be a free port under international control. He also agreed on the need to obtain the Chinese Government's concurrence with regard to these proposals. But this was more lip service on his—and Roosevelt's and Churchill's —part. No provision was made in case of failure to get this agreement, and, as 'the heads of the three Great Powers have agreed that these claims of the Soviet Union shall be unquestionably

[12] Vl. Vilensky, *Kitai i Sovetskaya Rossia*, Moscow, 1919, p. 41, quoted by J. Degras, editor, *Soviet Documents on Foreign Policy*, London, 1951, Volume I, pp. 159–60. This passage does not occur in any subsequent Russian text. It is included in the English translation from the French original published by the Chinese Ministry for Foreign Affairs and reproduced in the *China Year Book*, 1924, p. 868.

[13] A. K. Wu, *China and the Soviet Union*, London, 1950, p. 73.

fulfilled after Japan has been defeated', China was left no choice in the matter.[14]

To justify the high price he asked for entering the Pacific War, Stalin said to Roosevelt:

> . . . if these conditions were not met, it would be difficult for him and Molotov to explain to the Soviet people why Russia was entering the war against Japan . . . they would not understand why Russia should enter a war against a country with which they had no great trouble.[15]

A sudden and strange solicitude for Soviet public opinion! The readiness of the United States and Britain to pay Stalin the price he asked was due to two factors: first, it was believed at the time that the Japanese forces on the Asian continent, backed by the war industries in Manchuria, might, even after the surrender of Japan herself, put up a long and bitter resistance, unless attacked by Russia; secondly, after the defeat of Germany, it was obvious that Russia was strong enough to take whatever she demanded at Yalta whether or not the United States and Britain consented. Dean Acheson, United States Secretary of State, said:

> . . . unquestionably the Russians had in their power not only to take what was conceded to them, but much more besides.
>
> There was very little likelihood that anybody would have the will, and few people could have the power, to throw them out of any area on the mainland which they might occupy, and where they might wish to remain . . .[16]

China was kept completely in the dark as regards the contents of the Yalta Agreement until June 15, 1945, when it was divulged to Chiang Kai-shek by General Hurley, United States Ambassador to China.[17] China's foreign minister, T. V. Soong, immediately went to Moscow, where he was given the drafts of three

[14] The text of the Yalta Agreement is to be found in *United States Relations with China, op. cit.*, pp. 113–14.
[15] Feis, *op. cit.*, p. 243.
[16] *American Policy Toward China*, Secretary of State Dean Acheson's Statement to a Joint Senate Committee, June 4, 1951, Washington.
[17] *United States Relations with China, op. cit.*, p. ix.

agreements: A Treaty of Friendship and Alliance; An Agreement Regarding the Ports of Dairen and Port Arthur; and An Agreement Regarding the Manchurian Railroads. The first promised that the Soviet Government would work *solely* with Chiang Kai-shek's regime, and would not aid his enemies (presumably Mao Tse-tung). The other two named the price Stalin demanded for this promise, viz., that the Manchurian Railways and connected enterprises (factories, coal mines, etc.) should be the exclusive property of Russia. These demands exceeded the terms of the Yalta Agreement.[18] Soong complained of this to President Truman, and was advised in reply not to go beyond the terms laid down. When Soong accordingly proved adamant, Stalin retreated, with the result that on August 14, 1945, China and Russia signed agreements congruent with the secret Yalta Agreement.

Having obtained the prize he coveted, Stalin was now prepared to join battle with Japan.

RUSSIA IN THE WAR AGAINST JAPAN

The Japanese did not know that Stalin had agreed in February 1945 at Yalta, to attack them three months after the end of the war in Europe. On February 22, Molotov, in response to an enquiry, assured Sato, the Japanese Ambassador, that Far Eastern questions had been entirely excluded from the discussions at Yalta and that the U.S.S.R. would continue its policy of neutrality in the Far Eastern War.[19]

While keeping Japan in the dark as regards her intentions, Russia tried to get as much material aid as possible from the United States, so as to cut her costs in any future military engagement. She accordingly gave the United States a list of supplies which, in her view, were essential for the offensive against Japan. The United States was asked to provide a two-months' supply of food, fuel, transport equipment and other material for a force of $1\frac{1}{2}$ million troops, 3,000 tanks, 75,000 motor vehicles, and 5,000

---

[18] Feis, *op. cit.*, p. 317.
[19] Evidence of Sato, IMFTE, Record, p. 23579, quoted by F. C. Jones, *Japan's New Order in East Asia. Its Rise and Fall, 1937–1945*, London, 1954, p. 433.

aeroplanes. These supplies were additional to other supplies covered by the current Lend-Lease agreement. The list was slightly revised by Washington, and up to June 30, 1945, 80 per cent of it was delivered.[20]

On August 6 the A-bomb was dropped on Hiroshima, followed two days later by another on Nagasaki. On the same day Russia declared war on Japan, and the Potsdam Agreement was published. Two days later, on August 10, Japan accepted the Potsdam Agreement with a sole reservation regarding the Imperial House, and on August 14, the Emperor declared Japan's surrender. The Soviet Command, however, completely ignored this declaration and continued to advance until the whole of Manchuria and some areas in the adjoining provinces were in their hands.

Russia did not suffer any loss of equipment in the war against Japan, as she had received supplies for two months of war from the United States, while her actual engagement lasted for only nine days. Her casualties were 8,219 killed and 22,264 wounded, while she put Japanese losses at 80,000 killed.[21]

[20] General J. R. Deane, *The Strange Alliance*, London, 1947, pp. 248–9.
[21] *The Times*, September 11, 1945.

CHAPTER XXVII

RUSSIA'S LOOTING OF MANCHURIA

On November 24, 1945, Slatekovsky, economic adviser to Marshal Malinovsky, Commander-in-Chief, Soviet troops in Manchuria, put before Chang Chia-ngau, Chairman of the Economic Commission at the Chinese Government headquarters in Manchuria the proposal that 80 per cent of Manchuria's heavy industry should be placed under joint Sino-Soviet ownership. On December 4, Chang Chia-ngau declared that no economic discussion would be possible prior to the withdrawal of Soviet troops from Manchuria. To this Marshal Malinovsky retorted that the date of withdrawal would not be fixed until the question of Soviet economic rights in Manchurian industry were settled. While these negotiations were going on, Soviet troops began dismantling industrial equipment on a large scale. The Soviet Government stated in a note delivered at Chungking on January 21, 1946, that all the equipment removed was 'war booty', by which the Russians understood all those industrial enterprises which had been of use to the Japanese army;[1] such a definition could, of course, cover practically all industry. On March 27, 1946, the Soviet Ambassador again proposed to the Chinese Foreign Minister that the main industrial enterprises, mines and airfields in Manchuria be placed under joint Sino-Soviet companies for a period of thirty years, the remaining enterprises to be returned to China immediately. These proposals also were rejected by the Chinese government.[2]

The Soviet troops now continued the dismantling at full speed, doing the job so thoroughly that by the time they had finished, practically no machinery was left within the bare factory walls.

In no way can war destruction or demolition by the Japanese he held responsible for the disembowelling of Manchurian enterprises. Japan's collapse in Manchuria was too rapid for a scorched

[1] M. Beloff, *Soviet Policy in the Far East, 1944–1951*, London, 1953, pp. 38–9.
[2] *United States Relations with China, op. cit.*, pp. 596–8.

earth policy to be operated, and so the Russians occupied Manchuria intact. Furthermore, over 80 per cent of Manchuria's industry was concentrated in the south, outside the zone of military operations.

The only survey of the extent of dismantlement is to be found in a report by a United States reparations commission headed by Edwin Pauley, which in May and June 1946, investigated industrial conditions in Manchuria. The report states that in dismantling, the Russians

> concentrated on certain categories of supplies, machinery and equipment. In addition to taking stockpiles and certain complete industrial installations, the Soviets took by far the larger part of all functioning power-generating and transforming equipment, electric motors, experimental plants, laboratories and hospitals. In machine-tools, they took only the newest and best, leaving antiquated tools behind.[3]

Other causes of the devastation of Manchuria's industry were pointed out in the Report:

> How much of the wrecked condition is a direct result of Soviet removals and how much may be ascribed to pillage, civil war, and indirect consequences of the Soviet occupation cannot be accurately determined.

Everett D. Hawkins, who in 1946 was Director of the Mukden Office of the United States Information Service, said:

> The general belief is that the Japanese had to cannibalise a certain number of their machines towards the close of the war to keep certain plants going, that the small tools, equipment and materials which are being sold in some of the black 'open' markets in Mukden were looted by the Chinese, but that the generators and heavy equipment were systematically taken by the Soviets, put in railroad cars and sent up north, probably to Siberia.

[3] NYT, December 14, 1946.

Summing up the situation, the Pauley Commission gave an estimate of the total damage done to basic Manchurian industries from all causes:

Industry	Monetary Loss (in U.S. $ millions)	Percentage Reduction in Productive Capacity
Electric power	201	71
Coal	100	—
Iron and steel	141·26	51–100
Railroads	137·16	—
Metal working	150	80
Non-ferrous mining (coal excepted)	10	75
Liquid fuels and lubricants	11·68	65
Cement	23	50
Chemicals	14	50
Textiles	38	75
Paper and pulp	7	30
Radio, telegraph, telephones	25	20–100
Total	858·10	

Source: Pauley Report, quoted in F. C. Jones, *Manchuria Since 1931*, London, 1949, p. 229.

The Russians did not deny that they dismantled at least some of Manchurian industry. Replying to foreign correspondents in February 1946, the Russian Commander in Mukden, Major General Kovtoun-Stankevich, admitted that industrial equipment had been removed from Manchuria and taken to Russia, but he justified this action on the ground that the equipment was war booty.[4]

At that time Li Li-san, leader of the Communists in Manchuria, newly-arrived from Moscow, declared in a speech in Harbin:

I feel that the movement of the machinery is not an important problem at all. Of course the Soviet Union moved some machinery but not a large amount compared with its war losses.[5]

[4] G. W. Atkinson, 'The Sino-Soviet Treaty of Friendship and Alliance', *International Affairs*, London, July 1947.
[5] *Daily Worker*, New York, July 26, 1946, quoted by Dallin, *op. cit.*, p. 245.

393

CHAPTER XXVIII

DID STALIN HELP MAO TO COME TO POWER? *

Soviet diplomatic relations with Kuomintang China from the end of the war until the complete victory of Mao were very 'proper' —full support for Chiang Kai-shek and no recognition of Mao. During the war, Stalin took pains to belittle and deride the Chinese Communists before United States statesmen. For instance, he told Harriman, U.S. Ambassador, on June 10, 1944: 'The Chinese Communists are not real Communists. They are "margarine" Communists.' Later he called them 'cabbage' Communists, and on another occasion 'radish' Communists (red outside and white inside).[1]

He repeatedly affirmed that he recognised only Chiang's Nationalist Government. On May 28, 1945, he is said to have 'made the categorical statement that he would do everything he could to promote unification of China under the leadership of Chiang Kai-shek.' He stated that 'he would welcome representatives of the Generalissimo (Chiang) to be with his troops entering Manchuria in order to facilitate the organisation in Manchuria of Chinese administration'.[2]

Again at Potsdam, Stalin declared that 'Chiang Kai-shek's Government was the only possible government in China and that the Chinese Communists were not real Communists at all'.[3] Six

---

* The evidence on which this Chapter is based is extremely inadequate, because the Chinese and Russian archives dealing with the subject—if they exist—have not been opened, nor have those who carried out the liaison between the Russian and Chinese Communists disclosed what happened. Some students of Chinese affairs who have read my book (as, for instance, Professor K. A. Wittfogel and Mr. J. Menken), entirely disagree with the whole Chapter—not without good reason. However, their reading of these events, which are so shrouded in mystery, is as much conjecture as mine. My interpretation gains support from other students of China, notably Brandt and Associates, in *Documentary History of Chinese Communism, op. cit.*, and B. I. Schwartz, *Chinese Communism and the Rise of Mao*, (Cambridge, Mass., 1951).

[1] Feis, *op. cit.*, pp. 140–1.
[2] R. E. Sherwood, *The White House Papers of Harry L. Hopkins*, Volume II, London 1949, pp. 891–2.
[3] J. F. Byrnes, *Speaking Frankly*, London, 1946, p. 288.

months later General Hurley, United States Ambassador to Chungking could make the following statement to the Senate Foreign Relations Committee: 'Russia . . . does not recognise the Chinese armed Communist Party as Communist at all. Russia is not supporting the Chinese Communist Party.'[4]

More important than the diplomatic make-believe was Moscow's real attitude expressed in her actions. Unaware of the treaty just signed in Moscow between T. V. Soong and Molotov, under which the Soviet Government pledged itself to render 'moral support and assistance' only to the Kuomintang Government 'as the Central Government of China', Chu Teh, Commander-in-Chief of the Chinese Communist armies, sought the right on August 10, 1945, for his soldiers to participate in accepting the surrender of Japanese troops. Chu's claim was rejected out of hand by all the Powers, including Russia. Nevertheless, on August 11, Chu Teh ordered Communist forces to proceed to Manchuria. The Russian military authorities refused to allow them to enter as military units, although they permitted them to enter unarmed.[5]

There were not enough Russian troops in Manchuria to occupy the countryside, so they concentrated on the big cities and railway lines where they installed and protected Kuomintang officials for many months. In fact, because he feared Manchuria might fall into the hands of the Chinese Communists, Chiang Kai-shek begged Russia to retain her troops longer than was originally stipulated between Molotov and Soong. Thus at the end of November 1945 the Soviet command in Manchuria obligingly agreed to postpone the evacuation of its troops 'in order to assist the Chinese Government in the difficult task of establishing its authority in Manchuria'—against Chinese Communist resistance, needless to say. The official Soviet news agency, *Tass*, published a report stating that the Soviet Army had been prepared to evacuate Manchuria by December 3, but that General Hsiung Shih-hui, the Chinese Commander in Manchuria, had told Marshal Malinovsky that 'non-Governmental troops have made it difficult to introduce Chinese troops and administration into Manchuria'. Therefore, the Soviet Government had 'given its

---

[4] Feis, *op. cit.*, p. 410. [5] Jones, *Manchuria Since 1931, op. cit.*, p. 231.

consent to postponing the removal of troops from Manchuria for one month, and this has been acknowledged by the Chinese Government with great satisfaction'. [6] Month after month Chiang renewed his request for the Russians to stay on, and it was not until May 1946—six months after the originally agreed date—that the Soviet evacuation was finally completed.

Long after the events, Chiang Kai-shek accused Russia of arming the Communists in Manchuria. But this was denied by as authoritative a spokesman as America's General Marshall, who stated on his return journey from China in January 1947, that there was no evidence whatsoever to indicate that the Chinese Communists were being supported by Russia. [7] The United States ambassador to China, J. Leighton Stuart, said in October 1947, that there was 'little if any evidence of material assistance from Moscow' to the Chinese Communists. [8] Again, every foreign observer that witnessed the entry of Communist troops into Tientsin or Peking agreed on the large amount of American arms borne by these troops (mainly brought over by Kuomintang troops that changed sides), but not one mentioned any Russian arms. Russia did not even turn any Japanese arms over to the Chinese Communists, as both the Chinese Communist and Russian authorities confirmed. What Japanese arms they possessed were taken from dumps in places which the Russians had not occupied. [9] When H. R. Lieberman, *New York Times* correspondent, pointed out to Chou En-lai that 'the Communists had benefited considerably in Manchuria during the Soviet occupation of Japanese arms and by being permitted to enter evacuated cities before the arrival of Government forces', Chou retorted: 'The Russians held the railway lines. We got our arms from the countryside. Also we took cities held by the Nationalists and not by the Russians'. [10]

Chiang's *post hoc* version of Russian aid to the Chinese Communists falls down on another count. Manchuria was *not* the principal area of battle. The Communists had far greater forces deployed in North and Central China, south of the Great Wall

[6] *Soviet Monitor*, November 3, 1945.
[7] NYT, January 12, 1947.
[8] L. K. Rosinger and associates, *The State of Asia*, London, 1951, pp. 37–8.
[9] NYHT, March 15, 1946.
[10] NYT, September 9, 1946.

than they had in Manchuria, and it was in these areas that the main fighting between Mao's army and that of Chiang Kai-shek took place, that is, areas that the Russians did not penetrate. With victory secure in North China the fate of Manchuria was in any case sealed, as the Kuomintang forces were far distant in the west and south.

No military aid was given.[10a] But perhaps Stalin helped Mao in another field, with political assistance in his rise to the top of the Communist movement, with advice in the civil war? But in this sphere too Mao has little to thank Stalin for.

As regards the first point, it need but be mentioned that Moscow repeatedly appointed the leaders of the Chinese Communist Party. There were Ch'u Ch'iu-pai, Li Li-san, Wang Ming, Po Ku, and the last (appointed in 1934), Chang Wen-t'ien. Mao Tse-tung was not one of the Moscow appointees. Quite the contrary, he was not in Moscow's good books at all, and was even, on its orders, dismissed from the Politbureau (September 1927). This information he himself gave in an interview with Edgar Snow.[11] (According to another source he was even reduced to probationary membership of the Party.)[12] In the same interview, Mao Tse-tung put the responsibility for the defeat of the Chinese Revolution of 1925–7 squarely at the door of Moscow's main representative in China at the time, Borodin.[13]

[10a] A very different picture, showing Russia's great military assistance to Mao, is drawn by a number of students of China. See, for instance, H. Feis, *op. cit.*, pp. 264, 377, 381–2; J. L. Stuart, *Fifty Years in China*, New York, 1954, p. 180; and Carsun Chang, *The Third Force in China*, New York, 1952, p. 172. These writers believe that the Soviet army in Manchuria played a decisive role in giving Mao's troops Japanese equipment and opportunities for reorganisation and training, thus transforming them from a guerilla force to a regular army. The published evidence is probably too inadequate for a safe generalisation, but on the whole the present author is inclined to think that Mao would have won the civil war against the Kuomintang even without Russia's help, and that if this was forthcoming at all, it was of secondary importance.

[11] E. Snow, *Red Star over China*, London, 1937, p. 165.

[12] Schwartz, *op. cit.*, p. 100

[13] Snow, *Red Star over China*, *op. cit.*, p. 161. One should not, of course, take Mao's words at their face value. There is ample evidence to show that Mao was on the extreme right of the Chinese Communist Party at the time of the 1925–27 Revolution. (See, for instance, what M. N. Roy, who was in China in 1927 as a Comintern representative, writes in his book, *Revolution and Counter-Revolution in China*, Calcutta, 1946, p. 615). The fact that Mao's *Selected Works* includes only one entry written prior to March 1927, also speaks volumes about his role in the defeated Revolution, for, as editor of a weekly paper for about four years before 1927, he must certainly have written more than one short article.

Even when the Chinese Soviets, the edifice on which Mao rose, were already in existence, Moscow showed little appreciation, or even knowledge of them. Thus, for instance, in his Report to the Sixteenth Congress of the Communist Party of the Soviet Union (June 1930), Stalin remarked: 'It is said that a Soviet Government has already been created there! I think that if this is true then there is nothing surprising in it.'[14]

Whatever the details of the struggle for power inside the Communist Party of China, it is undeniable that Mao rose in spite of Moscow, and not thanks to her. The record of his rise, explored painstakingly in an excellent study by B. I. Schwartz, leads to two unavoidable conclusions: one,

> That Mao established his leadership within the Chinese Communist movement by dint of the real military, financial, and mass power which had been created by his own successful strategy; that the gravitation of power into the hands of Mao Tse-tung and Chu Teh was the result of circumstances and power relations existing within the Chinese Communist movement rather than of any decision made in Moscow.

Two,

> . . . that Moscow's recognition of the Mao Tse-tung leadership was essentially in the nature of an acquiescence to a *fait accompli*.[15]

After taking control of the Party, Mao gained little ideological inspiration from Stalin. One of the chief CCP theoreticians, Chen Po-ta, could candidly say in an article written on the occasion of Stalin's seventieth birthday:

> It was only after the 1942 movement of ideological reorientation that Stalin's numerous works on China were systematically published by our Party . . . Many comrades of our Party who in fact led the Chinese revolution never had occasion to make a systematic study of Stalin's numerous works on China. Among them was Comrade Mao Tse-tung.[16]

[14] Schwartz, *op. cit.*, p. 136.
[15] *Ibid.*, p. 187.
[16] Chen Po-ta, *Stalin and the Chinese Revolution*, Peking, 1953. In subsequent editions of the same work the last sentence is omitted.

But perhaps Mao's debt to Stalin is in the realm of civil war strategy? The mere fact of Russia's looting of Manchurian industry shows unequivocally, however, that Stalin had entirely misjudged the situation and the prospects of the civil war in China. Had Stalin counted on a Communist victory, with the Communists in control of the Manchurian countryside, he could simply have kept the industries in Manchuria intact and handed them over to the Chinese Communists to give them a strong industrial and military basis in their fight against the Kuomintang. Stalin himself, it seems, admitted he was wrong in his estimate of the situation in China at a meeting with Kardelj and some other Yugoslav Communist leaders in February 1948. He said:

> It is true, we also have made mistakes. For instance, after the war we invited the Chinese comrades to come to Moscow and we discussed the situation in China. We told them bluntly that we considered the development of the uprising in China had no prospects, that the Chinese comrades should seek a *modus vivendi* with Chiang Kai-shek, and that they should join the Chiang Kai-shek government and dissolve their army. The Chinese comrades . . . acted quite otherwise. They mustered their forces, organised their armies, and now, as we see, they are beating Chiang Kai-shek's army. Now, in the case of China, we admit we were wrong. It has proved that the Chinese comrades and not the Soviet comrades were right.[17]

After his spasm of 'self-criticism', however, Stalin continued to misinterpret events in China. At a conference of Chinese Communists held in Southern Hopei in July 1948 to determine strategy for the coming campaign, the Soviet view was expressed that the Communists should continue to wage guerrilla warfare but not undertake an all-out offensive. This would weaken the United States, who would continue to pour military aid into China and so be bogged down in a war of attrition. The Moscow proposal was defeated by the Conference.[18]

There are many other pointers to show that the civil war in China did not develop according to the perspectives held, or the blueprint drawn up, in Moscow.

[17] V. Dedijer, *Tito Speaks*, London, 1953, p. 331.
[18] C. P. Fitzgerald, *Revolution in China*, London, 1952, pp. 102–4; and Beloff, *op. cit.*, pp. 60–1.

Until nearly the end of the civil war Soviet policy was orientated on a compromise between the Chinese Communists and the Kuomintang, not on a decisive victory of Mao. Some points in the record of her dealings will show this clearly.

On February 21, 1948, *Pravda* noted that since the non-aggression treaty of the U.S.S.R. with the Kuomintang Government had not been abrogated within the prescribed period, it had been prolonged automatically for a further two years. In April *Pravda* vigorously attacked a member of Chiang's Foreign Affairs Committee for demanding that the Sino-Soviet Treaty of August 1945 be denounced. Despite the formation of the Chinese Communist Government of the Liberated Areas, the U.S.S.R. continued to hold diplomatic relations with Chiang's Government *only*. Mao's resounding victories in November 1948, which completed the conquest of Manchuria and brought hundreds of thousands of Chiang's troops and a vast amount of American military supplies over to the side of the Communists found little echo in the Soviet Press. On the 31st anniversary of the Russian Revolution, November 7, 1948, Molotov made much of the progress of the 'Liberation movements' in Asia, but did not refer specifically to the Chinese Communist successes. 'This gives support to the view that the Russians were still contemplating a settlement in which the Kuomintang would be left in control of a part of the country'.[19] Further confirmation can be gained from several reports that Moscow was ready to mediate between the Kuomintang and the Chinese Communist Party. A notable example came after the resignation of Chiang Kai-shek and the assumption of the post of Acting President by General Li Tsung-jen, in January 1949, when negotiations along these lines were conducted between him and the Soviet Ambassador. According to the official American version, they reached tentative agreement on the following three points: (1) Chinese neutrality in any future war, (2) elimination of United States influence, and (3) establishment of a 'basis of real co-operation' between China and Russia. Li then approached the Americans for support for this agreement, but was rebuffed.[20] The Soviet Government has never

[19] C. P. Fitzgerald, *Revolution in China*, London, 1952, p. 62.
[20] *U.S. Relations with China, op. cit.*, p. 293.

denied this version. Even after the PLA had taken Peking (January 21, 1949), Moscow continued to maintain diplomatic relations with the Kuomintang Government, and the Soviet ambassador had the singular distinction of being the only ambassador to follow the Kuomintang Government to Canton. At the same time the Soviet consulates in Communist-occupied China were closed by Moscow. As late as March 1949, Russia initiated talks with Kuomintang representatives at Urumchi (Sinkiang) over Soviet proposals for economic co-operation between the two governments in Sinkiang.

It was only after the final victory of Mao Tse-tung was established beyond doubt, and a matter of a few days or even weeks old, that Moscow changed its cautious attitude to the Chinese Communists and gave full support to Mao Tse-tung. On April 25, five days after the Communist armies crossed the Yangtze, *Pravda* declared that the 'liberation of Nanking' had put an end to 'the reactionary rule of the Kuomintang'. Li Tsung-jen was now referred to as the 'so-called Acting President', and references to 'New China' began to multiply in the Soviet press.[21]

In sum, the history of Stalin's intervention in China's affairs has been one long series of blunders and defeats. Indeed, it is symbolical of Moscow's role in Mao's rise to power that Mao was the only important Communist leader in the world who had never made a pilgrimage to Moscow or met Stalin. His one and only visit took place in February 1950, well after his final victory.

However, past quarrels and misunderstandings have little influence on present-day relations between Mao and Moscow.

[21] Beloff, *op. cit.*, p. 65.

CHAPTER XXIX

RUSSIA'S ECONOMIC AID TO CHINA

China is, and for many years will be, in the throes of industrialisation. The element overriding all others in her relations with Russia is the ability and readiness of Moscow to aid her in her economic construction.

The economic relations existing between China and Russia have already been dealt with. It has been pointed out that in their trading relations Moscow's position is much stronger than that of Peking, and that China needs Russia more than Russia needs China; that Russia drives a hard bargain in trade negotiations with China; that she charges high prices for the goods she supplies to China, while paying low prices for the goods she buys; that the credit she grants China is not at all generous.

All this, however, does not discount the vital role the Soviet connection plays in China's economic growth. As Russia and her European satellites supply some four-fifths of China's imports, and practically all her imports of capital goods, they hold a strategic place in China's economy. As long as the general international situation does not change radically, and especially while the Western embargo on trade with China in strategic goods continues, Peking will continue to be economically dependent on Moscow.

Above all, the most decisive factor in Sino-Soviet relations is the fact that in *1980* China will probably have raised herself economically to Russia's position thirty years earlier, in *1950*. And as long as the major centres of heavy industry—so decisive for military and economic world mastery—are in the heart of Eurasia—in Russia—Mao will have to submit to being Number Two, a big, but very definitely junior, partner.

CHAPTER XXX

CHINA AND RUSSIA CONTEND FOR THE BORDER REGIONS

There are three regions inhabited by non-Chinese, bordering on both Russia and China, where the two countries struggle for influence and mastery. These are Mongolia, Sinkiang and Korea.

CHINA, RUSSIA AND MONGOLIA

Mongolia is divided geographically into two parts: Outer Mongolia or the Mongolian People's Republic which is officially an independent state, with an area ten times larger than Britain and $1-1\frac{1}{2}$ million inhabitants; and Inner Mongolia, which is a part of the Chinese People's Republic and in which there are some 800,000 Mongols. These contain the major part of the Mongol people, although there are Mongols in a few other territories as well. There are about half a million living in Russia around the Baikal in the areas adjoining Mongolia; these are divided mainly between the Tuvinian Autonomous Region of the RSFSR and the Buryat Mongol Autonomous Soviet Republic. Another branch of the Mongolian people, the Kalmuks, used to live between the Don and the Volga, but after the Second World War their republic was abolished and they were deported to Siberia.[1]

The Tsars had not attempted to annex Mongolia to Russia. Their policy was to use her as a buffer against China, Japan and Britain. They therefore opposed any attempt at unifying all the Mongols into one state. Stalinist Russia has inherited this policy. Her central theme is to try to bring the Mongol countries under her influence, but at the same time to avoid uniting them and annexing all their territories. In this policy she is enjoying much greater success than her predecessor.

Tsarist imperialism had shown an active interest in Mongolia since the turn of the century, and especially after the 1904-5

[1] Gluckstein, *op. cit.*, p. 310.

403

Russo-Japanese war. In 1907, Russia asked for Japan's recognition of Mongolia as a Russian zone of influence in return for Russia's recognition of Manchuria as a Japanese colony. A compromise was reached whereby Mongolia was carved into two parts, Outer Mongolia, recognised as a Russian zone of influence, and Inner Mongolia, whose status was not affected by this treaty. With the overthrow of the Manchu dynasty in Peking by the 1911 revolution, Mongolia seceded from China. Her princes kept in close touch with Russia and chose a pro-Russian to be the Mongolian Emperor. In 1915 a Tripartite Agreement was entered into by China, Russia and Mongolia, by which Outer Mongolia was declared an autonomous region under the nominal suzerainty of China and special privileges were reserved for Russia. Outer Mongolia had in reality become a protectorate under a Russian and Chinese condominium. With the Russian revolution the Mongol princes sought to revert to Chinese sovereignty. But in the meanwhile Mongolia had become a battlefield for the Russian White and Red Armies. To cut a long story short, after the defeat of the White Armies in 1921, and with Soviet troops present in Outer Mongolia, Soviet influence became predominant. Nevertheless Moscow continued to accept Chinese suzerainty over Outer Mongolia. Thus an agreement between China and Russia dated May 31, 1924, stated: 'The Government of the Union of Soviet Socialist Republics recognises that Outer Mongolia is an integral part of the Republic of China, and respects China's sovereignty therein.'[2]

However, Moscow did not cease, turning the Mongolian People's Republic into her satellite. When, for instance, Danzan, the Commander-in-Chief of the Mongolian Army, delivered an anti-Russian speech at the third congress of the Mongolian People's Revolutionary Party, he was arrested and executed.[3] During the period 1924–30 great efforts were made by the Soviets to increase their own and diminish China's trade with Outer Mongolia (in 1934, 91 per cent of all Mongolia's external trade was with Russia).[4] Again, the building of the Turksib

[2] A. K. Wu, *op. cit.*, p. 348.
[3] G. M. Friters, *Outer Mongolia and Its International Position*, London, 1951, p. 130.
[4] *Ibid.*, pp. 136–7.

railway (1930) made Outer Mongolia much more accessible from the Russian than the Chinese side. This factor became even more important when Ulan Bator, the capital of the Mongolian People's Republic, was connected by rail with Russia (a fact first mentioned in a Soviet news item in November 1949).[5] To enhance Russian influence, the Mongolian People's Republic adopted the Russian (Cyrillic) script for its press and official publications in 1941.

It became quite obvious that the Mongolian People's Republic was in fact completely outside Chinese suzerainty. The Sino-Soviet Treaty negotiated in 1945 by Molotov and Soong declared, subject to affirmation by a plebiscite, the independence of the Mongolian People's Republic; and, so as to forestall any idea of unity with Inner Mongolia, added the words 'in her existing boundaries'. The plebiscite took place on October 20, 1945. Of 494,960 eligible voters, 487,490, or 98·4 per cent, cast their vote. The result was remarkable in that 100 per cent of the voters declared themselves in favour of separation from China—there was not a single dissentient.[6]

The Treaty of February 1950 between Russia and Communist China nullified the 1945 Sino-Soviet Treaty, but affirmed the independence of the Mongolian People's Republic. The actual text of the notes on the Mongolian People's Republic has not been published, which probably means that it does not differ much from the 1945 text.

From all that has been said, it is quite obvious that the Mongolian People's Republic is completely under the tutelage of Moscow.

The Mongols in the Tuvinian Autonomous Region, also called Tannu-Tuva, or Tuva, are also in the Russian sphere being actually within the RSFSR. Almost as big as Britain in area, Tuva

---

[5] *Ibid* p. iv.

[6] That such a perfect result was achieved, when at least the Chinese population of the Mongolian People's Republic—making up some 5 per cent of the total population (W. Kolarz, *The Peoples of the Soviet Far East*, London, 1954, p. 153)—probably opposed the separation of the country from China, is not to be wondered at seeing that the following provision was included in the 1945 plebiscite decree for the Mongolian People's Republic:

'On the election list, each citizen shall indicate opposite his name whether he is for independence or against it, and sign the document. In case of illiteracy, the citizen shall indicate his identity by the fingerprint of his right thumb' (*Pravda*, November 22, 1945).

has an extremely small population, estimated in 1941 at 95,000.[7]
In 1915, it was incorporated into the Russian Empire, but Outer
Mongolia continued to claim jurisdiction over it, and the Tuvi-
nians themselves wished to join the—for them—great nation,
whose written language they used, for lack of one of their own. So
in 1924 Tuva rebelled and declared her affiliation with Outer
Mongolia. Soviet troops suppressed this revolt.[8] Tannu-Tuva was
declared an independent state in 1921, but was completely under
Moscow's control, and in 1944 was officially annexed to the
U.S.S.R., becoming the Tuvinian Autonomous Region of the
RSFSR. Moscow was set upon having a more direct and tight
control over Tuva than she has over the Mongolian People's
Republic, because of the former's great strategic importance, the
Kuznetsk oilfield lying north-west of it. (The fact that a big por-
tion of the population of Tuva are Russian facilitates this control
for Moscow.)

The Buryat Mongol Autonomous Soviet Republic, also part of
the RSFSR, was established in 1923. It has a population of some
quarter of a million, the majority of whom are Russians.[9] Having
formed part of the U.S.S.R. for so many years, it is the bridge-head
for Russian expansion amongst the Mongols in general. Buryat
was the first Mongol language to introduce the Russian script.[10]
Whenever Moscow decides to send administrators (as distinct
from military advisers) to the Mongolian People's Republic, it
prefers Buryat Mongols to Great Russians.[11]

The Russian policy of holding on leash several Mongolian tribes
while preventing their unity, and of using them as buffers against
China (in the past also against Japan and Britain), cannot be
viewed too favourably by Mao. Often in the past Mao has made
clear his wish to include the whole of Mongolia as part of China.
Thus in 1936 he said to Edgar Snow:

[7] Kolarz, op. cit., p. 161.
[8] Friters, op. cit., pp. 130–1.
[9] Kolarz, op. cit., p. 115.
[10] Ibid., p. 123.
[11] R. Bollenbach, 'The Mongol People's Republic (Democracy of a New Type)',
Papers on China, Volume 3, May 1949.

When the people's revolution has been victorious in China the Outer Mongolian Republic will automatically become a part of the Chinese federation, at their own will.[12]

Eight years later Mao said:

When they took that right for themselves and set up their own democratic republic, the Outer Mongolians issued a declaration to the effect that they would rejoin China as soon as they were recognised as one of the national entities which, according to Dr. Sun Yat-sen, are to enjoy equal autonomous rights under the Chinese Republic.

I hope and have no doubt that they will rejoin China the moment the National Government lives up to the promise of the founder of the Republic and the Kuomintang.[13]

But there is hardly any doubt that Mao will have to content himself with far less than this. In Mongolian affairs, his wicket—Inner Mongolia—is much weaker than Moscow's.

One of the themes in Chinese history is the struggle between peasants and herdsmen along the line where agricultural land meets grazing land. This struggle still continues today. Not only does it split the Mongols of China, the majority of whom are agriculturists, away from all other Mongols, who are mainly nomads, but even more, it separates the Chinese as a whole from the Mongols as a whole. The Chinese peasant has encroached and is still encroaching on the preserves of the Mongolian nomad, and consequently no love is lost between Mongols and Chinese. These elements of conflict make for deep national and social antagonisms in the Inner Mongolian Autonomous Region itself (of whose population, 5 million are Han Chinese, and less than a million Mongols). And with Inner Mongolia divided against itself, it is unlikely to become a point of attraction for an irredentist movement among the rest of the Mongolians.

Nevertheless some change in the Russo-Chinese balance of power as regards Mongolian affairs is sure to come about as a result of the strengthening of China herself as well as of Peking's

[12] E. Snow, *Scorched Earth*, *op. cit.*, Volume II, p. 289.
[13] G. Stein, *The Challenge of Red China*, London, 1945, p. 356.

increasing efforts to multiply economic ties with the Mongolian People's Republic. This is very likely one of the motives behind the newly-opened railway line between Chining (in China) and Ulan Bator, the capital of the Mongolian People's Republic. In the past trade between China and the Mongolian People's Republic was carried by means of the Manchurian railways. The Chining–Ulan Bator railroad shortens the distance by three-fifths. (Though this is one of the motives for the building of the Chining–Ulan Bator line, this is not the most important; the need to improve railway connection between China and Russia is the prime factor.)

SINKIANG

Another area bordering on China and Russia, and inhabited by non-Chinese, is Sinkiang. Sinkiang is much larger than the British Isles, France and Germany together. Its population of 4,873,000 is made up of 13 nationalities, among which the Uighurs predominate, making up more than 74 per cent of the total; the Kazakhs follow with 10·3 per cent. Together with the other Turkic peoples they make up 90 per cent of Sinkiang's population. The Turkic peoples are all Moslems, and many of them (the Kazakhs, Kirghiz, Uzbeks, Tatars) have brethren over the border in Soviet Turkestan. The Uighurs also have close affinity with these peoples.

Sinkiang is mostly desert, but it has important deposits of oil, coal, iron, copper, lead, manganese, sulphur, saltpetre, and allegedly, uranium. Its importance is enhanced by the fact that it has common frontiers with Russia, China, Afghanistan, Tibet and India.

Russia has been encroaching upon Sinkiang since the middle of the nineteenth century. She got a firm foothold in the district of Ili, at the time of the Taiping Rebellion, when the Manchus were so weakened that they could not oppose the Tsar's demand for—in the main—free Russian trade in Ili. Additional privileges in the area were conferred upon Russia by the Russo-Chinese Treaty of St. Petersburg (1881). After that, despite the ebb and flow of Russian influence in the wake of the Revolution, the situation on the whole remained fairly static, Russia's interests being confined mainly to trade. A radical turn came with the *coup d'état* of Sheng Shih-tsai in April 1933. He ruled the country for eleven years, for the first eight or nine being actively supported by Russia, who supplied him with ammunition, machine-guns, armoured trucks and aeroplanes, as well as with generous loans. For a time, Sinkiang became an economic domain of Russia for all practical purposes.[14] However, when the fortunes of the war in Europe frowned upon Russia, in 1942, Sheng turned on his Soviet advisers and Communist supporters, arrested tens of thousands and executed many. But his independence was to be brief. On November 7, 1944, a revolt broke out in the three North-western districts of Sinkiang bordering on Russia—Ili, Tacheng and Ashan—leading to the establishment of a pro-Soviet East Turkestan Republic, with its own Kazakh-Uighur army. The agricultural and mineral resources of this region make it the richest in Sinkiang.

The next act in the drama occurred in March 1949 when Soviet representatives held talks with representatives of the Kuomintang government in Urumchi in which they tried hard to come to agreement on a common Sino-Soviet development of Sinkiang. The negotiations broke down.[15]

With the surrender of the whole Province of Sinkiang by the Kuomintang authorities to the Chinese Communists on September 19, 1949, the East Turkestan Republic was abolished, and its troops absorbed into the People's Liberation Army. Some of the leaders of this Moscow-controlled republic, for instance, Saifudin (at present vice-governor of Sinkiang), were absorbed into the new administration. Others were purged. Among those purged were Ghani Bator, one of the heroes of the 1944 revolt; Aisa Abdullah, manager of the former East Turkestan Republic's Economic Development Company; and Abdul Gafoor Sabri Hodjaev, former head of the military court.[16] Some years later a Peking paper went so far as to refer to the East Turkestan leaders as 'a bunch of

---

[14] During the early 1930's only 12·5 per cent of Sinkiang's foreign trade was with China (O. Lattimore, *Pivot of Asia*, Boston, 1950, p. 172) while Russia's share was 82·5 per cent (*Ibid.*, pp. 173–4).

[15] It is possible that this anxiety to secure a foothold in Sinkiang before the collapse of the Kuomintang government was to some extent connected with Moscow's desire to have a position of strength from which to conduct future bargaining with Mao Tse-tung.

[16] H. R. Lieberman, NYT, December 23, 1951.

pro-imperialist elements' who 'launched an East Turkestan movement in Sinkiang to stir up hatred against one another among the nationalities'.[17]

Sinkiang's special status was underlined in the Sino-Soviet negotiations of 1950, when a special economic delegation from Sinkiang was added to the delegation of the Central People's Government of China in Moscow. The Sinkiang contingent stayed on after the conclusion of the main talks, and signed a separate economic agreement, by which two mixed Sino-Soviet companies, one for oil, the other for non-ferrous metals, were to be established.[18] A few years later, however, Mao managed to dislodge the Soviets from their foothold in Sinkiang, wringing agreement on the liquidation of the joint companies and their transference to full Chinese ownership in October 1954.[19]

National affinity with the peoples of Russian Turkestan makes for irredentist tendencies in Sinkiang. Moreover, Russian influence in Sinkiang has a geographical prop: vast deserts separate Sinkiang from China, but no natural barriers cut her off from Russia. Geography has, in addition, brought the main centres of Sinkiang much nearer to the Soviet railway line than to the Chinese. Thus the main oilfield, near Wusu, is only 300 miles from the Russian railhead at Sergiopol, while the nearest Chinese railway is some 1,600 miles away, and can be reached only by very difficult mountain tracks. As a result transport costs to China are prohibitive and Sinkiang oil has for many years been transported to Russia for refining and disposal. (This situation will be radically changed when the Lanchow–Urumchi–Alma Ata railway, at present under construction, linking China proper with Sinkiang and then going on to Russia, is completed.)

CHINA, RUSSIA AND KOREA

The third region to be dealt with in this section is Korea. Korea borders on Manchuria and Russia; Vladivostok is only 100 miles from North Korean ports, while Shantung is a similar

[17] KMJP, September 20, 1955.
[18] *Soviet Monitor*, March 29, 1950.
[19] See p. 67.

distance away to the West. Add to this Korea's position some 120 miles from Japan—the present basis of U.S. power in the Pacific—and her importance in Chinese foreign policy, above all in her relations with the U.S. on the one hand and Russia on the other, becomes obvious.

In the contest between China and Russia for influence in Korea, Russia had a great initial advantage in that the North Korean regime was established by Russian bayonets long before the Chinese Communists achieved power in China. It seems that as early as 1945 Moscow saw in North Korea a reliable future vassal, unlike Manchuria, or China as a whole. Consequently she left North Korean industries intact.[20] It is evident from North Korea's complete dependence on Soviet arms that her advance on the South on June 25, 1950, could not have taken place except by Moscow's dictate. Possibly Moscow sought through the Korean war to embroil China in a war with the United States, weaken her and increase her dependence on Russia. Of course Russia hit another bird with the same stone, involving the United States in a long, exhausting and indecisive localised military conflict.

When the Korean war broke out the Soviet press immediately repeated the version broadcast by the North Korean radio, which alleged that the attack had come from the South and that the North Korean Army had been ordered to repel it.[21] Peking, on the contrary, was clearly not prepared for the event, and for the first 24 hours of the war, the Chinese press was in complete confusion.[22] But whether or not she wanted the war, Peking came out solidly on the side of North Korea when United Nations troops approached the Yalu River. The reason for this is obvious: the Yalu River power plant on the border of Manchuria and Korea, is the most important supplier of electric power for Manchurian industry.

[20] The U.S. Reparations Commissioner, Edwin W. Pauley, when visiting North Korea and Manchuria in May and June, 1946, reported that whereas in Manchuria the Russians had removed a tremendous amount of industrial equipment, there was 'little if any' evidence of stripping in North Korea (NYT, July 20, 1946 and December 15, 1946. Quoted in G. M. McCune, *Korea Today*, London, 1950, p. 214.)

[21] *Pravda*, June 26, 1950. Beloff, *op. cit.*, p. 183.

[22] Fitzgerald, *op. cit.*, p. 220.

As the war dragged on, however, Peking felt the burden growing too heavy for her, particularly as it interfered with her plans for industrialisation. It seems that Peking was ready for an armistice long before it was actually reached. In December 1952, with Peking's knowledge and backing, India presented the United Nations with a resolution on the question of the P.O.W.'s, the last impediment to armistice in Korea. This, however, was promptly and unceremoniously turned down by Vyshinsky. It was only after the death of Stalin and the disarray in the Kremlin which led to a strengthening in Mao's position, that an armistice was reached. On March 6, 1953, Stalin's death was announced. On March 30, four days after his return from Moscow, Chou En-lai issued a statement making an agreement on the question of the P.O.W.'s possible. Two days later, on April 1, Molotov endorsed Chou En-lai's proposal.

Since then there have been a number of pointers to show that Peking's influence in Pyongyang is much stronger than it was. The clearest is China's aid to North Korea. In September 1953, Kim Il Sung, Premier of North Korea, went to Moscow to discuss Soviet economic aid. An agreement was signed giving North Korea assistance to the tune of 1,000 million roubles (nominally about 250 million U.S. dollars or £90 million). But Peking was not to be outbid, and in November it announced a gift of JMP 8 million million (nominally about 317 million U.S. dollars, or £114 million) [23]. The goods supplied by China to North Korea include 'railway locomotives, goods wagons and passenger-coaches, coal and coke, pumps, electric motors, cement, timber of various kinds, and steel products'. [24] It is clear from the type of products supplied that China's aid to North Korea is no mean burden for her. Peking must set very great store on influence over North Korea to be prepared to make such a sacrifice.

Another event which might reflect Peking's increasing influence in Pyongyang was the purge that took place in North Korea in August 1953. Among those purged was Ho Kai Ye, Vice-Premier and head of the Secret Police, Lee Sung Yup, Minister of Justice and Mayor of Seoul during the North Korean occupation of the

[23] NCNA, Peking, November 23, 1953.
[24] PC, December 16, 1954.

city, and Kwon O Dik, North Korean Ambassador to Peking (March 1952–February 1953). It was announced that Ho Kai Ye committed suicide while Lee Sung Yup and another nine were sentenced to death for espionage on behalf of the United States.[25] The leader of this group was Ho Kai Ye. He was born in Siberia, was a Soviet citizen until 1945, came to Korea with the Soviet troops and was then installed at the top of the North Korean administration. (There is another possible explanation for this purge, namely, that Ho Kai Ye was a Beria protégé, and the fall of the one followed the fall of the other.)

It should always be borne in mind, however, that the rivalry between Peking and Moscow over influence in Korea is overshadowed by and subordinated to their united front against the United States and South Korea.

[25] *The Economist*, August 29, 1953.

CHAPTER XXXI

CHINA, RUSSIA AND THE WEST

Mao's victory brought a second Communist Power into being. Russia's economic and military strength is incomparably greater than that of China, but China has nearly three times the population of Russia, a vast area, considerable military strength, great industrial potentialities, and the possibility (because of geography, race and past historical associations) of assuming leadership in Asia. This last point has become of special significance for Russia since the 'cold war' between East and West reached an impasse in Europe, while the situation in Asia, the underbelly of the Western capitalist Powers, is yet fluid. Stalled in Europe, Moscow must look to the East as she has done many times since the Crimean War. Indeed, 'it becomes a law in Russian history that every time Russia finds herself checked in Europe she intensifies her drive in Asia.'[1]

There is another, secondary reason for Russia to encourage China's expansion in Asia. Inasmuch as there is friction between Russia and China over Mongolia and Sinkiang, it is to her advantage that China be preoccupied elsewhere, in her South and South-western borders: in Tibet, Korea or Taiwan (Formosa). This makes less likely clashes between China and Russia and, simultaneously, may lead to the diversion of a considerable portion of the resources of the Western Powers from Europe, the more decisive theatre of struggle between the West and Russia.

In this context of the world struggle of the Powers, Russia and China find themselves allies, with Russia the senior partner. China finds it necessary to rely on Russia's aid.

Whatever their relative strength, Sino-Soviet relations are those of allies, not of master and servant. China, the greatest and oldest nation in the world, cannot become a satellite of any foreign power. That is why her administration, unlike those of the Eastern European satellites, is totally independent of Russia,

---

[1] A. Lobanov-Rostovsky, *Russia and Asia*, New York, 1933, p. 147.

and suffers no intervention on Russia's part. Even if Moscow could intervene in the internal affairs of the country, she has probably learnt, from the fiasco of Stalin's policy in Yugoslavia, to be very wary of such an attempt.

To sum up, if China is in the orbit of Moscow, it can only be because her own needs constrain her in that direction.

The Moscow-Peking axis will have to face great trials. It is clear that if the alliance were ever to break, Mao's China would be a much greater menace to Moscow than Kuomintang China could ever have been. The Kuomintang, despite its ruthless terrorism, was a weak government unable to unite the country, to construct its economy or to build up its military strength. During its rule, too, Moscow could rely to a certain extent on internal opposition—the Chinese Communists—to harass Chiang Kai-shek. Today the position is quite different. Mao has united China and is turning her into an economic and military power far surpassing anything her past has seen, while Moscow is helpless to intervene in her internal affairs.

MOSCOW, PEKING AND THE ADVANCE OF COMMUNISM
IN ASIA

Communism, whether in its Russian or Chinese version, has a tremendous appeal in Asia, for obvious economic, social and political reasons. If one were somewhat schematically to date the era of capitalism from the fifteen hundreds, one could say that in four centuries capitalism has become the predominant mode of production in the whole world, yet it embraces *directly* only a minority of the world's population. Intensive industrial development has taken exclusive hold of only a few countries: Western and Central Europe, North America and a few other areas. More than two-thirds of humanity live in countries with primitive, pre-capitalist modes of production—the largest area being Asia, where more than half the world's population lives, and where capitalism comprises only a few tiny islands in a backward agrarian sea. The great Asian revolt is rooted chiefly in resentment agaimt this division of the world into advanced and backward countries. The peoples of Asia, and especially their vocal intelligentsia, do not believe that the backwardness is divinely ordained (a conviction strengthened by the industrial and military successes of Japan). Their revolt against backwardness and hunger is expressed in a national and social uprising against imperialism and feudalism. To believe, like McCarthy, that the revolt of Asia and the victory of Mao Tsetung in China are merely the fruits of a Moscow or Peking plot is about as enlightened and intelligent as to believe that the French revolution was the act of a handful of demagogues, or that the revolution in Hungary in October, 1956, was the work of a few American agents. Hundreds of millions of people are on the move, because they wish no longer to accept the crushing burden of imperialism and landlordism, not because the local agitator has said his part.

Into this upsurge Moscow and, after Mao's victory, Peking, beam their propaganda. A number of factors aid Russia in its appeal to Asia. First, a large part of the Soviet Union is made up of Asiatic provinces. Secondly, Russia abolished feudal land tenure, a fact which appeals strongly to Asians who strive for agrarian reform. A third, and perhaps over-riding factor, is Russia's industrial attainments.

Beside the United States and Western Europe, Russia may be somewhat backward industrially, but to Asiatic eyes she is a giant. The output per person in Russia, while less than a third of that of the United States, and about a third of that of Britain, is four or five times higher than in India or China. The annual *per capita* consumption of energy of all kinds (in coal equivalents, metric pounds) was, in 1937, 13,310 in the U.S.A.; 9,600 in the United Kingdom; and 2,430 in the U.S.S.R., Russia had thus reached only about one-fifth of the United States level, or a little over a quarter of that of Britain. But here again the U.S.S.R. far surpasses India and China, their consumption figures being 190 and 170 respectively.[2]

True, Russia knows neither political democracy nor personal liberty. But the illiterate and oppressed Asian peasant is hardly likely to pine for the freedom of the press or personal liberty; even the intellectual, enamoured of 'national greatness', would

[2] Woytinsky, *op. cit.*, p. 299.

scarcely consider this a factor of overriding importance. Thus Russia's reputation goes before her in her drive to the East as a country highly developed technically, with high living standards, a symbol of anti-feudal revolution and industrialism. The fact that the Russian rulers support the revolutionary waves of national liberation and agrarian reform in Asia only as a means of self-aggrandisement in no way impairs their influence—at least, so long as the Kremlin's interests and the needs of the Asiatic peoples do not clash headlong in practice.

In many ways, the appeal of Mao's China to Asians is even greater. China is part of Asia, her population a good half of its total population. She was a semi-colonial country, and is now waking to become an industrial and military giant.

Peking seems to have gained the upper hand in the rivalry for influence over the Communist movement in Asia. Moscow appears to have accepted Peking as the source of inspiration for the Communist movements of the East, and Peking has openly staked her claim to this leadership. Thus, in his inaugural speech at the Trade Union Conference of Asian and Australasian Countries in 1949, Liu Shao-chi said:

> The way taken by the Chinese people in defeating imperialism and its lackeys and in founding the People's Republic of China is the way that should be taken by the peoples of the various colonial and semi-colonial countries in their fight for national independence and people's democracy.
>
> This way is the way of Mao Tse-tung. [3]

Again, on the occasion of the thirtieth anniversary of the Chinese Communist Party, a leading member of the Party, Lu Ting-yi, wrote an article entitled 'The World Significance of the Chinese Revolution', which contained the following: 'The classic type of revolution in imperialist countries is the October Revolution. The classic type of revolution in colonial and semi-colonial countries is the Chinese revolution.' [4] It is true that the Soviet press until a couple of years ago stressed the great debt owed by

[3] Chen Po-ta, *Mao Tse-tung on the Chinese Revolution*, Peking, 1953, p. 86.
[4] NCNA, Peking, June 25, 1951.

the Chinese revolution to Soviet inspiration, and above all, to the advice given by Stalin. But nevertheless no Soviet spokesman has denounced the doctrine pronounced by Liu Shao-chi.[5]

However, Chinese hegemony over the Communist Parties in different Asian countries is not everywhere unchallenged.

In the case of Indo-China, both Moscow and Peking made it absolutely clear that Vietminh was Peking's satellite. Moscow did not recognise Ho Chi Minh's government (established on August 22, 1945), until after Peking did. Peking's recognition came on January 18, 1950 (immediately after Mao had established his power over practically the whole of China), and Moscow's on January 31, 1950. Again, when Ho Chi Minh went to Moscow (in July 1955) he was given a grant of £35,800,000,[6] while Peking was ready to grant £115 million.[7]

The Japanese Communist Party is also more under the influence of Peking than of Moscow. A survey of the Japanese Party publication, *Akhata* (Red Flag) between June 1952 and December 1953, shows that there were 85 articles on the U.S.S.R. (many of them dealing in part with relations with China) as against 168 articles dealing exclusively with China.[8] Furthermore, the Japanese Communist Party programme of November 1951 defined Japan as a colonial or semi-colonial country, thus putting her in the same category to which China belonged before 1949. This suggests that the strategy and tactics employed in Japan would be learnt from Chinese mentors.

The position in India is much less clear. The Indian Communist Party is split on different issues, one of the main being whether to follow the line of Chou En-lai and Molotov on friendship with Nehru, while treating the United States as the main enemy, or to continue with propaganda against British Imperialism as 'Enemy No. 1'. This issue, in which Moscow and Peking are united, cuts across another—whether the Chinese example should be

[5] It was ignored in an essay on Asian national liberation struggles by the Orientalist E. M. Zhukov, who explained Asian revolutionary successes in terms of the lessons of the October Revolution and the history of the Bolshevik Party (*Crisis of the Colonial System*, Reports presented in 1949 to the Pacific Institute of the Academy of Sciences, U.S.S.R., Bombay, 1951).

[6] NCNA, Hanoi, August 13, 1955.

[7] NCNA, Peking, July 7, 1955.

[8] R. Swearingen, 'The Communist Line in Japan', FES, April 1954.

applied to India. Here, loyalties seem confused. In July 1949 the Editorial Board of the Bombay *Communist* attacked those Indian comrades who wanted to follow Mao's line. Mao, the editorial board charged, had paid no regard to the hegemony of the proletariat, co-operated with rich peasants, and brought sections of the bourgeoisie into the government. This open attack on Mao was rejected by the Cominform, a Moscow agency, and the Indian leadership was reprimanded in its paper.[9] Since then, no word of criticism has been levelled against Mao in the Indian Communist Party press.

Most other Asian Communist Parties leave no doubt as to where their Mecca lies. Hundreds of delegates from Party, youth, trade union, student and other organisations make the pilgrimage to Peking all the year round, while Moscow is relatively neglected.

Russia's and China's attitudes to the advance of Communism in Asia are both rent with deep contradictions. From Russia's standpoint it is by no means an unmixed blessing. True, the movement could weaken the Western capitalist powers considerably by intensifying their raw material problems, and at the same time give the Communist bloc control over half the world's oil resources (instead of 6 per cent as at present) and virtually all the world's natural rubber supply as well as vast quantities of other strategic materials. True, Communist domination of Asia could sharpen marketing difficulties for the Western capitalist countries, and so handicap them in the race against Russia for world domination. Last, but not least, it is true that such a victory could provide a tremendous human reservoir for Russian military purposes—a factor of grave importance as the Korean War has demonstrated. But, on the other hand, an expansion of Asian Communism could heighten the tensions within the Russian system to breaking point: the more the backward countries come under the aegis of the Communist movement, the more numerous and clamant will be the demands for Russian equipment, the more pressing will become the latter's crisis of under-production and the more threatening will be the danger of Titoism.

On the face of it, it seems that this analysis is contradicted by Moscow's recent move to give economic aid to India, Burma and

[9] *For a Lasting Peace, for a People's Democracy!* January 27, 1950.

Afghanistan. This is not so, however. The move is of a piece with Moscow's policy of drawing the neutral countries away from the West, while preserving the social *status quo* in them. To give one million tons of steel to India over a period of three years (and not as a gift, but in exchange for Indian goods) [10] is much easier than to supply the needs of a Communist India set upon the speedy development of industry with emphasis on heavy industry, and isolated from the West. This policy is also sure to tip the scale in Moscow's favour and against Peking in the struggle between them for influence in Asia: after all China is much less able to aid the countries of Asia than Russia is.

China's attitude to the advance of Communism in Asia is complicated by the thought that while advancing Communism in Asia will tend to look to Peking for leadership, thus increasing her prestige and power, this same advance can gravely harm China's efforts at industrialisation, first, as a greater portion of the resources of Russia and Eastern Europe will have to be diverted from China elsewhere, and secondly, as the advance of Communism in Asia will increase international tensions, causing a greater portion of the industrial output of Russia and her European satellites, as well as of China herself, to be diverted to armaments, a terrible burden on China as it is.

Chinese demands for help in her industrialisation might have any of a number of possible results, depending upon the current international situation. In certain circumstances, they could lead the Kremlin to a more 'pacifist' foreign policy in order to save on armaments and supply the requisite amount of steel, machinery, locomotives, and so on, to China. In other circumstances, they might have the opposite effect and drive Moscow to the military conquest of Western Europe, whose great industrial resources could provide the steel and industrial equipment for China's growth. Chinese pressure could produce equally contradictory effects upon Russian domestic policy: the imposition upon the Russian people of an austere regimen so that heavy industry might wax at the cost of home consumption, to satisfy Chinese demands; [11]

[10] *The Times*, London, December 14, 1955.

[11] It is not yet safe to say what role Mao played in the fall of Malenkov with his 'soft' policies, and the rise of Bulganin and Khrushchev. But that there is some connection is obvious.

or the opposite, the granting of popular concessions in order to increase the mass support and the stability of the regime in face of Mao's pressure. And of course, the internal situation in Russia can in turn condition the effect—in kind and extent—of Chinese pressure upon the Kremlin tremendously: if stable, the regime in Russia will react quite differently to the way it will when it is shaky. The same applies, *mutatis mutandis*, to the relation between tensions in the Moscow-Peking axis and tensions between Russia and her East-European satellites: Mao's pressure on Moscow can lead to intensified pressure on the Eastern European satellites, or to its opposite, a relaxation of demands, depending on circumstances.

Again, China's interest in lifting the Western Powers' trade embargo may lead to 'pacifism', to greater 'friendliness' with the Western Powers. This might fit in with Moscow's wish to shed some of the burden of China's industrialisation. On the other hand, it might not fit Moscow's book, as a rapprochement between Peking and the West can lead to the weakening of the Moscow-Peking axis.

The attitude of Moscow, as well as Peking, to the advance of Communism in Asia, and to the 'cold war', is thus neither simple nor one-sided. The number of variables is much too big to be able to arrive at any useful conclusions regarding the probable future developments in China's foreign policies.

However, the following may safely be said of China's general role in world Communism: that it will be the strongest and most impregnable citadel of Stalinism. As China's backwardness is so much greater than Russia's—not to speak of Russia's European satellites—her working class so small, and lacking in cohesion and culture, the forces compelling the bureaucracy to grant concessions, perhaps even threatening to blow up the regime through

---

In September–October 1954 a Soviet delegation headed by Khrushchev visited Peking. This delegation promised China a Soviet credit of 520 million rubles. In addition four important Soviet-Chinese enterprises were handed over entirely to China (an oil company in Sinkiang, a non-ferrous metal company in Sinkiang, the Dairen Shipbuilding Company, and a company for civil aviation). (See pp. 66–7). It was immediately after this promise of a large supply of capital goods to China that the protagonists of a slackening of emphasis on heavy industry were severely attacked in the Russian press, an attack culminating in an article by D. Shepilov, future Russian Foreign Minister, called 'The Party General Line and the Vulgarizers of Marxism'. (*Pravda*, January 24, 1955). A month later Malenkov was removed from the Premiership.

revolutionary explosions, are much weaker in China than in Russia, and even more, than in Eastern Europe. In all probability, if revolutionary events elsewhere do not cause China's course to be steered along a different path, she will have to pass through a generation, perhaps two, before the rule of the bureaucracy is threatened. The present regime in China, if she is kept in isolation, will probably make its Russian Stalinist precursor seem mild by comparison.

Mao's China is and will be an important factor strengthening Stalinist exploitation, oppression and rigidity in the 'Socialist Third of the World.'[12]

[12] In this respect it is interesting to note the major pronouncement in the *People's Daily* of December 29, 1956, called 'More on the Historical Experience of the Dictatorship of the Proletariat.' This approves the general course of Soviet policy, in the main justifies Stalin's career, support Soviet policy in Hungary and reproves Tito. It emphasises the 'leading role of the Soviet Union in the Socialist Camp.' Throughout his trip to Moscow, Warsaw and Budapest in January 1957, Chou En-lai harped on the same theme. Symbolically his applause was loudest after Khrushchev's statement: 'All of us Communists . . . consider it a matter of pride for us to be as true to Marxism-Leninism as was Stalin himself." (*Manchester Guardian*, January 18, 1957).

NOTE ON DRAFT OF THE SECOND
FIVE YEAR PLAN (1958–1962)

As, at the time of this book going to press, the Chinese Communist authorities had only started discussing the Second Five Year Plan, and had not yet drawn any definite conclusions, the discussion of this Plan was avoided in the body of the book. It is, however, useful to cast a glimpse at the proposals for the Second Five Year Plan adopted by the Eighth Congress of the Chinese Communist Party on September 27, 1956. The main items are as follows:

Output Targets

		1952 actual	1957 goal	1962 approx. goal
Steel	000 tons	1,350	4,120	10,500–12,000
Coal	,,	63,530	113,000	190,000–210,000
Electricity	000,000 kwh	7,260	15,900	40,000–43,000
Crude petroleum	000 tons	436	2,012	5,000–6,000
Cement	,,	2,860	6,000	12,500–14,500
Machine-made paper	,,	370	650	1,500–1,600
Cotton piece-goods	000 bolts	111,630	163,720	235,000–260,000
Grain	000,000,000 catties	3,087·9	3,631.8	5,000
Cotton	0,000 *tan*	2,607·4	3,270·0	4,800

Sources: 1952 and 1957: Li Fu-chun, *op. cit.*, pp. 32, 36.
1962: *Proposals of the Eighth National Congress of the Communist Party of China for the Second Five Year Plan for Development of the National Economy (1958–1962)*, Peking, 1956, pp. 14–15, 18.

The total value of industrial output in 1962 will be about 100 per cent more than in 1957.[1] (The increase planned for the First Five Year Plan was 90·83 per cent.) The value of agricultural output in 1962 is planned to be about 35 per cent more than in 1957.[2] (In the First Five Year Plan the increase was set at 23·3 per cent.) New railways are planned to cover 8,000–9,000

---

[1] Chou En-lai's speech to the Eighth National Congress of the Communist Party of China, NCNA, Peking, September 16, 1956).
[2] *Ibid.*

kilometres in the Second Five Year Plan[3] (as against some 4,084 kms. in the First Five Year Plan).

Capital investments for the Second Five Year Plan are set at JMP 80,000 million, while the First Five Year Plan target was JMP 42,740 million.[4] 'Of all capital investments, investments in industry will be raised from 58·2 per cent in the First Five Year Plan to about 60 per cent in the Second Five Year Plan, and investments in agriculture, forestry and water conservancy will be raised from 7·6 per cent to about 10 per cent.'[5]

Whereas the First Five Year Plan aims to raise the portion of capital goods in total industrial production to 38 per cent (consumer goods thus making up 62 per cent), the Second Five Year Plan aims to increase the share of capital goods to 'about 50 per cent'.[6]

In the Second Five Year Plan 'the number of university and college graduates is expected to reach approximately 500,000, which is roughly 80 per cent more than the number aimed at in the First Five Year Plan. In 1962 the total enrolment in universities and colleges is expected to reach approximately 850,000, which is roughly double the number aimed at in 1957.'[7]

One should be careful not to accept as final the present rough proposals of the Communist Party Congress regarding the Second Five Year Plan. In the case of the First Five Year Plan it was two years after its initiation that final figures about its targets were published, and these differed widely from the original figures announced.

---

[3] *Proposals of the Eighth National Congress*, etc., *op. cit.*, p. 22.
[4] 'Answers to Some Questions on the Second Five Year Plan,' SSST, October 25, 1956.
[5] *Ibid.*
[6] *Ibid.*
[7] *Proposals*, etc., *op. cit.*, p. 29.

REFERENCE INDEX

GENERAL INDEX[1]

Absenteeism, 219–22

Afforestation, 33

Agrarian reform, *see* Land reform

Agriculture: as affecting ability to industrialise, 19, 36–7, 53; backwardness of, 19–24; smallness of farm, 19; low productivity of labour in, 22–3; unemployment in, 23, 129; standard of living in, 23–4; possibilities of enlarging cultivated areas, 31–3; possibilities of increasing agricultural output, 31–4; investments during First Five Year Plan, 60; output targets and achievements during First Five Year Plan, 58–60; draft output targets during Second Five Year Plan, 423. *See also* Afforestation, Agricultural taxation, Cadres, Collectivisation, Fertilisers, Insects, Land reform, Livestock, State grain trade monopoly, Water conservancy

Agricultural Producer Co-operatives, *see* Collectivisation

Agricultural taxation: increasing burden of, 98–101; violence against peasants in collecting, 99–101; peasants' resistance to, 101; on goods consumed by peasants, 101–2

All-China Federation of Democratic Women, 353

All-China Federation of Democratic Youth, 353, 355

All-China Federation of Trade Unions, *see* Trade Unions

All-China Students' Federation, 353

An Tzu-wen, Deputy Director CC CCP Organisation Department, Member CC: on cadres in land reform, 94; on persecution of peasants by cadres, 125–6; on corruption of cadres ('3-anti'), 370

Banking, 107–10, 189–91

Birth control, *see* Population

Bond campaigns, 256

Bonuses, 256–7

Books, State control on publication of, 331

Brewing, illicit, 135

'Bureaucratic Capitalism', 188–90

Bureaucratic mismanagement: causes of, 293–4; overstaffing and red tape, 294–5; production of shoddy goods, 295–7; fits of overactivity alternating with slackness, 297; wastage of materials, 297–302; cheating by managements, 297–8; lack of tie-in between plants, 298–9; commodities wasted, 302–5

Cadres: role in land reform, 93–5; in collection of agricultural taxes, 99–101; in granting credits to peasants, 108–10; in collecting deposits from peasants, 110–11; in directing peasants' production, 125–7; in grain trade, 133–4; KMT personnel among, 367–9; typical daily schedule of, 336; overworking of and fatigue, 336–7; political ignorance of, 339; as targets of 'purge', *see* '3-anti'

Capital: amount needed for industrialisation, 29–31; accumulation of (1931–6), 30; compared with other countries, 30–1; increase of agricultural output as means of raising c., 31–3; syphoning off of agricultural surpluses as means of c. accumulation, 36–7; peasants' corvée as means of c. construction, 37; bias towards heavy industry affecting c. accumulation, 37–9, 54–5; Russian aid in raising c., 65–7; c. accumulation during First Five Year Plan, 49–50; compared with other countries, 50–1; targets of c. investment during Second Five Year Plan, 424. *See also* Foreign capital

Capitalists: suffering under KMT, 188–92; welcome of 'Liberation', 192–3; Mao's promises to, 192–7; defended from workers, 194–5; fulfilling State contracts, 202–3; squeezing out of, 199–207. *See also* '5-anti'

Censorate, 359, 371

Chen Po-ta, Vice-President Chinese Academy of Sciences, Deputy-Director of CC CCP Rural Works Department, Alternate member PB: on antagonism of some Party members towards collectivisation, 158; on Mao and Stalin's writings, 398

[1] Biographical notes refer to the positions held by the person in question as of September, 1956.

Wages: level, 251–4; compared with pre-war, 254–5; deductions from, 256; bonuses, 256–7; in State industry compared with private industry, 257–9; lagging behind rising productivity of labour, 260–1; compared with peasants' income, 261; increasing inequalities in, 225–30; piece work, 224–30; raising of norms, 228–30; workers' proposals of voluntary reduction in, 196, 241; of apprentices, 254

Water conservancy: under Empire, 287, 311–12; under Mao, 62–4; payment to peasants on, 127–8. *See also* Huai River Project, Yellow River Project

Workers, role in Mao's rise to power, 183–4, 209–13

Yalta Conference, 387–9

Yeh Chi-chuang, Minister of Foreign Trade, Member CC, 68–70, 72

Yellow River Project, 63–4

Young Pioneers: membership, 353; relations to NDYL, 355

Yung Erh-jen, 197–8